CONGRESSIONAL POLICIES, PRACTICES AND PROCEDURES

THE DODD-FRANK WALL STREET REFORM AND CONSUMER PROTECTION ACT

CONGRESSIONAL POLICIES, PRACTICES AND PROCEDURES

Additional books in this series can be found on Nova's website
under the Series tab.

Additional E-books in this series can be found on Nova's website
under the E-books tab.

CONGRESSIONAL POLICIES, PRACTICES AND PROCEDURES

THE DODD-FRANK WALL STREET REFORM AND CONSUMER PROTECTION ACT

NATHAN L. MORRIS
AND
PHILIP O. PRICE
EDITORS

Nova Science Publishers, Inc.
New York

Copyright © 2011 by Nova Science Publishers, Inc.

All rights reserved. No part of this book may be reproduced, stored in a retrieval system or transmitted in any form or by any means: electronic, electrostatic, magnetic, tape, mechanical photocopying, recording or otherwise without the written permission of the Publisher.

For permission to use material from this book please contact us:
Telephone 631-231-7269; Fax 631-231-8175
Web Site: http://www.novapublishers.com

NOTICE TO THE READER

The Publisher has taken reasonable care in the preparation of this book, but makes no expressed or implied warranty of any kind and assumes no responsibility for any errors or omissions. No liability is assumed for incidental or consequential damages in connection with or arising out of information contained in this book. The Publisher shall not be liable for any special, consequential, or exemplary damages resulting, in whole or in part, from the readers' use of, or reliance upon, this material. Any parts of this book based on government reports are so indicated and copyright is claimed for those parts to the extent applicable to compilations of such works.

Independent verification should be sought for any data, advice or recommendations contained in this book. In addition, no responsibility is assumed by the publisher for any injury and/or damage to persons or property arising from any methods, products, instructions, ideas or otherwise contained in this publication.

This publication is designed to provide accurate and authoritative information with regard to the subject matter covered herein. It is sold with the clear understanding that the Publisher is not engaged in rendering legal or any other professional services. If legal or any other expert assistance is required, the services of a competent person should be sought. FROM A DECLARATION OF PARTICIPANTS JOINTLY ADOPTED BY A COMMITTEE OF THE AMERICAN BAR ASSOCIATION AND A COMMITTEE OF PUBLISHERS.

Additional color graphics may be available in the e-book version of this book.

Library of Congress Cataloging-in-Publication Data
The Dodd-Frank Wall Street Reform and Consumer Protection Act / editors,
Nathan L. Morris and Philip O. Price.
   p. cm.
 Includes index.
 ISBN 978-1-61324-101-1 (hardcover)
 1. United States. Dodd-Frank Wall Street Reform and Consumer Protection
Act. 2. Financial services industry--Law and legislation--United States. 3.
Financial institutions--Law and legislation--United States. I. Morris,
Nathan L. II. Price, Philip O.
 KF969.58201.A2 2011b
 346.73'082--dc22
2011008485

Published by Nova Science Publishers, Inc. † New York

CONTENTS

Preface		vii
Chapter 1	The Dodd-Frank Wall Street Reform and Consumer Protection Act: Issues and Summary *Baird Webel*	1
Chapter 2	Brief Summary of the Dodd-Frank Wall Street Reform and Consumer Protection Act	23
Chapter 3	The Dodd-Frank Wall Street Reform and Consumer Protection Act: Systemic Risk and the Federal Reserve *Marc Labonte*	37
Chapter 4	The Dodd-Frank Wall Street Reform and Consumer Protection Act: Titles III and VI, Regulation of Depository Institutions and Depository Institution Holding Companies *M. Maureen Murphy*	65
Chapter 5	Hedge Funds: Legal History and the Dodd-Frank Act *Kathleen Ann Ruane and Michael V. Seitzinger*	85
Chapter 6	The Dodd-Frank Wall Street Reform and Consumer Protection Act: Regulations to be Issued by the Consumer Financial Protection Bureau *Curtis W. Copeland*	93
Chapter 7	The Dodd-Frank Wall Street Reform and Consumer Protection Act: Title VII, Derivatives *Mark Jickling and Kathleen Ann Ruane*	131
Chapter 8	Dodd-Frank Act, Title VIII: Supervision of Payment, Clearing, and Settlement Activities *Donna Nordenberg and Marc Labonte*	147
Chapter 9	The Dodd-Frank Wall Street Reform and Consumer Protection Act: Title IX, Investor Protection *Mark Jickling*	181

Contents

Chapter 10 The Dodd-Frank Wall Street Reform and Consumer Protection Act: Executive Compensation **203**
Michael V. Seitzinger

Chapter 11 The Dodd-Frank Wall Street Reform and Consumer Protection Act: Title X, The Consumer Financial Protection Bureau **207**
David H. Carpenter

Chapter 12 The Dodd-Frank Wall Street Reform and Consumer Protection Act: Standards of Conduct of Brokers, Dealers, and Investment Advisers **225**
Michael V. Seitzinger

Chapter 13 Rulemaking Requirements and Authorities in the Dodd-Frank Wall Street Reform and Consumer Protection Act **235**
Curtis W. Copeland

Chapter 14 The Dodd-Frank Wall Street Reform and Consumer Protection Act Changes to the Regulation of Derivatives and Their Impact on Agribusiness **317**
Michael K. Adjemian and Gerald E. Plato

Chapter Sources **339**

Index **339**

PREFACE

Beginning in 2007, U.S. financial conditions deteriorated, leading to the near collapse of the U.S. financial system in September 2008. Major banks, insurers, government-sponsored enterprises and investment banks either failed or required hundreds of billions in federal support to continue functioning. Congress responded to the crisis by enacting the most comprehensive financial reform legislation since the 1930s. The Dodd-Frank Act creates a new regulatory umbrella group with authority to designate certain financial firms as "systemically significant" and subjecting them to increased prudential regulation, including limits on leverage, heightened capital standards and restrictions on certain forms of risky trading. This new book reviews issues related to financial regulation and provides brief descriptions of major provisions of the Dodd-Frank Act.

Chapter 1- Beginning in 2007, U.S. financial conditions deteriorated, leading to the near collapse of the U.S. financial system in September 2008. Major banks, insurers, government-sponsored enterprises, and investment banks either failed or required hundreds of billions in federal support to continue functioning. Households were hit hard by drops in the prices of real estate and financial assets, and by a sharp rise in unemployment. Congress responded to the crisis by enacting the most comprehensive financial reform legislation since the 1930s.

Chapter 2- Years without accountability for Wall Street and big banks brought us the worst financial crisis since the Great Depression, the loss of 8 million jobs, failed businesses, a drop in housing prices, and wiped out personal savings.

The failures that led to this crisis require bold action. We must restore responsibility and accountability in our financial system to give Americans confidence that there is a system in place that works for and protects them. We must create a sound foundation to grow the economy and create jobs.

Chapter 3- The recent financial crisis contained a number of systemic risk episodes, or episodes that caused instability for large parts of the financial system. The lesson some policymakers have taken from this crisis is that a systemic risk or "macroprudential" regulator is needed to prevent similar episodes in the future. But what types of risk would this new regulator be tasked with preventing, and is it the case that those activities are currently unsupervised?

Chapter 4- The Dodd-Frank Wall Street Reform and Consumer Protection Act of 2010, P.L. 111-203, has as its main purpose financial regulatory reform. Titles III and VI effectuate changes in the regulatory structure governing depository institutions and their holding companies and, thus, constitute a substantial component of the reform effort. Under Title III, there will no longer be a single regulator of federal and state-chartered savings associations, also known as thrifts or savings and loan associations. Title III abolishes the Office of the Thrift Supervision (OTS) and contains extensive provisions respecting the rights of affected employees as well as other administrative matters. It allocates the OTS functions among three existing regulators: the Comptroller of the Currency (OCC) will regulate federally chartered thrifts; the Federal Deposit Insurance Corporation (FDIC), state-chartered thrifts; and the Board of Governors of the Federal Reserve System (FRB), savings and loan holding companies. Title III also makes certain changes to deposit insurance: it makes permanent the increase of deposit insurance coverage to $250,000, and makes that increase retroactive to January 1, 2008. It extends full insurance coverage of non-interest bearing checking accounts for two additional years and authorizes a similar program for credit unions. Included in Title III is also a requirement that the Department of the Treasury and each federal financial regulatory agency establish an office of Minority and Women Inclusion.

Chapter 5- Hedge funds have received a great deal of media coverage in the past several years because large sums of money have been gained or lost in a relatively short time by some hedge funds. Most hedge funds are not required to register with the Securities and Exchange Commission (SEC) under the Investment Company Act of 1940 or the Investment Advisers Act of 1940. In 2004, the SEC implemented a rule that would have required all hedge fund advisers to register with the SEC under the Investment Advisers Act. Hedge funds challenged the rule in federal court, arguing that the SEC had misinterpreted provisions of the Investment Advisers Act. The U.S. Court of Appeals for the D.C. Circuit agreed with the hedge funds and struck down the SEC's rule. Following that decision, it appeared that congressional action would be necessary to require all hedge funds to register.

Chapter 6- Title X of the Dodd-Frank Wall Street Reform and Consumer Protection Act (P.L. 111-203, July 21, 2010) consolidates many federal consumer protection responsibilities into a new Bureau of Consumer Financial Protection (often referred to as the Consumer Financial Protection Bureau, or CFPB) within the Federal Reserve System. The act transfers supervisory and enforcement authority over a number of consumer financial products and services to the Bureau on a still-tobe-determined transfer date during calendar year 2011. Title X and Title XIV of the act contain numerous provisions that require or permit the CFPB to issue regulations implementing the statute's provisions. This report describes those provisions, notes that certain regulatory oversight tools will not be available for CFPB rules, and discusses the authority of a council of bank regulators to "set aside" the Bureau's rules.

Chapter 7- The financial crisis implicated the unregulated over-the-counter (OTC) derivatives market as a major source of systemic risk. A number of firms used derivatives to construct highly leveraged speculative positions, which generated enormous losses that threatened to bankrupt not only the firms themselves but also their creditors and trading partners. Hundreds of billions of dollars in government credit were needed to prevent such losses from cascading throughout the system. AIG was the best-known example, but by no means the only one.

Chapter 8- The U.S. financial system processes millions of transactions each day representing daily transfers of trillions of dollars, securities, and other assets to facilitate purchases and payments. Concerns had been raised, even prior to the recent financial crisis, about the vulnerability of the U.S. financial system to infrastructure failure. These concerns about the "plumbing" of the financial system were heightened following the market disruptions of the recent crisis.

Chapter 9- Title IX of the Dodd-Frank Wall Street Reform and Consumer Protection Act (P.L. 111-203) contains 10 subtitles and 113 separate sections amending federal securities laws intended to improve investor protection. The range of Title IX's provisions is very broad: some sections will bring significant changes to the securities business, while others are little more than technical clarifications of the Securities and Exchange Commission's (SEC's) authority. This report provides brief summaries of those provisions that create new SEC authority, that were controversial during the legislative process, or that appear likely to have far-reaching consequences.

Chapter 10- As part of their financial regulatory reform legislation, both the House and the Senate passed bills with provisions applying to executive compensation. The House- and Senate-passed executive compensation provisions differed, in some cases significantly.

The House and Senate conferees on Wall Street reform passed an executive compensation subtitle. On June 30, 2010, the House agreed to the conference report for H.R. 4173, now referred to as the Dodd-Frank Wall Street Reform and Consumer Protection Act. The Senate agreed to the conference report on July 15, 2010. The President signed the bill into law as P.L. 111-203 on July 21, 2010.

Among the provisions of the bill are say-on-pay requirements, the establishing of independent compensation committees, the clawback of unwarranted excessive compensation, and requirements on the executive compensation at financial institutions.

On October 18, 2010, the Securities and Exchange Commission (SEC or Commission) proposed rules to implement Dodd-Frank's executive compensation provisions.

Chapter 11- In the wake of what many believe is the worst U.S. financial crisis since the Great Depression, the Obama Administration proposed sweeping reforms of the financial services regulatory system— including the creation of an executive agency with authority over consumer financial issues, the broad outline of which has been encompassed in a document called the Administration's White Paper (the White Paper). The House of Representatives began consideration of bills seeking similar reform, which in large part were shepherded by Representative Barney Frank, Chairman of the Committee on Financial Services. On December 11, 2009, the House approved H.R. 4173, the Wall Street Reform and Consumer Protection Act of 2009. On May 20, 2010, the Senate approved its own financial reform measure, H.R. 4173, the Restoring American Financial Stability Act of 2010. (For an analysis of the consumer protection provisions of these proposals and how they varied, see CRS Report R40696, *Financial Regulatory Reform: Consumer Financial Protection Proposals*, by David H. Carpenter and Mark Jickling; for an overview of the overall financial reform proposals, see CRS Report R40975, *Financial Regulatory Reform and the 111th Congress*, coordinated by Baird Webel.)

Chapter 12- Brokers and dealers and investment advisers have been held to different standards of conduct in their dealings with investors. In very general terms, a broker-dealer is held to a suitability standard, and an investment adviser is held to a fiduciary duty standard. With passage of the Dodd-Frank Wall Street Reform and Consumer Protection Act (P.L. 111-203), which tasks the Securities and Exchange Commission (SEC) with issuing rules concerning the standards of conduct for brokers, dealers, and investment advisers, the current standards may be changed.

Chapter 13- The Dodd-Frank Wall Street Reform and Consumer Protection Act (P.L. 111-203, July 21, 2010) contains more than 300 provisions that expressly indicate in the text that rulemaking is required or permitted. However, it is unclear how many rules will ultimately be issued pursuant to the act because, among other things, (1) most of the provisions appear to be discretionary (e.g., stating that an agency "may" issue a rule); (2) individual provisions may result in multiple rules; (3) some provisions appear to provide rulemaking authorities to agencies that they already possess; and (4) rules may be issued to implement provisions that do not specifically require or permit rulemaking.

Chapter 14- A severe credit crunch in the United States in 2007 marked the beginning of a global financial crisis, which was symbolized by a series of surprising bank acquisitions and failures.[1] In spite of repeated efforts by the United States Federal Reserve Board and Federal Open Markets Committee to boost liquidity by lowering the primary credit rate and the Federal funds rate target, the American economy slid into a deep recession beginning in December 2007 (National Bureau of Economic Research, 2008). In 2008, Bear Stearns and Merrill Lynch, two investment banks in business for a century, collapsed and were bought out. In September of that year, the financial services firm Lehman Brothers, founded in 1850, filed for Chapter 11 bankruptcy protection. Because the Federal National Mortgage Corporation (Fannie Mae) and the Federal Home Loan Mortgage Corporation (Freddie Mac) were deeply involved in the home mortgage derivatives market, which lay at the heart of the financial crisis, the Federal Government took conservatorship of both, and it acquired an ownership stake in American International Group (AIG) to provide confidence to the financial system. In the agricultural sector, the credit squeeze, in combination with a concurrent price boom in commodities markets, may have contributed to difficulties for some established cotton merchants to finance *margin calls*,[2] forcing them into bankruptcy or mergers.

In: The Dodd-Frank Wall Street Reform...
Editors: Nathan L. Morris and Philip O. Price

ISBN: 978-1-61324-101-1
© 2011 Nova Science Publishers, Inc.

Chapter 1

THE DODD-FRANK WALL STREET REFORM AND CONSUMER PROTECTION ACT: ISSUES AND SUMMARY[*]

Baird Webel

SUMMARY

Beginning in 2007, U.S. financial conditions deteriorated, leading to the near collapse of the U.S. financial system in September 2008. Major banks, insurers, government-sponsored enterprises, and investment banks either failed or required hundreds of billions in federal support to continue functioning. Households were hit hard by drops in the prices of real estate and financial assets, and by a sharp rise in unemployment. Congress responded to the crisis by enacting the most comprehensive financial reform legislation since the 1930s.

Treasury Secretary Timothy Geithner issued a reform plan in the summer of 2009, which served as a template for legislation in both the House and Senate. House committees reported a number of bills on an issue-by-issue basis, which were then consolidated into a comprehensive bill, the Wall Street Reform and Consumer Protection Act of 2009 (H.R. 4173). H.R. 4173, as passed by the House on December 11, 2009, contained elements of H.R. 1728, H.R. 2571, H.R. 2609, H.R. 3126, H.R. 3269, H.R. 3817, H.R. 3818, H.R. 3890, and H.R. 3996. On May 20, 2010, the Senate passed H.R. 4173, after substituting the text of Senator Christopher Dodd's bill, the Restoring American Financial Stability Act of 2010 (S. 3217), as amended. Following a conference committee, the House accepted changes to H.R. 4173, now titled the Dodd-Frank Wall Street Reform and Consumer Protection Act, on June 30, 2010, and the Senate followed suit on July 15, 2010. President Obama signed the bill, now P.L. 111-203, on July 21, 2010.

Perhaps the major issue in financial reform has been how to address the systemic fragility that was revealed by the crisis. The Dodd-Frank Act creates a new regulatory umbrella group chaired by the Treasury Secretary—the Financial Stability Oversight Council—with authority to designate certain financial firms as "systemically significant"

---

[*] This is an edited, reformatted and augmented version of a Congressional Research Services publication, dated July 29, 2010.

and subjecting them to increased prudential regulation, including limits on leverage, heightened capital standards, and restrictions on certain forms of risky trading. These firms will also be subject to a special resolution process similar to that used in the past to address failing depository institutions.

Other aspects of financial reform address particular sectors of the financial system or selected classes of market participants. The Dodd-Frank Act consolidates consumer protection responsibilities in a new Bureau of Consumer Financial Protection within the Federal Reserve. The act consolidates bank regulation by merging the Office of Thrift Supervision (OTS) into the Office of the Comptroller of the Currency (OCC). It requires more derivatives to be cleared and traded through regulated exchanges, and it mandates reporting for derivatives that remain in the over-the-counter market. Hedge funds have new reporting and registration requirements. Credit rating agencies are subject to greater disclosure and legal liability provisions, and references to credit ratings will be removed from statute and regulation. A federal office is created to collect insurance information. Executive compensation and securitization reforms attempt to reduce incentives to take excessive risks. Intermediaries who provide investment advice to retail investors and municipalities may be subject to a fiduciary duty. The Federal Reserve's emergency authority is amended and its activities are subject to greater public disclosure and oversight by the Government Accountability Office (GAO).

This report reviews issues related to financial regulation and provides brief descriptions of major provisions of the Dodd-Frank Act.

INTRODUCTION

Comprehensive Financial Reform Proposals

The 111th Congress considered several proposals to reorganize financial regulators and to reform the regulation of financial markets and financial institutions. Following House committee markups on various bills addressing specific issues, House Committee on Financial Services Chairman Barney Frank introduced the Wall Street Reform and Consumer Protection Act of 2009 (H.R. 4173), incorporating elements of numerous previous bills.[1] After two days of floor consideration, the House passed H.R. 4173 on December 11, 2009, on a vote of 232-202.

Chairman Christopher Dodd of the Senate Committee on Banking, Housing, and Urban Affairs issued a single comprehensive committee print on November 16, 2009, the Restoring American Financial Stability Act of 2009.[2] This proposal was revised over the following months and a committee print of the Restoring American Financial Stability Act of 2010[3] was issued on March 15, 2010. This bill was amended in committee on March 22, 2010, and was reported as S. 3217 on April 15, 2010. The full Senate took up S. 3217 and amended it several times, finishing consideration on May 20, 2010, when it substituted the text of S. 3217 into H.R. 4173. The Senate then passed its version of H.R. 4173 on a vote of 59-39.

Following a conference committee, the House on June 30, 2010, agreed to the H.R. 4173conference report—now titled the Dodd-Frank Wall Street Reform and Consumer Protection Act—by a vote of 237-192. The Senate agreed to the report on July 15, 2010, by a vote of 60-39. The legislation was signed into law on July 21, 2010, as P.L. 111-203.

In addition to Chairman Dodd's and Chairman Frank's bills, other proposals were made but not scheduled for markup. For example, House Financial Services Committee Ranking

Member Spencer Bachus introduced a comprehensive reform proposal, the Consumer Protection and Regulatory Enhancement Act (H.R. 3310), and offered a similar amendment (H.Amdt. 539) during House consideration of H.R. 4173.[4] In March 2008, Treasury Secretary Hank Paulson issued a "Blueprint for a Modernized Financial Regulatory Structure."[5] The Obama Administration released "Financial Regulatory Reform: A New Foundation" in June 2009, and followed this with specific legislative language that provided a base text for congressional consideration.[6]

This report discusses related major provisions of the enacted version of the Dodd-Frank Act.

Understanding the fabric of financial reform proposals requires some analysis both of the Panic of 2008, as well as of more enduring concerns about risks in the financial system. This report begins with that analysis.

The Panic of September 2008[7]

The financial disruptions that peaked in September 2008 focused policy attention on systemic risk, which had previously been a subject of interest to academics and central bankers, but was not seen as a significant threat to economic stability. The last major systemic risk episode was bank runs in the Great Depression; the main elements of the current bank regulatory regime and federal safety net were put in place to prevent its recurrence. Between the end of the Great Depression and the early 2000s, the financial system weathered numerous shocks, failures, and crashes, with limited spillover into the real economy. Typically, the Federal Reserve (Fed) would announce that it stood ready to provide liquidity to the system, and that proved sufficient to stem panic. The idea that a financial shock could cause the entire system to spin out of control and collapse, and that the flow of credit might stop altogether, seemed to many to be a remote prospect. De facto policy was to rely on the Fed to deal with crises after the fact.

The events of 2007 and 2008 caused a sharp reassessment of the robustness and the self-stabilizing capacity of the financial system. As Treasury Secretary Timothy Geithner noted in written testimony delivered to the House Financial Services Committee on September 23, 2009, "The job of the financial system ... is to efficiently allocate savings and risk. Last fall, our financial system failed to do its job, and came precariously close to failing altogether."[8]

A number of discrete failures in individual markets and institutions led to global financial panic. U.S. financial firms suffered heavy losses in 2007 and 2008, primarily because of declines in the value of mortgage-related assets. During September 2008, Fannie Mae and Freddie Mac were placed in government conservatorship. Merrill Lynch was sold in distress to Bank of America in a deal supported by the Fed and Treasury. The Fed and Treasury failed to find a buyer for Lehman Brothers, which subsequently filed for bankruptcy, disrupting financial markets. A money market mutual fund (the Reserve Primary Fund) that held Lehman-related paper announced losses, triggering a run on other money market funds, and Treasury responded with a guarantee for money market funds. The American International Group (AIG), an insurance conglomerate with a securities subsidiary that specialized in financial derivatives, including credit default swaps, was unable to post collateral related to its derivatives and securities lending activities. The Fed intervened with an $85 billion loan to prevent bankruptcy and to ensure full payment to AIG's counterparties. In response to the general panic, Congress approved the $700 billion Troubled Asset Relief Program (TARP); the Fed introduced several lending facilities to provide liquidity to different parts of the financial system; and the Federal Deposit Insurance Corporation (FDIC) introduced a debt guarantee program for banks. The panic largely subsided through the latter part of 2008, although confidence in the financial system returned very slowly.

It was widely understood that the panic had its roots in the subprime mortgage market, in which years of double-digit housing price increases had fed a bubble mentality and caused lenders to relax their customary prudence. That the housing market would cool, as it began to do in 2006, was not a great surprise. What was generally unexpected was the way losses caused by rising foreclosures and bad loan rippled through the system. Major financial institutions had constructed highly leveraged speculative positions that magnified the subprime shock, so that a setback in a $1 trillion segment of the U.S. housing market generated many times that amount in financial losses.

Giant financial institutions were shown to be vulnerable to liquidity runs, and many failed or had to be rescued as short-term credit dried up. The value of complex financial instruments created through securitization became completely uncertain, and market participants lost confidence in each others' creditworthiness. Risks that were thought to be unrelated became highly correlated; a negative spiral that showed all financial risk taking to be interconnected and all declines to be self-reinforcing took hold. Doubts about counterparty exposure were magnified by opacity in derivatives markets.

Disruption to the financial system exacerbated recessionary forces already at work in the economy. Asset prices plunged and consumers suffered sharp losses in their retirement and college savings accounts, as well as in the value of their homes. The financial crisis accelerated declines in consumption and business investment, which in turn made banks' problems worse. Overall, the recession proved to be the deepest and longest since the Great Depression.

Against this background, Congress took up financial reform legislation in 2009. The legislation included measures to improve systemic stability, improve policy options for coping with failing financial firms, increase transparency throughout financial markets, and protect consumers and investors. By the time of final passage, the Dodd-Frank Act included provisions that affect virtually every financial market and to amend existing or grant new authority and responsibility to nearly every federal financial regulatory agency.

THE DODD-FRANK ACT (P.L. 111-203)

Systemic Risk

Policy Issues[9]

Systemic risk refers to sources of instability for the financial system as a whole, often through "contagion" or "spillover" effects that individual firms cannot protect themselves against.[10] Although regulators took systemic risk into account before the crisis, and systemic risk can never be eliminated, analysts have pointed to a number of ostensible weaknesses in the regulatory regime's approach to systemic risk. First, there has been no regulator with overarching responsibility for mitigating systemic risk. Some analysts argue that systemic risk can fester in the gaps in the regulatory system where one regulator's jurisdiction ends and another's begins. Second, the crisis revealed that liquidity crises and runs were not just a problem for depository institutions. Third, the crisis revealed that nonbank, highly leveraged firms, such as Lehman Brothers and AIG, could be a source of systemic risk and "too big (or too interconnected) to fail." Finally, there were concerns that the breakdown of different payment, clearing, and settlement (PCS) systems, which are not regulated consistently (or, in some cases, at all), would be another source of systemic risk.

Provisions in the Dodd-Frank Act (Titles I and VIII)

The Dodd-Frank Act does not create a dedicated systemic risk regulator with powers to neutralize sources of systemic risk as they arise. Instead, it creates a Financial Services Oversight Council (FSOC), chaired by the Treasury Secretary and consisting of eight heads of federal regulatory agencies (including the newly created Consumer Financial Protection Bureau) and a presidential appointee with insurance experience. The act creates an Office of Financial Research to support the council. The council is authorized to identify and advise regulators on sources of systemic risk and "regulatory gap" problems, but would have no rulemaking, examination, or enforcement powers of its own. The council is to identify systemically important financial firms regardless of their legal charter, and the Fed will subject them to stricter prudential oversight and regulation, including short-term debt limits, a 10% liability concentration limit, counterparty exposure set at 25% of total capital, risk-based capital requirements (that account for off-balance sheet activities), annual stress tests, and a 15-to-1 leverage limit. The details of this stricter oversight will be determined by the Fed in yet-to-be issued implementing rules. Many large firms are already regulated by the Fed for safety and soundness because they are bank holding companies; the act prevents a firm from changing its charter in order to escape Fed regulation. In addition, the Dodd-Frank Act includes mechanisms by which the Fed would be empowered to curb the growth or reduce the size of large firms to prevent systemic risk.

The Dodd-Frank Act (Section 619) puts limits on commercial banks' proprietary trading activities and investments in hedge funds or private equity firms.[11] It also provides for many PCS systems and activities deemed systemically important by the council to be regulated by the Fed, unless those systems are registered with the Securities and Exchange Commission (SEC) or the Commodities Futures Trading Commission (CFTC), in which case the system would be regulated by those entities. Title XI would also allow the FDIC to set up emergency liquidity programs to guarantee the debt of bank holding companies, similar to the 2008 Temporary Liquidity Guarantee Program.

Federal Reserve Emergency Authority and Congressional Oversight

Policy Issues[12]

During the recent financial turmoil, the Fed engaged in unprecedented levels of emergency lending to nonbank financial firms through its authority under Section 13(3) of the Federal Reserve Act. This statute states that "in unusual and exigent circumstances, the Board of Governors of the Federal Reserve System, by the affirmative vote of not less than five members, may authorize any Federal reserve bank ... to discount for any individual, partnership, or corporation, notes, drafts, and bills of exchange...."[13]

Such loans can be made only if secured to the Fed's satisfaction and if the targeted borrower is unable to obtain the needed credit through other banking institutions. In addition to the level of lending, the form of the lending has been novel, particularly the creation of three limited liability corporations controlled by the Fed, to which the Fed lent a total of $72.6 billion to purchase illiquid assets from Bear Stearns and AIG. The Fed's recent actions under Section 13(3) generated debate in Congress about whether measures were needed to amend the institution's emergency lending powers.

Provisions in the Dodd-Frank Act (Title XI)

The Dodd-Frank Act includes several provisions related to Federal Reserve lending authority. In particular, this legislation stipulates that, although the Fed may authorize a Federal Reserve Bank to make collateralized loans as part of a broadly available credit facility, it may not authorize a Federal Reserve Bank to lend to only a single and specific individual, partnership, or corporation. When using emergency authority, the Fed will be required to seek approval from the Treasury Secretary. In addition, the Dodd-Frank Act allows the Government Accountability Office (GAO) to audit the Fed's lending facilities and open market operations for internal controls and risk management, and it calls for a GAO audit of the Fed's actions during the crisis. The act requires disclosure of Fed borrowers and borrowing terms, with a lag. The act also prohibits firms regulated by the Fed from participating in the selection of directors of the regional Federal Reserve Banks.

Resolution Regime for Failing Firms

Policy Issues[14]

Most companies that fail in the United States are resolved in accordance with the bankruptcy code. Depository institutions that hold FDIC-insured deposits are subject to a special resolution regime, called a conservatorship or receivership. Under normal circumstances, bankruptcies are judicial in nature with no additional public resources available to support the process. The FDIC's conservatorship/receivership regime is a largely nonjudicial, administrative process, requiring the FDIC to resolve depositories such that the total to be expended will cost the Deposit Insurance Fund less than any other possible method. Under limited circumstances, the FDIC may waive this "least-cost resolution" requirement in order to minimize systemic risk.[15] Some believe that the speed and discretion available in the FDIC's conservatorship/receivership regime is a useful model for resolving other types of systemically important financial firms. The collapse of Lehman Brothers (and the near collapse of AIG, Bear Stearns, and others) during the recent financial crisis has focused congressional attention on policy options for resolving systemically significant nondepository financial institutions.[16] Proponents argue that creating a special resolution regime for such firms would make future taxpayer bailouts unnecessary. Opponents argue that it would provide a way for policymakers to provide "backdoor bailouts" to favored creditors and counterparties of failing firms.

Provisions in the Dodd-Frank Act (Title II)

The Dodd-Frank Act establishes a new system for certain financial companies whose resolution under otherwise available law is determined by various federal regulators to pose dangers to the U.S. financial system. This resolution system is modeled after the FDIC's existing receivership regime for depository institutions. Many types of financial companies and their subsidiaries are eligible for this special resolution regime; however, subsidiaries that are insurance companies, certain broker-dealers, and insured depositories are not eligible.

For an eligible financial company to be resolved under the special regime, a group of regulators, including two-thirds of the Federal Reserve Board, must recommend the company for the resolution based on standards delineated by the Dodd-Frank Act. After the recommendation, the Secretary of the Treasury (Secretary), in consultation with the President, must make a determination that the "company is in default or in danger of default;" the company's resolution under otherwise available law would "have serious adverse effects on financial stability of the United States; no viable private sector alternative is available;" and other considerations.[17] A company that disputes the determination by the Secretary will have limited rights to appeal the determination in federal court.

Although the special resolution regime is modeled after the FDIC's receivership power, there are some important distinctions between the two. For instance, the Dodd-Frank Act emphasizes that

> creditors and shareholders will bear the losses of the financial company; management responsible for the condition of the financial company will not be retained; and the [FDIC] and other appropriate regulators will take all steps necessary and appropriate to assure that all parties ... having responsibility for the condition of the financial company bear losses consistent with their responsibility, including actions for damages, restitution, and recoupment of compensation and other gains not compatible with such responsibility.[18]

The act also states that "[a]ll financial companies put into receivership under this title shall be liquidated, [and n]o taxpayer funds shall be used to prevent the liquidation of any financial company under this title."[19]

The funding mechanism for resolutions under the Dodd-Frank Act also differs from the conservatorship/receivership regime for depositories. The Orderly Liquidation Fund established by the Dodd-Frank Act will not be prefunded. Instead, the FDIC, upon being appointed receiver of a particular financial company, is authorized to borrow funds from the Treasury subject to explicit caps based on the value of the failed firm's consolidated assets. If necessary to pay off such obligations to the Treasury, the FDIC would have the authority to assess claimants of the failed institution that received more compensation through the receivership than they would have received had the failed firm been liquidated in bankruptcy, as well as with the power to assess certain large financial institutions (bank holding companies and nonbank financial companies eligible for the special resolution regime that have more than $50 billion in assets and all nonbank financial institutions supervised by the Fed as systemically significant). The Dodd-Frank Act also imposes a three-year time limit on any receivership with the possibility of up to two one-year extensions.

Securitization and Shadow Banking

Policy Issues[20]

Shadow banking refers to financial activity either conducted by nonbanks or sponsored by banks off of their balance sheets. Securitization supports the shadow banking system. Securitization is the process of turning mortgages, credit card loans, and other debt into marketable securities. Securitizers acquire and pool many loans from primary lenders and then issue new securities based on the flow of payments through the pool. This process can allow banks to reduce the risk of their retained portfolios. Securitization also finances nonbank lenders specializing in mortgage loans, credit cards, and other loan products, and thus can increase the amount of credit available to businesses and consumers. If the risks of securitized products are adequately managed and understood, securitization can enhance financial stability by shifting financial risk to those most willing and able to bear it.

Securitization risks were not properly managed during the period leading up to the crisis, which contributed to the housing bubble and financial turmoil in a variety of ways. Lenders planning to sell their loans have a reduced stake in the borrower's long-term capacity to repay the loan. Bank underwriting standards are subject to guidances issued by bank regulators because loans to risky borrowers might be unsafe and unsound for the banks themselves. These guidances, however, do not apply to nonbank mortgage lenders that are funded through securitization (although the Fed has separate authority to regulate lending). Private securitization was especially prevalent in the subprime mortgage market, the nonconforming mortgage market, and in regions where loan defaults have been particularly severe. As loans were made that the lender never expected to hold, mortgage underwriting standards deteriorated.

Opaqueness in the shadow banking system also caused problems. When defaults rose among home buyers, the complexity of mortgage-backed securities (MBSs) made it more difficult to identify which firms would suffer the largest losses. Furthermore, a drop in the credit rating of a MBS could require some holders to sell, even though the security was still performing. In addition to holding the securities of nonbank subprime lenders, some banks also sponsored their own mortgage funding facilities off their balance sheets in special purpose vehicles. When the liquidity of MBSs declined, some of these sponsoring banks had to pull the assets of such special purpose vehicles back on to their balance sheets and recognize more losses.

One approach to address incentives in securitization is to require loan securitizers to retain a portion of the long-term default risk. An advantage of this "skin in the game" requirement is that it may help preserve underwriting standards among lenders funded by securitization. Another advantage is that securitizers would share in the risks faced by the investors to whom they market their securities. A possible disadvantage is that if each step of the securitization chain must retain a portion of risk, then relatively little risk may ultimately be shifted out of the financial sector to investors. To the extent that securitization is seen as a device to shift risk to those more willing and able to bear it, concentration of risk in the financial sector may be self-defeating.

Provisions in the Dodd-Frank Act (Title IX)

The Dodd-Frank Act generally requires securitizers to retain some of the risk if they issue asset-backed securities. The amount of risk required to be retained depends in part on the quality of the underlying assets. Regulators are instructed to write risk retention rules requiring less than 5% retained risk if the securitized assets meet prescribed underwriting standards. For assets that do not meet these standards, regulators are instructed to require not less than 5% retention of risk. Securitizers are prohibited from hedging the retained credit risk.

The Dodd-Frank Act requires separate risk retention rules for different asset classes that are securitized (residential mortgages, commercial mortgages, auto loans, etc.). The risk retention rules for securitization of nonmortgage assets are to be jointly issued by the SEC and Federal Banking Agencies (FDIC, Office of the Comptroller of the Currency [OCC], and Federal Reserve). The risk retention rules for the securitization of mortgage assets are to be jointly issued by the SEC, the Federal Banking Agencies, the Department of Housing and Urban Development (HUD), and the Federal Housing Finance Agency (FHFA). Regulators are also directed to craft risk retention rules appropriate to collateralized debt obligations (CDOs) and other complex securities if the underlying assets are tranches of other asset-backed securities.

Regulators may also impose retained risk requirements on originators of assets after taking into account the riskiness of the assets, whether securitization markets are causing a decline in prudent underwriting, and the effect on the ability of consumers and businesses to obtain credit on reasonable terms.

In the case of residential mortgages that are securitized, the Dodd-Frank Act allows for a complete exemption from risk retention if all of the mortgages in the securitization meet the standards of a "qualified residential mortgage," which regulators will define according to certain factors, but which must be no broader than the definition of "qualified mortgage" in Section 1412 of Dodd-Frank. Some of the factors are full documentation of borrowers' financial resources, debt-to-income ratio limits, and payment shock mitigation. The act also provides an exemption from retained risk requirements for certain Farm Credit Administration loans and related guarantees. Also exempt are loans guaranteed by the United States or an agency of the United States, as well as municipal securities. Notably, securities guaranteed by Fannie Mae and Freddie Mac are not automatically exempt.

The act requires securitizers to perform due diligence on the underlying assets of the securitization and to disclose the nature of the due diligence. In addition, investors in asset-backed securities are to receive more information about the underlying assets.

Consolidation of Bank Supervision

Policy Issues[21]

Commercial banks and similar institutions are subject to regulatory examination for safety and soundness. Prior to the crisis, depending on their charter, commercial banks, thrifts, and credit unions may have been examined by the OCC, the Office of Thrift Supervision (OTS), the Federal Reserve, the National Credit Union Administration (NCUA), or a state authority. State bank examiners often coordinated through the Conference of State Bank Supervisors. Federal bank examiners often conducted joint rulemaking and coordinated through the Federal Financial Institutions Examinations Council (FFIEC). In addition, some firms engage in bank-like activities, but are not subject to oversight by bank regulators.

The system of multiple bank regulators was believed to have problems, some of which could be mitigated by regulatory consolidation. Multiple regulators may find it challenging to implement consistent enforcement even if they employ joint rulemaking. To the extent that regulations are applied inconsistently, institutions may have an incentive to choose the regulator that they feel will be the weakest or least intrusive. If so, competition among the regulators for covered institutions (regulatory arbitrage) could lead to less effective financial supervision. Among the arguments against consolidation are that regulatory consolidation could change the traditional U.S. dual banking system in ways that put smaller banks at a disadvantage. Another argument for maintaining the current system is that competition among regulators encourages the regulators to monitor each other and alert policymakers if one regulator lowers standards.

During the Dodd-Frank policy debate, there was concern about the Fed's roles in both bank holding company regulation and conducting monetary policy. Some argued that the Fed should concentrate on monetary policy and have fewer regulatory responsibilities, especially if the institution's independence is to be preserved. In contrast, the Fed argued that its bank regulation responsibilities provided it with helpful information for the conduct of monetary policy.

Provisions in the Dodd-Frank Act (Title III)

The Dodd-Frank Act did not effect a complete consolidation of banking agencies, nor did it remove the Fed's bank regulatory responsibilities. Title III eliminates the Office of Thrift Supervision as an independent agency and reassigns its duties to the FDIC, the OCC, and to the Federal Reserve. The Fed will be the holding company level regulator for institutions formerly regulated by OTS. The OCC will be the depository institution level regulator for federally chartered thrifts. The FDIC will be the depository institution level regulator for state chartered thrifts. The Fed remains the regulator for state chartered member banks. Title III also expands the assessment base for the FDIC's deposit insurance fund. The new formula will be based upon the total assets of the insured depository minus the average tangible equity of the insured depository. Title VI also creates a three-year moratorium on chartering new credit card banks, industrial loan companies, and trust banks.

Consumer Financial Protection[22]

Policy Issues

In the United States, depository institutions—banks, thrifts, and credit unions—have been subject to comprehensive supervision, examination, and enforcement by a number of federal regulators. These regulators have monitored the institutions that they supervise for both safety and soundness and for compliance with other federal laws, including the various federal consumer protection laws. Many nondepository financial companies, such as payday lenders and nonbank mortgage lenders, have been primarily regulated by the states. However, the financial products that these nondepositories offer may still be subject to federal consumer protection laws, such as the Truth in Lending Act (TILA).[23] The Federal Reserve largely has been charged with promulgating the regulations to implement the TILA and most other federal consumer protection laws, and the Federal Trade Commission (FTC) primarily has been responsible for enforcing these laws and regulations against institutions that do not have a primary federal regulator.

In light of this fragmented system, some have proposed legislation to consolidate consumer financial protection functions. These proposals raise policy questions regarding how best to balance safety and soundness regulation with consumer compliance. Although a loan that cannot be repaid is typically bad for both the borrower and the lender, there are some areas in which there can be a conflict between safety and soundness regulation and consumer protection. When a banking activity is profitable, safety and soundness regulators tend to look upon it favorably, because it enables the bank to meet capital requirements and withstand financial shocks. A consumer protection regulator, however, may look at such activity less favorably, especially if the profit is seen to have been gained unfairly at the expense of consumers. Removing consumer compliance authority from the federal bank regulators may weaken the safety and soundness regulation of banks if, for example, the separation results in a less complete picture of bank operations for the prudential regulator. The Fed has argued that its role in consumer protection aids its other authorities, including bank supervision and systemic risk. On the other hand, some, including the Obama Administration, have argued that professional bank examiners are trained "to see the world through the lenses of institutions and markets, not consumers,"[24] and separating compliance and safety and soundness into a different agency is the best way to protect both consumers and financial institutions. The extent to which the cost and availability of credit will be affected by a new regulator will depend on exactly what rules it prescribes and how aggressively it and the other regulators enforce consumer protection laws and regulations.

Provisions in the Dodd-Frank Act (Title X)

The Dodd-Frank Act establishes a Bureau of Consumer Financial Protection within the Federal Reserve System to have authority over an array of consumer financial products and services (including deposit taking, mortgages, credit cards and other extensions of credit, loan servicing, check-guaranteeing, collection of consumer report data, debt collection, real estate settlement, money transmitting, financial data processing, among others). It will serve as the primary federal consumer financial protection supervisor and enforcer of federal consumer protection laws over many of the institutions that offer these products and services. The bureau will be required to consult with the prudential regulators when prescribing regulations.

The bureau's authority over financial institutions varies according to the type of company: (1) depository institutions with more than $10 billion in assets (i.e., "larger depositories"); (2) depositories institutions with $10 billion or less in assets (i.e., "smaller depositories"); and (3) nondepositories. The Dodd-Frank Act explicitly exempts a number of different entities and consumer financial activities from the bureau's supervisory and enforcement authority. Within a year and a half of enactment, primary consumer protection supervisory and enforcement powers over larger depositories that are currently held in those institutions' prudential regulators will be transferred to the bureau.

The bureau will not acquire primary supervisory and enforcement powers over smaller depositories. Instead, these powers will remain with those institutions' primary regulators. The bureau will have some ability to participate in the examination of these smaller depositories, refer potential enforcement actions against smaller depository institutions to their prudential regulators, and require reports directly from these depositories. While the bureau's supervisory and enforcement powers are limited with regard to these smaller depositories, they, along with their larger depository counterparts, generally will be subject to the consumer protection rules prescribed by the bureau.

Regarding nondepository institutions that offer consumer financial products and services, the bureau would only be the primary supervisor and enforcer over entities that

1) are engaged in consumer mortgage related activities (i.e., mortgage origination, brokerage, or servicing activities, mortgage modification or foreclosure relief activities);
2) are nonmortgage related consumer financial entities that are "larger participant[s] in a market" as determined by the Bureau in regulations and after consultation with the FTC;
3) the Bureau has reasonable cause to believe are "engaging, or ha[ve] engaged, in conduct that poses risks to consumers with regard to the offering or provision of consumer financial products or services;"
4) provide or offer to provide private student loans; or
5) provide or offer to provide a payday loan.[25]

The bureau's supervisory powers over these covered nondepositories include the authority to require them to register with the bureau, submit to background checks, or adhere to other measures "to ensure that such persons are legitimate entities and are able to perform their obligations to consumers."[26]

The Dodd-Frank Act authorizes the bureau to prescribe rules and issue orders and guidance. The act also transfers to the bureau rulemaking authority for many of the existing federal consumer protection laws (referred to as the "enumerated consumer laws"), including the TILA, Real Estate Settlement Procedures Act, and Home Ownership and Equity Protection Act. As a check on the bureau's rulemaking powers, the Financial Stability Oversight Council has the ability to set aside a regulation prescribed by the bureau if the regulation "would put the safety and soundness of the United States banking system or the stability of the financial system of the United States at risk."

As previously mentioned, the Dodd-Frank Act explicitly exempts some activities and entities from the bureau's jurisdiction. For instance, the bureau generally will not have any power to regulate insurance activities or to impose interest rate caps on products. The act also significantly limits the bureau's supervisory, enforcement, and rulemaking powers over a

> merchant, retailer, or seller of nonfinancial goods or services ... to the extent that such person (i) extends credit directly to a consumer ... exclusively for the purpose of enabling that consumer to purchase such nonfinancial good or service directly from the merchant, retailer, or seller; (ii) ... collects debt arising from [such] credit ... or (iii) sells or conveys [such] debt ... that is delinquent or otherwise in default.[27]

The bureau's authority is further restricted on certain merchants, retailers, and sellers of nonfinancial goods that are also small businesses. It generally does not have supervisory, rulemaking, or enforcement powers over automobile dealers, but the Dodd-Frank Act makes it easier for the FTC to regulate them.[28] Other entities for which the act provides certain exemptions include real estate brokers, real estate agents, sellers of manufactured and mobile homes, income tax preparers, and accountants, each to the extent that they are acting in their normal capacity (e.g., a real estate broker would be exempt to the extent that s/he brings parties together to purchase a property). However, the bureau will be able to exert authority over these entities to the extent that they are subject to an enumerated consumer law.

Mortgage Standards

Policy Issues

Beginning around the middle of 2006, residential mortgage delinquency and foreclosure rates began to rise sharply in many regions of the United States. In addition to the negative effects on some homeowners, the increase in nonperforming mortgages contributed to the financial crisis by straining the balance sheets of financial firms that held those mortgages. Although all kinds of mortgages experienced increases in delinquency and foreclosure, many poorly performing mortgages exhibited increasingly complex features, such as adjustable interest rates, or nontraditional mortgage features, such as negative amortization.[29] Such nontraditional or complex mortgage features may be appropriate for some borrowers in some circumstances, many were made available more widely than the purposes for which they were originally intended. In addition, some observers view certain mortgage features, such as high prepayment penalties, as predatory. Although not all troubled mortgages exhibited these or similar features, and not all loans that exhibited such features became troubled, some observers point to the widespread use of such mortgage terms as having exacerbated the housing "bubble" and its subsequent collapse.

The role that nonperforming mortgages played in the recent financial crisis have led some to suggest that actions should be taken both to protect consumers from risky mortgage products and to protect the U.S. financial system from experiencing major losses due to troubled mortgages in the future. One possible way to minimize mortgage defaults and foreclosures is to limit or prohibit certain mortgage features that are viewed as especially risky. Another would be to require mortgage lenders to offer consumers basic mortgage products with traditional terms alongside any loan with nontraditional features. Although either of these approaches may reduce the chances of widespread mortgage failures, and might help preserve financial stability, both could also limit consumer choice or prevent borrowers from taking out loans with nontraditional features that may be advantageous given their specific circumstances. Some argue that such approaches could limit financial innovation in mortgage products or reduce competition among lenders.

Provisions in the Dodd-Frank Act (Title XIV)

The Dodd-Frank Act amends the Truth in Lending Act to set minimum standards for certain residential mortgages. Lenders will be required to determine that mortgage borrowers have a reasonable ability to repay the mortgages that they receive, based on the borrowers' verified income and other factors, subject to regulations promulgated by the Fed. Certain "qualified mortgages" with traditional mortgage terms will be presumed to have met these requirements. The Fed is also directed to issue regulations prohibiting mortgage originators from "steering" consumers to mortgages that (1) those consumers do not have a reasonable ability to repay, (2) exhibit certain features that are determined to be predatory, or (3) meet certain other conditions. It is also directed to issue regulations prohibiting any practices related to residential mortgage lending that it deems to be "abusive, unfair, deceptive, [or] predatory." The legislation restricts the use of prepayment penalties. Mortgage originators are prohibited from receiving compensation that varies in any way based on the applicable mortgages terms or conditions, other than the principal amount. The legislation also requires increased disclosures to consumers on a range of topics, including disclosures related to how certain features of a mortgage may affect the consumer.

New requirements related to "high-cost mortgages" are included in the legislation, such as limitations on the terms of such mortgages and a requirement that lenders verify that borrowers have received pre-purchase counseling before obtaining such a mortgage. The legislation also imposes additional restrictions on residential mortgage loans and includes additional housing-related provisions that are not discussed in this report.

Derivatives

Policy Issues[30]

Derivatives are financial contracts whose value is linked to some underlying price or variable. Derivatives are traded both on organized exchanges with central clearing houses that guarantee payment on all contracts, and in a previously unregulated over-the-counter (OTC) market, where credit risk is borne by the individual counterparties. The CFTC regulates commodity futures and options on futures, whereas the SEC regulates options on securities.

The Commodity Futures Modernization Act of 2000 (CFMA)[31] largely exempted swaps and other derivatives in the OTC market from regulation. The collapse of AIG in 2008 illustrated the risks of large OTC derivatives positions that are not backed by collateral or margin (as a central clearing house would require). If AIG had been required to post margin on its credit default swap contracts, it would not have been able to build such a large position, which may have reduced the threat to systemic stability and resulting a costly taxpayer bailout. Such disruptions in markets for financial derivatives during the recent crisis led to calls for changes in derivatives regulation, particularly in the OTC market. Further, opacity in the OTC market made it difficult for policymakers and market participants to gauge firms' risk exposures, arguably exacerbating the panic.

Derivatives reform focused on requiring the OTC markets to adopt features of the regulated markets, including mandatory clearing through derivatives clearing organizations, trading on exchanges or exchange-like facilities, registration of certain market participants, and the like.

Provisions in the Dodd-Frank Act (Titles VII and XVI)

The Dodd-Frank Act mandates centralized clearing and exchange-trading of many OTC derivatives, but provides exemptions for certain market participants.[32] The act creates a process by which federal regulators (either the CFTC or the SEC) will determine which types of swaps and security-based swaps will be subject to the clearing requirement. It also requires reporting of all swaps and security-based swaps, including those that are not subject to or are exempt from the clearing requirement, to regulated entities or to regulators themselves. The act requires regulators to impose capital requirements on swap dealers, security-based swap dealers, major swap participants, and major security-based swaps participants. The CFTC is to regulate "swaps," which include contracts based on interest rates, currencies, physical commodities, some credit default swaps, whereas the SEC will have authority over "security-based swaps," including other credit default swaps and equity swaps.[33] Both agencies will be given the power to promulgate rules to prevent the evasion of the clearing requirements created by the act.

In general, swaps and security-based swaps that must be cleared must also be traded on an exchange or exchange-like facility that provides price transparency. The regulators are given considerable discretion to define the forms of trading that will meet this requirement.

The Dodd-Frank Act includes an exemption from the clearing requirement, if desired, if at least one party to the trade is an "end user,"[34] defined as parties that are not financial entities[35] and are using the swaps to hedge or mitigate commercial risk. An exempted party must inform the CFTC or SEC (depending on the contract) on how they generally meet their financial obligations when entering into noncleared swaps or security-based swaps.

Section 716, a widely debated section of the act, prohibits federal assistance to any swaps entity with respect to any swap, security-based swap, or other activity of the swaps entity.[36] Swaps entities are defined as swap dealers, security-based swap dealers, major swap participants, and major security-based swap participants that are registered under either the CEA or the Exchange Act. However, swap entities do not include any major swap participant or major security-based swap participant that is an insured depository institution. This exemption appears to address concerns that under previous language large commercial banks would have been unable to hedge their risk without becoming ineligible for federal assistance, including access to the Federal Reserve's discount window or any other Fed credit facility and FDIC insurance.

Depository institutions will be able to act as swap dealers in limited circumstances, such as when they are permitted to deal in the underlying interest, but not with regard to credit default swaps. Furthermore, depository institutions are permitted to establish an affiliate that is a swap entity as long as it is supervised by the Fed and comports with Sections 23A and 23B of the Federal Reserve Act.

Credit Rating Agencies

Policy Issues[37]

Credit rating agencies provide investors with an evaluation of the creditworthiness of bonds issued by a wide spectrum of entities, including corporations, sovereign nations, and municipalities. The grading of the creditworthiness is typically displayed in a letter hierarchical format: for example, AAA being the safest, with lower grades representing a greater risk. Credit rating agencies are typically paid by the issuers of the securities being rated by the agencies, which could be seen as a conflict of interest. In exchange for adhering to various reporting requirements, the SEC provides interested credit rating agencies with a Nationally Recognized Statistical Rating Organization (NRSRO) designation. The designation is particularly important because a variety of state and federal laws and regulations have referenced NRSRO ratings.[38]

In recent years, credit rating agencies have come under increased public scrutiny following several alleged performance failures. For instance, during the recent housing boom cycle the three dominant agencies (Fitch, Moody's, and Standard & Poor's) initially rated many mortgage-backed securities as AAA, before sharply downgrading the securities as the subprime mortgage market collapsed, resulting in heavy losses for investors that relied on these ratings. In some circumstances, downgrades forced financial firms to sell or hold more capital against the security, thereby exacerbating liquidity and deleveraging problems. The perceived agency failings have led to a focus on strengthening the accountability of credit rating agencies and reducing potential conflicts of interest that may compromise the integrity of their ratings.

Provisions in the Dodd-Frank Act (Title IX)

The Dodd-Frank Act contains provisions that enhance SEC regulation; impose new reporting, disclosure, and examination requirements on NRSROs; establish new standards of legal liability, create a new mechanism to prevent issuers of structured finance securities from choosing the agency that will perform the initial rating; and require removal of references to NRSRO ratings from federal statutes and regulations.

The act establishes an Office of Credit Ratings in the SEC to examine NRSROs and issue related regulations, including rules requiring that each credit rating be accompanied by extensive disclosures about the assumptions and methodologies underlying the rating. To permit users of ratings to compare NRSRO performance, the SEC will publish information on initial credit ratings and on subsequent changes to such ratings. After notice and opportunity for a hearing, the SEC will be permitted to temporarily suspend or permanently revoke an NRSRO's registration for a particular class of securities if it determines that the NRSRO lacks adequate financial and managerial resources for producing ratings with integrity.

Under the Dodd-Frank Act, NRSROs will be subject to the same standards of accountability as are statements made by registered public accounting firms and securities analysts. The act also permits investors to bring private rights of action against NRSROs for a knowing or reckless failure to conduct a reasonable investigation while performing a credit rating. The act requires the SEC to promulgate rules designed to prevent the sales and marketing considerations of an NRSRO from influencing the ratings that it produces and gives it the authority to revoke or suspend the registration of NRSROs that violated such rules.

The Dodd-Frank Act removes the references to credit ratings in selected sections in specific federal financial statutes.[39] Federal regulatory agencies will also be required to review and remove references to NRSRO ratings. The act also directs the SEC to conduct a study that would result in it establishing a system under which the initial rating assignments for structured finance securities would be made on a random or semirandom basis.

Investor Protection

Policy Issues

The multi-billion dollar Madoff Ponzi scheme raised concerns over the effectiveness of the SEC's efforts to protect investors. Madoff's operation was a registered broker-dealer subject to both SEC and Financial Industry Regulatory Authority (FINRA, the self regulatory organization for broker-dealers) oversight, as well as a registered investment adviser subject to SEC oversight. Reform initiatives seek to improve the SEC's performance by providing it with more funding and by amending the regulation of investment advisers and others.

Under prior law, broker-dealers were required to make recommendations "suitable" to their customers, while investment advisers have a fiduciary duty to act in the customers' best interests, without regard to their own compensation, and with an affirmative duty to disclose any potential conflicts of interest. The services provided by broker-dealers and investment advisers, however, often overlap—both can provide investment advice and there are some concerns that customers may falsely assume that the person advising them is committed to acting in their best interests.

Provisions in the Dodd-Frank Act (Title IX)

The Dodd-Frank Act gives the SEC the authority to impose a fiduciary duty on broker-dealers who offer personalized investment advice about securities to a retail customer following a study.

The SEC collects fees from securities transactions and registration fees, which go to an account available to congressional appropriators. The SEC's budget has often been much less than the annual fees that it collects and there has been interest in permitting the agency to be self-funded as is the case with the federal banking regulators. Under the Dodd-Frank Act, some fees will be available to appropriators to fund the SEC, while others will go to the Treasury General Fund. The SEC's budget will remain subject to the congressional appropriations process, but it will submit its budget request directly to Congress, without changes by the Administration. In addition, the Dodd-Frank Act authorizes increased funding levels for FY2011 to FY2015, subject to appropriations, which would result in almost a doubling of SEC funding. It also enables the SEC to access up to $100 million annually from a "Reserve Fund" for what the SEC "determines is necessary to carry out the functions of the agency,"[40] funded from the agency's fee collections.

The act creates an Office of Investor Advocate within the SEC. The Investor Advocate will assist retail investors in resolving significant problems they may have with the commission or with self-regulatory organizations; identify areas in which investors would benefit from changes in regulations; and identify problems that investors have with financial service providers and investment products.

The Dodd-Frank Act also establishes an Investor Advisory Committee within the SEC, whose purpose is to advise and consult with the SEC on regulatory priorities; issues relating to the regulation of securities products, trading strategies, fee structures, and the effectiveness of disclosure; initiatives to protect investor interest; and initiatives to promote investor confidence and the integrity of the securities marketplace. The committee will include an Investor Advocate, a representative of the state securities commissions, senior citizen advocates, and persons representing the interests of individual equity and debt investors, and of institutional investors.

Previously, publicly traded corporations with a market value of less than $75 million (known as nonaccelerated filers) enjoyed a temporary exemption from Section 404(b) of the Sarbanes-Oxley Act of 2002, which requires publicly traded companies to audit their internal accounting controls (a process aimed at ensuring the reliability of a firm's financial reporting).[41] In 2009, the SEC adopted rules to remove the small company exemption, for the fiscal year ending on or after June 15, 2010. The Dodd-Frank Act effectively reverses that SEC rulemaking, making the exemption permanent.

The Dodd-Frank Act creates a new class of SEC registrant, the "municipal advisor." Intermediaries who provide financial advice to municipalities will be required to register with the SEC, abide by rules written by the Municipal Securities Rulemaking Board (MSRB), and will have a fiduciary duty to their clients. The MSRB membership will be reconstituted, so that board members who are independent of the municipal securities industry constitute a majority.

Hedge Funds

Policy Issues[42]

Hedge funds are not explicitly defined in federal securities law. They are generally described as privately organized, pooled investment vehicles not available to the public whose primary investors are wealthy individuals or institutions. Some hedge funds can also be distinguished from other investment funds by their pronounced use of leverage and their use of trading strategies based on short selling. The funds have a significant capital market presence. According to some estimates, they have been responsible for about one-fifth of the daily trading on the New York Stock Exchange and have over a trillion dollars in assets.

Hedge funds can provide benefits to financial markets by enhancing liquidity and efficiency and by reallocating financial risk. Some potential risks were revealed in 1998 when the hedge fund Long-Term Capital Management (LTCM) teetered on the brink of collapse. Concerns over the systemic implications of LTCM's collapse resulted in the New York Fed engineering a multibillion dollar rescue of the fund. Hedge fund failures did not play a prominent role in precipitating or spreading the recent financial crisis, however.

Under the "private adviser" exemption, hedge fund managers, who do not hold themselves to be investment advisers and who have fewer than 15 clients, have been exempted from registering with the SEC as investment advisers under the Investment Advisers Act (IAA).[43] Although some hedge fund managers registered voluntarily, it has been argued that the absence of comprehensive hedge fund data that would accompany mandatory fund registration, could deprive regulators of potentially critical information on the size and nature of the funds and the risks that they may or may not pose to the economy.

Provisions in the Dodd-Frank Act (Title IV)

The Dodd-Frank Act eliminates the "private adviser" exemption in the IAA, generally requiring advisers to private funds such as hedge funds with more than $150 million in assets under management to register with the SEC and to provide such information about their investment portfolios and strategies as the SEC and the FSOC deem necessary to monitor systemic risk. Advisers to venture capital funds and family offices (but not private equity funds) will be exempt from the registration requirement. The Dodd-Frank Act also raises the asset threshold for SEC registration from $25 million to $100 million. Smaller advisers will generally register with the states, although SEC registration is required if an adviser's home state does not regulate advisers or if an adviser is registered to do business in more than 15 states.

Executive Compensation and Corporate Governance

Policy Issues[44]

The financial crisis led to policy concerns about a possible link between excessive financial firm risk taking and executive compensation practices. Beginning in 2008, the

Troubled Asset Relief Program subjected recipients to various executive pay restrictions and corporate governance requirements. In the fall of 2009, as part of its safety and soundness regulatory oversight of banks, the Fed proposed to review bank pay structures to identify any compensation arrangements that provide incentives to take excessive.[45] In June 2010, final guidance was issued. These initiatives are significantly premised on the widely held belief that large financial firm incentive pay structures significantly contributed to excessive risk taking. However, at least one major academic study has raised questions concerning the premise.[46]

Provisions in the Dodd-Frank Act (Title IX)

Under the Dodd-Frank Act, at least once every three years, public company shareholders will be able to cast a nonbinding vote to approve executive compensation and where applicable, executive golden parachutes, known generally as "say on pay." The SEC will be permitted to adopt exemptions for small public companies. The act also authorizes the SEC to promulgate rules that would allow shareholders to nominate candidates for a public company's board through the company's proxy materials, a process called proxy access. The SEC may exempt small companies from these provisions.

The Dodd-Frank Act also requires the SEC to amend its rules to require additional disclosure on the relationship between executive compensation and corporate financial performance with respect to such metrics as changes in the value of an issuer's stock and dividend distributions. The SEC must issue rules prohibiting stock exchanges from listing the stock of any company that does not adopt an executive incentive pay "clawback" policy. Specifically, when there is an accounting restatement from material noncompliance with federal financial disclosure laws, a company is required to recover incentive-based compensation awarded to current or former executives based on the erroneous disclosures during three years preceding the restatement.

The Dodd-Frank Act also directs federal financial regulators to jointly adopt guidance requiring applicable financial institutions (including depository institutions, broker-dealers, credit unions, investment advisers, Fannie Mae, and Freddie Mac) with more than $1 billion in assets to prohibit incentive-based pay arrangements for executives, employees, directors, or principal shareholders deemed to be excessive, or that could lead to material financial loss at the financial institution.

Insurance[47]

Policy Issues

Under the McCarran-Ferguson Act of 1945,[48] insurance regulation is generally left to the individual states. For several years prior to the financial crisis, some Members of Congress have introduced legislation to federalize insurance regulation along the lines of the dual regulation of the banking sector, although none of this legislation has reached the committee markup stage.[49]

The financial crisis, particularly the involvement of insurance giant AIG and the smaller monoline bond insurers, changed the tenor of the debate around insurance regulation, with increased emphasis on the systemic importance of some insurance companies. Although it could be argued that insurer involvement in the financial crisis demonstrated the need for full-scale federal regulation of insurance, the financial regulatory reform proposals in the 111th Congress generally have not included language implementing such a system. Instead, such proposals have tended to include the creation of a somewhat narrower federal office focusing on gathering information on insurance and setting policy on international insurance issues. Provisions on consumer protection, investor protection, and systemic risk provisions also have the potential to affect insurance, though insurance has been largely exempted from these aspects of the legislation as well.

Provisions in the Dodd-Frank Act (Title V)

The Dodd-Frank Act creates a new Federal Insurance Office within the Treasury Department. In addition to gathering information and advising on insurance issues, this office would have limited preemptive power over state insurance laws and regulations. This preemption is limited to cases in which the state measures result in less favorable treatment of non-U.S. insurers and in which the case is covered by an existing international agreement. Insurers are exempted from oversight by the act's new Bureau of Consumer Financial Protection. Under the act, systemically significant insurers could be subject to identification by the Financial Stability Oversight Council, regulation by the Federal Reserve and resolution by the special authority created by the act, although resolution of state-chartered insurance companies would continue to occur under the state insurer insolvency regimes. In addition, the Dodd-Frank Act streamlines the state regulation of surplus lines insurance and reinsurance.[50]

Miscellaneous Provisions in the Dodd-Frank Act

The Dodd-Frank Act contains several miscellaneous provisions in various titles of the legislation, including the following:

- *Section 1075: Interchange Fees.* This section authorizes the Federal Reserve to prescribe regulations regarding interchange transaction fees with respect to electronic debit transactions. The amount of such interchange fees must be reasonable and proportional to the costs incurred by the debit card issuer in the transaction. This provision applies to all banks that have $10 billion or more in assets.
- *Title III, Subtitle C: Federal Deposit Insurance Corporation.* This subtitle reforms deposit insurance by altering the assessment base, placing a floor on reserve ratios, and permanently increasing the insured deposit limit to $250,000.
- *Title XII: Improving Access to Mainstream Financial Institutions.* This title includes provisions to expand access to the banking system for families with low and moderate incomes by (1) authorizing a program to help such individuals open low-cost checking or savings accounts at banks or credit unions; and (2) creating a pool of capital to enable community development financial institutions to provide small, local, retail loan programs as alternatives to "pay day" or automobile title loans in local communities.
- *Title XIII: The TARP Pay it Back Act.* This title reduces the amount authorized to be outstanding under the TARP to $475 billion; it was originally $700 billion. It will

The Dodd-Frank Wall Street Reform and Consumer Protection Act 21

also prohibit the Treasury from using repaid TARP funds to make new TARP investments.

- *Title XV: Miscellaneous Provisions.* This title requires the Administration to assess proposed loans by the International Monetary Fund to middle-income nations. If it determines that the loan recipient's public debt exceeds its annual gross domestic product, it will have to oppose the loan unless it can certify to Congress that the loan is likely to be repaid. The act also stipulates that entities responsible for production processes or manufactured output that depend on minerals originating in the Democratic Republic of Congo and adjoining countries will be required to provide disclosures to the SEC on the measures taken to exercise due diligence with respect to the source and chain of custody of the materials, and products manufactured from them. In addition, companies will be required to disclose (1) payments to foreign governments for mineral extraction rights, and (2) information regarding mine safety violations.

End Notes

[1] Initially incorporated bills included H.R. 2609, H.R. 3126, H.R. 3269, H.R. 3817, H.R. 3818, H.R. 3890, and H.R. 3996.

[2] The Restoring American Financial Stability Act of 2009 committee print is available at http://banking.senate.gov/public/_files/111609FullBillTextofTheRestoringAmericanFinancialStabilityActof2009.pdf.

[3] The Restoring American Financial Stability Act of 2010 committee print is available at http://banking.senate.gov/public/_files/ChairmansMark31510AYO10306_xmlFinancialReformLegislationBill.pdf. The amendment adopted in committee is available at http://banking.senate.gov/public/_files/032310Mangers Amendment AYO10627.pdf.

[4] See http://republicans.financialservices.house.gov/index.php?option=com_content&task=view&id= 601& Itemid=42.

[5] "Blueprint for a Modernized Financial Regulatory Structure" U.S. Treasury, available at http://www.treas.gov/press/ releases/reports/Blueprint.pdf.

[6] Treasury has created websites to track financial intervention and financial reform. See http://ustreas.gov/initiatives/ regulatoryreform/ and http://www.financialstability.gov.

[7] See, for example, "The Panic of 2008," a speech given by Federal Reserve Governor Kevin Warsh on April 6, 2009, for discussion of aspects of typical financial panics and historical examples, available at http://www.federalreserve.gov/ newsevents/speech/warsh20090406a.htm.

[8] Treasury Secretary Timothy F. Geithner, Written Testimony House Financial Services Committee, Financial Regulatory Reform, September 23, 2009, available at http://www.ustreas.gov/press/releases/tg296.htm.

[9] For more information, see CRS Report R40877, *Financial Regulatory Reform: Systemic Risk and the Federal Reserve*, by Marc Labonte.

[10] For an overview of systemic risk, see CRS Report R40417, *Macroprudential Oversight: Monitoring Systemic Risk in the Financial System*, by Darryl E. Getter.

[11] For more information, see CRS Report R41298, *The "Volcker Rule:" Proposals to Limit "Speculative" Proprietary Trading by Banks*, by David H. Carpenter and M. Maureen Murphy.

[12] See CRS Report RL34427, *Financial Turmoil: Federal Reserve Policy Responses*, by Marc Labonte.

[13] 12 U.S.C. § 343.

[14] See CRS Report R40530, *Insolvency of Systemically Significant Financial Companies (SSFCs): Bankruptcy vs. Conservatorship/Receivership*, by David H. Carpenter.

[15] 12 U.S.C. § 1823(c)(4).

[16] For a more in-depth analysis of these resolution regimes, see CRS Report R40530, *Insolvency of Systemically Significant Financial Companies (SSFCs): Bankruptcy vs. Conservatorship/Receivership*, by David H. Carpenter and CRS Report R40928, *Lehman Brothers and IndyMac: Comparing Resolution Regimes*, by David H. Carpenter.

[17] Dodd-Frank Act § 203.

[18] Dodd-Frank Act § 204.

[19] Dodd-Frank Act § 214.

[20] See CRS Report RS22722, *Securitization and Federal Regulation of Mortgages for Safety and Soundness*, by Edward V. Murphy.

[21] See CRS Report R41176, *Federal Financial Services Regulatory Consolidation: Structural Response to the 2007-2009 Financial Crisis*, by Walter W. Eubanks and CRS Report R40249, *Who Regulates Whom? An Overview of U.S. Financial Supervision*, by Mark Jickling and Edward V. Murphy.

[22] See CRS Report R41338, *The Dodd-Frank Wall Street Reform and Consumer Protection Act: Title X, The Consumer Financial Protection Bureau*, by David H. Carpenter.

[23] 15 U.S.C. §§ 1601 *et seq.*

[24] U.S. Department of the Treasury, *Financial Regulatory Reform: A New Foundation*, June 2009, pg. 56, available at http://www.financialstability.gov/docs/regs/FinalReport_web

[25] Dodd-Frank Act § 1024.

[26] Dodd-Frank Act § 1024.

[27] Dodd-Frank Act § 1027(a).

[28] The Dodd-Frank Act streamlines the FTC's rulemaking procedures for declaring trade practices to be unfair or deceptive under the FTC Act, but only with regards to auto dealers. Dodd-Frank Act § 1029. The FTC's general rulemaking procedures under the FTC Act are not altered by the Dodd-Frank Act. 15 U.S.C. § 57a.

[29] See CRS Report RL33775, *Alternative Mortgages: Causes and Policy Implications of Troubled Mortgage Resets in the Subprime and Alt-A Markets*, by Edward V. Murphy.

[30] For more information, see CRS Report R40965, *Key Issues in Derivatives Reform*, by Rena S. Miller.

[31] P.L. 106-554, 114 Stat. 2763.

[32] Dodd-Frank Act § 723 (swaps) and § 763 (security-based swaps (SBS).

[33] Contracts with a large number of underlying securities will be swaps; contracts based on single securities or narrow-based security indexes will be security-based swaps.

[34] Dodd-Frank Act § 723 (Swaps) and § 763 (SBS).

[35] Financial entities are defined, for the purposes of these subsections, as swap dealers, security-based swap dealers, major swap participants, major security-based swap participants, commodity pools, private funds, employee benefit plans, and persons predominantly engaged in activities that are in the business of banking or are financial in nature. The CFTC and SEC are given the power to exempt small banks, savings associations, farm credit system institutions, and credit unions from the definition of financial entities. § 723 (Swaps) and § 763 (SBS) of the Dodd-Frank Act.

[36] Dodd-Frank Act § 716.

[37] See CRS Report R40613, *Credit Rating Agencies and Their Regulation*, by Gary Shorter and Michael V. Seitzinger.

[38] See CRS Report RS22519, *Credit Rating Agency Reform Act of 2006*, by Michael V. Seitzinger.

[39] As an example, federally-insured thrifts were prohibited from owning bonds rated below investment grade by an NRSRO.

[40] Dodd-Frank Act § 991.

[41] See CRS Report RS22482, *Section 404 of the Sarbanes-Oxley Act of 2002 (Management Assessment of Internal Controls): Current Regulation and Congressional Concerns*, by Michael V. Seitzinger.

[42] See CRS Report R40783, *Hedge Funds: Legal History and the Dodd-Frank Act*, by Kathleen Ann Ruane and Michael V. Seitzinger and CRS Report R40783, *Hedge Funds: Legal History and the Dodd-Frank Act*, by Kathleen Ann Ruane and Michael V. Seitzinger.

[43] 15 U.S.C. § 80b-1 *et seq.*

[44] See CRS Report RS22583, *Executive Compensation: SEC Regulations and Congressional Proposals*, by Michael V. Seitzinger.

[45] See CRS Report R40540, *Executive Compensation Limits in Selected Federal Laws*, by Michael V. Seitzinger and Carol A. Pettit.

[46] Rudiger Fahlenbrach, Rene Stulz, and Rene M. Bank, "CEO Incentives and the Credit Crisis," *Charles A. Dice Center Working Paper No. 2009-13*, July 27, 2009, available at SSRN: http://ssrn.com/abstract=1439859.

[47] See CRS Report R41018, *Insurance and Financial Regulatory Reform in the 111th Congress*, by Baird Webel.

[48] 15 U.S.C. § 1011 *et seq.*

[49] See CRS Report R40771, *Insurance Regulation: Issues, Background, and Legislation in the 111th Congress*, by Baird Webel.

[50] See CRS Report RS22506, *Surplus Lines Insurance: Background and Current Legislation*, by Baird Webel.

In: The Dodd-Frank Wall Street Reform...
Editors: Nathan L. Morris and Philip O. Price

ISBN: 978-1-61324-101-1
© 2011 Nova Science Publishers, Inc.

Chapter 2

BRIEF SUMMARY OF THE DODD-FRANK WALL STREET REFORM AND CONSUMER PROTECTION ACT

Create a Sound Economic Foundation to Grow Jobs, Protect Consumers, Rein in Wall Street and Big Bonuses, End Bailouts and Too Big to Fail, Prevent Another Financial Crisis

Years without accountability for Wall Street and big banks brought us the worst financial crisis since the Great Depression, the loss of 8 million jobs, failed businesses, a drop in housing prices, and wiped out personal savings.

The failures that led to this crisis require bold action. We must restore responsibility and accountability in our financial system to give Americans confidence that there is a system in place that works for and protects them. We must create a sound foundation to grow the economy and create jobs.

HIGHLIGHTS OF THE LEGISLATION

Consumer Protections with Authority and Independence: Creates a new independent watchdog, housed at the Federal Reserve, with the authority to ensure American consumers get the clear, accurate information they need to shop for mortgages, credit cards, and other financial products, and protect them from hidden fees, abusive terms, and deceptive practices.

Ends Too Big to Fail Bailouts: Ends the possibility that taxpayers will be asked to write a check to bail out financial firms that threaten the economy by: creating a safe way to liquidate failed financial firms; imposing tough new capital and leverage requirements that make it undesirable to get too big; updating the Fed's authority to allow system-wide support but no longer prop up individual firms; and establishing rigorous standards and supervision to protect the economy and American consumers, investors and businesses.

Advance Warning System: Creates a council to identify and address systemic risks posed by large, complex companies, products, and activities before they threaten the stability of the economy.

Transparency & Accountability for Exotic Instruments: Eliminates loopholes that allow risky and abusive practices to go on unnoticed and unregulated -- including loopholes for over-the-counter derivatives, asset-backed securities, hedge funds, mortgage brokers and payday lenders.

Executive Compensation and Corporate Governance: Provides shareholders with a say on pay and corporate affairs with a non-binding vote on executive compensation and golden parachutes.

Protects Investors: Provides tough new rules for transparency and accountability for credit rating agencies to protect investors and businesses.

Enforces Regulations on the Books: Strengthens oversight and empowers regulators to aggressively pursue financial fraud, conflicts of interest and manipulation of the system that benefits special interests at the expense of American families and businesses.

STRONG CONSUMER FINANCIAL PROTECTION WATCHDOG

The Consumer Financial Protection Bureau

- **Independent Head:** Led by an independent director appointed by the President and confirmed by the Senate.
- **Independent Budget:** Dedicated budget paid by the Federal Reserve system.
- **Independent Rule Writing:** Able to autonomously write rules for consumer protections governing all financial institutions – banks and non-banks – offering consumer financial services or products.
- **Examination and Enforcement:** Authority to examine and enforce regulations for banks and credit unions with assets of over $10 billion and all mortgage-related businesses (lenders, servicers, mortgage brokers, and foreclosure scam operators), payday lenders, and student lenders as well as other non-bank financial companies that are large, such as debt collectors and consumer reporting agencies. Banks and Credit Unions with assets of $10 billion or less will be examined for consumer complaints by the appropriate regulator.
- **Consumer Protections:** Consolidates and strengthens consumer protection responsibilities currently handled by the Office of the Comptroller of the Currency, Office of Thrift Supervision, Federal Deposit Insurance Corporation, Federal Reserve, National Credit Union Administration, the Department of Housing and Urban Development, and Federal Trade Commission. Will also oversee the enforcement of federal laws intended to ensure the fair, equitable and nondiscriminatory access to credit for individuals and communities.
- **Able to Act Fast:** With this Bureau on the lookout for bad deals and schemes, consumers won't have to wait for Congress to pass a law to be protected from bad business practices.
- **Educates:** Creates a new Office of Financial Literacy.
- **Consumer Hotline:** Creates a national consumer complaint hotline so consumers will have, for the first time, a single toll-free number to report problems with financial products and services.
- **Accountability:** Makes one office accountable for consumer protections. With many agencies sharing responsibility, it's hard to know who is responsible for what, and

easy for emerging problems that haven't historically fallen under anyone's purview, to fall through the cracks.

- **Works with Bank Regulators:** Coordinates with other regulators when examining banks to prevent undue regulatory burden. Consults with regulators before a proposal is issued and regulators could appeal regulations they believe would put the safety and soundness of the banking system or the stability of the financial system at risk.
- **Clearly Defined Oversight:** Protects small business from unintentionally being regulated by the CFPB, excluding businesses that meet certain standards.

LOOKING OUT FOR THE NEXT BIG PROBLEM: ADDRESSING SYSTEMIC RISKS

The Financial Stability Oversight Council

- **Expert Members:** Made up of 10 federal financial regulators and an independent member and 5 nonvoting members, the Financial Stability Oversight Council will be charged with identifying and responding to emerging risks throughout the financial system. The Council will be chaired by the Treasury Secretary and include the Federal Reserve Board, SEC, CFTC, OCC, FDIC, FHFA, NCUA, the new Consumer Financial Protection Bureau, and an independent appointee with insurance expertise. The 5 nonvoting members include OFR, FIO, and state banking, insurance, and securities regulators.
- **Tough to Get Too Big:** Makes recommendations to the Federal Reserve for increasingly strict rules for capital, leverage, liquidity, risk management and other requirements as companies grow in size and complexity, with significant requirements on companies that pose risks to the financial system.
- **Regulates Nonbank Financial Companies:** Authorized to require, with a 2/3 vote and vote of the chair, that a nonbank financial company be regulated by the Federal Reserve if the council believe there would be negative effects on the financial system if the company failed or its activities would pose a risk to the financial stability of the US.
- **Break Up Large, Complex Companies:** Able to approve, with a 2/3 vote and vote of the chair, a Federal Reserve decision to require a large, complex company, to divest some of its holdings if it poses a grave threat to the financial stability of the United States – but only as a last resort.
- **Technical Expertise:** Creates a new Office of Financial Research within Treasury to be staffed with a highly sophisticated staff of economists, accountants, lawyers, former supervisors, and other specialists to support the council's work by collecting financial data and conducting economic analysis.
- **Make Risks Transparent:** Through the Office of Financial Research and member agencies the council will collect and analyze data to identify and monitor emerging risks to the economy and make this information public in periodic reports and testimony to Congress every year.

- **No Evasion:** Large bank holding companies that have received TARP funds will not be able to avoid Federal Reserve supervision by simply dropping their banks. (the "Hotel California" provision)
- **Capital Standards:** Establishes a floor for capital that cannot be lower than the standards in effect today and authorizes the Council to impose a 15-1 leverage requirement at a company if necessary to mitigate a grave threat to the financial system.

ENDING TOO BIG TO FAIL BAILOUTS

Limiting Large, Complex Financial Companies and Preventing Future Bailouts

- **No Taxpayer Funded Bailouts:** Clearly states taxpayers will not be on the hook to save a failing financial company or to cover the cost of its liquidation.
- **Discourage Excessive Growth & Complexity:** The Financial Stability Oversight Council will monitor systemic risk and make recommendations to the Federal Reserve for increasingly strict rules for capital, leverage, liquidity, risk management and other requirements as companies grow in size and complexity, with significant requirements on companies that pose risks to the financial system.
- **Volcker Rule:** Requires regulators implement regulations for banks, their affiliates and holding companies, to prohibit proprietary trading, investment in and sponsorship of hedge funds and private equity funds, and to limit relationships with hedge funds and private equity funds. Nonbank financial institutions supervised by the Fed also have restrictions on proprietary trading and hedge fund and private equity investments. The Council will study and make recommendations on implementation to aid regulators.
- **Extends Regulation:** The Council will have the ability to require nonbank financial companies that pose a risk to the financial stability of the United States to submit to supervision by the Federal Reserve.
- **Payment, clearing, and settlement regulation.** Provides a specific framework for promoting uniform risk-management standards for systemically important financial market utilities and systemically important payment, clearing, and settlement activities conducted by financial institutions.
- **Funeral Plans**: Requires large, complex financial companies to periodically submit plans for their rapid and orderly shutdown should the company go under. Companies will be hit with higher capital requirements and restrictions on growth and activity, as well as divestment, if they fail to submit acceptable plans. Plans will help regulators understand the structure of the companies they oversee and serve as a roadmap for shutting them down if the company fails. Significant costs for failing to produce a credible plan create incentives for firms to rationalize structures or operations that cannot be unwound easily.

- **Liquidation:** Creates an orderly liquidation mechanism for FDIC to unwind failing systemically significant financial companies. Shareholders and unsecured creditors bear losses and management and culpable directors will be removed.
- **Liquidation Procedure:** Requires that Treasury, FDIC and the Federal Reserve all agree to put a company into the orderly liquidation process to mitigate serious adverse effects on financial stability, with an up front judicial review.
- **Costs to Financial Firms, Not Taxpayers**: Taxpayers will bear no cost for liquidating large, interconnected financial companies. FDIC can borrow only the amount of funds to liquidate a company that it expects to be repaid from the assets of the company being liquidated. The government will be first in line for repayment. Funds not repaid from the sale of the company's assets will be repaid first through the claw back of any payments to creditors that exceeded liquidation value and then assessments on large financial companies, with the riskiest paying more based on considerations included in a risk matrix
- **Federal Reserve Emergency Lending:** Significantly alters the Federal Reserve's 13(3) emergency lending authority to prohibit bailing out an individual company. Secretary of the Treasury must approve any lending program, and such programs must be broad based and not aid a failing financial company. Collateral must be sufficient to protect taxpayers from losses.
- **Bankruptcy**: Most large financial companies that fail are expected to be resolved through the bankruptcy process.
- **Limits on Debt Guarantees:** To prevent bank runs, the FDIC can guarantee debt of solvent insured banks, but only after meeting serious requirements: 2/3 majority of the Board and the FDIC board must determine there is a threat to financial stability; the Treasury Secretary approves terms and conditions and sets a cap on overall guarantee amounts; the President activates an expedited process for Congressional approval.

REFORMING THE FEDERAL RESERVE

- **Federal Reserve Emergency Lending:** Limits the Federal Reserve's 13(3) emergency lending authority by prohibiting emergency lending to an individual entity. Secretary of the Treasury must approve any lending program, programs must be broad based, and loans cannot be made to insolvent firms. Collateral must be sufficient to protect taxpayers from losses.
- **Audit of the Federal Reserve:** GAO will conduct a one-time audit of all Federal Reserve 13(3) emergency lending that took place during the financial crisis. Details on all lending will be published on the Federal Reserve website by December 1, 2010. In the future GAO will have ongoing authority to audit 13(3), emergency lending , and discount window lending, and open market transactions.
- **Transparency - Disclosure:** Requires the Federal Reserve to disclose counterparties and information about amounts, terms and conditions of 13(3) emergency lending and discount window lending, and open market transactions on an on-going basis, with specified time delays.

- **Supervisory Accountability:** Creates a Vice Chairman for Supervision, a member of the Board of Governors of the Federal Reserve designated by the President, who will develop policy recommendations regarding supervision and regulation for the Board, and will report to Congress semi-annually on Board supervision and regulation efforts.
- **Federal Reserve Bank Governance:** GAO will conduct a study of the current system for appointing Federal Reserve Bank directors, to examine whether the current system effectively represents the public, and whether there are actual or potential conflicts of interest. It will also examine the establishment and operation of emergency lending facilities during the crisis and the Federal Reserve banks involved therein. The GAO will identify measures that would improve reserve bank governance.
- **Election of Federal Reserve Bank Presidents:** Presidents of the Federal Reserve Banks will be elected by class B directors - elected by district member banks to represent the public - and class C directors - appointed by the Board of Governors to represent the public. Class A directors - elected by member banks to represent member banks – will no longer vote for presidents of the Federal Reserve Banks.
- **Limits on Debt Guarantees:** To prevent bank runs, the FDIC can guarantee debt of solvent insured banks, but only after meeting serious requirements: 2/3 majority of the Federal Reserve Board and the FDIC board determine there is a threat to financial stability; the Treasury Secretary approves terms and conditions and sets a cap on overall guarantee amounts; the President initiates an expedited process for Congressional approval.

CREATING TRANSPARENCY AND ACCOUNTABILITY FOR DERIVATIVES

Bringing Transparency and Accountability to the Derivatives Market

- **Closes Regulatory Gaps:** Provides the SEC and CFTC with authority to regulate over-the-counter derivatives so that irresponsible practices and excessive risk-taking can no longer escape regulatory oversight.
- **Central Clearing and Exchange Trading:** Requires central clearing and exchange trading for derivatives that can be cleared and provides a role for both regulators and clearing houses to determine which contracts should be cleared.
- **Market Transparency:** Requires data collection and publication through clearing houses or swap repositories to improve market transparency and provide regulators important tools for monitoring and responding to risks.
- **Financial safeguards:** Adds safeguards to system by ensuring dealers and major swap participants have adequate financial resources to meet responsibilities. Provides regulators the authority to impose capital and margin requirements on swap dealers and major swap participants, not end users.
- **Higher standard of conduct:** Establishes a code of conduct for all registered swap dealers and major swap participants when advising a swap entity. When acting as

counterparties to a pension fund, endowment fund, or state or local government, dealers are to have a reasonable basis to believe that the fund or governmental entity has an independent representative advising them.

NEW OFFICES OF MINORITY AND WOMEN INCLUSION

- At federal banking and securities regulatory agencies, the bill establishes an Office of Minority and Women Inclusion that will, among other things, address employment and contracting diversity matters. The offices will coordinate technical assistance to minority-owned and women-owned businesses and seek diversity in the workforce of the regulators.

MORTGAGE REFORM

- **Require Lenders Ensure a Borrower's Ability to Repay**: Establishes a simple federal standard for all home loans: institutions must ensure that borrowers can repay the loans they are sold.
- **Prohibit Unfair Lending Practices**: Prohibits the financial incentives for subprime loans that encourage lenders to steer borrowers into more costly loans, including the bonuses known as "yield spread premiums" that lenders pay to brokers to inflate the cost of loans. Prohibits pre-payment penalties that trapped so many borrowers into unaffordable loans.
- **Establishes Penalties for Irresponsible Lending**: Lenders and mortgage brokers who don't comply with new standards will be held accountable by consumers for as high as three-years of interest payments and damages plus attorney's fees (if any). Protects borrowers against foreclosure for violations of these standards.
- **Expands Consumer Protections for High-Cost Mortgages**: Expands the protections available under federal rules on high-cost loans -- lowering the interest rate and the points and fee triggers that define high cost loans.
- **Requires Additional Disclosures for Consumers on Mortgages**: Lenders must disclose the maximum a consumer could pay on a variable rate mortgage, with a warning that payments will vary based on interest rate changes.
- **Housing Counseling**: Establishes an Office of Housing Counseling within HUD to boost homeownership and rental housing counseling.

HEDGE FUNDS

Raising Standards and Regulating Hedge Funds

- **Fills Regulatory Gaps:** Ends the "shadow" financial system by requiring hedge funds and private equity advisors to register with the SEC as investment advisers and provide information about their trades and portfolios necessary to assess systemic risk. This data will be shared with the systemic risk regulator and the SEC will report to Congress annually on how it uses this data to protect investors and market integrity.

- **Greater State Supervision:** Raises the assets threshold for federal regulation of investment advisers from $30 million to $100 million, a move expected to significantly increase the number of advisors under state supervision. States have proven to be strong regulators in this area and subjecting more entities to state supervision will allow the SEC to focus its resources on newly registered hedge funds.

CREDIT RATING AGENCIES

New Requirements and Oversight of Credit Rating Agencies

- **New Office, New Focus at SEC:** Creates an Office of Credit Ratings at the SEC with expertise and its own compliance staff and the authority to fine agencies. The SEC is required to examine Nationally Recognized Statistical Ratings Organizations at least once a year and make key findings public.
- **Disclosure:** Requires Nationally Recognized Statistical Ratings Organizations to disclose their methodologies, their use of third parties for due diligence efforts, and their ratings track record.
- **Independent Information:** Requires agencies to consider information in their ratings that comes to their attention from a source other than the organizations being rated if they find it credible.
- **Conflicts of Interest:** Prohibits compliance officers from working on ratings, methodologies, or sales; installs a new requirement for NRSROs to conduct a one-year look-back review when an NRSRO employee goes to work for an obligor or underwriter of a security or money market instrument subject to a rating by that NRSRO; and mandates that a report to the SEC when certain employees of the NRSRO go to work for an entity that the NRSRO has rated in the previous twelve months.
- **Liability:** Investors can bring private rights of action against ratings agencies for a knowing or reckless failure to conduct a reasonable investigation of the facts or to obtain analysis from an independent source. NRSROs will now be subject to "expert liability" with the nullification of Rule 436(g) which provides an exemption for credit ratings provided by NRSROs from being considered a part of the registration statement.
- **Right to Deregister:** Gives the SEC the authority to deregister an agency for providing bad ratings over time.
- **Education:** Requires ratings analysts to pass qualifying exams and have continuing education.
- **Eliminates Many Statutory and Regulatory Requirements to Use NRSRO Ratings:** Reduces over-reliance on ratings and encourages investors to conduct their own analysis.

- **Independent Boards:** Requires at least half the members of NRSRO boards to be independent, with no financial stake in credit ratings.
- **Ends Shopping for Ratings:** The SEC shall create a new mechanism to prevent issuers of asset backed-securities from picking the agency they think will give the highest rating, after conducting a study and after submission of the report to Congress.

EXECUTIVE COMPENSATION AND CORPORATE GOVERNANCE

Gives Shareholders a Say on Pay and Creating Greater Accountability

- **Vote on Executive Pay and Golden Parachutes:** Gives shareholders a say on pay with the right to a non-binding vote on executive pay and golden parachutes. This gives shareholders a powerful opportunity to hold accountable executives of the companies they own, and a chance to disapprove where they see the kind of misguided incentive schemes that threatened individual companies and in turn the broader economy.
- **Nominating Directors:** Gives the SEC authority to grant shareholders proxy access to nominate directors. These requirements can help shift management's focus from short-term profits to long-term growth and stability.
- **Independent Compensation Committees:** Standards for listing on an exchange will require that compensation committees include only independent directors and have authority to hire compensation consultants in order to strengthen their independence from the executives they are rewarding or punishing.
- **No Compensation for Lies:** Requires that public companies set policies to take back executive compensation if it was based on inaccurate financial statements that don't comply with accounting standards.
- **SEC Review:** Directs the SEC to clarify disclosures relating to compensation, including requiring companies to provide charts that compare their executive compensation with stock performance over a five-year period.
- **Enhanced Compensation Oversight for Financial Industry:** Requires Federal financial regulators to issue and enforce joint compensation rules specifically applicable to financial institutions with a Federal regulator.

IMPROVEMENTS TO BANK AND THRIFT REGULATIONS

- **Volcker Rule** Implements a strengthened version of the Volcker rule by not allowing a study of the issue to undermine the prohibition on proprietary trading and investing a banking entity's own money in hedge funds, with a *de minimis* exception for funds where the investors require some "skin in the game" by the investment advisor--up to 3% of tier 1 capital in the aggregate

- **Abolishes the Office of Thrift Supervision:** Shuts down this dysfunctional regulator and transfers authorities mainly to the Office of the Comptroller of the Currency, but preserves the thrift charter.
- **Stronger lending limits:** Adds credit exposure from derivative transactions to banks' lending limits.
- **Improves supervision of holding company subsidiaries:** Requires the Federal Reserve to examine non-bank subsidiaries that are engaged in activities that the subsidiary bank can do (e.g. mortgage lending) on the same schedule and in the same manner as bank exams, Provides the primary federal bank regulator backup authority if that does not occur.
- **Intermediate Holding Companies:** Allows use of intermediate holding companies by commercial firms that control grandfathered unitary thrift holding companies to better regulate the financial activities, but not the commercial activities.
- **Interest on business checking:** Repeals the prohibition on banks paying interest on demand deposits.
- **Charter Conversions:** Removes a regulatory arbitrage opportunity by prohibiting a bank from converting its charter (unless both the old regulator and new regulator do not object) in order to get out from under an enforcement action.
- **Establishes New Offices of Minority and Women Inclusion at the federal financial agencies**

INSURANCE

- **Federal Insurance Office:** Creates the first ever office in the Federal government focused on insurance. The Office, as established in the Treasury, will gather information about the insurance industry, including access to affordable insurance products by minorities, low- and moderate- income persons and underserved communities. The Office will also monitor the insurance industry for systemic risk purposes.
- **International Presence:** The Office will serve as a uniform, national voice on insurance matters for the United States on the international stage.
- **Streamlines** regulation of surplus lines insurance and reinsurance through state-based reforms.

INTERCHANGE FEES

- **Protects Small Businesses from Unreasonable Fees:** Requires Federal Reserve to issue rules to ensure that fees charged to merchants by credit card companies debit card transactions are reasonable and proportional to the cost of processing those transactions.

CREDIT SCORE PROTECTION

- **Monitor Personal Financial Rating:** Allows consumers free access to their credit score if their score negatively affects them in a financial transaction or a hiring decision. Gives consumers access to credit score disclosures as part of an adverse action and risk-based pricing notice.

SEC AND IMPROVING INVESTOR PROTECTIONS

SEC and Improving Investor Protections

- **Fiduciary Duty:** Gives SEC the authority to impose a fiduciary duty on brokers who give investment advice --the advice must be in the best interest of their customers.
- **Encouraging Whistleblowers:** Creates a program within the SEC to encourage people to report securities violations, creating rewards of up to 30% of funds recovered for information provided.
- **SEC Management Reform:** Mandates a comprehensive outside consultant study of the SEC, an annual assessment of the SEC's internal supervisory controls and GAO review of SEC management.
- **New Advocates for Investors:** Creates the Investment Advisory Committee, a committee of investors to advise the SEC on its regulatory priorities and practices; the Office of Investor Advocate in the SEC, to identify areas where investors have significant problems dealing with the SEC and provide them assistance; and an ombudsman to handle investor complaints.
- **SEC Funding:** Provides more resources to the chronically underfunded agency to carry out its new duties.

SECURITIZATION

Reducing Risks Posed by Securities

- **Skin in the Game:** Requires companies that sell products like mortgage-backed securities to retain at least 5% of the credit risk, unless the underlying loans meet standards that reduce riskiness. That way if the investment doesn't pan out, the company that packaged and sold the investment would lose out right along with the people they sold it to.
- **Better Disclosure:** Requires issuers to disclose more information about the underlying assets and to analyze the quality of the underlying assets.

MUNICIPAL SECURITIES

Better Oversight of Municipal Securities Industry

- **Registers Municipal Advisors**: Requires registration of municipal advisors and subjects them rules written by the MSRB and enforced by the SEC.
- **Puts Investors First on the MSRB Board:** Ensures that at all times, the MSRB must have a majority of independent members, to ensure that the public interest is better protected in the regulation of municipal securities.
- **Fiduciary Duty:** Imposes a fiduciary duty on advisors to ensure that they adhere to the highest standard of care when advising municipal issuers.

TACKLING THE EFFECTS OF THE MORTGAGE CRISIS

- **Neighborhood Stabilization Program:** Provides $1 billion to States and localities to combat the ugly impact on neighborhood of the foreclosure crisis -- such as falling property values and increased crime - by rehabilitating, redeveloping, and reusing abandoned and foreclosed properties.
- **Emergency Mortgage Relief:** Building on a successful Pennsylvania program, provides $1 billion for bridge loans to qualified unemployed homeowners with reasonable prospects for reemployment to help cover mortgage payments until they are reemployed.
- **Foreclosure Legal Assistance.** Authorizes a HUD administered program for making grants to provide foreclosure legal assistance to low- and moderate-income homeowners and tenants related to home ownership preservation, home foreclosure prevention, and tenancy associated with home foreclosure.

TRANSPARENCY FOR EXTRACTION INDUSTRY

- **Public Disclosure**: Requires public disclosure to the SEC of payments made to the U.S. and foreign governments relating to the commercial development of oil, natural gas, and minerals.
- **SEC Filing Disclosure:** The SEC must require those engaged in the commercial development of oil, natural gas, or minerals to include information about payments they or their subsidiaries, partners or affiliates have made to the U.S. or a foreign government for such development in an annual report and post this information online.

Congo Conflict Minerals

- **Manufacturers Disclosure:** Requires those who file with the SEC and use minerals originating in the Democratic Republic of Congo in manufacturing to disclose measures taken to exercise due diligence on the source and chain of custody of the materials and the products manufactured.
- **Illicit Minerals Trade Strategy:** Requires the State Department to submit a strategy to address the illicit minerals trade in the region and a map to address links between conflict minerals and armed groups and establish a baseline against which to judge effectiveness.
- **Deposit Insurance Reforms:** Permanent increase in deposit insurance for banks, thrifts and credit unions to $250,000, retroactive to January 1, 2008.
- **Restricts US Funds for Foreign Governments:** Requires the Administration to evaluate proposed loans by the IMF to a middle-income country if that country's public debt exceeds its annual Gross Domestic Product, and oppose loans unlikely to be repaid.

In: The Dodd-Frank Wall Street Reform...
Editors: Nathan L. Morris and Philip O. Price

ISBN: 978-1-61324-101-1
© 2011 Nova Science Publishers, Inc.

Chapter 3

THE DODD-FRANK WALL STREET REFORM AND CONSUMER PROTECTION ACT: SYSTEMIC RISK AND THE FEDERAL RESERVE[*]

Marc Labonte

SUMMARY

The recent financial crisis contained a number of systemic risk episodes, or episodes that caused instability for large parts of the financial system. The lesson some policymakers have taken from this crisis is that a systemic risk or "macroprudential" regulator is needed to prevent similar episodes in the future. But what types of risk would this new regulator be tasked with preventing, and is it the case that those activities are currently unsupervised?

Some of the major financial market phenomena that have been identified as posing systemic risk include liquidity problems; "too big to fail" or "systemically important" firms; the cycle of rising leverage followed by rapid deleverage; weaknesses in payment, settlement, and clearing systems; and asset bubbles. At the time of the crisis, the Federal Reserve (Fed) already regulated bank

holding companies and financial holding companies for capital and liquidity requirements, and it could influence their behavior in markets that it did not regulate. In addition, the Fed directly regulated or operated in some payment, settlement, and clearing systems. Many systemically significant firms are already regulated by the Fed because they are bank holding companies, although some may exist in what is referred to as the shadow banking system, which was largely free of federal regulation for safety and soundness. The Fed's monetary policy mandate was broad enough to allow it to prick asset bubbles, although it has not chosen to do so. Neither the Board of Governors of the Federal Reserve System (Fed) nor other existing regulators had the authority to address gaps in existing regulation that they believed pose systemic risk.

Opponents of giving regulators new systemic risk responsibilities argue that the crisis did not occur because regulators lacked the necessary authority to prevent it, but because they used their authority poorly and failed to identify systemic risk until it was

---

[*] This is an edited, reformatted and augmented version of a Congressional Research Services publication, dated August 27, 2010.

too late. They fear that greater regulation of financial markets will lead to moral hazard problems that increase systemic risk. The recent crisis has demonstrated that government intervention may become unavoidable, however, even when firms or markets are not explicitly regulated or protected by the government.

The Dodd-Frank Wall Street Reform and Consumer Protection Act (H.R. 4173, P.L. 111-203) was signed into law on July 21, 2010. Provisions of this legislation involving the Federal Reserve and systemic risk are discussed in this report. The act creates a Financial Stability Oversight Council (Council) to identify (but not rectify) emerging threats and regulatory gaps. It authorizes the Fed to regulate systemically significant firms identified by the Council for safety and soundness. If the Secretary of the Treasury believes that a failure of a firm would threaten financial stability, the firm can be placed in receivership. It prohibits banks from engaging in proprietary trading, limits their ability to invest in hedge funds and private equity funds, and authorizes the Fed to regulate those activities at systemically significant firms. It also authorizes the Fed to regulate certain payment, clearing, or settlement systems identified as systemically significant by the Council. To prevent assistance to failing firms, it limits the Fed's authority to lend to non-banks in emergencies and requires more oversight and disclosure of Federal Reserve activities. It imposes minimum capital requirements on a greater array of institutions and calls for capital requirements to be made counter-cyclical. It attempts to move more derivatives into clearinghouses and exchanges.

Although the act could be portrayed as an expansion of the Fed's powers, the legislation also strips the Fed of certain powers, such as consumer financial protection responsibilities, and creates new checks on other powers, such as requirements to obtain approval from the Council or the Treasury Secretary before undertaking certain decisions.

INTRODUCTION

In the wake of the recent financial crisis, many commentators have called for systemic risk or "macroprudential" regulation to help avoid future crises. The Obama Administration's financial regulatory reform proposal of 2009 included many of the proposed elements, giving many—but not all—of these responsibilities to the Board of Governors of the Federal Reserve System (Fed).[1] Using the Administration's plan as a starting point, Congress enacted the Dodd-Frank Wall Street Reform and Consumer Protection Act (H.R. 4173), which was signed into law on July 21, 2010, as P.L. 111-203. The Dodd-Frank Act was a broad-based reform package that included provisions affecting almost every part of the financial system. This report discusses only those provisions related to systemic risk or the Federal Reserve, found mostly in Titles I and XI of the act.[2]

This report first discusses systemic risk issues, relating them to events in the recent crisis. It then identifies the Fed's existing powers and responsibilities for systemic risk regulation at the time of the crisis. Finally, it discusses parts of the Dodd-Frank Act involving the Fed and systemic risk, including the creation of a Financial Stability Oversight Council; regulation of systemically significant firms; resolution authority; modifications to the Fed's emergency lending authority and new disclosure requirements; the Consumer Financial Protection Bureau; the regulation of payment, clearing, and settlement systems and activities; and limits on proprietary trading.

WHAT IS SYSTEMIC RISK?

All financial market participants face risk—without it, financial intermediation would not occur. Some risks, such as the failure of a specific firm or change in a specific interest rate, can be addressed through diversification, insurance, or financial instruments such as derivatives. One definition of systemic risk is risk that can potentially cause instability for large parts of the financial system.[3] Often, systemic risk will be caused by risks that individual firms cannot protect themselves against; some economists distinguish these types of risks as a subset of systemic risks called systematic risks.[4] Systemic risk can come from within or outside of the financial system. An example of systemic risk that came from outside of the financial system were fears (that largely proved unfounded in hindsight) that the September 11, 2001, terrorist attacks on the nation's financial center would lead to widespread disruption to financial flows because of the destruction of physical infrastructure and death of highly specialized industry professionals. Systemic risk within the financial system is often characterized as *contagion*, meaning that problems with certain firms or parts of the system spill over to other firms and parts of the system.

The financial crisis that intensified in September 2008 featured many examples of systemic risk, including runs on financial institutions and illiquidity of asset classes, that will be discussed below. Many of these examples were highly unusual and had not been experienced as acutely by industry participants or financial regulators in the past. Whether firms or regulators were carelessly unprepared for what occurred, or whether these incidents truly could not be reasonably predicted, prevented, or avoided is subject to debate.

Some experts, both within the regulatory community and outside of it, have argued that part of the reason regulators failed to prevent the crisis is that regulators were given a mandate to prevent microprudential risk, but no regulator had a mandate to prevent macroprudential risk.[5] (Whether this is actually the case will be discussed below.)[6] Microprudential regulation focuses on identifying risks to an individual firm and requiring firms to protect against those risks, whereas macroprudential regulation focuses on preventing or safeguarding against systemic risks. A scenario can be imagined where microprudential regulators focus on the risks of a firm's actions to itself, but overlook risks posed by those same actions to the system as a whole. Proponents argue that financial regulatory reform should feature a new mandate to regulate systemic risk.[7]

At least two arguments have been made against a systemic risk regulator.[8] One argument holds that regulators already had the authority to respond to the systemic risk episodes that occurred in the crisis. Thus, the failure was not the result of a lack of regulator authority but poor use of existing authority. Conversely, it has been argued that those systemic risk episodes could not have been prevented precisely because they were systemic risk episodes— by their nature, the problems that arose were unlikely to be foreseen or neutralized. Either argument produces the conclusion that even with a systemic risk regulator in place, the crisis would not have been avoided. From this logic flows the same conclusion: the creation of a systemic risk regulator would be ineffective at best and harmful to necessary risk-taking behavior at worst because a systemic risk regulator, by design, has incentives to be overly cautious. Specific examples in the following section will help elucidate the perceived need for systemic risk regulation, while the subsequent section explains what regulators could and could not do in each area before the Dodd-Frank Act.

What Are Sources of Systemic Risk?

Policymakers can manage systemic risk only if the sources of systemic risk can be identified and regulated. A systemic risk regulator's authority to act could be made very broad and open ended to cover all contingencies, or it could be made more narrow to limit discretion and curb "mission creep," increasing the likelihood that once a risk is identified, additional legislative action would be needed to respond to it. This choice has implications for the balance of power between the legislative and executive branches. This section reviews sources of systemic risk that arose during the recent crisis, with the caveat that future crises are unlikely to follow a similar path as past crises. The examples selected below are the types of specific activities that could potentially be regulated for systemic risk.

Runs and Liquidity

Firms are said to be liquid when they are able to meet current obligations or short-term demand for funds. A firm is said to be solvent but illiquid when its assets exceed its liabilities, but it is unable to liquidate assets rapidly enough to meet current obligations. Markets are said to be liquid when a large volume of financial securities can be traded without price distortions because there is a ready and willing supply of buyers and sellers. Liquid markets are a sign of normalcy—most of the time, investors can take liquidity for granted.

Banking and many other types of financial intermediation often involve borrowing on a short-term basis and using the funds to lend or invest on a long-term basis. This creates a mismatch, where a financial institution's assets tend to be less liquid than its liabilities. Under normal financial conditions, an institution's short-term liquidity needs are relatively predictable, allowing it to easily sell or borrow against its long-term assets to meet those needs.

In a liquidity crunch of the type that characterized the episode beginning in August 2007 and other historical financial panics, investors are no longer willing to buy a firm's assets (at least not at prices the firm would consider reasonable) or lend it new funds against those assets. In these circumstances, if creditors attempt to withdraw their deposits or call in their loans all at once, an institution will fail even if the value of the institution's assets exceeds its liabilities. This scenario is referred to as a run. Historically, depositors have caused runs on banks, and mainstream economic thought credits the creation of Federal Deposit Insurance Corporation (FDIC) deposit insurance for largely eliminating the threat of depositor runs (because depositors have less incentive to withdraw funds if those funds are guaranteed by the government). In the recent crisis, runs occurred on non-banks when lenders refused to roll over loans as they matured.

Money market mutual funds were another part of the "shadow banking" system that was revealed to be susceptible to runs during the crisis. When Lehman Brothers failed, the Reserve Fund, a money market fund holding Lehman Brothers commercial paper, "broke the buck" (the value of its assets fell below par), and this prompted widespread withdrawal requests that could not be met. This set off a run throughout the money market industry, including a run against funds that did not hold Lehman debt. Like any investment fund where funds can be withdrawn on demand, a run is possible when the assets of the fund cannot be immediately liquidated to meet unusually high redemption requests. Money market mutual funds are seen as more susceptible to runs than other types of investment funds because funds can be withdrawn on demand; some funds hold assets, such as commercial paper, that cannot be resold to meet redemption requests; and money market funds are marketed as a safe alternative to bank accounts, with some featuring bank-like options such as check-writing.

Runs are subject to contagion. Runs may begin at troubled institutions, but sometimes spread to healthy institutions because of the liquidity mismatch. Because an institution's liquidity is finite, all depositors or creditors have an incentive to withdraw their funds first if they believe that the firm will soon run out of funds, especially in the absence of a governmental guarantee. The sudden withdrawal of funds can cause losses for remaining creditors at an otherwise healthy institution and can ultimately lead to the firm's failure. Runs can also be set off by an otherwise healthy institution's "counterparty" exposure to an unhealthy institution. Financial firms do not operate in isolation—they depend on each other as sources of credit, liquidity, and risk-sharing, and to buy and sell securities. Through these transactions, they become counterparties to each other, with the failure of one counterparty potentially imposing losses on the other. The crisis saw a widespread breakdown in counterparty trust that greatly reduced these transactions, straining the basic functioning of the financial system. Creditors and depositors may not be able to clearly gauge counterparty exposure, but because of the first-mover advantage in a run, may decide to err on the side of caution and withdraw funds.

Institutions face a tradeoff between the desire to hold liquidity to avoid the sorts of problems described above and the cost of holding that liquidity, which typically means earning less than through alternative uses of the funds. One way regulators reduce the likelihood of liquidity problems is by requiring that financial firms hold sufficient liquid reserves to meet unforeseen circumstances. Another way is to limit reliance on short-term debt that may be difficult to roll over during periods of financial turmoil. In principle, these interventions can be justified on economic grounds based on the argument that liquidity creates *positive externalities* for the financial system as a whole that are not fully captured by the individual institution holding the liquidity. Because the individual firm does not receive all of the benefit generated by the liquidity, individual firms tend not to hold as much as would be optimal from a societal perspective. In addition, individual institutions may hold too little liquidity for their own needs if they know that they can access Federal Reserve liquidity inexpensively (as was possible during the recent crisis). In economics, this is called the *moral hazard* problem—anticipated rescue from bad outcomes leads to greater risk taking.

TOO BIG TO FAIL" OR SYSTEMICALLY IMPORTANT FIRMS

Systemic risk can spread if the failure of a firm causes contagion to other firms through counterparty losses that in turn cause the counterparty to fail or makes others doubt the counterparty's solvency. Most counterparties are not important enough to impose serious losses on a critical number of counterparties, but a large share of assets, deposits, and liabilities are concentrated in a few firms in the United States, and, according to the International Monetary Fund (IMF), a few large firms "dominate key market segments ranging from private securitization and derivatives dealing to triparty repo and leveraged investor financing."[9] Some policymakers perceive the bankruptcy process, in the case of a large or highly interconnected financial firm, produces losses or delays in payment to creditors and counterparties of bankrupt firms that cause systemic risk.[10]

Contagion can spread unpredictably. For example, because the investment bank Lehman Brothers was under stress since Bear Stearns was rescued in March, policymakers reasoned that Lehman's failure would not cause systemic risk because market participants had several months to prepare themselves. Nevertheless, when Lehman Brothers failed, it unexpectedly caused a money market mutual fund holding its commercial paper to "break the buck." This set off a widespread run on money market accounts, including those that did not hold Lehman's paper, that disrupted firms' access to short-term debt.

In 2008, regulators acted on the principle that some firms, such as American International Group (AIG), are "too big to fail" or, in the case of Bear Stearns, if not too big, then "too interconnected to fail."[11] To avoid the bankruptcy of those two firms, the Fed arranged an assisted sale of Bear Stearns and lent funds to AIG.[12] Although equity holders of Bear Stearns and AIG suffered heavy losses, all counterparties and creditors (including subordinated debt holders, who bought debt that was explicitly junior to regular debt holders) were paid in full thanks to government support. However, the knowledge or suspicion that a firm is too big to fail changes the behavior of a firm and its creditors because of moral hazard. If a firm and its creditors believe that they will be protected from any future losses, they have an incentive to take more risks in an attempt to increase potential profits, since there will be less downside if those risks turn out badly. Thus, moral hazard increases the likelihood that large firms will be a source of systemic risk.

Leverage

Financial institutions fund their loans and asset purchases through a combination of liabilities (deposits and debt) and capital. Leverage is a term that refers to the ratio of liabilities to capital held by an institution. Institutions have an incentive to hold more capital to safeguard against insolvency (when liabilities exceed assets), but they also have an incentive to hold less capital so that profits are not spread too thinly among capital holders. During the credit boom, leverage increased in the financial sector, as some institutions increased their liabilities to expand their loans and asset purchases.[13] Because interest rates were relatively low, liabilities could be financed at relatively low cost. Beginning in the second half of 2007, firms began to write off losses on loans and assets, depleting their capital. Some capital was replenished by issuing new equity, but eventually institutions needed more capital than investors were willing to supply. Thus, if firms wished to reduce their liabilities to reduce leverage, they would have to sell some of their assets. Financial institutions complained that the desire of all institutions to sell assets at once, when buyers were scared off by uncertainty about future asset prices, led to a situation where assets could only be sold at "fire sale" prices that further depleted the seller's capital. To the extent that assets were "marked to market" (recorded at prevailing market prices) on an institution's balance sheet, fire sales could cause "feedback effects" where all institutions holding similar assets—even those that had not sold—faced write downs that depleted capital.[14]

Some economists have argued that this cycle of leveraging when times are good and deleveraging when times are bad is a source of systemic risk. They propose that capital requirements should be made less pro-cyclical, meaning that regulators would require firms to hold more capital than needed when times are good, so that they could draw down capital rather than be forced into fire sales when faced with losses.[15]

Payment, Settlement, and Clearing Systems

Another potential source of systemic risk could be an event that leads to the breakdown of a payment, settlement, or clearing system. Such an event would focus, not on the activities of specific firms, but rather on the robustness of the system as a whole when something goes wrong. Adverse events could potentially include the failure of a major counterparty, exchange, or clearinghouse; technological disruptions; or fraud, any of which might disrupt timely payments to a large number of financial market participants.

Concerns about systemic risk in the payment systems in the recent crisis have focused on the derivatives market. Policymakers have expressed concern that over-the-counter derivative contracts were not processed promptly enough and suffered from inadequate record keeping. Regulators have expressed a concern that over-the-counter contracts were overly vulnerable to counterparty risk, since the holder of a contract, who is often trying to hedge risk of its own, is exposed to the risk that the provider of protection could fail to make contractual payments. Further, it was apparent that there was not enough transparency for markets or regulators to identify where these counterparty risks lay. The alternative to trading on the over-the-counter market is to clear derivatives through a central clearinghouse and/or trade derivatives on public exchange.

Derivatives have not been the only market to fail to function smoothly in the recent crisis. Repurchase agreement (repo) markets also saw a large increase in "fails" during the crisis. In a common repurchase agreement, the holder of a Treasury bond sells it, with an agreement to buy it back for a higher price the next day. Repurchase agreements are a common source of liquidity for financial firms such as investment banks. During the crisis, investor flight to Treasury securities caused scarcity and low yields that led many buyers of the Treasury security to be unwilling or unable to sell it back at the end of the repo contract. According to the Treasury Market Practices Group, "While some settlement fails are inevitable, these widespread and persistent fails prevent efficient market clearing and impose credit risk on market participants, and are therefore damaging to overall market liquidity."[16]

REGULATORY GAPS, DISCRETION, AND INFORMATION GATHERING

One criticism raised about the performance of regulators in the run-up to the crisis is that each regulator was given very narrow mandates, and had no responsibility for "seeing the forest for the trees." According to this view, there were gaps between the responsibilities of different regulators, as well as regulators who were unconcerned about whether activities undertaken by institutions they regulated posed risks to the system as a whole. For example, it was argued that the Office of Thrift Supervision inadequately supervised AIG's financial products subsidiary, instead focusing only on the fact that it posed no risk to the health of thrifts.[17] (AIG was officially a thrift holding company.) Gaps were identified in the regulation of institutions (such as investment banks), financial systems (such as over-the-counter derivatives), and products (such as mortgages issued by non-banks, pre-crisis) that contributed to the crisis. Sometimes the focus of the "gaps in regulation" argument was the shadow banking system, and the proposed solution was for regulators to close gaps are focused on creating a similar regulatory environment for banks and non-banks.[18]

Another critique was that the regulatory system was ineffective because there were too many overlapping regulators, and this contributed to the crisis. Five regulators have responsibilities for different types of depository institutions at the federal level, and some depositories are regulated solely at the state level, for example. An argument for reducing the number of regulators is that firms can "forum shop" in the current system, choosing the regulator whom they believe will be most sympathetic or have the lightest touch. This could lead to a "race to the bottom" in terms of regulatory standards, where other regulators ease up to avoid losing firms to other regulators. An argument in favor of multiple regulators is that competition among regulators makes it less likely that regulators will suffer from "blind spots" or "groupthink."

Asset Bubbles

From a macroeconomic perspective, fixing specific details of what went wrong in the recent crisis is arguably less important for preventing a future crisis than addressing the disequilibrium in underlying economic fundamentals that led to the crisis. Specifically, such a viewpoint would see the housing bubble, and the financial sector's large exposure to it, as inevitably producing a crisis. Thus, a proponent of that view would argue that when the bubble first emerged, policymakers should have taken steps to prevent the bubble from becoming so large, so that the when the bubble did burst, it would have been less disruptive. For example, the Federal Reserve could have raised interest rates to increase (indirectly) the financing costs of purchasing a house, and regulators could have set rules to tighten mortgage underwriting standards which, in hindsight, are generally believed to have been too lax. Because investors have shown a willingness to accept lower underwriting standards in booms when defaults are low, it has also been argued that regulators should have required underwriting standards high enough that borrowers would have been able to withstand a downturn in the housing market. According to this view, unless the bubble could have been avoided, focusing on measures such as overall capital and liquidity levels alone would not have prevented the boom and bust cycle.

SYSTEMIC RISK AND THE FED'S EXISTING AUTHORITY AND RESPONSIBILITIES AT THE TIME OF THE CRISIS

Systemic risk regulation is not a new concept. On page one of a 2005 Federal Reserve document entitled *Federal Reserve: Purposes and Functions*, the Fed identifies "maintaining the stability of the financial system and containing systemic risk that may arise in financial markets" as one of its four primary duties.[19] At the time of the crisis, the Fed could have used its existing regulatory powers over bank holding companies and certain consumer financial products to limit the likelihood of a systemic risk episode, and it could have used its existing lender-of last-resort powers to ameliorate the fallout following a systemic risk episode. Besides its authority to lend to banks through the discount window, it had authority to provide direct assistance to any firm through its emergency authority, found in Section 13(3) of the Federal Reserve Act. This emergency authority was used extensively during the recent crisis to provide assistance to non-bank parts of the financial system.[20] Finally, the Fed has an overall statutory mandate to keep inflation stable and unemployment low. Arguably, it would be impossible to meet this existing mandate if the Fed ignored systemic risk.

Although regulators may have used their powers to attempt to prevent systemic risk before and during the crisis, it may be the case that they did not have all the legal authority needed to respond to the types of systemic issues that emerged. This may be, in part, because regulation has not kept pace with the changes brought about by financial innovation. This section looks at the Fed's existing powers and gaps in its powers at the time of the crisis in light of the specific systemic issues raised in the previous section.

Runs and Liquidity

The potential for runs can never be fully eliminated because they are a by-product of the maturity mismatch[21] inherent in financial intermediation. Nevertheless, regulators could require that financial institutions take precautionary steps that minimize the likelihood of runs, namely by requiring firms to hold some of their assets in a liquid form and maintain access to long-term credit. Banking companies traditionally have been regulated to ensure that they hold sufficient liquidity. This regulation, however, was more concerned with the liquidity of depository institutions rather than non-depository affiliates of banking institutions.[22] An assumption made by banks and regulators before the crisis was that healthy banks would always have access to ample private sector liquidity, in part because the Federal Reserve could always flood the private market with liquidity through its open market operations. Beginning in August 2007 and becoming acute in September 2008, healthy banks could not access sufficient liquidity from private sources despite the Fed's efforts, as fear of counterparty risk caused the interbank lending market to freeze up.

When banks could not access liquidity from private markets, they began borrowing from the Fed's discount window, posting their illiquid assets as collateral. Borrowing from the discount window and another newly created lending facility called the Term Auction Facility, created for banks rose from less than $1 billion to over $500 billion during the crisis.[23] Lending by the Fed was not the only action taken to halt runs by debt-holders during the crisis; the FDIC created the Temporary Liquidity Guarantee Program. This program, which was financed through fees levied on participating banks, temporarily guaranteed newly issued bank debt. Access to the discount window and similar lending facilities creates a moral hazard problem since it gives financial firms less incentive to obtain liquidity from private markets, which regulation of liquidity can potentially offset.

A skeptic might note that because institutions can never hold enough liquidity to remain liquid (without access to central bank credit) in a true market panic, simply requiring higher liquidity is unlikely to prevent a reoccurrence of the events similar to those of September 2008. If one concludes that liquidity problems were a symptom of the collapse in counterparty trust, other structural changes may be necessary to ensure that the problem is not repeated. For example, to reduce fears of counterparty risk, regulators could limit maximum exposure to individual counterparties or require that such exposures be adequately collateralized. This would raise the cost of taking on counterparty risk, perhaps persuading firms to become better diversified.

Effective structural changes were complicated by the disparate regulatory regimes in place in the U.S. for banks and non-banks. Non-bank financial institutions generally have not been regulated at the federal level for liquidity even though they often are more dependent on short-term borrowing than are banks (not including federally insured demand deposits). For example, a recent study estimated that 38% of broker-dealers' liabilities were short-term repurchase agreements ("repos"), whereas for commercial banks they were less than 10% of liabilities.[24] The proximate cause of failure for many non-bank financial institutions was a "run" by debtholders—an inability to roll over short-term debt. The Fed arguably extinguished liquidity problems at this category of institutions by making liquidity available through its emergency lending authority, found in Section 13(3) of the Federal Reserve Act. For example, the Fed provided liquidity through new temporary lending facilities for primary dealers (major broker-dealers in the Treasury market) in March 2008. Between September and November 2008, the Fed also added liquidity to commercial paper markets and asset-backed securities markets by directly purchasing or financing the purchase of those assets through special facilities created temporarily.[25]

The Securities and Exchange Commission (SEC), not the Fed, had regulatory responsibility for money market mutual funds. The SEC's regulation covers the types of assets that money market funds are allowed to hold.[26] In spite of this regulatory scope, it was Treasury, not the Fed or the SEC, that intervened to provide money market mutual funds a temporary guarantee in September 2008.[27] Although investors may hope for similar assistance in the event of a future crisis, Treasury no longer has authority to use the Exchange Stabilization Fund, the fund it used in 2008 for this purpose, that is, "for the establishment of any future guaranty programs for the United States money market mutual fund industry."[28]

Too Big to Fail or Systemically Important Firms

The Fed had primary regulatory responsibility for bank holding companies and financial holding companies. These two categories already encompassed many of the largest financial firms in the financial system. Because the Fed could already regulate banks for safety and soundness, it already had authority to take the too big to fail problem into account when setting regulation for these types of holding companies. The closest regulatory scrutiny was applied to a holding company's depository subsidiaries, as discussed above. If the crisis has demonstrated that systemic risk can be caused by any of the too big to fail's subsidiaries, it may follow that all subsidiaries should receive similar regulation.

As previously mentioned, commercial banks and securities firms, which are commonly referred to as investment banks, are subject to distinct regulatory systems in the United States. Before the crisis, there also were five large investment banks that did not fall under the Fed's regulatory umbrella, but since the crisis, each of these firms either failed (Lehman Brothers), were acquired by bank holding companies (Bear Stearns and Merrill Lynch), or converted to bank holding companies (Goldman Sachs and Morgan Stanley). As a result of these conversions to or acquisitions by bank holding companies, the Fed became the umbrella supervisor over these institutions.

Several other types of financial firms, including hedge funds and broker-dealers, were not closely regulated for safety and soundness by the Fed or by other federal regulators before the crisis. Previously, banks were the only type of financial institutions considered to be a source of systemic risk. Although non-bank financial institutions have, over time, grown rapidly relative to banks,[29] policy remained unchanged—firms (banks or non-banks) were not explicitly identified as too big to fail, and thus non-banks received no special regulatory treatment to take into account any special systemic risks they might pose.

For firms that were already regulated for safety and soundness, like banks, prudential regulation could potentially be set to take into account the moral hazard posed by too big to fail. Otherwise, in hindsight, it seems as if policymakers were willing to live with the assumption that the ambiguity surrounding whether or not a company would be protected as too big to fail would prevent moral hazard. Intervening during the crisis to keep Bear Stearns, Fannie Mae, Freddie Mac, and AIG from failing made it unlikely that market participants would perceive a stated intent to allow a large institution to fail as credible.

During the crisis, when a non-bank financial firm faced failure, the policy options were to allow the firm to enter bankruptcy, as was done with the investment bank Lehman Brothers, or for the government to inject funds to keep the firm solvent, as was done with the insurance company AIG. The Fed used its emergency lending authority (Section 13(3) of the Federal Reserve Act), which is broad enough to allow it to lend to troubled firms, provided the loan is "secured to the satisfaction of the Federal Reserve bank."[30] With respect to the transactions involving Bear Stearns and AIG, the Fed determined that its loans were satisfactorily secured. In the case of Lehman Brothers, Fed Chairman Ben Bernanke indicated, after the fact, that Lehman Brothers was not provided a loan because it could not secure the loan to the Fed's satisfaction. The Fed did not make public (and was not required to make public) specific evidence as to how it has ensured that loans are secured to its satisfaction. Its lender-of-last-resort role was specifically aimed at assisting solvent firms (firms whose assets exceed their liabilities) with liquidity problems.[31] A commonly held principle is that the lender-of-last-resort function should not be employed for firms whose troubles stem from solvency issues, but in the heat of a crisis,[32] it can be difficult to differentiate between liquidity problems and solvency problems.

For banks, thrifts, credit unions, and the housing government-sponsored enterprises (GSEs) Fannie Mae and Freddie Mac, there were also the options of government receivership or conservatorship, where the government seizes control of the firm to either wind it down or keep it functioning, respectively.[33] Under a government receivership, the federal administrative agency operating the receivership is given authority to impose losses on specific creditors and infuse either government or deposit insurance funds to reduce losses on other creditors. In the case of bank and thrift insolvencies, for example, the FDIC used funds financed through deposit insurance premiums to make depositors of a failed bank whole.[34]

Leverage

Banks already faced capital requirements set by regulators (including the Fed) based on the Basel Accords.[35] Typically, capital requirements were seen as providing for the safety of the specific firm, without considering how the cycle of leverage and deleverage might pose systemic risk. Some economists argue that the crisis has demonstrated that existing requirements were either too low or too pro-cyclical. It is argued that capital requirements were pro-cyclical because a firm was required to hold less capital when asset prices were high and to raise capital when asset prices fell.

Federal capital requirements were applied to depository subsidiaries, not a holding company's non-depository subsidiaries. "Firewalls" were in place to prevent problems with a non-depository subsidiary from affecting the depository subsidiary. In the Fed's words, "The Federal Reserve's supervision of nonbank subsidiaries under the Bank Holding Company (BHC) Act is primarily directed toward, and focused on, ensuring that the nonbank subsidiary does not present material financial, legal, or reputational risks to affiliated depository institutions nor to the BHC's or FBO's [Foreign Banking Organization's] ability to support these depository institutions."[36] The logic behind this approach was that leverage limits or capital requirements are needed for the federally insured subsidiary because it has the advantage of the federal subsidy in terms of federally insured deposits, but less so for non-insured subsidiaries that are presumably subject to market discipline, including by stockholders. As discussed above, decisions during the recent financial crisis to rescue "systemically important" firms may be viewed as having undermined this logic, at least for large or interconnected firms.

Payment, Settlement, and Clearing Systems

The Fed had regulatory responsibility and played a key "clearinghouse" role in the check-clearing payment system for banks.[37] The Fed set regulations on banks' uses of the payment system to ensure its smooth functioning. (For example, the Fed has capped and assessed fees on a bank's overdrafts from its reserve account at the Federal Reserve bank.[38]) This system showed little sign of stress during the crisis. In addition, there are five private sector settlement systems supervised by the Fed, which operate in areas such as payments, securities, and foreign exchange.[39] Other payment, settlement, and clearing systems, as well as activities that did not occur through a clearinghouse, were not directly regulated by the Fed. (The Fed set best practice guidelines for any payment or settlement system, but these guidelines were not required for systems that the Fed does not regulate.)[40] The authority of Fed (and other bank regulators) over the institutions which they regulate is sufficient for them to monitor how banks operate in other payment, settlement, and clearing settings. Banks, particularly large banks, account for a considerable share of credit default swap and other derivative transactions. Thus, despite having no direct authority to regulate the private systems and clearinghouses handling these transactions, by overseeing how banks use and structure those transactions, the Fed could have a large role in affecting the overall operations of those systems.

Regulatory Gaps, Discretion, and Information Gathering

Regulators already coordinated policy through inter-agency groups such as the Federal Financial Institution Examinations Council (FFIEC) and the President's Working Group on

Financial Markets. FFIEC is composed of the federal bank regulators and is meant to set consistent regulation for banks across regulators. The President's Working Group includes the Secretary of the Treasury and the chairmen of the Federal Reserve, the SEC, and the CFTC. Those promoting the need to eliminate regulatory gaps argue that FFIEC's scope was too narrow to perceive systemic risk, while the President's Working Group's responsibilities were too ad hoc.

It can be said that during the recent crisis, there was no explicit statutory delegation of authority for systemic regulation. On the other hand, although the Fed lacked direct authority over many of the components of the financial services industry, it had a statutory directive sufficiently broad to provide a basis for it to monitor the financial system to inform Congress of potential systemic dangers.

Prior to enactment of the Dodd-Frank Act, the Fed lacked sufficient authority to intervene in financial markets even if it were to identify a gap in regulation that could lead to systemic risk. Under the type of functional regulation in place after the enactment of the Gramm-Leach-Bliley Act in 1999,[41] regulatory authority over holding companies was dispersed among an array of regulators. As the primary regulator of bank holding companies and financial holding companies, the Fed had broad powers over the banking subsidiaries of the holding company but limited powers over the non-banking subsidiaries such as insurance companies and securities firms.[42] Although the law provided the Fed with safety and soundness regulatory authority over the holding company itself, and over certain of its depository subsidiaries, federal banking and securities regulators, as well as state insurance regulators, were designated as primary functional regulators of other subsidiaries. The result was that there was no clear authority for the Fed or for any one regulator to oversee or to intervene in the entire operations of a holding company. Moreover, although the Fed had full access to information on transactions between banks and nonbanks and any public information on nonbanking concerns, neither the Fed nor any one regulator had access to all of the proprietary information that may have been needed to make a systemic risk determination.

On the other hand, the Fed's broad general policy mandate casts doubt on the argument that there was no "big picture" regulator tasked with identifying the broader problems mounting in financial markets. With its legal mandate to "promote effectively the goals of maximum employment, stable prices, and moderate long-term interest rates,"[43] it is difficult to argue that the Fed's outlook was too narrow for it to be aware of the fundamental macroeconomic imbalances that were arguably at the root of the crisis. The Fed may not have had the authority to act on systemic issues that were outside of its areas of responsibility, but the Fed regularly makes recommendations to Congress on issues that it believes affect its mandated goals. The argument that "everybody missed the warning signs that the Fed missed" has validity, but begs the question of whether a systemic risk regulator would have missed them as well.

Asset Bubbles

The Fed's legal mandate to "promote effectively the goals of maximum employment, stable prices, and moderate long-term interest rates"[44] gives it broad discretion to develop and pursue a monetary policy that will meet that mandate. Events since 2007 offer strong evidence that the bursting of an asset bubble can lead to macroeconomic results that are inconsistent with its mandate. If the Fed wished to raise interest rates to burst an asset bubble, its actions could be justified by its current mandate. But in the past, the Fed has chosen not to use monetary policy to respond to asset bubbles, arguing that to burst a bubble just for the sake of doing so would stray from its current mandate.

In the past, the Fed has argued that it would not be able to identify bubbles accurately until they had already burst. Although this may seem doubtful to some, a large body of economic theory supports the position that future movements in asset prices cannot be accurately predicted since current asset prices should incorporate all available information about their future movement. In other words, the Fed could successfully identify bubbles only if it were able to "outsmart" market participants, and it is questionable whether the Fed has more information or expertise than market participants. It could be argued that the evidence that the housing market was being driven by speculation as opposed to fundamentals was prevalent and obvious, and markets have demonstrated time and again that pricing is not always efficient. Even if it is accepted that markets are sometimes prone to bubbles, it does not necessarily follow that the Fed can accurately identify them. Fed officials are on record fairly late in the housing boom as dismissing the claim that a housing bust was a serious threat to the U.S. economy. For example, in June 2007, two months before liquidity problems emerged, Chairman Bernanke stated in a speech that "However, fundamental factors— including solid growth in incomes and relatively low mortgage rates— should ultimately support the demand for housing, and at this point, the troubles in the subprime sector seem unlikely to seriously spill over to the broader economy or the financial system."[45]

The Fed has also argued in the past that attempts to use higher interest rates to prick asset bubbles before they are fully inflated could be either ineffective or a cure that is worse than the disease. Instead, the Fed has argued it can use expansionary monetary policy to ensure a smooth landing after a bubble has burst. The aftermath of the dot-com bubble would seem to support this view— the 2001 recession was mild and brief, and it is not evident that attempts by the Fed to prick the dot-com bubble earlier would have led to a better outcome. On the other hand, it is doubtful that attempts by the Fed to prematurely prick the housing bubble could have ended worse than the 2008 financial crisis, and monetary policy was not powerful enough in this case to ensure a smooth landing.

EVALUATING SYSTEMIC RISK REGULATION

Systemic events have proven to be rare in modern times. When they occur, they are usually not predicted by many beforehand. This hampers the evaluation of a systemic risk regulator's performance. In years with good outcomes, it may be impossible to distinguish whether good outcomes were caused by the systemic risk regulator's vigilance or were simply the result of normal times. There is also the risk that a systemic risk regulator who is only rewarded for avoiding instability would allow too little risk-taking, and thus stifle financial innovation and efficient intermediation. Because systemic events have proven hard to predict, a systemic risk regulator could plead that its failure to predict the systemic event accorded with conventional wisdom.

Assuming that the Fed's mandate provides it with systemic risk authority, the law seems not to have offered any clear-cut mechanism to discipline the Fed for failure to prevent a systemic event—other than congressional intervention by amending federal law. Under the Federal Reserve Act, Fed governors serve 14-year terms and can only be removed for "cause," not for policy disputes.[46] The Federal Reserve System is self-financing; without changing the law, Congress cannot adjust its budget to influence its priorities. Adding specific systemic risk authority to the Fed's current wide-ranging remit, which some see as enabling the Fed to justify any action by pointing to some part of its mission, broadens the Fed's already wide-ranging authority and may enhance arguments that the broad mandate hampers effective oversight.

THE DODD-FRANK WALL STREET REFORM AND CONSUMER PROTECTION ACT

The Dodd-Frank Wall Street Reform and Consumer Protection Act (H.R. 4173) was signed into law on July 21, 2010, as P.L. 111-203. The Dodd-Frank Act was a broad-based reform package that included provisions affecting almost every part of the financial system. While the overall goal of the act was to prevent another systemic risk episode, this section discusses only those provisions of the act related to the types of systemic risk issues discussed in this report or the Federal Reserve. The provisions discussed are found mostly in Titles I and XI of the act.[47]

Systemic Risk Provisions

New systemic risk responsibilities in the Dodd-Frank Act were mostly divided between the newly created Financial Stability Oversight Council and the Federal Reserve, although resolution authority was largely shared between the Treasury Secretary and the Federal Deposit Insurance Corporation. Modifications to existing regulations generally applied to the existing regulator.

Financial Stability Oversight Council
Title I, Subtitle A of the Dodd-Frank Act creates the Financial Stability Oversight Council on the date of enactment. The Council is chaired by the Secretary of the Treasury, and the voting members consist of the heads of eight federal regulatory agencies (including the chairman of the Fed), the Treasury Secretary, and a member appointed by the President with insurance expertise. The Council is tasked with identifying risks to financial stability and responding to emerging systemic risks, while minimizing moral hazard arising from expectations that firms or their counterparties will be rescued from failure. The Council's duties include

- collecting information on financial firms from regulators and through the Office of Financial Research, which is created in Title 1, Subtitle B to support the Council;
- monitoring the financial system to identify potential systemic risks;

- proposing regulatory changes to Congress to promote stability, competitiveness, and efficiency;
- facilitating information sharing and coordination among financial regulators;
- making regulatory recommendations to financial regulators, including "new or heightened standards and safeguards";
- identifying gaps in regulation that could pose systemic risk;
- reviewing and commenting on new or existing accounting standards issued by any standard-setting body;
- providing a forum for the resolution of jurisdictional disputes among council members. The Council may not impose any resolution on disagreeing members, however.

The Council is required to provide an annual report and testimony to Congress.

In contrast to some proposals to create a systemic risk regulator, the Dodd-Frank Act does not give the Council authority (beyond the existing authority of its individual members) to eliminate emerging threats or close regulatory gaps it identifies. In many cases, the Council can only make regulatory recommendations—it cannot impose change. The fact that regulators are on the Council may make it less likely they would resist its recommendations, however.

Regulation of Systemically Significant Firms[48]

In addition to the duties listed above, the Council has authority to identify non-bank financial firms that are systemically significant by a "two-thirds vote of the voting members then serving," including the Treasury Secretary. A firm would be deemed systemically significant on the basis of a Council determination that it could pose a threat to financial stability because of material distress or because of "the nature, scope, size, scale, concentration, interconnectedness, or mix of the activities" of the firm. Foreign financial firms operating in the United States could be identified by the Council as systemically significant. The act exempts firms with consolidated assets under $50 billion, although the Council and Fed may raise that threshold. The Fed is given examination powers to help the Council determine whether a firm is systemically significant. A firm can contest its designation before the Council and, if unsuccessful, through appeal to a federal district court, which may set aside the Council's determination only if it finds it to be arbitrary and capricious. Any firm that has over $50 billion in consolidated assets and received assistance under the Troubled Asset Relief Program (TARP) that ceases to be a bank holding company would automatically be considered a systemically significant firm.

Under the new law, the Council may recommend that the Fed impose more stringent prudential safety and soundness standards on these firms than are applicable to other nonbank financial firms and bank holding companies which do not pose a systemic risk. In recommending these standards, the Council may recommend different standards for individual institutions or categories based on the risk they present.

Under Subtitle C of Title I, the Fed would regulate for safety and soundness the firms which the Council has subjected to Fed supervision on the basis of a systemic risk determination and any other bank holding company with total consolidated assets of $50 billion. At the recommendation of the Council or on its own initiative, the Fed may set different standards for different systemically significant firms or categories of firms based on various risk-related factors. The standards include risk-based capital requirements that account for off-balance-sheet activities and 15 to 1 leverage limits (if appropriate), liquidity requirements, risk management requirements, and exposure limits of 25% of a company's capital per counterparty. Other prudential standards may be applied at the Fed's discretion. The firms are required to submit resolution plans ("living wills") and credit exposure reports to the Fed. Regulated subsidiaries would continue to be regulated by their primary functional regulator, although the Fed may override the functional regulator if the Fed believes the firm is not adhering to regulatory standards or poses a threat to financial stability. The Fed must consult with the primary regulator before applying heightened prudential standards to a regulated subsidiary. The Fed must conduct annual stress tests on systemically significant firms and, in consultation with the Council and the FDIC, issue regulations establishing remediation measures to be imposed at an early stage of a firm's "financial decline" in an effort to prevent insolvency and its potential impact on the financial system.

If the Board determines, and at least two-thirds of the Council confirms, that a systemically significant firm poses a "grave threat" to financial stability, it may:

1) limit the ability of the company to merge with, acquire, consolidate with, or otherwise become affiliated with another company;
2) restrict the ability of the company to offer a financial product or products;
3) require the company to terminate one or more activities;
4) impose conditions on the manner in which the company conducts one or more activities; or
5) if the Board of Governors determines that the actions described in paragraphs (1) through (4) are inadequate to mitigate a threat to the financial stability of the United States in its recommendation, require the company to sell or otherwise transfer assets or off-balancesheet items to unaffiliated entities.[49]

In addition, Title VI prohibits any insured depository institution, bank holding company, or systemically significant institution from merging with or acquiring assets of another company which causes the total consolidated liabilities of the acquiring company to exceed 10% of the aggregate consolidated liabilities of all financial companies or, in the case of interstate mergers, 10% of the total amount of deposits of insured depository institutions in the United States. The Fed may make exceptions for a bank in default, an acquisition involving assistance provided by the FDIC to institutions in danger of default, an acquisition that results in minimal increase in the company's liabilities, or during severe financial conditions.

Resolution Authority[50]

Title II attempts to address the concern that failures of systemically important financial firms were too destabilizing under prior law by establishing a new system for certain financial companies whose resolution under otherwise available law is determined by various federal regulators to pose dangers to the U.S. financial system. This resolution system is modeled after the FDIC's existing receivership regime for depository institutions. Many types of financial companies and their subsidiaries are eligible for this special resolution regime;

however, subsidiaries that are insurance companies, certain broker-dealers, and insured depositories are not eligible.

In order for an eligible financial company to be resolved under the special regime, a group of regulators, including two-thirds of the Federal Reserve Board, must recommend the company for the resolution based on standards delineated by the Dodd-Frank Act. After the recommendation, the Treasury Secretary, in consultation with the President, must make a determination that the "company is in default or in danger of default;" the company's resolution under otherwise available law would "have serious adverse effects on financial stability of the United States;" "no viable private sector alternative is available;" and other considerations. A company that disputes the determination by the Treasury Secretary will have limited rights to appeal the determination in federal court.

While the special resolution regime is modeled after the FDIC's receivership power, there are some important distinctions between the two. For instance, the Dodd-Frank Act emphasizes that

> creditors and shareholders will bear the losses of the financial company; management responsible for the condition of the financial company will not be retained; and the [FDIC] and other appropriate agencies will take all steps necessary and appropriate to assure that all parties, including management, directors, and third parties, having responsibility for the condition of the financial company bear losses consistent with their responsibility, including actions for damages, restitution, and recoupment of compensation and other gains not compatible with such responsibility.[51]

The act also states that "[a]ll financial companies put into receivership under this title shall be liquidated [and n]o taxpayer funds shall be used to prevent the liquidation of any financial company under this title."[52]

The funding mechanism for resolutions under the Dodd-Frank Act also differs from the conservatorship/receivership regime for depositories. The Orderly Liquidation Fund established by the Dodd-Frank Act will not be prefunded. Instead, the FDIC, upon being appointed receiver of a particular financial company, is authorized to borrow funds from the Treasury subject to explicit caps based on the value of the failed firm's consolidated assets. If necessary to pay off such obligations to the Treasury, the FDIC would have the authority to assess claimants of the failed institution that received more through the receivership than they would have received had the failed firm been liquidated in bankruptcy, as well as the power to assess certain large financial institutions (bank holding companies and nonbank financial companies eligible for the special resolution regime that have more than $50 billion in assets and all nonbank financial institutions supervised by the Fed as systemically significant). The Dodd-Frank Act also imposes a three-year time limit on any receivership with the possibility of up to two one-year extensions."

Proprietary Trading[53]

Title VI contains an outright prohibition on proprietary trading by any FDIC-insured depository institution, company controlling an insured depository institution, company treated as a bank holding company for purposes of the International Banking Act of 1978, and any affiliate or subsidiary of such entity. Such institutions are also barred from owning interests in or sponsoring hedge funds or private equity funds. There are, however, certain exceptions to the prohibition— some transitional, some involving activities by foreign firms that take place solely outside the United States, and others designated as permitted activities, including purchasing and selling government or GSE securities, market making activities, risk mitigating hedging activities, small business investment company investments, insurance company portfolio investments, and other investments identified by regulators.

Rather than subjecting non-bank financial companies supervised by the Fed to a prohibition on proprietary trading and hedge fund ownership or sponsorship, the legislation authorizes the regulators to issue rules subjecting such companies to additional capital and quantitative limits on such activities unless the activity has been identified under one of the exceptions.

Payment, Clearing, and Settlement Systems and Activities

In addition to the duties listed above, the Council, by a two-thirds vote including the chairman, is authorized to identify systemically significant systems for payment, clearing, and settlement (PCS) of financial transactions (also called utilities) and (PCS) activities for regulation by the SEC or the CFTC if registered therewith; otherwise, by the Fed. Title VIII identifies activities that could potentially be regulated, including settling and netting of financial transactions; the provision and maintenance of trade, contract, or instrument information; risk management activities related to continuing transactions; transmittal and storage of payment instructions; and the movement of funds. The act identifies funds transfers, securities contracts, futures contracts, forward contracts, repurchase agreements, swaps, foreign exchanges contracts, financial derivatives contracts, and any similar transaction identified by the Council as financial instruments whose payment, clearing, or settlement could be regulated. It explicitly excludes designated contract markets, registered futures associations, swap data repositories, certain swap execution facilities, national securities exchanges and associations, alternative trading systems, security-based swap data repositories, broker dealers, investment companies, futures commission merchants, commodity trading advisors, and commodity pool operators from regulation.

The PCS regulator may make information requests, issue rules and take enforcement actions, and examine a designated PCS system or firm performing a PCS activity. For PCS systems and activities regulated by the SEC or CFTC, the Fed may make enforcement recommendations or take actions in case of "imminent risk or substantial harm." Once a PCS system is regulated, it may borrow from the Fed; the right to borrow is limited to "unusual or exigent circumstances" and requires a showing that the firm cannot secure credit elsewhere and a majority vote of the Fed Board taken after consultation with the Treasury Secretary.[54]

Derivatives[55]

Title VII seeks to remake the OTC market in the image of the regulated futures exchanges. The act includes a requirement that swap contracts be cleared through a central counterparty regulated by one or more federal agency. Clearing houses require traders to post initial margin at the time they open a contract to cover potential losses, and require subsequent deposits of cash (called maintenance margin) to cover actual losses to the position. The effect of margin requirements is to eliminate the possibility that any firm can build up an uncapitalized exposure so large that default would have systemic consequences. The size of a cleared position is limited by the firm's ability to post capital to cover its losses.

That capital protects its trading partners and the system as a whole. Counterparty risk is shifted from the firms engaged in the trade to the clearing house.

The new law provides exceptions to the clearing requirement for commercial end-users, or firms that use derivatives to hedge the risks of their nonfinancial business operations. Regulators may also provide exemptions for smaller financial institutions.

Swap dealers and major swap participants—firms with substantial derivatives positions— will be subject to margin and capital requirements above and beyond what the clearing houses mandate. Trades that are cleared will also be subject to trading on an exchange, or an exchange-like "swap execution facility," regulated by either the Commodity Futures Trading Commission (CFTC) or the Securities and Exchange Commission (SEC), in the case of security-based swaps. All trades will be reported to data repositories, so that regulators will have complete information about all derivatives positions. Data on swap prices and trading volumes will be made public. This would make more information available to regulators about the size and distribution of possible losses during periods of market volatility.

The act prevents insured depository institutions from dealing credit default swaps.

Capital Requirements[56]

Title I requires the federal banking regulators to establish minimum risk-based capital requirements and leverage requirements on a consolidated basis for depository institutions, depository holding companies, and firms designated as systemically significant by the Council that are no lower than those were set for depository institutions as of the date of enactment. Under this provision, no longer will holding companies be authorized to include trust-preferred securities in Tier I capital. These requirements are phased in, and certain small firms are exempted.

Title VI requires the federal banking regulators to make capital "requirements countercyclical, so that the amount of capital required to be maintained ... increases in times of economic expansion and decreases in times of economic contraction, consistent with ... safety and soundness."[57]

The Council is required to conduct a study on the feasibility of implementing a contingent capital requirement for systemically significant firms. Contingent capital is debt that can be converted into equity by the issuing firm under certain circumstances. Following the study, if the Council recommends, the Fed may impose contingent capital requirements on systemically significant firms.

Changes to Section 13(3) Emergency Lending Authority

Title XI amends Section 13(3) of the Federal Reserve Act to require the Fed to establish, in consultation with the Secretary, regulations governing the use of the Federal Reserve Act's Section 13(3) emergency lending authority, in contrast to the ad hoc use of Section 13(3) during the recent crisis. The policies and procedures prescribed in these regulations must include measures to prevent aid to failing firms or insolvent borrowers and may require borrowers to certify that they are solvent. Any program established under this authority must be approved by the Treasury Secretary and must be "for the purpose of providing liquidity to the financial system, and not to aid a failing financial firm or company." A program that is "structured to remove assets from the balance sheet of a single and specific company" is forbidden, as is any program designed to help a single company to avoid bankruptcy or an insolvency proceeding. The policies and procedures must ensure that any assistance be secured sufficiently to protect taxpayers from losses "consistent with sound risk management practices." This contrasts with the standard applicable during the recent crisis, which required that security for assistance be "indorsed [sic.], or otherwise secured to the satisfaction of the Federal reserve [sic.] bank." Any program under this authority must be "terminated in a timely and orderly fashion."[58]

FDIC Emergency Liquidity Program

In addition to the Fed, the Federal Deposit Insurance Corporation (FDIC) also set up emergency programs in response to the crisis. On October 14, 2008, the FDIC announced the creation of the Temporary Liquidity Guarantee Program to encourage liquidity in the banking system, including a Debt Guarantee Program and a Transaction Guarantee Program.[59] This program was not specifically authorized by Congress; it was authorized under the FDIC's standing systemic risk mitigation authority, 12 U.S.C. § 1823(c)(4)(G). The Debt Guarantee Program guarantees debt issued by banks, thrifts, and bank holding companies, including commercial paper, interbank funding, promissory notes, and any unsecured portion of secured debt.[60]

Title XI provides more specific, explicit authority for the FDIC to create a program to guarantee debt of solvent depository institutions or depository institution holding companies and their affiliates "during times of severe economic distress." This supersedes the authority in 12 U.S.C. 1823(c)(4)(G). To institute such a program, at the Treasury Secretary's request, two-thirds of the FDIC's Board and two-thirds of Fed governors must make a finding, that (1) a liquidity event exists, (2) failure to act would have serious adverse effects on financial stability, and (3) using this authority would ameliorate the effects. The program must be "widely available" to "solvent insured depository institutions or solvent depository institution holding companies (including any affiliates thereof" and may not include "the provision of equity in any form." There could, therefore, be no program under this authority similar to the Capital Purchase Program[61] undertaken under the Troubled Asset Relief Program (TARP) authorized by the Emergency Economic Stabilization Act of 2008.[62] Under the legislation, the FDIC, in consultation with the Treasury Secretary, must establish policies and procedures governing the terms and conditions of such a program "as soon as is practicable." The program must be financed by assessments on participants, although temporary funding will be available to the FDIC from the Treasury. Upon establishing a program, the Treasury Secretary, in consultation with the President, is to establish a maximum amount of debt that can be guaranteed, and obtain congressional approval before any guarantees may be issued. Congressional approval is to take the form of a joint resolution to be considered under expedited procedures.

Bank Holding Company Regulation[63]

Title VI makes modifications to the Fed's authority to regulate bank holding companies. It removes the strict limitations on Fed authority to take direct action against functionally regulated subsidiaries of bank holding companies. It expands Fed authority to examine bank holding company subsidiaries by specifically including risks to U.S. financial stability as a focus of the examination. It authorizes the Fed to monitor how the subsidiaries, except for functionally regulated subsidiaries and depository institution subsidiaries, are complying with any other applicable federal law (subject to the allocation of examination functions under the Consumer Financial Protection Act of 2010, Title X of the Dodd-Frank Act).

Title VI also sets standards for the Fed to examine activities of non-depository, non-functionally regulated subsidiaries of depository institution holding companies that "are permissible for the insured depository institution subsidiaries of the depository institution holding company in the same manner, subject to the same standards, and with the same frequency as would be required if such activities were conducted by the lead insured depository institution subsidiary of the holding company." The regulator of the lead depository institution may request a Fed examination of the non-depository, non-functionally regulated subsidiaries of the holding company, and if the Fed fails to begin such an examination, the regulator of the lead depository institution may commence to conduct the examination. Recommendations for supervisory actions are to be submitted to the Fed; if the Federal Reserve Board does not take enforcement action within 60 days, the agency making the recommendation may take action.[64]

Other Federal Reserve Provisions

This section discusses major provisions of the Dodd-Frank Act related to the Federal Reserve that do not involve systemic risk issues.

Consumer Financial Protection Bureau[65]

Title X establishes a Bureau of Consumer Financial Protection (Bureau) within the Federal Reserve System with authority over an array of consumer financial products and services (including deposit taking, mortgages, credit cards and other extensions of credit, loan servicing, check-guaranteeing, collection of consumer report data, debt collection, real estate settlement, money transmitting, and financial data processing, among others). It will serve as the primary federal consumer financial protection supervisor and enforcer of federal consumer protection laws over many of the institutions that offer these products and services. The Bureau will be required to consult with the prudential regulators when prescribing regulations.

The Dodd-Frank Act authorizes the Bureau to prescribe rules and issue orders and guidance. The legislation also transfers to the Bureau rulemaking authority for many of the existing federal consumer protection laws, including the Truth in Lending Act, the Real Estate Settlement Procedures Act, and the Home Ownership and Equity Protection Act. As a check on the Bureau's rulemaking powers, the Financial Stability Oversight Council has the ability to set aside a regulation prescribed by the Bureau if the regulation "would put the safety and soundness of the United States banking system or the stability of the financial system of the United States at risk."

The Bureau is established within the Federal Reserve System, but it has some measure of independence from the Fed. For instance, the Fed does not have the formal authority to stop, delay, or disapprove of a Bureau regulation, nor can it

A. intervene in any matter or proceeding before the Director [of the CFPB], including examinations or enforcement actions, unless otherwise specifically provided by law;
B. appoint, direct, or remove any officer or employee of the Bureau; or

C. merge or consolidate the Bureau, or any of the functions or responsibilities of the Bureau, with any division or office of the Board of Governors or the Federal Reserve banks.[66]

However, the Bureau is not completely independent of the Fed. As an example, the act allows, but does not require, the Fed to "delegate to the Bureau the authorities to examine persons subject to the jurisdiction of the [Board] for compliance with the Federal consumer financial laws."[67]

The Bureau is to be headed by a director appointed by the President, subject to the advice and consent of the Senate, to serve for a five-year term from which s/he could only be removed for "inefficiency, neglect of duty or malfeasance in office." The director has authority to hire the employees necessary to carry out the duties of the Bureau. The act establishes a procedure by which the existing regulators (including the Fed) will transfer employees to the Bureau as necessary to perform the consumer financial protection functions that are transferred from those agencies to the Bureau.

The Bureau will be funded "from the combined earnings of the Federal Reserve System [in an] amount determined by the Director to be reasonably necessary to carry out the authorities of the Bureau" subject to specified caps. The cap will be 10% of the total operating expenses of the Federal Reserve System for FY2011, 11% for FY2012, and 12% thereafter. As a gauge of how much money this will be, the system's total operating expenses for FY2009 were $4.98 billion, 10% of which is just under $500 million. These funds are not reviewable by either the House or Senate Committees on Appropriations. The act also authorizes appropriations if the director "determine[s] that sums available to the Bureau [as specified by the caps] under this section will not be sufficient to carry out the authorities of the Bureau under Federal consumer financial law for the upcoming year."[68]

GAO Audits

Previously, the Government Accountability Office (GAO) was not allowed to audit monetary policy actions, including interest rate changes, transactions with foreign governments, open market operations, and loans to financial firms. Actions taken by the Fed in response to the financial crisis were covered by this exemption. Title XI allows GAO to audit open market operations, discount window lending, actions taken under emergency authority, and actions taken in response to the financial crisis for

A. the operational integrity, accounting, financial reporting, and internal controls governing the credit facility or covered transaction;
B. the effectiveness of the security and collateral policies established for the facility or covered transaction in mitigating risk to the relevant Federal reserve bank and taxpayers;
C. whether the credit facility or the conduct of a covered transaction inappropriately favors one or more specific participants over other institutions eligible to utilize the facility; and
D. the policies governing the use, selection, or payment of third-party contractors by or for any credit facility or to conduct any covered transaction.[69]

The legislation does not authorize the GAO to conduct policy evaluations of the Fed's monetary actions. GAO may not disclose confidential information in its reports until that information was made public by the Fed. The GAO must audit the Fed's response to the recent crisis response within a year of enactment.

The legislation also calls for a separate GAO audit of Federal Reserve bank governance to assess whether it produces conflicts of interest or potential conflicts, and whether the existing system of selecting regional Federal Reserve bank directors results in directors who represent "the public without discrimination on the basis of race, creed, color, sex, or national origin, and with due but not exclusive consideration to the interests of agriculture, commerce, industry, services, labor, and consumers."[70]

Disclosure

Title XI of the Dodd-Frank Act establishes, for the first time, disclosure requirements relating to Federal Reserve lending. It requires that the Fed provide the congressional committees of jurisdiction details on the rationale for assistance, the identity of the recipient, the material terms of the assistance, and the expected cost to the taxpayer. This information is to be provided within seven days of an action taken under Section 13(3), with updates every 30 days following. The Fed can request that this information be kept confidential and limited to the chairmen and ranking members of the committees.

The act calls for public disclosure of the identities of borrowers, amount borrowed, rate charged, and collateral pledged or assets transferred within one year after a credit facility is terminated and within two years after the transaction for discount window loans or open market operations. For Fed programs created during the crisis, this information must be publicly disclosed by December 1, 2010.

Federal Reserve Governance

Previously, one of the seven governors of the Federal Reserve Board was designated (by the President with Senate confirmation) chairman and one was designated vice-chairman. In addition to these positions, Title XI creates a vice-chairman for supervision, nominated by the President with Senate confirmation. The vice-chairman for supervision is required to testify to the committees of jurisdiction semi-annually.

Previously, the presidents of the 12 Federal Reserve regional banks were chosen by each regional bank's Board of Directors. The board was comprised of nine members: three chosen by the member banks from the banking industry, three chosen by the member banks to represent non-banking interests, and three chosen by the Board of Governors in Washington to represent non-banking interests. Title XI allows only the directors representing non-banking interests to select the regional bank presidents. As noted in the previous section, the legislation also calls for a GAO audit of the selection process for regional bank directors.

Regulation of Thrift Holding Companies[71]

Previously, thrifts were regulated by the Office of Thrift Supervision (OTS). Title III abolishes OTS and transfers its authority to other regulators. The Fed gains the authority to supervise, issue rules, and take enforcement actions with respect to any savings and loan holding company and any of its subsidiaries, other than a depository institution.

Title VI authorizes the Fed to require a grandfathered unitary thrift holding company which conducts some commercial or other non-financial activities to conduct all or part of its financial activities in an intermediate savings and loan holding company regulated by the Fed.

Securities Holding Companies[72]

Title VI eliminates the investment bank holding company framework in section 17 of the Securities Exchange Act of 1934, under which a securities firm not having a depository institution subsidiary may choose to be supervised by the SEC as an investment bank holding company, coincidentally satisfying a foreign law requirement for consolidated supervision by its home country. Instead, a securities holding company (SHC) may submit to Fed regulation. It would then become subject to the record-keeping, reporting, and examination requirements imposed by the Fed as specified in section 618 of the Dodd-Frank Act. The Fed is also authorized to prescribe capital and risk management standards for SHCs.

ACKNOWLEDGMENTS

The author would like to thank M. Maureen Murphy and David Carpenter for their contributions and comments.

End Notes

[1] Treasury has created websites to track financial intervention and financial reform. See http://ustreas.gov/initiatives/ regulatoryreform/ and http://www.financialstability.gov.

[2] For an overview, see CRS Report R41350, *The Dodd-Frank Wall Street Reform and Consumer Protection Act: Issues and Summary*, coordinated by Baird Webel.

[3] A recent International Monetary Fund report points out that this definition is imprecise and that systemic risk "is often viewed as a phenomenon that is there 'when we see it,' reflecting a sense of a broad-based breakdown in the functioning of the financial system, which is normally realized, ex-post, by a large number of failures of financial institutions (usually banks)." See International Monetary Fund, *Global Financial Stability Report*, April 2009, p. 113.

[4] See, for example, Olivier De Bandt and Philipp Hartmann, "Systemic Risk: A Survey," European Central Bank, working paper 35, November 2000, http://www.ecb.int/pub/pdf/scpwps/ecbwp035.pdf.

[5] See CRS Report R40417, *Macroprudential Oversight: Monitoring Systemic Risk in the Financial System*, by Darryl E. Getter.

[6] See the section "Systemic Risk and the Fed's Existing Authority and Responsibilities" below.

[7] Leading proponents of this view are cited in International Monetary Fund, "How to Ensure Financial Stability after the Crisis," *IMF Survey Online*, May 14, 2009, http://www.imf.org/external/ pubs/ft/survey/so/2009/NEW051409A.htm.

[8] Criticisms of the proposal to create a systemic risk regulation include Alex Pollack, "Is a 'Systemic Risk Regulator' Possible?", *The American*, May 12, 2009; Dean Baker, "Making Financial Regulation Work: A Systemic Risk Regulator," *Washington Post*, June 22, 2009, http://voices.washingtonpost.com/hearing/2009/06/one_ofjhe_major_debates.html.

[9] International Monetary Fund, United States—Selected Issues, July 13, 2009, p. 24.

[10] For example, the Federal Reserve used this rationale to justify its assistance to Bear Stearns. See Chairman Ben S. Bernanke, "Developments in the Financial Markets," Testimony before the Committee on Banking, Housing, and Urban Affairs, U.S. Senate, April 3, 2008.

[11] Greg Ip, "Central Bank Offers Loans to Brokers, Cuts Key Rate," *Wall Street Journal*, March 17, 2008, p. A1.

[12] AIG would later receive more extensive assistance from the Fed and Troubled Asset Relief Program. For more information, see CRS Report R41073, *Government Interventions in Response to Financial Turmoil*, by Baird Webel and Marc Labonte.

[13] See, for example, U.S. Government Accountability Office, *Financial Crisis Highlights Need to Improve Oversight of Leverage at Financial Institutions and across System*, GAO 09-739, July 2009.

[14] For more information, see CRS Report R40423, *Fair Value Accounting: Context and Current Concerns*, by Gary Shorter.

[15] See, for example, Rafael Repullo and Javier Suarez, "The Procyclical Effects of Basel II," Centre for Economic Policy Research, working paper 0809, June 2008, http://www.cemfi.es/research/publications/workingpapersre.asp? lang=en.

[16] Treasury Market Practices Group, "Treasury Market Practices Group Endorses Several Measures to Address Widespread Settlement Fails," *press release*, November 12, 2008, http://www.newyorkfed.org/tmpg/pr081112.pdf.

[17] See, for example, Scott Polakoff, Testimony before the Senate Banking Committee, March 5, 2009; Jeff Gerth, "Was AIG Watchdog Not Up to the Job?", MSN Money, November 10, 2008, http://articles.money central.msn.com/Investing/Extra/was-aig-watchdog-not-up-to-the-job.aspx.

[18] This is related to, but distinct from, calls for the regulation of "too big to fail" firms because the latter would lead to regulation of only a subset of non-bank financial firms.

[19] Federal Reserve Board of Governors, *Federal Reserve: Purposes and Functions* (Washington, DC: June 2005), p. 1. The Fed is not the only regulator that already has systemic risk authority. For example, the FDIC has a systemic risk exception that allows it to waive its least cost resolution mandate when a bank failure could cause systemic risk.

[20] For more information on the Fed's recent emergency assistance, see CRS Report RL34427, *Financial Turmoil: Federal Reserve Policy Responses*, by Marc Labonte.

[21] "Maturity mismatch" is used to identify a traditional characteristic of balance sheets of financial intermediaries such as banks, which will generally have short-term liabilities, such as checking and savings deposits, to be balanced against assets, such as commercial loans and real estate mortgages, which mature at the end of a longer term..

[22] See, for example, CRS Report R41181, *Permissible Securities Activities of Commercial Banks Under the Glass-Steagall Act (GSA) and the Gramm-Leach-Bliley Act (GLBA)*, by David H. Carpenter and M. Maureen Murphy.

[23] For more information on these and other Fed actions during the recent crisis, see CRS Report R41073, *Government Interventions in Response to Financial Turmoil*, by Baird Webel and Marc Labonte.

[24] See Tobias Adrian, Christopher Burke, and James McAndrews, *The Federal Reserve's Primary Dealer Credit Facility*, Federal Reserve Bank of New York, Current Issues in Economics and Finance, vol. 15, no. 4, August 2009, p. 2.

[25] For more information, see CRS Report RL34427, *Financial Turmoil: Federal Reserve Policy Responses*, by Marc Labonte.

[26] The SEC issued new rules in January 2010 to strengthen regulation of money market mutual funds. See Securities and Exchange Commission, "SEC Approves Money Market Fund Reforms to Better Protect Investors," press release 2010-14, January 27, 2010.

[27] U.S. Department of the Treasury Press Release, "Treasury Announces Temporary Guarantee Program for Money Market Funds"(September 29, 2008). http://www.ustreas.gov/press/releases/hp1161.htm.

[28] P.L. 110-343, Tit. I, § 131, 122 Stat. 3797, 12 U.S.C. § 5236.

[29] According to a Federal Reserve study, assets held by broker-dealers increased from less than 3% of the size of commercial bank assets in 1980 to nearly 30% in 2007. Over the same period, hedge fund capital increased from less than 1% of the size of commercial bank capital to more than 100% of bank capital. See Tobias Adrian, Christopher Burke, and James McAndrews, *The Federal Reserve's Primary Dealer Credit Facility*, Federal Reserve Bank of New York, Current Issues in Economics and Finance, vol. 15, no. 4, August 2009, p. 5.

[30] 12 U.S.C. 343.

[31] *See,* Howard H. Hackley, Lending Functions f the Federal Reserve Banks: A History 129 (1973). The author, who served for a number of years as General Counsel of the Board of Governors of the Federal Reserve System, states that "it seems clear that it was the intent of Congress that loans should be made only to credit worthy borrowers; in other words; the Reserve Bank should be satisfied that a loan under this authority would be repaid in due course, either by the borrower or by resort to security."

[32] *See, e.g.,* Bart De Meester, "The Global Financial Crisis and Government Support for Banks: What Role for the GATS?" 13 J. Int'l Econ. L. 27, 42 (2010).

[33] See CRS Report RL34657, *Financial Institution Insolvency: Federal Authority over Fannie Mae, Freddie Mac, and Depository Institutions,* by David H. Carpenter and M. Maureen Murphy.

[34] Although it has not been used in the recent crisis and in currently occurring bank failures, the Federal Deposit Insurance Corporation has authority, if the Deposit Insurance Fund is depleted, to access a line of credit with Treasury, i.e., to borrow public funds, to operate bank resolution regimes. 12 U.S.C. § 1824(a).

[35] For more information, see CRS Report R40249, *Who Regulates Whom? An Overview of U.S. Financial Supervision,* by Mark Jickling and Edward V. Murphy; CRS Report RL33278, *The Basel Accords: The Implementation of II and the Modification of I,* by Walter W. Eubanks.

[36] Federal Reserve, *Bank Holding Company Supervisory Manual,* Washington, DC, July 2009, p. 77.

[37] Under 12 U.S.C. § 4008(c)(1), the Fed has the responsibility '[i]n order to carry out the provisions of the [Expedited Funds Availability Act ... to regulate ... any aspect of the payment system, including the receipt, payment, collection, or clearing of checks."

[38] See, "Policy on Payment System Risk, 73 Fed. Reg. 79109 (December 24, 2008).

[39] Information on these clearinghouses can be found at http://www.federalreserve.gov/paymentsystems/over_pssystems.htm.

[40] Federal Reserve, *Policy on Payment System Risk,* as amended effective December 18, 2008, http://federalreserve.gov/paymentsystems/psr_policy

[41] P.L. 106-102, 113 Stat. 1339.

[42] *For further information, see* CRS Report R41181, *Permissible Securities Activities of Commercial Banks Under the Glass-Steagall Act (GSA) and the Gramm-Leach-Bliley Act (GLBA),* by David H. Carpenter and M. Maureen Murphy.

[43] Section 2A of the Federal Reserve Act, 12 USC 225a.

[44] Section 2A of the Federal Reserve Act, 12 USC 225a.

[45] Chairman Ben S. Bernanke, "The Housing Market and Subprime Lending," Speech to the 2007 International Monetary Conference, June 5, 2007, http://www.federalreserve.gov/newsevents/speech/bernanke 20070605a.htm.

[46] 12 U.S.C. §§ 241-242.

[47] For an overview, see CRS Report R41350, *The Dodd-Frank Wall Street Reform and Consumer Protection Act: Issues and Summary,* coordinated by Baird Webel.

[48] This section prepared with M. Maureen Murphy, Legislative Attorney.

[49] P.L. 111-203, § 121(a).

[50] This section was prepared with David H. Carpenter, Legislative Attorney.

[51] P.L. 111-203, § 204(a).

[52] P.L. 111-203, § 214.

[53] This section prepared with M. Maureen Murphy, Legislative Attorney.

[54] P.L. 111-203, § 806(b).

[55] This section prepared with Mark Jickling, Specialist in Financial Economics.

[56] This section prepared with M. Maureen Murphy, Legislative Attorney.

[57] P.L. 111-203 § 616.

[58] P.L. 111-203, § 1101.

[59] See the initial announcement at http://www.fdic.gov/news/news/press/2008/pr08100.html. See http://www.fdic.gov/ news/news/press/2008/pr08105.html, which provides further details of the program.

[60] For more information, see CRS Report R41073, *Government Interventions in Response to Financial Turmoil,* by Baird Webel and Marc Labonte.

[61] http://www.financialstability.gov/roadtostability/capitalpurchaseprogram.html.

[62] P.L. 110-343, 110 Stat. 3765, § 101, 12 U.S.C. § 5211.

[63] This section prepared with M. Maureen Murphy, Legislative Attorney.

[64] P.L. 111-203 § 1105.

[65] This section was prepared with David H. Carpenter, Legislative Attorney. For more information, see CRS Report R41338, *The Dodd-Frank Wall Street Reform and Consumer Protection Act: Title X, The Consumer Financial Protection Bureau,* by David H. Carpenter.

[66] P.L. 111-203, § 1012(c)(2).

[67] P.L. 111-203§ 1112(c)(1).

[68] P.L. 111-203 § 1017.

[69] P.L. 111-203 § (b)(2).

[70] P.L. 111-203, § 1109(b) quoting 12 U.S.C. § 302.

[71] This section prepared with M. Maureen Murphy, Legislative Attorney.

[72] This section prepared with M. Maureen Murphy, Legislative Attorney.

In: The Dodd-Frank Wall Street Reform...
Editors: Nathan L. Morris and Philip O. Price

ISBN: 978-1-61324-101-1
© 2011 Nova Science Publishers, Inc.

Chapter 4

THE DODD-FRANK WALL STREET REFORM AND CONSUMER PROTECTION ACT: TITLES III AND VI, REGULATION OF DEPOSITORY INSTITUTIONS AND DEPOSITORY INSTITUTION HOLDING COMPANIES[*]

M. Maureen Murphy

SUMMARY

The Dodd-Frank Wall Street Reform and Consumer Protection Act of 2010, P.L. 111-203, has as its main purpose financial regulatory reform. Titles III and VI effectuate changes in the regulatory structure governing depository institutions and their holding companies and, thus, constitute a substantial component of the reform effort. Under Title III, there will no longer be a single regulator of federal and state-chartered savings associations, also known as thrifts or savings and loan associations. Title III abolishes the Office of the Thrift Supervision (OTS) and contains extensive provisions respecting the rights of affected employees as well as other administrative matters. It allocates the OTS functions among three existing regulators: the Comptroller of the Currency (OCC) will regulate federally chartered thrifts; the Federal Deposit Insurance Corporation (FDIC), state-chartered thrifts; and the Board of Governors of the Federal Reserve System (FRB), savings and loan holding companies. Title III also makes certain changes to deposit insurance: it makes permanent the increase of deposit insurance coverage to $250,000, and makes that increase retroactive to January 1, 2008. It extends full insurance coverage of non-interest bearing checking accounts for two additional years and authorizes a similar program for credit unions. Included in Title III is also a requirement that the Department of the Treasury and each federal financial regulatory agency establish an office of Minority and Women Inclusion.

Title VI addresses some perceived inadequacies with respect to prudential regulation of depository institutions and their holding companies, including the existence of certain exceptions to the Bank Holding Company Act's (BHC Act's) general prohibition on affiliation of banking institutions and commercial or manufacturing concerns; investment

---

[*] This is an edited, reformatted and augmented version of a Congressional Research Services publication, dated July 23, 2010.

in hedge funds or private equity funds and proprietary trading by banking institutions; gaps in the authority of the FRB to oversee all of the subsidiaries of bank holding companies; the need for greater coordination among the regulators with respect to enforcement actions, charter conversions, and mergers and acquisitions; and elimination of some of the differences affecting the regulation of thrifts and banks, state-chartered and federally chartered institutions, and bank and thrift holding companies.

The full implications of Titles III and VI will not be apparent until the agencies promulgate the many implementing regulations required before many of the provisions go into effect. Generally, the legislation specifies a time period for when a particular rulemaking is to be completed; in some cases, studies are required before the rulemaking may occur.

BACKGROUND AND OVERVIEW

Titles III and VI of the Dodd-Frank Wall Street Reform and Consumer Protection Act of 2010, P.L. 111-203, address certain issues that many Members of Congress, including the major drafters of the legislation, the House Committee on Financial Services and the Senate Committee on Banking, Housing, and Urban Affairs, perceived as impediments to effective regulation of the banking industry and possible contributing factors to certain aspects of the financial crisis of 2008. The version of Title III reported by the Senate Committee on Banking, Housing, and Urban Affairs, on which the final version is based, sought "to increase the accountability of the banking regulators by establishing clearer lines of responsibility and to reduce the regulatory arbitrage in the financial regulatory system whereby financial companies 'shop' for the most lenient regulators and regulatory framework."[1] The final version takes a step in that direction by abolishing one of the regulators, the Office of Thrift Supervision (OTS), the agency which had supervisory authority over Washington Mutual and Indy Mac Bank, the failures of which represented large losses to the Deposit Insurance Fund. The act distributes the OTS functions, regulating savings associations (thrifts or savings and loans) and savings and loan holding companies. Under Title X of the bill, the Consumer Financial Protection Bureau (CFPB) will assume much of the OTS responsibility for overseeing compliance by savings and loan associations with federal consumer protection laws. Title III allocates prudential supervision among three federal regulators. The Office of the Comptroller of the Currency (OCC) will now regulate federally chartered thrifts as well as national banks; the Federal Deposit Insurance Corporation (FDIC) will now regulate state-chartered thrifts as well as state-chartered banks which are not members of the Federal Reserve System (FRS); and the Board of Governors of the Federal Reserve System (FRB) will now regulate both bank holding companies (including financial holding companies) and thrift or savings and loan holding companies, as well as state-chartered banks which are members of the Federal Reserve System (FRS). Other provisions of Title III provide for reallocation of OTS personnel and property among those agencies, with various safeguards respecting employee rights and status.

Many of the provisions of Titles III and VI appear to be designed to correct perceived inadequacies in terms of the prudential regulation of banks, savings associations, bank holding companies, and savings and loan holding companies or discrepancies between the regulation of banks and savings associations. For example, there are provisions preventing depository institutions under supervisory or enforcement orders from changing their charters without full consent by the existing chartering authority and a plan for meeting the requirements of the enforcement order. There are numerous provisions requiring greater coordination among regulators and provisions enhancing the authority of FRB to oversee all of the components of holding companies. There are also provisions providing backup examination and enforcement authority in case the FRB's efforts fail to meet the standards imposed under the statute. There are various provisions designed to minimize regulatory differences applicable to different types of banking institutions and to address what have appeared to be loopholes permitting certain companies to own or control a depository institution without having to submit to consolidated regulation by the FRB under the Bank Holding Company Act (BHC Act).[2]

Miscellaneous matters addressed in Title III include changing the basis of deposit insurance assessments imposed on banks; permanently increasing deposit insurance coverage to $250,000; applying that increase retroactively to January 1, 2008; and establishing offices of Minority and Women Inclusion in the Department of the Treasury and in the federal financial regulatory agencies.

Title VI contains a number of provisions designed to tighten regulation of banking activities possibly threatening the safety and soundness of depository institutions and their holding companies. There are provisions tightening the controls on transactions with affiliates, derivative and swaps operations, and lending limits. There are also restrictions on banking companies making investments in hedge funds or private equity funds or engaging in proprietary trading, patterned on a proposal by a former FRB Chairman and current Chairman of the President's Economic Recovery Advisory Board.[3]

TITLE III: ENHANCING FINANCIAL INSTITUTION SAFETY AND SOUNDNESS ACT OF 2010

Overview of Title III

Title III consists of three subtitles. Subtitle A transfers the powers and duties of the OTS and establishes a transfer date for the transfers to become effective. Subtitle B provides for the transition to the new regulatory structure. Subtitle C contains several provisions affecting the FDIC and deposit insurance. Subtitle D includes various provisions including establishment of the Office of Minority and Women Inclusion within federal financial regulatory agencies and the Department of the Treasury, branching by depository institutions; and extension of temporary deposit insurance coverage of transaction accounts. What follows are summaries of sections of Title III relating to substantive changes in the regulation of depository institutions and their holding companies.

Transfer of OTS Functions to the OCC, FDIC, and FRB

Distribution of OTS Functions

Section 311 requires that OTS functions are to be distributed to the OCC, FDIC, and FRB one year after enactment, subject to a six-month extension.

Section 312 transfers the authority of OTS and the Director of OTS as follows:

- To the FRB, the authority to supervise, issue rules, and take enforcement actions respecting any savings and loan holding company and any of its subsidiaries, other than a depository institution;
- To the OCC, the authority to supervise, issue rules, and take enforcement actions respecting any federally chartered savings association or thrift; and,
- To the FDIC, the authority to supervise, issue rules, and take enforcement actions respecting any state-chartered savings association or thrift.

Section 313 abolishes the OTS and the position of Director of the OTS effective 90 days after the transfer.

Section 314 charges OCC, in addition to its other functions, with "assuring ... fair access to financial services and fair treatment of customers by the institutions and other persons subject to its jurisdiction, and requires the Comptroller of the Currency to designate a Deputy Comptroller for supervising and examining federal savings associations.

Transition from OTS to New Regulators

Sections 315, 316, 317, 318, and 319 are essentially technical in nature. For example, they include provisions that preserve OTS regulations, orders, agreements, regulations, and law suits and establish a method for the agencies to which OTS functions are transferred to effectuate the transition. There are provisions respecting funding, contracting and leasing authority, and setting forth a procedure for the agencies to which OTS functions are transferred to assume responsibility.

Sections 321, 322, 323, 324, 325, and 326 address various matters that arise during the transition period by outlining the type of consultation and cooperation to take place among the transferee agencies and the OTS with respect to payment of expenses; transfer of personnel; property and administrative services; and any other necessary actions for orderly implementation. OTS employees are to be transferred to the OCC and FDIC (and the Consumer Financial Protection Bureau) based on the functions they perform. Various provisions make allowances for employee retention rights with respect to salary and benefits, including retirement benefits. There are also provisions for transferring OTS property, contracts, and funds and for the OTS Director to wind up the affairs of the agency after the transfers have been accomplished.

Report Outlining Transition Implementation Plan

Section 327 requires the agencies jointly to submit, within 60 days of enactment, a plan for implementing Title III to the Senate Banking Committee and the House Financial Services Committee as well as to the Inspectors General (IGs) of Treasury, FDIC, OCC, OTS, and FRB. Within 60 days of receiving the plan, the IGs are to submit a written report on the proposed plan addressing various factors relating to the plan's fair, efficient, and orderly implementation of the requirements of the legislation. The Treasury, FDIC, and FRB IGs are to submit joint reports every six months on implementation of the plan.

Deposit Insurance Fund and Enhanced FDIC Authority

Assessments Based on Assets Rather Than Insured Deposits

Section 331 alters the basis on which assessments on depository institutions for deposit insurance are calculated. No longer will assessments be based on the amount of insured deposits; rather assessments generally are to be based on "the average consolidated total assets of the insured depository institution ... minus ... the sum of—the average tangible equity of the insured depository institution ...." There is authority for the FDIC to vary this for custodial banks (banks with a percentage of revenues generated by assets under custody) and banker's banks (banks providing banking services to other banks).

Elimination of Procyclical Assessments

Section 332 eliminates a requirement that the FDIC refund or credit to the next assessment any overpayments of assessments and authorizes it to suspend or limit the payment of dividends from excess reserves in the deposit insurance fund. The section also requires the FDIC to issue regulations on refunding overpayments or limiting dividend payments.

FDIC May Require Reports Without Getting Approval of Primary Regulator

Section 333 eliminates a requirement that FDIC receive a depository institution's primary federal regulator's approval before requiring additional reports from an insured depository institution. All that is now necessary is consultation with the primary federal regulator.

Increase in the Minimum Reserve Ratio

Section 334 increases the minimum reserve ratio for the Deposit Insurance Fund from 1.15% to 1.35% of estimated insured deposits or the comparable percentage of the assessment base. It requires the FDIC to take the steps necessary for the reserve ratio to reach that goal by September 30, 2020. It also requires the FDIC to "offset the effect [of this requirement] ... on insured depository institutions with total consolidated assets of less than" $10 billion.

Permanent Deposit Insurance Increase to $250,000; Applied Retroactively for Depositors of Institutions Which Failed in 2008

Section 335 effectuates a permanent increase in deposit insurance and share insurance for insured depository institutions and insured credit unions to $250,000, and applies this increase retroactively to the depositors of any institution for which the FDIC was appointed receiver after January 1, 2008. This will cover depositors in such institutions as IndyMac Bank, F.S.B., Pasadena, California, which was closed by the OTS, with the FDIC named as Conservator, on July 11, 2008.[4]

Director of the Consumer Financial Protection
Bureau, Ex-Officio Member of FDIC Board

Section 336 substitutes the Director of the Consumer Financial Protection Bureau for the OTS Director to serve with the Comptroller of the Currency as ex-officio members of the FDIC Board of Directors along with three presidentially appointed members. It provides for an acting official to serve in case of a vacancy or disability of an ex-officio board member.

Branching Authority of Savings Associations Converting to Bank Status

Section 341 authorizes a savings association converting to bank status to continue to operate any branch that it was operating immediately before the conversion and to acquire any additional branches in any state in which it operated a branch immediately before becoming a bank in any location in that state if the state law would permit a bank chartered in that state to operate a branch in that location.

Office of Minority and Women Inclusion in Federal
Financial Regulatory Agencies

Section 342 requires the Consumer Protection Bureau, Treasury, OCC, FDIC, FRB, each Federal Reserve bank, the Federal Housing Finance Agency, the National Credit Union Administration, and the Federal Trade Commission to establish an Office of Minority and Women Inclusion "responsible for all matters of the agency relating to diversity in management, employment, and business activities." The Director of these offices is to be a career reserved position in the Senior Executive Service, and is to develop standards on equal employment opportunity; increased participation of minority- and women-owned businesses in agency programs; and assessment of the diversity policies of the regulated entities. There is also a provision authorizing the Director to recommend termination of contractors "who have failed to include minority and women in their workforce." Section 342 requires annual reports from these offices and imposes upon the agencies obligations to make efforts to seek workforce diversity by recruiting practices and partnering with organization devoted to these goals, including inner-city high schools.

Deposit Insurance for Non-Interest Bearing Checking Accounts

Section 343 requires the FDIC and the NCUA to provide deposit insurance and share insurance coverage, without any cap or limit, for non-interest bearing transaction accounts. This authority sunsets January 1, 2013.

Sections 351- 378 consist of technical and conforming amendments to conform other sections of the law to changes made in Title III.

TITLE VI: IMPROVEMENTS TO REGULATION OF BANK AND SAVINGS ASSOCIATION HOLDING COMPANIES AND DEPOSITORY INSTITUTIONS

Title VI, the Bank and Savings Association Holding Company and Depository Institution Regulatory Improvements Act of 2010, addresses some of the issues that have been viewed as possibly weakening the ability of banking companies to focus on their main business of financial intermediation—accepting retail deposits that earn a modest return at no risk of loss to depositors and transforming them into capital that is available for lending and, thereby, fostering economic growth and activity. Title VI includes a temporary moratorium on FDIC approval of deposit insurance for new industrial loan companies and credit card banks; authority to segregate into intermediate holding companies the commercial activities of unitary thrift holding companies which have been able to combine an insured depository with commercial activities under exceptions to the BHC Act; broader authority for the FRB to supervise holding companies; further lending limits on depository institution loans to insiders; stricter capital levels for holding companies; prohibitions on proprietary trading and investment in hedge funds by banking companies; various requirements for studies (including a study on subjecting savings association holding companies to the BHC Act); and specific provisions aimed at such particular activities or powers of banks and thrifts.

What follows is a brief summary of each of the sections of Title VI except for those which are essentially technical in nature.

Moratorium and Study on Treatment of Credit Card Banks and Industrial Loan Companies

Section 603 establishes a three-year-moratorium during which the FDIC may not approve deposit insurance for any new credit card bank, industrial bank, or trust bank or any application for change in control of any existing institution of those types that has the result that a "commercial firm" acquires control of the institution, i.e., a firm which has 85% of its annual gross revenues derived from activities other than control of depository institutions and activities that are financial in nature. There are exceptions for change in control situations involving an institution which is in default or danger or default; for the merger or whole acquisition of the commercial firm; or for the acquisition of voting shares of less than 25% of the commercial firm.

This section also requires that, within eighteen months, the Government Accountability Office (GAO) must submit a study of whether it is necessary to eliminate certain exceptions to the BHC Act definition of "bank" or "bank holding company" that allow certain companies to avoid being subject to the requirement that companies owning or controlling banks be subject to FRB regulation under the BHC Act. In this study, GAO is to identify types and numbers of institutions, their size, geographic location, commercial affiliates, and their federal supervisor. GAO is to evaluate the adequacy of the applicable regulatory frameworks and the consequences of subjecting the institutions to the BHC Act. Among the exceptions that GAO is to study are (1) state-chartered banks owned by thrift associations and limited to taking deposits for thrift associations; (2) a bank controlled by a trust company or mutual savings bank in the same state as of December 31, 1970, provided that, subject to an exception for investments authorized for national banks, the trust company or mutual savings bank does not acquire any interest in a company which would give it 5% of the voting shares of the company; (3) institutions which function only in a trust or fiduciary capacity, subject to certain activities restrictions; (4) credit card banks; (5) industrial loan companies; and (6) savings associations.

Reports and Examinations of Holding Companies and Regulation of Holding Company Subsidiaries

Expanded FRB Authority

Section 604 expands the FRB's authority with respect to bank holding company subsidiaries in several ways and, thereby, modifies the "Fed-lite" provisions of the Gramm-Leach Bliley Act of 1999 (GLBA).[5] Section 604(c) removes the strict limitations on FRB authority to take direct action against functionally regulated subsidiaries[6] of bank holding companies.[7] Section 604(a) extends the authority of the FRB to require reports from bank holding companies and their subsidiaries to cover compliance with any applicable federal law in addition to those laws which the FRB has explicit authority to enforce. Exempted from this authority are functionally regulated subsidiaries and insured depository subsidiaries. In seeking reports from bank holding company subsidiaries, the FRB is to use existing reports and supervisory materials as much as possible. Section 604(b) expands FRB's authority to examine bank holding company subsidiaries by specifically including risks to U.S. financial stability as a focus of the examination and by authorizing it to monitor, except for functionally regulated subsidiaries and depository institution subsidiaries, how the subsidiaries are complying with any other applicable federal law (subject to the allocation of examination functions under the Consumer Financial Protection Act of 2010). Section 604(c) also adds to the definition of "functionally regulated subsidiaries" certain entities which are subject to regulation or registration with the Commodities Futures Trading Commission.[8] Sections 604(g) and (h) provide parallel authority for the FRB to require reports and make examinations of thrift holding companies. In examining holding companies, the FRB is required to coordinate with other regulators and avoid duplication. Section 604(i) modifies the definition of savings and loan holding company under the Home Owners Loan Act (HOLA)[9] to exclude bank holding companies, intermediate holding companies, and companies controlling a savings association "that functions solely in a trust or fiduciary capacity."

Risk to Financial System Must Be Considered in the Context of Any Holding Company Acquisition or Merger

Section 604(d) amends the BHC Act to require the FRB to consider, in addition to other enumerated factors,[10] the potential risks to the U.S. banking system or U.S. financial stability of any proposed acquisition, merger, or consolidation. Section 604(e) amends a provision of the BHC Act which permits financial holding company acquisitions of nonbanking concerns without prior notice to require prior notice for acquisitions involving savings associations and to require FRB approval for acquisitions involving assets of $10 billion or more.[11]

Standards for FRB Examination of Holding Company Subsidiaries

Section 605 sets standards for the FRB examination of non-depository, non-functionally regulated subsidiaries of depository institution holding companies by requiring that the examination cover "the activities ... that are permissible for the insured depository institution subsidiaries of the depository institution holding company in the same manner, subject to the same standards, and with the same frequency as would be required if such activities were conducted by the lead insured depository institution subsidiary of the holding company." If the FRB does not conduct such an examination, the regulator of the lead depository institution may provide the FRB with a written recommendation to conduct such an examination. If the FRB fails to begin such an examination or provide an explanation for not doing so within 60 days of receiving such a recommendation, the regulator of the lead depository institution may commence to conduct the examination. The focus of the examination is to determine whether the activities of these non-functionally regulated, non-depository institution subsidiaries of the holding company materially threaten a depository institution or the holding company, accord with law, and are subject to appropriate risk management systems. Such examinations are to be coordinated with the FRB not only to avoid duplication and share information but also to eliminate the possibility of "conflicting supervisory demands." Recommendations for supervisory actions are to be submitted to the FRB; if the FRB does not take enforcement action within 60 days, the agency making the recommendation may take action. Before taking any supervisory action against a non-depository, non-functionally regulated subsidiary, notice is to be provided to the appropriate state or federal regulator. Fees may be assessed as necessary for the cost of examinations by the regulator of the holding company's lead depository institution.

Increased Standards for a Bank Holding Company to Commence to Engage in Financial Activities or to Complete an Interstate Merger or Acquisition

Section 606 amends the BHC Act to add to the requirements for engaging in financial activities as a financial holding company a specification that the holding company (as well as its subsidiary depository institutions as required under GLBA) be well capitalized and well managed. This section contains a provision authorizing savings and loan holding companies to engage in activities that are permissible for financial holding companies provided they meet all the requirements and conduct the activities subject to the same regime as is applicable to financial holding companies.

Section 607 amends the BHC Act and the Bank Merger Act[12] to increase the capital standards for interstate acquisitions of a bank by a bank holding company or interstate bank mergers by requiring that the bank holding company or, in the case of mergers, the resulting bank be well managed and well capitalized.

Increased Restrictions on Interaffiliate Transactions Within Holding Companies

Section 608 amends sections 23A[13] and 23B[14] of the Federal Reserve Act,[15] which impose restrictions on interaffiliate transactions between member banks (and their subsidiaries) and their bank holding company or any of their holding company affiliates, by expanding the transactions covered under section 23A. For example, purchases of assets subject to repurchase agreements are included within the category of extensions of credit, and there is no authority for the FRB to exempt purchases of real or personal property within this category. Securities borrowing and derivative transactions also are covered to the extent of any credit exposure of the member bank to the affiliate. Section 608 also limits the FRB's authority to grant exemptions by removing the FRB's authority to grant an exemption for a transaction by order, thus, requiring all exemptions to be by regulation. It provides the FRB with authority to determine, jointly with the appropriate federal banking agency, how to calculate the amount of a covered transaction in the case of netting agreements. Before any exemption may take effect, the FDIC must be notified and not object in writing within 60 days of notice on the basis of the exemption's presenting "an unacceptable risk to the Deposit Insurance Fund." It also provides authority for the FRB and the OCC or the FDIC to grant exemptions for a transaction by national banks or state-chartered banks, provided that there is a finding that the exemption is in the public interest and the FDIC determines that the exemption does not present "an unacceptable risk to the Deposit Insurance Fund."

Section 608 also amends section 23B of the FRA to further reduce the FRB's flexibility in granting exceptions to the requirements that interaffiliate transactions under the BHC Act be on market terms by requiring that the FRB notify the FDIC and not receive a written objection from the FDIC within 60 days of notice that contends that the proposed exception presents "an unacceptable risk to the Deposit Insurance Fund."

Similar amendments are added to the HOLA transactions involving savings associations and savings and loan holding companies.

Section 609. makes transactions between banks and their subsidiaries subject to FRA section 23A by removing an exemption for transactions entered into after enactment, effective one year after the transfer date, i.e., the date on which OTS functions are actually assumed by the transferee agencies.[16]

Lending Limits

Section 610 includes within the lending limits applicable to national banks, and, thus, to limits on loans to one person or insiders and interaffiliate transactions, any credit exposures arising from derivative transactions, repurchase agreements, reverse repurchase agreements, and securities lending or borrowing transactions.

Derivative Transactions by State-Chartered Banks

Section 611 permits state-chartered banks to engage in derivative transactions only if the law of the bank's chartering state "takes into consideration credit exposure to derivative transactions."

Charter Conversions by Institutions Under Enforcement Order

Section 612 prohibits depository institutions from converting from one charter—state to federal or vice-versa or thrift to bank—while under a formal enforcement order or a memorandum of understanding unless the proposed new regulator notifies the prospective former regulator that a conversion is proposed and of a plan to address the supervisory concerns, and the former regulator does not object. The new regulator must see to it that the plan is implemented. If there has been a final enforcement action by a state attorney general, the conversion must be conditioned on compliance with its requirements.

De Novo Interstate Branching

Section 613 expands the authority of banks to establish *de novo* branches on an interstate basis to permit *de novo* branching to any location in a state allowed for branching by an in-state bank. No longer will state laws placing conditions on *de novo* branching by out-of-state banks act as a bar to an out-of-state bank wishing to establish its first branch in the state.[17]

Loans to Insiders

Section 614 adds credit exposure by virtue of derivative transactions, reverse repurchase agreements, securities lending or borrowing transactions to the restrictions on loans by member banks to insiders; authorizes the FRB to issue implementing rules; and requires the FRB to consult with OCC and FDIC when doing so.

Countercyclical Capital Requirements

Section 616 amends the BHC Act, the Savings & Loan Holding Company Act,[18] and the International Lending Supervision Act of 1983[19] to require the federal banking regulators to make capital "requirements countercyclical, so that the amount of capital required to be maintained by a [holding company, insured depository institution] ... increases in times of economic expansion and decreases in times of economic contraction, consistent with ... safety and soundness ...." The section also adds a new section 38A to the FDI Act to specify that the federal regulators of bank holding companies and savings and loan holding companies or any depository institution controlled by any company that is neither a bank holding company nor a savings and loan holding company must require them "to serve as a source of financial strength for any depository institution subsidiary." The regulators are to issue implementing rules to this effect within a year of enactment. Section 616 also authorizes the regulators to require reports under oath from such companies in order to assess the ability of the company to comply with the law and to enforce compliance. For this purpose "source of financial strength" is the "ability ... to provide financial assistance to such insured depository institution in the event of the financial distress of the insured depository institution."

Elimination of SEC-Regulated Investment Bank Holding Company; Establishment of FRB-Regulated Securities Holding Company

Section 617 eliminates the investment bank holding company framework in section 17 of the Securities Exchange Act of 1934,[20] under which a securities firm not having a depository institution subsidiary may choose to be supervised by the SEC as an investment bank holding company, coincidentally satisfying a foreign law requirement for consolidated supervision by its home country. The securities holding company regime established in section 618 serves as a replacement.

Section 618 establishes a framework whereby a securities holding company may submit to FRB regulation as a supervised securities holding company. Under this provision, "a person (other than a natural person) that owns or controls 1 or more brokers or dealers registered with the ... [SEC]... and the associated persons" may elect to register with FRB and, thereby, meet a foreign regulator's requirement for supervision on a consolidated basis. A securities holding company would then become subject to the recordkeeping, reporting, and examination requirements imposed by the FRB as specified in section 618. This section provides the FRB with a full range of civil enforcement authority under section 8 of the FDI Act; authorizes it to apply BHC Act requirements on the company; and requires the FRB to prescribe capital and risk management standards, taking into account the differences in types of business, financial assets, liabilities, off-balance sheet exposure, transactions and relationships with other financial companies, importance as a source of credit and liquidity, and the scope of activities of the supervised securities holding company.

The "Volcker Rule" Provision[21]

Overview

Section 619 includes certain prohibitions on proprietary trading and hedge fund investments by banking companies. Subsection (a) contains an outright prohibition on proprietary trading by and ownership of interests in or sponsorship of hedge funds or private equity funds by a "banking entity." "Banking entity" is defined in subsection (h) to mean any FDIC-insured depository institution, company controlling an insured depository institution, company treated as a bank holding company for purposes of the International Banking Act of 1978, and any affiliate or subsidiary of such entity.[22] The exact language provides a broad prohibition. It reads: "a banking entity shall not ... engage in proprietary trading, or ... acquire or retain any equity, partnership, or other ownership interest in or sponsor a hedge fund or a private equity fund." There are, however, certain exceptions, some transitional and others designated as permitted activities under subsection (d) of the legislation.

Rather than subjecting nonfinancial companies supervised by the FRB to a prohibition on proprietary trading and hedge fund ownership or sponsorship, the legislation authorizes the regulators to issue rules subjecting such companies to additional capital and quantitative limits on such activities unless the activity has been identified as a permitted activity under section (d) and has not been subjected to capital and quantitative requirements for safety and soundness purposes.

Subsection 619(h) sets forth definitions of various terms, in some cases providing a degree of discretion to the regulators to expand the reach of the prohibitions and limitations. For example:

> A "hedge fund" or a "private equity fund" is defined as "an issuer that would be an investment company ... but for section 3(c)(1) or 3(c)(7) of [the Investment Company Act of 1940], *or such similar funds as the ... [appropriate regulatory agencies] may, by rule, ... determine.*"[23]
>
> "Proprietary trading" is "engaging as a principal for the trading account of the banking entity or nonbank financial company supervised by the Board in any transaction to purchase or sell, or otherwise acquire or dispose of, any security, any derivative, any contract of sale of a commodity for future delivery, any option on any such security, derivative, or contract, or *any other security or financial instrument that the appropriate ... agencies ...may, by rule ..., determine.*"[24]

Financial Stability Oversight Council Study on Implementation of Restrictions on Proprietary Trading and Investment in Hedge Funds and Private Equity Funds

Subsection 619 (b) requires the Financial Stability Oversight Council to complete a study not later than six months after enactment and make recommendations on how implementation may be geared to (1) promote banking entity safety and soundness; (2) limit inappropriate transfers to "unregulated entities" of the federal subsidies embodied in FDIC deposit insurance and FRS liquidity programs; (3) "protect taxpayers and consumers and enhance financial stability" by minimizing risky activities by banking entities; (4) reduce conflicts of interest between customer interests and the self-interest of the covered entities; (5) limit unduly risky activities of the covered entities; (6) accommodate insurance company investment authority while safeguarding both affiliated banking entities and the financial stability of the United States;[25] and (7) devise appropriate timing for divestiture of illiquid assets affected by implementation of section 619.

Joint Rulemaking

Subsection 619(b) requires the federal banking regulators and the SEC and CFTC to conduct joint rulemaking and to adopt these rules no later than nine months after the Council completes its study. The regulators must coordinate the regulations for safety and soundness and elimination of the possibility of advantaging or disadvantaging some companies. Subsection (c) specifies that final rules are to become effective the earlier of (1) 12 months after they are issued or (2) two years after enactment.

Divestiture of Non-Conforming Activities Within Two Years

In general, banking entities will be given two years to divest nonconforming activities. Subsection 619(c) requires divestiture of nonconforming activities generally within two years of enactment subject to certain exceptions. The FRB is to issue rules on the divestiture provisions within six months of enactment. Additional capital and other restrictions, including margin requirements, on ownership interests in or sponsorship of hedge funds or private equity funds by banking entities are to be implemented by rules promulgated within the context of the joint rulemaking. The two-year divestiture requirement may be extended under certain circumstances: (1) the FRB may approve extensions for one-year periods not to exceed three additional years, and (2) if a contractual obligation in effect on May 1, 2010, requires a banking entity to take or retain its ownership interest in, or provide additional capital to, an illiquid fund, the entity may apply to the FRB for an extension which may be granted for no more than five years; divestiture would be required at the end of the five years or on the contractual date—whichever is earlier.

Exceptions

Subsection 619(d) identifies exceptions to the blanket prohibitions of subsection 619(a) by listing permitted activities and setting conditions under which those activities may be conducted. It excludes from permitted activities any transaction or class of activities, otherwise permitted, that would involve or result in a material conflict of interest; a material exposure by the banking entity to "high-risk assets or high-risk trading strategies" as defined by the regulators; or a threat to safety and soundness of the banking entity or to the financial stability of the United States. It provides standards by which the regulators may set further limits or conditions on these activities and includes authority for the regulators to add to the list of permitted activities. The regulators may impose additional capital and quantitative limits as "appropriate to protect the safety and soundness of banking entities engaged in such activities." Among the conditions specified for conducting these activities are that the activity must (1) be permitted under other federal or state law; (2) be subjected to restrictions as determined by the appropriate federal regulators; and (3) not involve or result in a material conflict of interest, expose the banking entity to "high-risk assets or high-risk trading strategies," or threaten safety and soundness of the banking entity or the financial stability of the United States. Subject to those conditions, the exceptions or permitted activities are:

- **Government and GSE Obligations.** Subsection (d)(1)(A) authorizes the purchase and sale of U.S. obligations; obligations of federal agencies; obligations of Ginnie Mae, Fannie Mae, Federal Home Loan Banks, Farmer Mac, and Farm Credit System institutions; and obligations of any state or political subdivision of a state.
- **Market Making Activities.** Subsection (d)(1)(B) authorizes the "purchase, sale, acquisition, or disposition of securities and various instruments which the regulators have determined by rule to fall within the definition of "proprietary trading" under subsection (h)(4), provided the transactions are "in connection with underwriting or market-making related activities, to the extent that ... [such transactions] are designed not to exceed the reasonably expected near term demands of clients, customers, or counterparties."
- **Risk Mitigating Hedging Activities.** Subsection (d)(1)(C) authorizes "risk-mitigating hedging activities" that are related to "positions, contracts, or other holdings of the banking entity and are designed to reduce specific risks in connection with and related to such holdings.
- **Small Business Investment Company Investments.** Subsection (d)(1)(E) authorizes specified small business investment company investments and investments qualified as rehabilitation expenditures with respect to a qualified rehabilitated building or certified historic structure as defined in section 47 of the Internal Revenue Code or similar state historic tax credit program.
- **Insurance Company Portfolio Investments.** Subsection (d)(1)(F) authorizes the "purchase, sale, acquisition, or disposition of securities and other instruments" which the regulators have determined by rule to fall within the definition of "proprietary trading" under subsection (h)(4) if the transactions are "by a regulated insurance company directly engaged in the business of insurance for the general account of the company by any affiliate of such regulated insurance company, provided that such activities by any affiliate are solely for the general account of the regulated insurance company." The transactions must also comply with applicable law, regulation, or guidance, and there must be no determination by the regulators that a relevant law, regulation, or guidance is insufficient to protect the safety and soundness of the banking entity or the financial stability of the United States.
- **Proprietary Trading by Foreign Companies Conducted Outside the United States.** Subsections (d)(1)(H) and (I) authorize investments permitted under sections 4(c)(9) and 4(c)(13) of the Bank Holding Company Act,[26] provided they are

conducted solely outside the United States by a company not controlled directly or indirectly by a company organized under the laws of the United States or of a state.

- **Other Investments.** Subsection (d)(1)(J) provides the regulators with authority to permit "[s]uch other activity ... by rule, ... [as] would promote and protect the safety and soundness of the banking entity and the financial stability of the United States."

Exceptions to the Ban on Investing in Hedge Funds or Private Equity Funds

Subsection 619(d)(1)(G) authorizes banking entities to organize and offer private equity or hedge funds only if (1) the banking entity provides "bona fide trust, fiduciary, or investment advisory services"; (2) the fund is offered only in connection with trust, fiduciary, or investment advisory services to "persons that are customers of such services of the banking entity"; (3) the banking entity retains only a de minimis interest in the funds;[27] (4) the banking entity and its affiliates engage in no transaction with the fund that would be designated as a covered transaction under FRA section 23A and other transactions with the fund are conducted only on terms specified in FRA section 23B, as if the banking entity were a member bank, and the fund an affiliate of that bank; (5) the banking entity does not guaranty the obligations of the hedge fund or private equity fund; (6) the banking entity does not share a name with the hedge fund or private equity fund; (7) no director or employee of the banking entity, other than a director or employee directly engaged in providing investment advisory or other services to the hedge fund or private equity fund, takes or retains an interest in the fund; and (8) the banking entity takes certain steps to assure the investors in the hedge fund or private equity fund that losses of the fund will be borne solely by its investors.

De Minimis Investment in Hedge Fund or Private Equity Fund

Subsection 619(d)(4) permits banking entities, subject to certain limitations, to make and retain a "de minimis investment" in a hedge fund or private equity fund or to make an initial investment in a hedge fund or private equity fund that the banking entity organizes. Among the limitations is a requirement to seek unaffiliated investors to reduce, within one year (subject to a possible extension for two more years), the banking entity's initial investment to the prescribed de minimis amount, as defined in subsection (d)(4). A de minimis investment must be (1) "not more than 3 percent of the total ownership interests of the fund," (2) "immaterial to the banking entity, as defined by rule," and (3) such that the aggregate investment of the banking entity in all such funds does not exceed 3% of its Tier 1 capital. There is also a requirement that a banking entity's aggregate outstanding de minimis or initial investments in hedge funds or private equity funds organized by the banking entity, including retained earnings, must be deducted from assets and tangible equity of the banking entity and the amount of the deduction to "increase commensurate with the leverage of the hedge fund or private equity fund."

Under subsection 619(f), a banking entity serving as "an investment manager, investment advisor, or investment sponsor to a hedge fund or private equity fund" or a banking entity which organizes and offers a hedge fund or private equity fund in connection with fiduciary or trust services as specified in subsection (d)(1)(G) or any affiliates thereof may enter into a transaction with the fund which would be a covered transaction under FRA section 23A if the banking entity and affiliate were a member bank and the fund were an affiliate thereof. In addition, any transaction between the banking entity and the fund must comply with Section 23B of the FRA as if the banking entity were a member bank and the fund, an affiliate, thereof. The FRB may permit a banking entity to enter into a prime brokerage transaction with any hedge fund or private equity fund in which a hedge fund or private equity fund managed, sponsored, or advised by the banking entity or nonbank financial company has an ownership interest under certain conditions. The banking entity must be in compliance with all of the conditions under which a banking entity may organize and advise a hedge fund or private equity fund in connection with fiduciary or trust services under subsection (d)(1)(G). Moreover, the banking entity's chief executive officer must provide an annual, and updated as necessary, written certification of compliance. The FRB must have determined that the primary brokerage agreement is consistent with the safe and sound operation of the banking entity; moreover, the prime brokerage transaction is subject to FRA section 23B as if the counterparty were an affiliate of the banking entity. Additional capital charges or other restrictions for nonbank financial companies are to be covered by rules issued by the appropriate regulators in the prescribed joint rulemaking proceedings.

Regulatory Authority to Grant Exceptions and Rules of Statutory Construction

Subsection 619(d)(1)(J) provides the regulators with authority to permit "[s]uch other activity ... by rule, ... [as] would promote and protect the safety and soundness of the banking entity and the financial stability of the United States."

Subsection 619(g) provides three rules of statutory construction for interpreting section 619: (1) the prohibitions and restrictions of section 619 apply, except as provided in the section, notwithstanding the existence of other provisions of law authorizing such activities; (2) nothing in section 619 is to "be construed to limit the ability of a banking entity or nonbank financial company ... to sell or securitize loans in a manner otherwise permitted by law"; and (3) nothing in section 619 is to "be construed to limit the inherent authority of any Federal agency or State regulatory authority under otherwise applicable provisions of law."

Evasions

Subsection 619(e) authorizes the appropriate regulator, having reasonable cause to believe that a banking entity or a nonbank financial company supervised by the FRB, is engaged in activities functioning as an evasion of section 619, or in violation of section 619, to order, subject to notice and opportunity for a hearing, termination of the activity and disposition of the investment. This subsection also requires the regulators to issue internal control and recordkeeping rules to insure compliance with section 619.

Report

Section 620 requires the federal banking agencies to prepare a joint report within 18 months of enactment on the investments and activities which banking companies may engage in under federal and state law, focusing on the types of activities, associated risks, and risk mitigation activities. The report is to be forwarded to the House Committee on Banking and Financial Services and the Senate Banking, Housing and Urban Affairs Committee two months after its completion with recommendations on whether activities present safety and soundness risks to banking concerns or to the U.S. financial systems, whether each investment or activity is appropriate, and any additional necessary restrictions.

Conflicts of Interest Relating to Certain Securitizations

Section 621 prohibits, subject to certain exceptions, asset-backed securities underwriters and sponsors and related entities from engaging in transactions with investors in those securities under circumstances giving rise to a conflict of interest and requires the SEC to issue implementing rules. Specifically, section 621 amends the Securities Act of 1933[28] to prohibit any "underwriter, placement agent, initial purchaser, or sponsor or any affiliate or subsidiary of any such entity, of an asset-backed security ...at any time for ... one year after the date of the first closing of the sale of the asset-backed security [from engaging in] any transaction that would involve in or result in any material conflict of interest with respect to any investor in a transaction arising out of such activities." The SEC is to issue rules within 270 days of enactment to implement this provision. There are specific exceptions for risk-mitigating hedging activities designed to reduce related risks and for purchases of the securities made pursuant to and consistent with commitments to provide liquidity for the security or market making for the security.

Concentration Limit of 10% of Aggregated Consolidated Assets of All Financial Companies

Section 622 prohibits any insured depository institution, bank holding company, savings and loan holding company, company controlling an insured depository institution, nonbank financial company supervised by the FRB, or any foreign bank or company treated as a bank holding company to merge or acquire assets of another company if the total consolidated liabilities of the acquiring company upon consummation of the transaction exceeds 10% of the aggregate consolidated liabilities of all financial companies at the end of the previous calendar year. The FRB may make exceptions with respect to the acquisition of a bank in default, an acquisition involving assistance provided by the FDIC under its authority to provide assistance to insured depository institutions in danger of default or during severe financial conditions under 12 U.S.C. § 1823(c), or an acquisition that results in minimal increase in the company's liabilities. Rulemaking authority is provided to the FRB; however, the rules must be "in accordance with the recommendations of the Council" after the Council completes a study on the potential effect of this concentration limit. The Council is to complete its study within six months of enactment; the FRB, to issue rules within nine months thereafter.

Section 623 amends the FDIA, the BHC Act, and the Savings and Loan Holding Company Act to prohibit the federal banking agencies from approving any application for an interstate merger transaction in which the resulting depository institution, bank holding company, or savings and loan holding company would control more than 10% of the total amount of deposits of insured depository institutions in the United States. There are exceptions for acquisitions of a depository institution in default or involving assistance provided by the FDIC under its authority under 12 U.S.C. § 1823(c).to provide assistance to insured depository institutions in danger of default or during severe financial conditions and for transactions resulting in only a minimal increase in the liabilities of the financial company.

Qualified Thrift Lenders

Section 624 applies to savings associations which fail to remain qualified thrift lenders, i.e., to qualify as a domestic building and loan association under 26 U.S.C. § 7701(a)(19) or generally to maintain 65% or more of portfolio assets in qualified thrift investments. It adds to the restrictions in place prior to enactment of the Dodd-Frank legislation a provision that limits their ability to pay dividends unless they are permissible for a national bank; necessary to meet obligations of the company which controls the savings association; and are specifically approved by OCC. The OCC may employ a full range of enforcement authority, under section 8 of the FDIA, against a savings association failing to remain a qualified thrift lender, which is deemed to be a violation of section 5 of the Home Owners' Loan Act, 12 U.S.C. §1464.

Treatment of Dividends by Certain Mutual Holding Companies

Section 625 imposes restrictions on the declaration or waiver of dividends by mutual holding companies. It requires every savings association subsidiary of a mutual holding company to provide the appropriate federal banking agency and the FRB 30-days' notice before declaring a dividend on any nonwithdrawable stock of the savings association. It permits a mutual holding company to waive dividends declared by a subsidiary if (1) no insider or tax-qualified or non-taxqualified employee stock benefit plan of the mutual holding company holds any of the subject stock or (2) the FRB is given 30-days' notice of the intended waiver and the FRB does not object. The FRB may object to the waiver only on the following grounds; (1) the waiver would be detrimental to the safe and sound operation of the savings association; (2) the mutual holding company's board of directors has not determined that the waiver is consistent with its fiduciary duties to the mutual members of the holding company; or (3) prior to December 1, 2009, the mutual holding company reorganized into a mutual holding company, issued minority stock from its mid-tier stock holding company or its subsidiary stock savings association, and waived dividends which it had a right to receive from the subsidiary stock savings association.

Intermediate Holding Company for Unitary Thrift Holding Companies

Section 626 authorizes the FRB to require a grandfathered unitary thrift holding company which conducts commercial or manufacturing activities or other non-financial activities in addition to financial activities to conduct all or part of its financial activities in an intermediate savings and loan holding company. If the FRB determines that the establishment of such an intermediate holding company is necessary to supervise the financial activities or to keep the FRB from supervising the non-financial activities, it must establish an intermediate holding company.

Financial activities that are internal to the company need not be placed in the intermediate holding company if the FRB finds that the grandfathered unitary thrift holding company engaged in the activities during the year prior to enactment and at least 2/3's of the assets or revenues generated from the activities are attributable to the grandfathered unitary thrift holding company. If an intermediate holding company is required, the grandfathered unitary thrift holding company must serve as a source of strength for it; the FRB may require periodic reports from the parent company. The FRB is required to issue regulations regarding interaffilate transactions between the intermediate holding company and its parent and non-subsidiary affiliates, but it may not "restrict or limit any transaction in connection with the bona fide acquisition or lease by an unaffiliated person of assets, goods, or services." FRB may use the full array of enforcement authorities under section 8 of the FDIA to enforce the provisions of the section against the grandfathered unitary thrift holding company. A savings clause states that nothing in the section is to be construed as requiring a unitary savings and loan holding company to conform its activities to those permissible for a savings and loan holding company, i.e., to divest its non-conforming commercial or manufacturing activities.

Interest on Business Checking Accounts

Section 627 repeals the prohibition applicable to banks and thrifts on paying interest on business checking accounts, effective one year after enactment.

Credit Card Bank Small Business Lending

Section 628 permits credit card banks to make one kind of commercial loan without satisfying the BHC Act definition of "bank," and, thereby, being subject to FRB regulation on a consolidated basis. The type of loan authorized is credit card loans to small businesses meeting the Small Business Administration eligibility criteria for business loans under 13 C.F.R., Part 121.[29]

End Notes

[1] S.Rept. 111-176, 111th Cong., 2d Sess. 23 (2010).

[2] 12 U.S.C. 1841 *et seq.*

[3] For further information see, CRS Report R41298, *The "Volcker Rule": Proposals to Limit "Speculative" Proprietary Trading by Banks*, by David H. Carpenter and M. Maureen Murphy.

[4] FDIC, Failed Bank Information, Failed Bank Information for IndyMac Bank, F.S.B., and IndyMac Federal Bank, F.S.B., Pasadena, CA, http://www.fdic.gov/bank/individual/failed/IndyMac.html#Introduction.

[5] Act of Nov. 12, 1999, P.L. 106-102.

[6] The term "functionally regulated subsidiary" of a bank holding company is defined in 12 U.S.C. § 1844(c)(5) to mean a bank holding company subsidiary which is not a bank holding company or depository institution. Such a subsidiary may be a broker or dealer registered under the Securities Exchange Act of 1934, 15 U.S.C. §§ 78a et seq.; an investment advisor registered with the SEC or any state; an investment company registered under the Investment Company Act of 1940, 15 U.S.C. §§ 80a-1 et seq.; an insurance company subject to supervision by a state insurance regulator; or an entity subject to regulation by the Commodity Futures Trading Commission "with respect to the commodities activities of such entity....". *Id.*

[7] P.L. 106-102, tit. I, subtit. B., sec. 112, 113 Stat. 1338, added section 10A to the Federal Reserve Act, 12 U.S.C. § 1849. Under this provision, prior to the enactment of the Dodd-Frank legislation, the FRB was precluded from taking action against a functionally regulated subsidiary of a bank holding company unless the action was necessary to address an unsafe or unsound practice posing a material risk to an affiliated depository institution

or the payment system and the FRB finds that an action against the affiliated depository institution or depository institutions in general would not provide adequate protection against the material risk.

[8] The specific language, found in section 604(c), reads: "an entity that is subject to regulation by, or registration with, the Commodity Futures Trading Commission, with respect to activities conducted as a futures commission merchant, commodity trading adviser, commodity pool, commodity pool operator, swap execution facility, swap data repository, swap dealer, major swap participant, and activities that are incidental to such commodities and swaps activities."

[9] Act of June 13, 1933, c. 64, 48 Stat. 128, 12 U.S.C. §§ 1461 et seq.

[10] The types of factors to be considered include competitive factors, supervisory factors, treatment of certain bank stock loans, managerial resources, and money laundering.

[11] For Hart-Scott-Rodino (antitrust filing under 15 U.S.C. § 18a(c)(8)) purposes, such acquisitions are to be treated as if FRB approval is not required.

[12] 12 U.S.C. § 1828(c).

[13] 12 U.S.C. § 371c.

[14] 12 U.S.C. § 371c-1.

[15] Act of December 23, 1913, ch. 6, 38 Stat. 251, 12 U.S.C. §§ 221 et seq.

[16] Under section 311 of the Dodd-Frank legislation, the transfer date is to take place one year of enactment unless the Secretary of the Treasury notifies the House Financial Services Committee and the Senate Committee on Banking, Housing, and Urban Affairs of a transfer date within the succeeding 18 months and provides information on why the transfer cannot be effectuated within the year and what steps are being taken to meet the new transfer date in an orderly fashion.

[17] 12 U.S.C. §§ 36(g) and 1831u(b) set conditions on interstate *de novo* branching by out-of-state national and state-chartered banks, respectively.

[18] 12 U.S.C. § 1730a.

[19] P.L. 98-181, tit. IX, § 901, 97 Stat. 1278, 12 U.S.C. § 3901 note.

[20] 15 U.S.C. § 78q.

[21] *See* CRS Report R41298, *The "Volcker Rule": Proposals to Limit "Speculative" Proprietary Trading by Banks,* by David H. Carpenter and M. Maureen Murphy.

[22] Excluded from the definition of "banking entity" are institutions functioning solely in a trust capacity under specified conditions: substantially all the deposits must be in trust funds; none of its insured deposits are marketed through an affiliate; no demand deposits are accepted or commercial loans made; and the institution does not accept payment, discount, or borrowing services from the Federal Reserve banks.

[23] Emphasis supplied.

[24] Emphasis supplied.

[25] The actual language reads: "appropriately accommodate the business of insurance within an insurance company subject to regulation in accordance with the relevant insurance company investment laws, while protecting the safety and soundness of any banking entity with which such insurance company is affiliated and of the United States financial system."

[26] 12 U.S.C. §§ 1843(c)(3) and 1843(c)(9).

[27] A de minimis investment, as defined in subsection (d)(4), is "not more than 3 percent of the total ownership interests of the fund," and "immaterial to the banking entity, as defined by rule" but such that the aggregate investment of the banking entity in all such funds does not exceed 3% of its Tier 1 capital.

[28] 15 U.S.C. §§ 77a et seq.

[29] The Small Business Administration regulations include a table setting size standards for various businesses (13 C.F.R. § 121.201); some are stated in millions of dollars, others in numbers of employees.

In: The Dodd-Frank Wall Street Reform...
Editors: Nathan L. Morris and Philip O. Price

ISBN: 978-1-61324-101-1
© 2011 Nova Science Publishers, Inc.

Chapter 5

HEDGE FUNDS: LEGAL HISTORY AND THE DODD-FRANK ACT[*]

Kathleen Ann Ruane and Michael V. Seitzinger

SUMMARY

Hedge funds have received a great deal of media coverage in the past several years because large sums of money have been gained or lost in a relatively short time by some hedge funds. Most hedge funds are not required to register with the Securities and Exchange Commission (SEC) under the Investment Company Act of 1940 or the Investment Advisers Act of 1940. In 2004, the SEC implemented a rule that would have required all hedge fund advisers to register with the SEC under the Investment Advisers Act. Hedge funds challenged the rule in federal court, arguing that the SEC had misinterpreted provisions of the Investment Advisers Act. The U.S. Court of Appeals for the D.C. Circuit agreed with the hedge funds and struck down the SEC's rule. Following that decision, it appeared that congressional action would be necessary to require all hedge funds to register.

In the wake of the financial crisis, Congress and President Obama's Administration debated proposals for financial regulatory reform. One of the main thrusts of the proposals was to allow regulatory agencies better access to information regarding large market participants whose failure may have a detrimental effect on the entire financial system. It is widely believed that many hedge funds could fall into the category of market participants that pose this sort of risk. Accordingly, much of the debate centered around eliminating the exemption from registration for hedge fund advisers and creating reporting requirements.

This report will discuss the SEC's previous rule requiring hedge fund advisers to register with the agency and the appeals court decision that struck it down. These events formed the basis for the eventual reforms enacted by the Dodd-Frank Act. The report will then discuss Title IV of the Dodd-Frank Act, which will create new registration and reporting requirements for private fund advisers. Further discussion of the various policy perspectives on this topic may be found in CRS Report 94-511, *Hedge Funds: Should They Be Regulated?*, by Mark Jickling.

---

[*] This is an edited, reformatted and augmented version of a Congressional Research Services publication, dated July 16, 2010.

INTRODUCTION

The term "hedge fund" is at times difficult to define for legal purposes, since it does not appear to be defined anywhere in federal securities laws. No single definition of the term appears to be used by industry participants, but perhaps one of the most useful definitions of a hedge fund is that it is "any pooled investment vehicle that is privately organized, administered by professional investment managers, and not widely available to the public."[1] Legally, however, they have historically been exempt from registration under the Investment Company Act of 1940 (15 U.S.C. 80a-3), because they qualify for exemptions from registration under either section 3(c)(1) or 3(c)(7). Therefore, the Dodd-Frank Act will define "private funds" to mean issuers that would be investment companies under the Investment Company Act, but for their qualification for the exemption in either 3(c)(1) or 3(c)(7).[2]

Hedge funds have received a great deal of media coverage in the past several years because large sums of money have been gained or lost in a relatively short time by some hedge funds. Some have argued that the Securities and Exchange Commission (SEC) should be given specific statutory authority to require the registration of hedge funds or their advisers. Arguments for other kinds of registration or for no regulation have also been urged.[3] With the passage of the Dodd-Frank Act, discussed below, hedge fund advisers will be required to register with the SEC. These new requirements are based, in part, on events that occurred in 2004.

2004 SECURITIES AND EXCHANGE COMMISSION RULE

In 2004 the SEC issued a rule[4] which resulted in requiring many hedge fund advisers to register with the SEC as investment advisers under the Investment Advisers Act.[5] This rule first defined a "private fund" as an investment company that is exempt from registration under the Investment Company Act[6] because it has fewer than 100 investors or only qualified investors,[7] allows its investors to redeem their interests within two years of investing, and markets itself based upon the "skills, ability, or expertise of the investment adviser."[8] The rule went on to state that these private funds, "[f]or purposes of section 203(b)(3) of the [Investment Advisers] Act (15 U.S.C. § 80b-3(b)(3), ... must count as clients the shareholders, limited partners, members, or beneficiaries ... of [the] Fund."[9] In general, prior to the rule, hedge fund advisers were exempt from registration with the SEC so long as they had "fewer than 15 clients."[10] Referred to collectively as "Goldstein," various hedge fund advisers brought suit to challenge the equation under the rule of "client" with "investor."

Goldstein v. Securities and Exchange Commission[11]

Goldstein argued that the SEC misinterpreted Section 203 of the Investment Advisers Act, which exempts from registration "any investment adviser who during the course of the preceding 12 months has had fewer than 15 clients.... "[12] In response to Goldstein's argument, the SEC argued that, because the Investment Advisers Act does not define "client," the term is therefore ambiguous. The SEC in its argument for authority to issue the hedge fund rule relied upon the decision in *Chevron, U.S.A., Inc. v. Natural Resources Defense Council*[13] that "[i]f ... the court determines Congress has not directly addressed the precise question at issue, the court does not simply impose its own construction on the statute, [footnote omitted] as would be necessary in the absence of an administrative interpretation. Rather, if the statute is silent or ambiguous with respect to the specific issue, the question for the court is whether the agency's answer is based on a permissible construction of the statute [footnote omitted]."[14] The SEC argued in *Goldstein* that, because the Investment Advisers Act does not define "client," it was a "permissible construction of the statute" for it to issue the hedge fund rule equating "client" with "investor."

The U.S. Court of Appeals for the District of Columbia in a three-judge panel unanimously found that this argument with respect to the SEC's hedge fund rule did not mesh with an amendment by Congress to Section 203 and that it was counter to interpretations that the SEC itself had made over the years about hedge fund advisers and investors.[15]

According to the court, a 1970 amendment, in which Congress eliminated a separate exemption from registration under the Investment Advisers Act for advisers who advised only investment companies and explicitly made the fewer than 15 clients exemption unavailable to such advisers,[16] would have been unnecessary if the shareholders of investment companies could be counted as "clients." The court went on to state that another section of the Investment Advisers Act suggests that Congress did not intend "shareholders, limited partners, members, or beneficiaries" of a hedge fund to be considered clients. In its definition of investment adviser as "any person who, for compensation, engages in the business of advising others, either directly or through publications or writings, as to the value of securities or as to the advisability of investing in, purchasing, or selling securities,"[17] the Investment Advisers Act does not cover a hedge fund manager whose job is to control the disposition of the pool of money in the fund and not to give investment advice. If, according to the court, the person controlling the fund is not an investment adviser to each individual investor, each investor cannot be a client of that person.

The SEC itself, before issuing the hedge fund rule, had apparently argued that an investment adviser of an entity like a hedge fund does not directly advise others. In 1997 the SEC stated that a "client of an investment adviser typically is provided with individualized advice that is based on the client's financial situation and investment objectives. In contrast, the investment adviser of an investment company need not consider the individual needs of the company's shareholders when making investment decisions, and thus has no obligation to ensure that each security purchased for the company's portfolio is an appropriate investment for each shareholder."[18]

The court then discussed a United States Supreme Court case to buttress further its position. The case, *Lowe v. Securities and Exchange Commission*,[19] held that certain financial newsletters were not investment advisers. After looking at the legislative history of the Investment Advisers Act, the Court found that the existence of an advisory relationship depended primarily upon the character of the advice given. An investment adviser "provide[s] personalized advice attuned to a client's concerns."[20] According to the court in *Goldstein*, the adviser/manager of a hedge fund is concerned with the fund's performance and not with the financial condition of each investor.

The D.C. Circuit concluded that "[t]he Commission has, in short, not adequately explained how the relationship between hedge fund investors and advisers justifies treating the former as clients of the latter"[21] and held that the SEC's hedge fund rule was arbitrary and vacated and remanded the rule.

On August 6, 2006, SEC Chairman Christopher Cox stated that the SEC would not seek en banc review of the court of appeals decision and would not petition the United States Supreme Court for a writ of certiorari.

Subsequent SEC Action

On December 13, 2006, the SEC voted unanimously to issue a proposal for a new antifraud rule under Section 206(4)[22] that would prohibit an investment adviser from defrauding investors in a hedge fund or certain other pooled investments. According to Chairman Cox, this proposal by the SEC responded to the *Goldstein* decision.[23]

On July 11, 2007, the SEC unanimously voted to approve new Rule 206(4)-8 under Section 206 of the Investment Advisers Act.[24] The rule, passed in the wake of *Goldstein*, would clarify the SEC's authority to pursue fraudulent misconduct by hedge fund advisers.

THE DODD-FRANK ACT: TITLE IV— REGULATION OF ADVISERS TO HEDGE FUNDS AND OTHERS

In light of recent economic events, a movement occurred toward financial regulatory reform. The main goal of the reform efforts was to allow regulatory agencies access to the information that they would need to determine whether a given financial firm, regardless of its regulatory status, may pose systemic risk in the event of its failure. Because hedge funds typically were structured in such a way as to avoid registration and disclosure under the securities laws, the Dodd-Frank Act eliminates some of the exemptions most often used by these entities in order to allow the SEC and the Financial Services Oversight Council access to the information necessary to achieve these goals. The theory of their proposals is that the elimination of these exemptions will require hedge funds to register and disclose to regulators, thereby allowing regulators access to the information that they might need to ward off potential catastrophe in the event of a hedge fund failure.[25] This section will discuss the exemptions from registration most commonly used by hedge funds, prior to the enactment of the Dodd-Frank Act. It will then discuss Title IV of the Dodd-Frank Act, eliminating certain exemptions and creating reporting requirements for advisers to private funds.

Exemptions Commonly Used by Hedge Funds

The Investment Company Act[26]
Many hedge funds are not investment companies under the Investment Company Act of 1940.[27] They are not merely exempt from registration or from the provisions of the Investment Company Act; rather, they are not included in the definition of "investment company" at all, because they generally avail themselves of one of two exemptions from the definition of investment company.

Section 3(c)(1) of the Investment Company Act states that issuers with fewer than 100 beneficial owners will not be deemed investment companies.[28] Many hedge funds limit themselves to 99 beneficial owners or fewer.[29] If one of these owners is a company, the company is counted as one owner for purposes of calculating the number of beneficial owners.[30] However, if the company owns more than 10% of the outstanding voting securities, each shareholder in the company is counted as a beneficial owner.

The other widely used exemption is Section 3(c)(7) of the Investment Company Act, which exempts funds that sell shares only to "qualified purchasers."[31] Qualified purchasers are (1) any natural person who owns not less than $5 million in investments as defined by the SEC; (2) a family-owned company that owns not less than $5 million in investments; (3) certain trusts; and (4) any other person who owns and invests on a discretionary basis at least $25 million in investments.[32] Funds using this exception are deemed investment companies for the purposes of limiting their ability to acquire securities in or sell their own securities to other investment companies.[33]

The Investment Advisers Act of 1940[34]

Many managers of private funds are investment advisers within the meaning of the Investment Advisers Act. Investment advisers are persons "who, for compensation, engage in the business of advising others, either directly or through publications or writings, as to the value of securities or as to the advisability of investing in, purchasing, or selling securities, or who, for compensation and as part of a regular business, issue or promulgate analyses or reports concerning securities."[35] In general, investment advisers are required to register with the SEC under the Investment Advisers Act.[36] Prior to the Dodd-Frank Act taking effect, advisers to private funds may not be required to register as long as, within the preceding 12-month period, they have not had more than 15 clients and do not hold themselves out to the public as an investment adviser, nor act as an investment adviser to a registered investment company or business development company.[37] "Clients," as discussed above, in this circumstance has been interpreted to refer to each pooled investment fund and not to each investor in the fund.[38] Therefore, if a particular private fund company consists of fewer than 15 individual pooled investment vehicles, the investment adviser to those funds is not required to register with the SEC under the Investment Advisers Act. The Dodd-Frank Act would eliminate this exemption.

Other Securities Laws

Private funds also may tend to structure the sales of their shares in such a way as to be exempt from registration and reporting obligations under the Securities Act of 1933[39] and the Securities Exchange Act of 1934.[40] In fact, in order to avail themselves of the common exemptions in the Investment Company Act, the fund may not make a "public offering" of its securities.[41] Offerings of securities that are not public offerings are defined under Section 4(2) of the Securities Act of 1933.[42] The Dodd-Frank Act would not change the ability of hedge funds to fit within these exemptions; therefore, the exemptions are not discussed in detail here.

Provisions of the Dodd-Frank Act

The Dodd-Frank Act will require the registration of investment advisers to private funds under the Investment Advisers Act of 1940. Private funds would be defined as those funds that would be investment companies under the Investment Company Act of 1940 but for their use of exemptions 3(c)(1) or 3(c)(7).[43]

Foreign private fund advisers would remain exempt from registration.[44] Foreign private fund advisers would be defined as advisers with no place of business in the United States having fewer than 15 clients and investors in the United States in private funds advised by the investment adviser and with aggregate assets under management attributable to U.S. clients and investors of less than $25 million (or such other higher number as the SEC may designate).[45] A foreign private fund adviser may not hold itself out as an investment adviser in the U.S., nor may it advise an investment company or a business development company as either term is defined by the Investment Company Act of 1940. Also exempt are investment advisers that solely advise small business investment companies that are licensees under the Small Business Investment Act[46] and venture capital fund advisers.[47] Private fund advisers with assets under management of less than $150 million would qualify for a limited exemption from registration if they comply with records and reporting requirements to be established by the SEC.[48] The bill would also provide for an exemption from the definition of investment adviser for "family offices" as defined by the SEC by rule.[49] Lastly, advisers registered with the Commodity Futures Trading Commission (CFTC) as commodity trading advisers are exempt from registration, unless the business of the adviser becomes predominantly securities-related after the Dodd-Frank Act takes effect.[50]

Registered advisers to private funds would be required to maintain records and file reports with the SEC, which would be made available to other relevant regulators including the Financial Services Oversight Council (FSOC).[51] The records would be required to include the amount of assets under management and use of leverage, counterparty credit exposure, trading and investment positions, valuation policies and practices, types of assets held, side arrangements, trading practices, and other information deemed necessary by the SEC in consultation with the FSOC for the public interest and/or the assessment of systemic risk.

The SEC is required to conduct periodic examinations of the records of private fund advisers.[52] The agency would also have the power to conduct examinations outside of the regular periodic examinations as it deemed necessary. The SEC would be required to make those records available to the FSOC. The FSOC would be required to maintain the confidentiality of information it receives from the SEC and the information would be exempt from the Freedom of Information Act (FOIA).[53] The SEC would also be exempt from disclosing reports and information required to be filed with it under this subsection, except that the SEC would be unable to withhold information from Congress and would not be prevented from complying with requests for information from other federal agencies or orders of a court of the United States in an action brought by the United States or the SEC. Furthermore, any federal agency or department receiving information, reports, documents, etc., pursuant to this subsection would be exempt from FOIA with respect to that information. The confidentiality of proprietary information, as defined by the bill, would also be safeguarded.

Private fund investment advisers would be required to safeguard client assets over which they have custody, including verification of such assets by independent accountants.[54] Taking into account the public interest and the economy, the SEC must increase the financial threshold for accredited investors, and is required to adjust that threshold every four years to determine whether the requirements of the definition should be adjusted or modified for the protection of investors.[55]

End Notes

[1] President's Working Group on Financial Markets, HEDGE FUNDS, LEVERAGE, AND THE LESSONS OF LONG-TERM CAPITAL MANAGEMENT 1 (1999) (hereinafter Working Group Report). Another useful definition of the term is an "entity that holds a pool of securities and perhaps other assets, whose interests are not sold in a registered public offering and which is not registered as an investment company under the Investment Company Act." United States Securities and Exchange Commission, STAFF REPORT TO THE UNITED STATES SECURITIES AND EXCHANGE COMMISSION ON THE IMPLICATIONS OF THE GROWTH OF HEDGE FUNDS 3 (2003).

[2] Discussed *infra*.

[3] *See* CRS Report 94-511, *Hedge Funds: Should They Be Regulated?*, by Mark Jickling.

[4] 69 FED. REG. 72,054 (December 10, 2004), *codified at* 17 C.F.R. Parts 275 and 279.

[5] 15 U.S.C. §§ 80b-1 *et seq.*

[6] 15 U.S.C. §§ 80a *et seq.*

[7] 15 U.S.C. § 80a-3(c)(1), (7).

[8] 17 C.F.R. § 275.203(b)(3)-1(d)(1).

[9] 17 C.F.R. § 275.203(b)(3)-2(a).

[10] Exempted from registration is "any investment adviser who during the course of the preceding 12 months has had fewer than 15 clients and who neither holds himself out generally to the public as an investment adviser nor acts as an investment adviser to any investment company.... " 15 U.S.C. § 80b-3(b)(3).

[11] 451 F.3d 873 (D.C. Cir. 2006).

[12] 15 U.S.C. § 80b-3(b)(3).

[13] 467 U.S. 837, 842-843 (1984).

[14] *Id.* at 843.

[15] *Goldstein v. Securities and Exchange Commission*, 451 F.3d 873 (D.C. Cir. 2006).

[16] P.L. 91-547, § 24, 84 Stat. 1413, 1430 (1970).

[17] 15 U.S.C. § 80b-2(11).

[18] *Status of Investment Advisory Programs Under the Investment Company Act of 1940*, 62 FED. REG. 15,098, 15,102 (March 31, 1997).

[19] 472 U.S. 181 (1985).

[20] *Id.* at 208.

[21] *Goldstein* at 882.

[22] 15 U.S.C. § 80b-6(4).

[23] DAILY REPORT FOR EXECUTIVES (BNA), A-41 (December 14, 2006).

[24] 17 C.F.R. § 275.206(4)-8.

[25] Financial Regulatory Reform, Obama Administration White Paper, available at http://www.financialstability.gov/docs/regs/FinalReport_web.pdf.

[26] 15 U.S.C. §§ 80a *et seq.*

[27] Working Group Report at 3, Appendix B available at http://www.ustreas.gov/press/releases/reports/hedgfund.pdf.

[28] 15 U.S.C. § 80a-3(c)(1).

[29] Working Group Report at 3, Appendix B.

[30] 15 U.S.C. § 80a-3(c)(1).

[31] 15 U.S.C. § 80a-3(c)(7). *See also*, Working Group Report at 3, Appendix B.

[32] 15 U.S.C. §80a-2 (a)(51)(A).

[33] 15 U.S.C. § 80a-12(d)(1)(A)(i), (B)(i).

[34] 15 U.S.C. §§ 80b-1 *et seq.*

[35] 15 U.S.C. §80b-2(a)(11). There are enumerated exemptions from this definition into which private fund or hedge fund managers do not typically fall.

[36] 15 U.S.C. § 80b-3(a).

[37] 15 U.S.C. § 80b-3(b)(3).

[38] *Goldstein v. Securities and Exchange Commission*, 451 F.3d 873 (D.C. Cir. 2006).

[39] 15 U.S.C. §§ 77 *et seq.*

[40] 15 U.S.C. §§ 78 *et seq.*; Working Group Report at Appendix B.

[41] 15 U.S.C. §§ 80a-3(c)(1), (c)(7).

[42] 15 U.S.C. § 77d(2). *See also*, Working Group Report at Appendix B.

[43] Section 403 of the Dodd-Frank Act.

[44] *Id.*

[45] Section 402 of the Dodd-Frank Act.

[46] Section 403 of the Dodd-Frank Act.

[47] Section 407 of the Dodd-Frank Act. Venture capital fund advisers would be required to maintain records and submit reports as the SEC designates by rule.

[48] Section 408 of the Dodd-Frank Act.

[49] Section 409 of the Dodd-Frank Act.

[50] Section 403 of the Dodd-Frank Act.

[51] Section 404 of the Dodd-Frank Act.

[52] *Id.*

[53] 5 U.S.C. § 552.

[54] Section 411 of the Dodd-Frank Act.

[55] Section 413 of the Dodd-Frank Act.

In: The Dodd-Frank Wall Street Reform...
Editors: Nathan L. Morris and Philip O. Price

ISBN: 978-1-61324-101-1
© 2011 Nova Science Publishers, Inc.

Chapter 6

THE DODD-FRANK WALL STREET REFORM AND CONSUMER PROTECTION ACT: REGULATIONS TO BE ISSUED BY THE CONSUMER FINANCIAL PROTECTION BUREAU[*]

Curtis W. Copeland

SUMMARY

Title X of the Dodd-Frank Wall Street Reform and Consumer Protection Act (P.L. 111-203, July 21, 2010) consolidates many federal consumer protection responsibilities into a new Bureau of Consumer Financial Protection (often referred to as the Consumer Financial Protection Bureau, or CFPB) within the Federal Reserve System. The act transfers supervisory and enforcement authority over a number of consumer financial products and services to the Bureau on a still-tobe-determined transfer date during calendar year 2011. Title X and Title XIV of the act contain numerous provisions that require or permit the CFPB to issue regulations implementing the statute's provisions. This report describes those provisions, notes that certain regulatory oversight tools will not be available for CFPB rules, and discusses the authority of a council of bank regulators to "set aside" the Bureau's rules.

Section 1022 alone gives the CFPB broad rulemaking powers, authorizing it to prescribe such rules "as may be necessary or appropriate" to enable the Bureau to administer federal consumer financial protection laws. The act contains many other provisions that require or permit the Bureau to issue rules, most of which give the Bureau substantial discretion regarding whether rules need to be issued, the contents of those rules, and when they must be issued. The Bureau also assumes responsibility for certain transferor agencies' existing rules, proposed rules that have not been made final, and final rules that have not taken effect. Therefore, other than for about 20 rules that are specifically required in the statute, it is not currently possible to determine how many rules the Bureau will issue, or the contents of those rules. Although most of the Bureau's rulemaking authority and discretion is the same as it was before being transferred from

---

[*] This is an edited, reformatted and augmented version of a Congressional Research Services publication, dated August 25, 2010.

the safety and soundness (prudential) regulators, it is not clear that those authorities and discretion will be exercised in the same way.

Like other independent regulatory agencies, some regulatory oversight methods will not be available for CFPB rules. The Bureau's significant rules will not be reviewed by the Office of Management and Budget (OMB) under Executive Order 12866, and those rules will not be subject to the cost-benefit analysis requirements in the order. The Bureau may be able to void OMB disapprovals of its collections of information under the Paperwork Reduction Act. Because the CFPB might not receive appropriated funds, Congress may not be able to control the Bureau's rulemaking through appropriations restrictions. Also, the effectiveness of new requirements placed on the Bureau to examine its rules within five years, and to take certain actions under the Regulatory Flexibility Act, may depend on how the Bureau interprets key terms.

Congress did, however, empower the newly created Financial Stability Oversight Council (composed primarily of the heads of the prudential regulatory agencies from which the CFPB was formed) to "stay" or "set aside" all or part of a Bureau rule that it concludes would put the safety and soundness of the U.S. banking or financial systems at risk. No other executive branch entity (including OMB) has previously been given the authority to nullify an agency's rules, and the authority to set aside a portion of a rule is greater than the expedited authority Congress gave itself through the Congressional Review Act (CRA). However, several aspects of the Council review process are currently unclear (e.g., whether the Council must vote to stay a rule).

Although Congress may not be able to use appropriations restrictions to control CFPB rulemaking, Congress still has an array of oversight tools available, including confirmation hearings, oversight hearings, meetings between individual Members and the Bureau, and CRA resolutions of disapproval. This report will not be updated.

INTRODUCTION

The Dodd-Frank Wall Street Reform and Consumer Protection Act (P.L. 111-203, July 21, 2010, hereafter, the "Dodd-Frank Act") was enacted in the wake of what many believe was the worst U.S. financial crisis since the Great Depression. The legislation addresses a variety of issues that arose as a result of that crisis, one of which was the perception that the federal system of consumer protection was fragmented and, in some cases, inconsistent with other regulatory functions.[1] For example, safety and soundness (prudential) regulators and consumer protection regulators may look on the same activity differently. Therefore, some argued that separating prudential and consumer protection regulation into separate agencies is the best way to protect both consumers and financial institutions.

Until the Dodd-Frank Act fully goes into effect, the Board of Governors of the Federal Reserve System will continue to write rules to implement most of the consumer financial protection laws. Enforcement of these laws is shared by a variety of prudential regulators, including the Office of the Comptroller of the Currency for national banks; the Federal Reserve Board for domestic operations of foreign banks and for state-chartered banks that are members of the Federal Reserve System; the Federal Deposit Insurance Corporation for state-chartered banks and other state-chartered banking institutions that are not members of the Federal Reserve System; the National Credit Union Administration for federally insured credit unions; and the Office of Thrift Supervision for federal savings and loan associations and thrifts. The Federal Trade Commission is the primary federal regulator for non-depository financial institutions (e.g., payday lenders and mortgage brokers) and many other non-financial commercial enterprises.[2]

Consumer Financial Protection Bureau

Title X of the Dodd-Frank Act, entitled the "Consumer Financial Protection Act of 2010,"[3] consolidates many federal consumer protection responsibilities into a new Bureau of Consumer Financial Protection (often referred to as the Consumer Financial Protection Bureau, CFPB, or Bureau) within the Federal Reserve System. [4] The act gives the CFPB rulemaking, enforcement, and supervisory authority over a variety of consumer financial products and services (and many of the entities that offer these products and services), and transfers to the Bureau rulemaking and enforcement authority over many previously enacted consumer protection laws. The Bureau's authority varies according to the type of company,[5] and the act explicitly exempts certain entities and activities from the Bureau's authority.[6]

Congress created the CFPB as an independent regulatory agency within the Federal Reserve System (which is, itself, an independent regulatory agency).[7] Such agencies are intended to be more independent of the President than cabinet departments and other executive branch agencies.[8] The Bureau is to be headed by a director, who is appointed by the President, with the advice and consent of the Senate, to a five-year term of office. The director can only be removed from office for "inefficiency, neglect of duty, or malfeasance in office."[9] Until a director is confirmed, the Secretary of the Treasury assumes all of the powers of the director. The CFPB is funded, up to certain caps, using proceeds from the combined earnings of the Federal Reserve System, which the Dodd-Frank Act says are not reviewable by either the House or the Senate appropriations committees.[10] Using the Federal Reserve System's operating expenses as a baseline, the CFBP could receive up to about $550 million for FY2011. However, if the director of the CFPB determines that these funds are insufficient, the act authorizes appropriations of up to $200 million per year for FY2010 through FY2014.

Some portions of the Consumer Financial Protection Act went into effect on the date of enactment, while many other parts of the act go into effect on the "designated transfer date," which the Secretary of the Treasury is required to establish not later than 60 days after the date of enactment (i.e., by September 19, 2010).[11] The act generally requires that the transfer date "be not earlier than 180 days, nor later than 12 months, after the date of enactment of this Act" (i.e., between January 17, 2011, and July 21, 2011).[12] Between the date of enactment and that transfer date, the Board of Governors of the Federal Reserve System ("Board of Governors") is required to transfer to the Bureau "the amount estimated by the Secretary needed to carry out the authorities granted to the Bureau under Federal consumer financial law."[13]

Section 1063(i) of the Dodd-Frank Act requires the Bureau, no later than the designated transfer date, to consult with the head of each agency transferring consumer protection functions and "identify the rules and orders that will be enforced by the Bureau." The agreed-upon list of rules and orders must be published in the *Federal Register*. Section 1063(j) states that "Any proposed rule of a transferor agency which that agency, in performing consumer financial protection functions transferred by this title, has proposed before the designated transfer date, but has not been published as a final rule before that date, shall be deemed to be a proposed rule of the Bureau." It also says that "any interim or final rule of a transferor agency which that agency, in performing consumer financial protection functions transferred by this title, has published before the designated transfer date, but which has not become effective before that date, shall become effective as a rule of the Bureau according to its terms."[14]

This Report

In addition to the above-mentioned general provisions making the CFPB responsible for transferor agencies' existing and pending rules, Title X of the Dodd-Frank Act contains numerous specific provisions that require or permit the Bureau to issue new regulations implementing the act's provisions. Title XIV of the act, entitled the "Mortgage Reform and Anti-Predatory Lending Act,"[15] also contains several provisions that require or permit the Bureau to issue rules. Commenters on the Dodd-Frank Act have expressed both concerns and hopes regarding the effects that these and other financial reform rules will have on the economy and on consumer protection,[16] with the operation of the CFPB a particular concern to some observers. [17] By one count, the legislation mentions a total of 243 "rulemakings" that are expected to occur pursuant to the act, with the Bureau accounting for 24 of those actions.[18] Others have placed the number of rules expected to be issued pursuant to the act even higher.[19]

This report describes the rulemaking provisions in Titles X and XIV of the Dodd-Frank Act that pertain to the CFPB.[20] To identify those provisions, CRS searched through the text of Titles X and XIV in the enrolled version of H.R. 4173 as passed by the House of Representatives and the Senate (because the text of the public law was not yet available) using certain words and terms ("regulation," "final rule," "proposed rule," "rulemaking," "prescribe rules," "prescribe regulations," "by rule," and "such rules"). The results of that effort are provided in a table in the **Appendix** to this report. Although this process identified more than 50 CFPB-related rulemaking provisions, it is unclear whether the searches identified all such provisions in the legislation. (For example, other rulemaking provisions may have used other terms.) The report also notes that while some regulatory oversight procedures and requirements will not apply to CFPB rules, the Dodd-Frank Act gives a council composed primarily of prudential regulators substantial authority to dispose of the Bureau's rules.

The table in the **Appendix** is organized into two groups: (1) provisions that require the CFPB to issue regulations (e.g., stating that the Bureau "shall prescribe regulations..."); and (2) provisions that permit, but do not require, the issuance of regulations (e.g., stating that the CFPB "may prescribe rules..."). For each such provision, the table provides the section number in the Dodd-Frank Act, the relevant text of the provision, whether the act requires the participation of other agencies in the development or issuance of the rule, and any deadlines delineated in the act regarding the issuance or implementation of the rules.

Provisions Not Included in the Table

The table in the **Appendix** does not include some general regulatory provisions in Titles X and XIV, including certain wholesale transfers of rulemaking authority from one agency to the CFPB. For example, Section 1061(b)(5)(A) states that the "authority of the Federal Trade

Commission under an enumerated consumer law to prescribe rules, issue guidelines, or conduct a study or issue a report mandated under such law shall be transferred to the Bureau on the designated transfer date." While it is possible that the Bureau may issue regulations pursuant to these types of transferred authorities, cataloguing all of the rulemaking authorities covered by this provision is beyond the scope of this report. Also, as noted previously, the CFPB and the prudential regulators have until the designated transfer date to decide which existing rules the Bureau will enforce.

The table also does not include provisions in the Dodd-Frank Act that may result in regulations, but that do not specifically require or permit rulemaking. For example, Section 1463(a) of the act amended Section 6 of the Real Estate Settlement Procedures Act of 1974 (12 U.S.C. 2605), and states (in part) that

> A servicer of a federally related mortgage shall accept any reasonable form of written confirmation from a borrower of existing insurance coverage, which shall include the existing insurance policy number along with the identity of, and contact information for, the insurance company or agent, or as otherwise required by the Bureau of Consumer Financial Protection.

Pursuant to this provision, the Bureau may issue regulations establishing written confirmation requirements. However, because the legislation did not specifically require or permit the issuance of rules, this provision is not included in the table.

Finally, the table does not include any rulemaking authorities involving the internal operation of the Bureau. For example, Section 1012(a)(1) of the Dodd-Frank Act authorizes the Bureau to establish general policies with respect to all executive and administrative functions, including "the establishment of rules for conducting the general business of the Bureau." This provision is not included in the table.

CFPB, Like Transferor Agencies, Has Broad Rulemaking Authority

In addition to the previously mentioned provisions in Section 1063 of the Dodd-Frank Act making the CFPB generally responsible for transferor agencies' existing and pending rules, Titles X and XIV of the act contain more than 50 provisions that transfer certain rulemaking authorities to the CFPB, or that give the Bureau new rulemaking authority. These provisions sometimes require the Bureau to issue certain rules, but they more often give the agencies the discretion to decide whether to issue rules within a particular area, and if so, what those rules will contain. Although most of the Bureau's legal rulemaking authority and discretion is the same as it was before being transferred from the prudential regulators, it is not clear that those authorities and discretion will be exercised in the same way.

Section 1022 and CFPB Rulemaking

Section 1022 of the act alone ("Rulemaking Authority") gives the CFPB broad rulemaking powers and responsibilities. For example, Section 1022(a) states that the Bureau is "authorized to exercise its authorities under Federal consumer financial law to administer, enforce, and otherwise implement the provisions of Federal consumer financial law." Section 1022(b)(1) permits the director of the Bureau to "prescribe rules and issue orders and guidance, as may be necessary or appropriate to enable the Bureau to administer and carry out the purposes and objectives of the Federal consumer financial laws, and to prevent evasions thereof."

The term "Federal consumer financial laws" is defined as including the new authorities provided in Title X, the authorities that were transferred to the Bureau under subtitles F and H, and the authorities in certain "enumerated consumer laws,"[21] which generally include[22]

- the Alternative Mortgage Transaction Parity Act of 1982 (12 U.S.C. 3801 et seq.);
- the Consumer Leasing Act of 1976 (15 U.S.C. 1667 et seq.);
- the Electronic Fund Transfer Act (15 U.S.C. 1693 et seq.), except with respect to section 920 of that act;
- the Equal Credit Opportunity Act (15 U.S.C. 1691 et seq.);
- the Fair Credit Billing Act (15 U.S.C. 1666 et seq.);
- the Fair Credit Reporting Act (15 U.S.C. 1681 et seq.), except with respect to sections 615(e) and 628 of that act (15 U.S.C. 1681m(e), 1681w);
- the Home Owners Protection Act of 1998 (12 U.S.C. 4901 et seq.);
- the Fair Debt Collection Practices Act (15 U.S.C. 1692 et seq.);
- subsections (b) through (f) of section 43 of the Federal Deposit Insurance Act (12 U.S.C. 1831t(c)-(f));
- Sections 502 through 509 of the Gramm-Leach-Bliley Act (15 U.S.C. 6802- 6809) except for section 505 as it applies to section 501(b);
- the Home Mortgage Disclosure Act of 1975 (12 U.S.C. 2801 et seq.);
- the Home Ownership and Equity Protection Act of 1994 (15 U.S.C. 1601 note);
- the Real Estate Settlement Procedures Act of 1974 (12 U.S.C. 2601 et seq.);
- the S.A.F.E. Mortgage Licensing Act of 2008 (12 U.S.C. 5101 et seq.);
- the Truth in Lending Act (15 U.S.C. 1601 et seq.);
- the Truth in Savings Act (12 U.S.C. 4301 et seq.);
- Section 626 of the Omnibus Appropriations Act, 2009 (P.L. 111-8); and
- the Interstate Land Sales Full Disclosure Act (15 U.S.C. 1701).

As discussed in detail in the next section of this report, the CFPB's rulemaking activities are subject to all of the applicable government-wide requirements (e.g., the Administrative Procedure Act), as well as the specific requirement in the enumerated consumer laws being transferred to the Bureau. In addition, Section 1022(b)(2) of the Dodd-Frank Act says that, in prescribing a rule under the federal consumer financial laws, the Bureau must "consider...the potential benefits and costs to consumers and covered persons," "the impact of proposed rules on covered persons," and "the impact on consumers in rural areas."[23] It also requires the Bureau to "consult with the appropriate prudential regulators or other Federal agencies prior to proposing a rule and during the comment process regarding (the rule's) consistency with prudential, market, or systemic objectives administered by such agencies." If a prudential regulator provides the CFPB with a written objection to all or part of a proposed rule, the Bureau is required to "include in the adopting release a description of the objection and the basis for the Bureau decision, if any, regarding such objection."[24] Notably, however, while these federal regulators and agencies can file objections to the Bureau's draft rules, Section 1022 does not permit them to prevent the rules from going forward.

Also, Section 1022(b)(4) states that, with one exception,[25]

> to the extent that a provision of Federal consumer financial law authorizes the Bureau and another Federal agency to issue regulations under that provision of law for purposes of assuring compliance with Federal consumer financial law and any regulations thereunder, the Bureau shall have the exclusive authority to prescribe rules subject to those provisions of law.

It also says that "the deference that a court affords to the Bureau with respect to a determination by the Bureau regarding the meaning or interpretation of any provision of a Federal consumer financial law shall be applied as if the Bureau were the only agency authorized to apply, enforce, interpret, or administer the provisions of such Federal consumer financial law."[26]

Related Authorities and Duties

To support its rulemaking functions, the CFPB is required to "monitor for risks to consumers in the offering or provision of consumer financial products or services."[27] As part of this monitoring effort, the Bureau is authorized to

> require covered persons and service providers participating in consumer financial services markets to file with the Bureau, under oath or otherwise, in such form and within such reasonable period of time as the Bureau may prescribe by rule or order, annual or special reports, or answers in writing to specific questions.[28]

To determine whether a nondepository institution (e.g., a payday lender or a mortgage broker) is a "covered person," the CFPB is authorized to require the nondepository "to file with the Bureau, under oath or otherwise, in such form and within such reasonable period of time as the Bureau may prescribe by rule or order, annual or special reports, or answers in writing to specific questions."[29] In addition, Section 1022(c)(7) of the act permits the CFPB to prescribe rules regarding registration requirements applicable to "covered persons" (other than an insured depository institution, insured credit union, or related person). The section also permits the Bureau to issue rules regarding the disclosure of that registration information to the public.[30]

The Bureau is required to publish at least one report per year regarding the "significant findings of its monitoring," with the first report required "beginning with the first calendar year that begins at least 1 year after the designated transfer date."[31] However, the Bureau is also allowed to make public, through reports or "other appropriate formats," any other information that it obtains from its monitoring effort that it determines is "in the public interest," provided that any confidential information that it collects is protected.[32] To the extent that the Bureau's rulemaking is an outgrowth of such monitoring, the interested public may be able to review those reports and determine what CFPB rules could be forthcoming.[33]

Rule Effectiveness Reports

Section 1022(d) of the act requires the CFPB to publish a report assessing the effectiveness of each "significant rule or order" within five years of it taking effect.[34] The act requires these assessments to address, among other things, "the effectiveness of the rule or order in meeting the purposes and objectives of this title and the specific goals stated by the Bureau." Before publishing the required report, the CFPB is required to obtain comments from the public about any recommendations for modifying, expanding, or eliminating the significant rule or order.

Other Rulemaking Requirements and Authorities

In addition to the broad rulemaking powers provided by Section 1022, Titles X and XIV of the Dodd-Frank Act also contain dozens of other provisions that require or permit the CFPB to issue regulations. Most of those provisions give the Bureau substantial discretion regarding whether, and if so, how rules should be crafted. Some sections are more specific, and describe what the rules should contain and/or how they should be promulgated. Most of the provisions in Title X authorize only the Bureau to issue rules, whereas almost all of the provisions in Title XIV require the rules to be issued jointly with a group of other agencies. Also, while a few of the rulemaking provisions in Title X indicate when the rules must be issued or implemented, in most cases the title is silent regarding the timing of the rules. Title XIV, on the other hand, contains a general provision stipulating when rules issued under the title must be published and take effect.

Most Provisions Provide Bureau Discretion

The non-mandatory rulemaking provisions in the Dodd-Frank Act arguably provide the CFPB with the greatest amount of discretion, allowing the Bureau to decide whether any regulations will be developed at all, and if issued, what the rules will contain. For example:

- Section 1071(a) of the act (amending the Equal Credit Opportunity Act (15 U.S.C. 1691 et seq.)) states that the Bureau "shall prescribe such rules and issue such guidance as may be necessary to carry out, enforce, and compile data pursuant to this section (on small business data collection)." Therefore, the Bureau can decide whether regulations or guidance in this area are "necessary," and if so, what any such rules will require.
- Section 1097(1) (amending Section 626 of the Omnibus Appropriations Act, 2009 (15 U.S.C. 1638 note)) says the Bureau "shall have authority to prescribe rules with respect to mortgage loans in accordance with section 553 of title 5, United States Code. Such rulemaking shall relate to unfair or deceptive acts or practices regarding mortgage loans, which may include unfair or deceptive acts or practices involving loan modification and foreclosure rescue services."[35] The Bureau can decide whether or not to use this rulemaking authority, and (within the parameters provided in this section) can determine the content of any rules that it decides to issue.

Although the mandatory provisions in the act require that certain rules be issued, they often give the Bureau substantial discretion regarding how the required rules will be crafted. For example:

- Section 1022(c)(6)(A) states that the Bureau "shall prescribe rules regarding the confidential treatment of information obtained from persons in connection with the exercise of its authorities under Federal consumer financial law." This provision does not prescribe either the content of the required rules or how they should be developed.
- Section 1024(b)(7)(A) requires the Bureau to "prescribe rules to facilitate supervision of persons described in subsection (a)(1) and assessment and detection of risks to consumers." Section 1024 relates to "Supervision of Nondepository Covered Persons," and subsection (a)(1) states that the section applies to any covered person who, among other things, "offers or provides origination, brokerage, or servicing of loans secured by real estate for use by consumers primarily for personal, family, or household purposes, or loan modification or foreclosure relief services in connection with such loans;" or "offers or provides to a consumer a payday loan." The section does not indicate how the required rules should be crafted or what they should contain.
- Section 1042(c) requires the Bureau to "prescribe regulations to implement the requirements of this section" (on "Preservation of Enforcement Powers of the States"). Although Section 1042 prescribes certain legal authorities and consultation requirements, the section does not otherwise indicate what the required regulations must contain.
- Section 1053(e) states that the Bureau "shall prescribe rules establishing such procedures as may be necessary to carry out this section" (on "Hearings and Adjudication Proceedings"). Section 1053 delineates special rules for cease-and-desist proceedings and enforcement of orders, but does not otherwise prescribe the contents of those rules.
- Section 1100(6)(B) states that the Bureau "is authorized to promulgate regulations setting minimum net worth or surety bond requirements for residential mortgage loan originators and minimum requirements for recovery funds paid into by loan originators." In issuing those regulations, the section requires the Bureau to "take into account the need to provide originators adequate incentives to originate affordable and sustainable mortgage loans, as well as the need to ensure a competitive origination market that maximizes consumer access to affordable and sustainable mortgage loans." Otherwise, the section does not indicate what those rules should contain.

As was the case with the discretionary provisions, some of the mandatory rulemaking provisions in Title X and Title XIV of the Dodd-Frank Act amend other statutes, and give the CFPB broad transferred authority within those amended statutes. For example, Section 1084 of the act amends the Electronic Fund Transfer Act (15 U.S.C. 1693 et seq.) and states that, with certain exceptions, the Bureau "shall prescribe rules to carry out the purposes of this title." (This section transferred certain rulemaking authorities from the Board of Governors of the Federal Reserve System to the CFPB.)

Certain sections of the act appear to allow the Bureau to take other, non-rulemaking actions to satisfy the underlying requirement. For example, Section 1002(25) states that the definition of a "related person" includes "any shareholder, consultant, joint venture partner, or other person, as determined by the Bureau (by rule or on a case-by-case basis) who materially participates in the conduct of the affairs of such covered person." Therefore, the Bureau could issue a rule defining these terms, or could adjudicate each case individually. Also, Section 1079(c) of the act requires the Bureau to "propose regulations or otherwise establish a program to protect consumers who use exchange facilitators." Therefore, the Bureau could issue a rule to protect consumers, or could do so by establishing a program.

Some Provisions Prescribe Rule Contents or Process

In contrast to the previously mentioned broad grants of rulemaking authority, some CFPB-related rulemaking provisions in Titles X and XIV, or the statutes amended by those titles, prescribe the contents of the rules that the statute requires or permits the Bureau to issue. For example, Section 1473(f)(2) of the act requires the Bureau and other agencies to "jointly, by rule, establish minimum requirements to be applied by a State in the registration of appraisal management companies." That provision also states the following:

> Such requirements shall include a requirement that such companies—(1) register with and be subject to supervision by a State appraiser certifying and licensing agency in each State in which such company operates; (2) verify that only licensed or certified appraisers are used for federally related transactions; (3) require that appraisals coordinated by an appraisal management company comply with the Uniform Standards of Professional Appraisal Practice; and (4) require that appraisals are conducted independently and free from inappropriate influence and coercion pursuant to the appraisal independence standards established under section 129E of the Truth in Lending Act.

Section 1094(3)(B) of the act (amending the Home Mortgage Disclosure Act of 1975 (12 U.S.C. 2801 et seq.)) also specifies the content of the required rule. That section requires the Bureau to

> develop regulations that (A) prescribe the format for such disclosures, the method for submission of the data to the appropriate agency, and the procedures for disclosing the information to the public; (B) require the collection of data required to be disclosed under subsection (b) with respect to loans sold by each institution reporting under this title; (C) require disclosure of the class of the purchaser of such loans; (D) permit any reporting institution to submit in writing to the Bureau or to the appropriate agency such additional data or explanations as it deems relevant to the decision to originate or purchase mortgage loans; and (E) modify or require modification of itemized information, for the purpose of protecting the privacy interests of the mortgage applicants or mortgagors, that is or will be available to the public.

Some of the rulemaking authorities transferred to the Bureau also contain specific requirements. For example, Section 1088(a)(9) of the act amended the Fair Credit Reporting Act (15 U.S.C. 1681 et seq.) and states that the Bureau "shall prescribe rules to carry out this subsection." (Previously, this rulemaking authority had been jointly provided to the Federal Trade Commission and the Board of Governors.) As had been the case with regard to the agencies who were previously required to issue these rules, the Bureau's rules are required to address

> (i) the form, content, time, and manner of delivery of any notice under this subsection; (ii) clarification of the meaning of terms used in this subsection, including what credit terms are material, and when credit terms are materially less favorable; (iii) exceptions to the notice requirement under this subsection for classes of persons or transactions regarding which the agencies determine that notice would not significantly benefit consumers; (iv) a model notice that may be used to comply with this subsection; and (v) the timing of the notice required under paragraph (1), including the circumstances under which the notice must be provided after the terms offered to the consumer were set based on information from a consumer report.[36]

Procedural Requirements

Some provisions in Titles X and XIV specify the process by which CFPB rules should be developed or issued. For example, Section 1041(c)(1) of the act requires the Bureau to "issue a notice of proposed rulemaking whenever a majority of states has enacted a resolution in support of the establishment or modification of a consumer protection regulation by the Bureau." The next paragraph states that

> Before prescribing a final regulation based upon a notice issued pursuant to paragraph (1), the Bureau shall take into account whether (A) the proposed regulation would afford greater protection to consumers than any existing regulation; (B) the intended benefits of the proposed regulation for consumers would outweigh any increased costs or inconveniences for consumers, and would not discriminate unfairly against any category or class of consumers; and (C) a Federal banking agency has advised that the proposed regulation is likely to present an unacceptable safety and soundness risk to insured depository institutions.

The section goes on to require the Bureau to include a discussion of these considerations in the *Federal Register* notice of any final regulation. If the Bureau decides not to issue a final regulation, the statute requires it to "publish an explanation of such determination in the Federal Register, and provide a copy of such explanation to each State that enacted a resolution in support of the proposed regulation, the Committee on Banking, Housing, and Urban Affairs of the Senate, and the Committee on Financial Services of the House of Representatives."[37]

Other provisions also establish certain procedural requirements for rulemaking. For example:

- Section 1024(a)(2) states that the Bureau "shall consult with the Federal Trade Commission prior to issuing a rule...to define covered persons subject to this section" (on "Supervision of Nondepository Covered Persons").
- Section 1094 requires the Bureau to issue certain rules "in consultation with other appropriate agencies."

As noted previously in this report, although these and other provisions require the CFPB to consult with other agencies before issuing their rules, the act does not permit those agencies to prevent the issuance of the rules.

Most of the provisions in Title X require or permit the CFPB alone to issue the required or permitted rules. Exceptions include (1) Section 1025(e)(4)(E), which requires the Bureau to prescribe certain rules with the "prudential regulators;" and (2) Section 1088(b)(3), which requires the Bureau, the Commodity Futures Trading Commission, and the Securities and Exchange Commission to each issue regulations carrying out Section 624 of the Fair Credit Reporting Act. In contrast, the provisions in Title XIV of the act almost always require that the Bureau issue the required rules jointly with the Board of Governors, the Comptroller of the Currency, the Federal Deposit Insurance Corporation, the National Credit Union Administration Board, and the Federal Housing Finance Agency.[38]

Publication and Effective Dates

Most of the individual provisions in Titles X and XIV of the Dodd-Frank Act that require or permit CFPB to issue rules do not specify when those rules must be published or take effect. To the extent that the timing of the rules is mentioned in those provisions, the issuance is always keyed to the designated transfer date. For example:

- Section 1024(a)(2) states that the "initial rule" must be issued within one year of the transfer date.
- Section 1079(c) requires that a proposed rule be issued (or a program be established) within two years after the submission of a report, which is required within one year of the transfer date.
- Section 1083(a) of the act (amending the Alternative Mortgage Transaction Parity Act of 1982 (12 U.S.C. 3801 et seq.)) requires that regulations be promulgated "after the designated transfer date."

In contrast to the timing discretion given to the Bureau in Title X, Section 1400(c) of the legislation states that all of the regulations required under Title XIV must "(A) be prescribed in final form before the end of the 18-month period beginning on the designated transfer date; and (B) take effect not later than 12 months after the date of issuance of the regulations in final form." It goes on to say that sections or provisions in that title "shall take effect on the date on which the final regulations implementing such section, or provision, take effect." Sections for which regulations have not been issued are required to take effect 18 months after the designated transfer date.

Rulemaking Authority and Discretion Generally the Same

Although the Dodd-Frank Act gives the CFPB some new responsibilities, most of its rulemaking authority and discretion was transferred to the Bureau through the enumerated consumer laws. With regard to those laws, the Bureau has the same amount of rulemaking authority and discretion as the prudential regulators that previously were responsible for them. What is different, however, is that the consumer protection powers provided by those laws are now vested in a single agency, and that agency now has as its primary mission to "regulate the offering and provision of consumer financial products or services."[39] Whether those contextual differences will result in different regulations, or different application of existing rules, is currently unclear.

SOME FEDERAL RULEMAKING REQUIREMENTS NOT APPLICABLE TO CFPB RULES

During the past 65 years, Congress and various presidents have developed an elaborate set of procedures and requirements to guide and oversee the federal rulemaking process. Statutory requirements include the Administrative Procedure Act, the Regulatory Flexibility Act, the Paperwork Reduction Act, the Unfunded Mandates Reform Act, and the Congressional Review Act—each of which requires that certain procedural and/or analytical requirements be addressed before agencies' rules can be published and take effect.[40] The scope and effectiveness of these and other congressional efforts to control the rulemaking process vary. For example, although Congress has used the Congressional Review Act (5 U.S.C. 801-808) to disapprove only one final rule in more than 14 years,[41] every year Congress adds a number of provisions to agencies' appropriations bills stating that "none of the funds" provided through the legislation can be used to initiate rulemaking in certain areas, to make certain proposed rules final, or to implement certain final rules.[42]

Presidential review of agency rulemaking is currently centered in Executive Order 12866, which requires covered agencies to submit their "significant" regulatory actions to the Office of Information and Regulatory Affairs (OIRA) within the Office of Management (OMB) before they are published in the *Federal Register*.[43] OIRA reviews the rules to determine their consistency with the analytic requirements in the executive order, the statutes under which they are issued, the President's priorities, and the rules issued by other agencies. The executive order requires that the agencies "propose or adopt a regulation only upon a reasoned determination that the benefits of the intended regulation justify its costs."[44] Covered agencies are required to estimate the costs and benefits of their "significant" rules, and to conduct a full cost-benefit analysis before issuing any "economically significant" rule (e.g., one that is expected to have a $100 million annual impact on the economy).[45] That analysis is required to include an assessment of not only the underlying benefits and costs, but also the costs and benefits of "potentially effective and reasonably feasible alternatives to the planned regulation."[46]

OIRA also plays a key role in implementing the requirements of the Paperwork Reduction Act (PRA, 44 U.S.C. 3501-3520). The PRA created OIRA, and generally requires that agencies receive OIRA approval for certain information collection requests before they are conducted. Before approving a proposed collection of information, OIRA must determine whether the collection is "necessary for the proper performance of the functions of the agency."[47] OIRA's information collection approvals must be renewed at least every three years if the agency wishes to continue collecting the information.

Many Rulemaking Requirements, and Exceptions, Apply to CFPB Rules

Many of the government-wide rulemaking requirements appear to apply to rulemaking by the CFPB, but the exceptions and exemptions to those requirements also apply. For example, the Administrative Procedure Act (APA, 5 U.S.C. 551 *et seq.*) generally requires that federal agencies publish a notice of proposed rulemaking in the *Federal Register*, give "interested persons" an opportunity to comment on the rule, consider those comments and publish a final rule with a general statement of its basis and purpose, and make the final rule effective no less than 30 days after its publication.[48] However, the APA also says that these "notice and comment" procedures do not apply when the agency finds, for "good cause," that those procedures are "impracticable, unnecessary, or contrary to the public interest."[49] Also, agencies can make their rules take effect less than 30 days after they are published if there is "good cause."[50] Therefore, for example, if the CFPB concludes that time constraints or other factors make public comments "impracticable," the agency can publish the final rule without a prior proposed rule or comment period. Agencies' use of the APA's good cause exceptions are subject to judicial review.

Also, the Regulatory Flexibility Act (RFA, 5 U.S.C. 601-612) requires federal agencies to assess the impact of their forthcoming rules on "small entities," which includes small businesses, small governmental jurisdictions, and small not-for-profit organizations.[51] Under the RFA, federal agencies must prepare a regulatory flexibility analysis at the time that proposed and certain final rules are published in the *Federal Register*. The act requires the analyses to describe, among other things, (1) why the regulatory action is being considered and its objectives; (2) the small entities to which the rule will apply and, where feasible, an estimate of their number; (3) the projected reporting, recordkeeping, and other compliance requirements of the rule; and, for final rules, (4) steps the agency has taken to minimize the impact of the rule on small entities. However, these requirements are not triggered if the head of the issuing agency certifies that the rule would not have a "significant economic impact on a substantial number of small entities." The RFA does not define "significant economic impact" or "substantial number of small entities," thereby giving federal agencies substantial discretion regarding when the act's analytical requirements are initiated.[52] Also, the RFA's analytical requirements do not apply when an agency publishes a final rule without publishing a prior proposed rule.[53] Therefore, if the CFPB publishes a final rule using the APA's "good cause" exception, the RFA's analytical requirements do not apply.

Some Rulemaking Requirements and Controls Are Not Applicable to the CFPB

In addition to these exceptions and exclusions, some notable regulatory oversight mechanisms do not appear to apply to the CFPB's rules at all, or may be able to be voided by the Bureau. These requirements are also not applicable to most, if not all, of the independent regulatory agencies from whom rulemaking authorities were transferred.

Executive Order 12866

For example, most of the requirements in Executive Order 12866 do not apply to independent regulatory agencies like the CFPB.[54] Therefore, the Bureau does not have to submit its proposed or final significant rules to OIRA for review before they are published. Also, CFPB does not have to conduct cost-benefit analyses for its economically significant rules, and does not have to show that the benefits of its significant rules "justify" the costs. Although Sections 1022 and 1041(c)(1) of the Dodd-Frank Act require the Bureau to "consider" and "take into account" the potential benefits and costs of its rules, these provisions appear to establish somewhat lower analytical thresholds than the requirement in Executive Order 12866 that the benefits of agencies' rules "justify" the costs.

Paperwork Reduction Act

Also, although the Paperwork Reduction Act covers independent regulatory agencies like the CFPB, and permits OIRA to disapprove their proposed collections of information, the Bureau may be able to collect the information even if OIRA objects. The PRA states that

> An independent regulatory agency which is administered by 2 or more members of a commission, board, or similar body, may by majority vote void (A) any disapproval by the Director (of OMB), in whole or in part, of a proposed collection of information of that agency; or (B) an exercise of authority under subsection (d) of section 3507 concerning that agency (regarding information collections that are part of a proposed rule).[55]

Although the CFPB is an independent regulatory agency, it is headed by a single director, not a multi-member body. Therefore, this provision would not appear to apply to the Bureau. However, Section 1100D(c) of the Dodd-Frank Act amends the PRA, and states that

> Notwithstanding any other provision of law, the Director (of OMB) shall treat or review a rule or order prescribed or proposed by the Director of the Bureau of Consumer Financial Protection on the same terms and conditions as apply to any rule or order prescribed or proposed by the Board of Governors of the Federal Reserve System.

Applying this subsection, because the Board of Governors, a multi-member board, is authorized to void OIRA disapprovals of its information collections, the director of the CFPB may arguably be authorized to do so as well.

Unfunded Mandates Reform Act

The Unfunded Mandates Reform Act (UMRA) of 1995 was enacted in an effort to reduce the costs associated with federal imposition of responsibilities, duties, and regulations upon state, local, and tribal governments and the private sector without providing the funding appropriate to the costs imposed by those responsibilities. Title II of UMRA (2 U.S.C. 1532-1538) generally requires cabinet departments and other agencies to prepare a written statement containing specific descriptions and estimates for any proposed rule that is expected to result in the expenditure of $100 million or more in any year to state, local, or tribal governments, or to the private sector.

However, UMRA does not apply to independent regulatory agencies, and therefore does not apply to any of the CFPB's rules. Even if UMRA did apply to the CFPB, UMRA contains so many other exceptions and exclusions that its requirements might not apply to most of the agency's rules.[56]

Appropriations Restrictions

Appropriations restrictions may also be unavailable as a way for Congress to control the Bureau's rulemaking. As noted earlier in this report, the CFPB is funded (up to certain caps) using money from the combined earnings of the Federal Reserve System, and the Dodd-Frank Act states that those funds are not reviewable by either the House or the Senate appropriations committees.[57] Therefore, since the Bureau might not receive appropriated funds, Congress may not be able to encourage or restrict rulemaking through the kinds of appropriations restrictions that it has frequently used with regard to other agencies' rules.

Effectiveness of New Rulemaking Requirements Depends on How the Bureau Interprets Key Terms

The Dodd-Frank Act made three amendments to the Regulatory Flexibility Act, adding requirements that are particular to the CFPB. Also, as noted previously, the Dodd-Frank Act requires the Bureau to examine certain rules within five years of their issuance. The effectiveness of these new rulemaking requirements may depend on how the CFPB interprets certain key terms.

Regulatory Flexibility Act Amendments

As noted previously in this report, the RFA requires all covered federal agencies (including independent regulatory agencies like the CFPB) to conduct a "regulatory flexibility analysis" before publishing any proposed or final rule that is expected to have a "significant economic impact on a substantial number of small entities." Section 1100G(b) of the Dodd-Frank Act adds a Bureau-specific provision to the government-wide requirements for proposed rule analyses, stating that the CFPB must also describe

> (A) any projected increase in the cost of credit for small entities; (B) any significant alternatives to the proposed rule which accomplish the stated objectives of applicable statutes and which minimize any increase in the cost of credit for small entities; and (C) advice and recommendations of representatives of small entities relating to issues described in subparagraphs (A) and (B) and (the initial regulatory flexibility analysis).

Also, Section 1100G(c) of the Dodd-Frank Act adds a Bureau-specific requirement to the existing requirements for a final rule analysis, stipulating that the Bureau must include "a description of the steps the agency has taken to minimize any additional cost of credit for small entities."

Since 1996, the RFA has required the Environmental Protection Agency and the Occupational Safety and Health administration to hold "advocacy review panels" before developing proposed rules that are expected to have a "significant economic impact on a substantial number of small entities."[58] Section 1100G(a) of the Dodd-Frank Act amended the RFA and requires the CFPB to hold such panels as well.

However, the CFPB does not have to convene an advocacy review panel or conduct an RFA analysis if it issues a final rule without a prior notice of proposed rulemaking (e.g., by using the APA's "good cause" exception), or if it certifies that the rule is not expected to have a "significant economic impact on a substantial number of small entities." Because the RFA does not define the terms "significant economic impact" or "substantial number of small entities," the CFPB, like other federal agencies, will have a substantial amount of discretion regarding when the act's requirements are triggered.

"Lookback" Requirement

The previously mentioned "lookback" provision in Section 1022(d) of the Dodd-Frank Act requires that the CFPB examine and report on the effectiveness of its "significant' rules and orders within five years of their issuance. However, Section 1022(d) does not define what rules should be considered "significant," and does not indicate how "effectiveness" should be measured. Therefore, the Bureau appears to have considerable discretion in determining which rules will have to be reviewed, and whether they will be considered "effective" or not.

Also, although the Dodd-Frank Act requires the Bureau to allow the public to comment before publishing its report, those comments are only required regarding any recommendations for modifying, expanding, or eliminating a rule or order. Thus, if the Bureau determines that a rule is effective, and therefore decides not to change the rule, the act does not appear to require public comments.

OVERSIGHT COUNCIL IS PERMITTED TO "STAY" OR "SET ASIDE" CFPB REGULATIONS

Although certain regulatory oversight mechanisms appear to be inapplicable or subject to interpretation by the CFPB, the Dodd-Frank Act establishes a new oversight mechanism that is arguably more powerful than any that had previously existed. Section 1023 of the act ("Review of Bureau Regulations") puts in place a procedure by which a Bureau rule, or a provision thereof, can be stayed or "set aside" by the newly-established Financial Stability Oversight Council if the Council concludes that the regulation or provision would "put the safety and soundness of the United States banking system or the ability of the financial system of the United States at risk."[59]

The Financial Stability Oversight Council was established by Section 111 of the Dodd-Frank Act. Voting members of the Council are (1) the Secretary of the Treasury, who serves as Chairperson of the Council; (2) the Chairman of the Board of Governors; (3) the Comptroller of the Currency; (4) the Director of the Bureau; (5) the Chairman of the Securities and Exchange Commission; (6) the Chairperson of the Federal Deposit Insurance Corporation; (7) the Chairperson of the Commodity Futures Trading Commission; (7) the Director of the Federal Housing Finance Agency; (8) the Chairman of the National Credit Union Administration Board; and (9) "an independent member appointed by the President, by and with the advice and consent of the Senate, having insurance expertise." Nonvoting members are (A) the Director of the Office of Financial Research within the Department of the Treasury;[60] (B) the Director of the Federal Insurance Office within the Department of the Treasury;[61] (C) "a State insurance commissioner, to be designated by a selection process determined by the State insurance commissioners"; (D) "a State banking supervisor, to be designated by a selection process determined by the State banking supervisors"; and (E) "a State securities commissioner (or an officer performing like functions), to be designated by a selection process determined by such State securities commissioners."

Section 1023(b) states that an "agency represented by a member of the Council" may petition the Council in writing to stay the effectiveness or set aside a Bureau regulation.[62] First, however, the agency must have, "in good faith," attempted to work with the Bureau to resolve its concerns regarding the effect of the rule on the banking or financial systems. Also, the petition must have been filed within 10 days after the rule was published in the *Federal Register*, and the petition must be published in the *Federal Register* and transmitted "contemporaneously" to the Senate Committee on Banking, Housing, and Urban Affairs, and to the House Committee on Financial Services.

If any "member agency" of the Council so requests, the Chairperson is permitted to stay the effectiveness of a CFPB rule for up to 90 days to permit the Council to consider the petition.[63] A decision to issue a stay of, or to set aside, a Bureau rule requires an affirmative vote by two-thirds "of the Members of the Council then serving," and must be taken within 45 days following the date the petition is filed, or by the expiration of a stay issued by the Council, whichever is later.[64] A decision by the Council to set aside a rule (or a provision therein) renders it "unenforceable," and the Council must publish that decision and its reasoning in the *Federal Register* "as soon as practicable after the decision."[65] The Council's decision to set aside a rule or a provision thereof is subject to judicial review under Chapter 7 of Title 5, *United States Code*.[66]

Unique Authority

The authority of the Financial Stability Oversight Council to stay or "set aside" final rules issued by the CFPB is unique. No other agency or organization in the executive branch of the federal government is currently permitted to unilaterally stop or nullify another agency's published final rule. Executive Order 12866 allows OIRA within OMB to return a covered agency's draft rule to the agency for "reconsideration" before it is published, but the executive order does not permit OIRA to simply "set aside" an agency's published final rule.

Also, Section 1023 permits the Council to revoke either an entire final rule or a "provision thereof." In this respect, the Council's authority is greater than the expedited disapproval authority that Congress granted to itself through the Congressional Review Act, which only permits revocation of final rules in their entirety.[67] (Congress could, of course, use its regular legislative authority to disapprove all or part of a CFPB rule.)

The Dodd-Frank Act does not provide any procedure by which the actions of the Council can be checked by the President or Congress. Nevertheless, if Congress and the President wanted a revoked Bureau rule to go into effect, legislation could be enacted that would reverse the Council's decision and/or place the rule in statute. Also, Section 1023(c)(8) of the Dodd-Frank Act subjects a Council revocation to judicial review.

It is notable that the voting members of the Financial Stability Oversight Council are the heads of the agencies from which the CFPB's consumer protection rulemaking and enforcement authorities were drawn. Therefore, these prudential regulatory agencies, relieved of most of their consumer protection functions, will potentially be able to stop the Bureau's consumer protection regulations if they conclude, by a two-thirds vote, that those regulations would put the banking or financial systems "at risk."

There are several aspects of the Council's revocation procedures that are currently unclear. For example:

- Before filing a petition, an agency must have acted "in good faith" to resolve its concerns regarding the effect of the rule on the banking or financial systems. It is unclear who determines whether the agency has, in fact, acted "in good faith," or what types of actions will be considered to meet that standard.
- The act states that the chairperson of the Council is permitted to stay the effectiveness of any rule for up to 90 days, upon a request by a "member agency." However, the statute also says that a decision to stay a rule requires an affirmative vote by two-thirds of the Council. It is unclear whether the chairperson can stay a rule for 90 days without such a vote.
- The act states that the Council can void a CFPB final rule if it concludes that it would put the safety and soundness of the banking or financial systems "at risk," but it is not clear what types of rules would meet that standard.
- Also, as discussed in the final section of this report on "Oversight Options," it is unclear whether the Council's decision to set aside a CFPB rule is, itself, a "rule" that must be submitted to Congress under the Congressional Review Act, and that can be disapproved by Congress using the expedited procedures contained therein.

Concluding Observations

Although Titles X and XIV of the Dodd-Frank Act contain more than 50 provisions that specifically require or permit the CFPB to issue regulations, the actual number of rules that will be issued by the Bureau pursuant to the act's authority is currently unknowable. For example:

- About 20 sections in the act specifically require that the CFPB issue rules, but the agency may issue multiple rules under a single provision.
- Other sections of the act allow the Bureau to promulgate such rules "as may be necessary" to implement those sections, including the broad rulemaking authority provided in Section 1022(b)(1). Therefore, subject to the consultation and considerations attendant to this provision (as well as the constraints of applicable government-wide rulemaking requirements), the CFPB will arguably be able to issue whatever rules it decides are "necessary or appropriate," even if no other sections of the statute provided specific rulemaking authority. On the other hand, the Bureau may decide to issue no new rules under these types of authorities.
- Still other sections of the Dodd-Frank Act do not mention rulemaking at all, but may be implemented through CFPB rules.[68]
- Section 1063 of the Dodd-Frank Act makes the CFPB responsible for certain rules that have been issued by an agency transferring consumer protection functions to the Bureau, any proposed rule that a transferor agency has not made final as of the designated transfer date, and any final rule issued by a transferor agency that has not taken effect. It is currently unclear how many rules that the Bureau will assume pursuant to these provisions, or how many amendments to those transferred rules that the Bureau will issue in the future.

Because of these and other factors, efforts to determine with precision how many rulemaking provisions are in the statute seem misplaced, for they will not necessarily provide useful clues as to how many or what type of rules the Bureau is likely to issue.

Congressional Oversight Options

Even though it is impossible to predict with any certainty what rules the CFPB will issue, it is clear that the Bureau has been given significant rulemaking authority. However, several of the mechanisms that have been used for decades to oversee and control rulemaking do not appear to be available with regard to the CFPB. The substance of the Bureau's significant rules will not be reviewed by OIRA under Executive Order 12866, it appears that the Bureau can void OIRA disapprovals of its collections of information under the PRA, and Congress may not be able to require or restrict rulemaking in particular areas through appropriation restrictions (because the Bureau, at least initially, may not receive appropriated funds). Also, the effectiveness of provisions in the Dodd-Frank Act that increased the Bureau's requirements under the RFA, as well as a provision requiring an evaluation of the Bureau's rules within five years of their issuance, appear dependent on how the CFPB interprets those provisions.

Nevertheless, Congress still has a number of oversight tools available to affect the nature of CFPB rulemaking, including

- confirmation hearings for the still-to-be-selected director of the Bureau;
- oversight hearings on the Bureau's implementation of the act; and
- meetings between individual Members and representatives of the Bureau regarding pending rules, and filing comments on the rules.[69]

As one author indicated,

[I]nvestigations conducted by congressional committees constitute another powerful device of formal political supervision.... The public legislative hearings, in which administrative action is carefully scrutinized and a commissioner or staff member is plied with questions, symbolizes the unparalleled sophistication of American congressional control over administrative action, in general and by [independent regulatory agencies], in particular. Individual oversight by representatives or senators also takes place. Through correspondence or meetings, the latter convey the concerns of their constituents.[70]

Congressional Review Act

Another congressional oversight option regarding the Bureau's rules is the Congressional Review Act, which was enacted in 1996 in an attempt to reestablish a measure of congressional authority over rulemaking "without at the same time requiring Congress to become a super regulatory agency."[71] The act generally requires all federal agencies (including independent regulatory agencies) to submit all of their covered final rules to both houses of Congress and GAO before they can take effect.[72] It also established expedited legislative procedures (primarily in the Senate) by which Congress may disapprove agencies' final rules by enacting a joint resolution of disapproval.[73] The definition of a covered rule in the CRA is quite broad, arguably including any type of document (e.g., legislative rules, policy statements, guidance, manuals, and memoranda) that the agency wishes to make binding on the affected public.[74] After a rule is submitted, Congress can use the expedited procedures specified in the CRA (particularly in the Senate) to disapprove of the rule. CRA resolutions of disapproval must be presented to the President for signature or veto.

For a variety of reasons, however, the CRA has been used to disapprove only one rule in the more than 14 years since it was enacted.[75] Perhaps most notably, it is likely that a President would veto a resolution of disapproval to protect rules developed under his own administration, and it may be difficult for Congress to muster the two-thirds vote in both houses needed to overturn the veto. Congress can also use regular (i.e., non-CRA) legislative procedures to disapprove agencies' rules, but such legislation may prove even more difficult to enact than a CRA resolution of disapproval (primarily because of the lack of expedited procedures in the Senate), and if enacted may also be vetoed by the President. These difficulties notwithstanding, even if the use of the CRA does not result in the disapproval of a rule, just the threat of filing of a resolution of disapproval can sometimes exert pressure on agencies to modify or withdraw their rules.[76]

Are Council Decisions "Rules" Under the CRA?

Although it is clear that the Bureau's rules are subject to the CRA, it is not clear whether a decision by the Financial Stability Oversight Council to "set aside" a Bureau rule is, itself, a "rule" under the CRA. Section 1023(c)(6) of the Dodd-Frank Act requires the Council's decisions to stay or set aside a rule be published in the *Federal Register*, and Section 1023(c)(7) states that the APA's notice and comment rulemaking procedures (5 U.S.C. 553) "shall not apply" to such decisions. Notably, however, the act does not state that the Council's decisions are not rules under Section 551 of the APA, and says that a Council decision to set aside a Bureau regulation is subject to judicial review (i.e., in the same manner as an agency rule would be). On the other hand, it is not clear that Congress intended the Council's actions to be considered "rules" that could be disapproved using CRA procedures. The Council itself appears to have been delegated no specific rulemaking authority.

If the Council's action to stay or set aside a Bureau rule is itself a rule, then it would have to be submitted to GAO and both houses of Congress before it could take effect, and Congress could use the expedited procedures in the CRA to disapprove of the Council's action. On the other hand, if the Council's action is not a rule, then Congress would have to use regular legislative procedures to revoke the Council's action, or to put the Bureau's revoked rule into law.

APPENDIX. REGULATIONS TO BE ISSUED BY THE CONSUMER FINANCIAL PROTECTION BUREAU

Section	Text of the Provision	Other Agencies	Deadlines for Rules
Mandatory Regulations (e.g., "shall prescribe rules ... ")			
Section 1022(c)(6)(A)	"…shall prescribe rules regarding the confidential treatment of information obtained from persons in connection with the exercise of its authorities under Federal consumer financial law."	None	None
Section 1024(a)(2)	"…shall consult with the Federal Trade Commission prior to issuing a rule, in accordance with paragraph (1)(B), to define covered persons subject to this section…" (on "Supervision of Nondepository Covered Persons").	Consultation with the Federal Trade Commission	"Initial rule" required within one year after the designated transfer date.
Section 1024(b)(7)(A)	" ... shall prescribe rules to facilitate supervision of persons described in subsection (a)(1) and assessment and detection of risks to consumers."	None	None
Section 1025(e)(4)(E)	"…shall prescribe rules to provide safeguards from retaliation against the insured depository institution, insured credit union, or other covered person described in subsection (a) instituting an appeal under this paragraph, as well as their officers and employees."	Rules to be issued with the "prudential regulators."	None
Section 1033(d)	"…by rule, shall prescribe standards applicable to covered persons to promote the development and use of standardized formats for information, including through the use of machine readable files, to be made available to consumers under this section" (on "Consumer Rights to Access Information").	None	None

Section	Text of the Provision	Other Agencies	Deadlines for Rules
Section 1035(c)	"The Ombudsman designated under this subsection (re private education loans) shall…in accordance with regulations of the Director, receive, review, and attempt to resolve informally complaints from borrowers of loans described in subsection (a), including, as appropriate, attempts to resolve such complaints in collaboration with the Department of Education and with institutions of higher education, lenders, guaranty agencies, loan servicers, and other participants in private education loan programs."	None	None
Section 1041(c)(1)	"The Bureau shall issue a notice of proposed rulemaking whenever a majority of the States has enacted a resolution in support of the establishment or modification of a consumer protection regulation by the Bureau."	Impetus for rulemaking is the enactment of resolutions by a majority of the States.	None
Section 1042(c)	"…shall prescribe regulations to implement the requirements of this section…" (on "Preservation of Enforcement Powers of the States").	None	None
Section 1053(e)	"…shall prescribe rules establishing such procedures as may be necessary to carry out this section" (on "Hearings and Adjudication Proceedings").	None	None
Section 1071(a) (amending the Equal Credit Opportunity Act (15 U.S.C. 1691 et seq.))	"Each financial institution shall compile and maintain, in accordance with regulations of the Bureau, a record of the information provided by any loan applicant pursuant to a request under subsection (b)."	None	None

Section	Text of the Provision	Other Agencies	Deadlines for Rules
Section 1071(a) (amending the Equal Credit Opportunity Act (15 U.S.C. 1691 et seq.))	"Information compiled and maintained under this section ("Small Business Loan Data Collection") shall be—(A) retained for not less than 3 years after the date of preparation; (B) made available to any member of the public, upon request, in the form required under regulations prescribed by the Bureau; (C) annually made available to the public generally by the Bureau, in such form and in such manner as is determined by the Bureau, by regulation."	None	None
Section 1079(c)	"…shall, consistent with subtitle B ("General Powers of the Bureau"), propose regulations or otherwise establish a program to protect consumers who use exchange facilitators."	None	Rule or program must be established within two years after the submission of a report (which is required within one year of the transfer date).
Section 1083(a) (amending the Alternative Mortgage Transaction Parity Act of 1982 (12 U.S.C. 3801 et seq.))	Bureau is required to determine whether the existing regulations applicable under paragraphs (1) through (3) of subsection (a) are "fair and not deceptive and otherwise meet the objectives of the Consumer Financial Protection Act of 2010," and "(3) promulgate regulations under subsection (a)(4)…."	None	Regulations to be promulgated "after the designated transfer date."
Section 1084 (amending the Electronic Fund Transfer Act (15 U.S.C. 1693 et seq.)	" … shall prescribe rules to carry out the purposes of this title" (with certain exceptions).	None	None
Section 1088(a)(9) (amending the Fair Credit Reporting Act (15 U.S.C. 1681 et seq.)	"…shall prescribe rules to carry out this subsection" (on amendments to the Fair Credit Reporting Act).	None	None

Section	Text of the Provision	Other Agencies	Deadlines for Rules
Section 1088(a)(11)(C) (amending the Fair Credit Reporting Act (15 U.S.C. 1681 et seq.))	"…shall, with respect to persons or entities that are subject to the enforcement authority of the Bureau under section 621…prescribe regulations requiring each person that furnishes information to a consumer reporting agency to establish reasonable policies and procedures for implementing the guidelines established pursuant to subparagraph (A)."	None	None
Section 1088(b)(3)	"Regulations to carry out section 624 of the Fair Credit Reporting Act (15 U.S.C. 1681s-3), shall be prescribed, as described in paragraph (2), by…."	Rules to be issued by (1) the Commodity Futures Trading Commission, with respect to entities subject to its enforcement authorities; (2) the Securities and Exchange Commission, with respect to entities subject to its enforcement authorities; (3) the Bureau, with respect to other entities subject to this legislation.	None
Section 1094(3)(B) (amending the Home Mortgage Disclosure Act of 1975 (12 U.S.C. 2801 et seq.))	"…. shall develop regulations that (A) prescribe the format for such disclosures, the method for submission of the data to the appropriate agency, and the procedures for disclosing the information to the public; (B) require the collection of data required to be disclosed under subsection (b) with respect to loans sold by each institution reporting under this title; (C) require disclosure of the class of the purchaser of such loans; (D) permit any reporting institution to submit in writing to the Bureau or to the appropriate agency such additional data or explanations as it deems relevant to the decision to originate or purchase mortgage loans; and	Rule to be developed in consultation with "appropriate banking agencies," the Federal Deposit Insurance Corporation, the National Credit Union Administration Board, and the Secretary of Housing and Urban Development.	None

Section	Text of the Provision	Other Agencies	Deadlines for Rules
	(E) modify or require modification of itemized information, for the purpose of protecting the privacy interests of the mortgage applicants or mortgagors, that is or will be available to the public."		
Section 1094(3)(F) (amending the Home Mortgage Disclosure Act of 1975 (12 U.S.C. 2801 et seq.))	"The data required to be disclosed under subsection (b) shall be submitted to the Bureau or to the appropriate agency for any institution reporting under this title, in accordance with regulations prescribed by the Bureau."	None	None
Section 1463(a) (amending Section 6 of the Real Estate Settlement Procedures Act of 1974 (12 U.S.C. 2605))	"A servicer of a federally related mortgage shall not…charge fees for responding to valid qualified written requests (as defined in regulations which the Bureau of Consumer Financial Protection shall prescribe) under this section" (or) "fail to comply with any other obligation found by the Bureau of Consumer Financial Protection, by regulation, to be appropriate to carry out the consumer protection purposes of this Act."	None	Per Section 1400(c), final rule to be published within 18 months after designated transfer date, and to take effect within 12 months after issuance.
Section 1471 (amending Chapter 2 of the Truth in Lending Act (15 U.S.C. 1631 et seq.))	"…shall jointly prescribe regulations to implement this section" ("Property Appraisal Requirements"). It goes on to say that the agencies "may jointly exempt, by rule, a class of loans from the requirements of this subsection or subsection (a) if the agencies determine that the exemption is in the public interest and promotes the safety and soundness of creditors."	Rule to be issued jointly with the Board of Governors, Comptroller of the Currency, Federal Deposit Insurance Corporation, National Credit Union Administration Board, and the Federal Housing Finance Agency	Per Section 1400(c), final rule to be published within 18 months after designated transfer date, and to take effect within 12 months after issuance.

Section	Text of the Provision	Other Agencies	Deadlines for Rules
Section 1473(f)(2) (amending Title XI of the Financial Institutions Reform, Recovery, and Enforcement Act of 1989 (12 U.S.C. 3331 et seq.))	"…shall jointly, by rule, establish minimum requirements to be applied by a State in the registration of appraisal management companies."	Rule to be issued jointly with the Board of Governors, the Comptroller of the Currency, the Federal Deposit Insurance Corporation, the National Credit Union Administration Board, and the Federal Housing Finance Agency	Per Section 1400(c), final rule to be published within 18 months after designated transfer date, and to take effect within 12 months after issuance.
Section 1473(f)(2) (amending Title XI of the Financial Institutions Reform, Recovery, and Enforcement Act of 1989 (12 U.S.C. 3331 et seq.))	"…shall jointly promulgate regulations for the reporting of the activities of appraisal management companies to the Appraisal Subcommittee in determining the payment of the annual registry fee."	Rule to be issued jointly with the Board of Governors of the Federal Reserve System, the Comptroller of the Currency, the Federal Deposit Insurance Corporation, the National Credit Union Administration Board, and the Federal Housing Finance Agency	Per Section 1400(c), final rule to be published within 18 months after designated transfer date, and to take effect within 12 months after issuance.
Section 1473(q) (amending Title XI of the Financial Institutions Reform, Recovery, and Enforcement Act of 1989 (12 U.S.C. 3331 et seq.))	"…shall promulgate regulations to implement the quality control standards required under this section" (on automated valuation models used to estimate collateral value for mortgage lending purposes).	Rule to be issued jointly with the Board of Governors, the Comptroller of the Currency, the Federal Deposit Insurance Corporation, the National Credit Union Administration Board, and the Federal Housing Finance Agency, in consultation with the staff of the Appraisal Subcommittee and the Appraisal Standards Board of the Appraisal Foundation	Per Section 1400(c), final rule to be published within 18 months after designated transfer date, and to take effect within 12 months after issuance.

Appendix. (Continued).

Section	Text of the Provision	Other Agencies	Deadlines for Rules
Discretionary Regulations (e.g., "may prescribe rules…")			
Section 1002(9)	The term "deposit-taking activity" includes "the receipt of funds or the equivalent thereof, as the Bureau may determine by rule or order, received or held by a covered person (or an agent for a covered person) for the purpose of facilitating a payment or transferring funds or value of funds between a consumer and a third party."	None	None
Section 1002(15)(A)	The definition of the term "financial product or service" includes "…such other financial product or service as may be defined by the Bureau, by regulation, for purposes of this title, if the Bureau finds that such financial product or service is—(I) entered into or conducted as a subterfuge or with a purpose to evade any Federal consumer financial law; or (II) permissible for a bank or for a financial holding company to offer or to provide under any provision of a Federal law or regulation applicable to a bank or a financial holding company, and has, or likely will have, a material impact on consumers."	None	None
Section 1002(25)	The definition of a "related person" includes "any shareholder, consultant, joint venture partner, or other person, as determined by the Bureau (by rule or on a case-by-case basis) who materially participates in the conduct of the affairs of such covered person."	None	None
Section 1022(b)(1)	"…may prescribe rules and issue orders and guidance, as may be necessary or appropriate to enable the Bureau to administer and carry out the purposes and objectives of the Federal consumer financial laws, and to prevent evasions thereof."	None	None

Section	Text of the Provision	Other Agencies	Deadlines for Rules
Section 1022(b)(3)(A)	"…by rule, may conditionally or unconditionally exempt any class of covered persons, service providers, or consumer financial products or services, from any provision of this title, or from any rule issued under this title, as the Bureau determines necessary or appropriate to carry out the purposes and objectives of this title, taking into consideration the factors in subparagraph (B)."	None	None
Section 1022(c)(4)(B)	"…may…require covered persons and service providers participating in consumer financial services markets to file with the Bureau, under oath or otherwise, in such form and within such reasonable period of time as the Bureau may prescribe by rule or order, annual or special reports, or answers in writing to specific questions, furnishing information described in paragraph (4), as necessary for the Bureau to fulfill the monitoring, assessment, and reporting responsibilities imposed by Congress."	None	None
Section 1022(c)(5)	"In order to assess whether a nondepository is a covered person, as defined in section 1002, the Bureau may require such nondepository to file with the Bureau, under oath or otherwise, in such form and within such reasonable period of time as the Bureau may prescribe by rule or order, annual or special reports, or answers in writing to specific questions."	None	None
Section 1022(c)(7)(A)	"…may prescribe rules regarding registration requirements applicable to a covered person, other than an insured depository institution, insured credit union, or related person."	None	None

Appendix. (Continued).

Section	Text of the Provision	Other Agencies	Deadlines for Rules
Section 1024(b)(7)(C)	"…may prescribe rules regarding a person described in subsection (a)(1), to ensure that such persons are legitimate entities and are able to perform their obligations to consumers. Such requirements may include background checks for principals, officers, directors, or key personnel and bonding or other appropriate financial requirements."	None	None
Section 1027(b)(2)	"…may exercise rulemaking, supervisory, enforcement, or other authority under this title with respect to a person described in paragraph (1) when such person is (A) engaged in an activity of offering or providing any consumer financial product or service…or (B) otherwise subject to any enumerated consumer law or any law for which authorities are transferred under subtitle F or H…."	None	None
Section 1027(g)(3)(B)(iii)	"Subject to a request or response pursuant to clause (i) or clause (ii) by the agencies made under this subparagraph (Departments of the Treasury and Labor), the Bureau may exercise rulemaking authority, and may act to enforce a rule prescribed pursuant to such request or response, in accordance with the provisions of this title."	None	None
Section 1031(b)	"…may prescribe rules applicable to a covered person or service provider identifying as unlawful unfair, deceptive, or abusive acts or practices in connection with any transaction with a consumer for a consumer financial product or service, or the offering of a consumer financial product or service. Rules under this section may include requirements for the purpose of preventing such acts or practices."	None	None

Section	Text of the Provision	Other Agencies	Deadlines for Rules
Section 1032(a)	"…may prescribe rules to ensure that the features of any consumer financial product or service, both initially and over the term of the product or service, are fully, accurately, and effectively disclosed to consumers in a manner that permits consumers to understand the costs, benefits, and risks associated with the product or service, in light of the facts and circumstances."	None	None
Section 1057(d)(3)	"…an arbitration provision in a collective bargaining agreement shall be enforceable as to disputes arising under subsection (a)(4), unless the Bureau determines, by rule, that such provision is inconsistent with the purposes of this title."	None	None
Section 1071(a) (amending the Equal Credit Opportunity Act (15 U.S.C. 1691 et seq.))	"…shall prescribe such rules and issue such guidance as may be necessary to carry out, enforce, and compile data pursuant to this section" (on small business data collection).	None	None
Section 1071(a) (amending the Equal Credit Opportunity Act (15 U.S.C. 1691 et seq.))	"…by rule or order, may adopt exceptions to any requirement of this section (on small business data collection) and may, conditionally or unconditionally, exempt any financial institution or class of financial institutions from the requirements of this section, as the Bureau deems necessary or appropriate to carry out the purposes of this section."	None	None
Section 1076(b)	The Bureau should issue rules if it "determines through the study required under subsection (a) (on reverse mortgage transactions) that conditions or limitations on reverse mortgage transactions are necessary or appropriate for accomplishing the purposes and objectives of this title…."	None	Study must be conducted within one year of enactment (i.e., by July 21, 2011), but no deadline established for possible regulations.

Appendix. (Continued).

Section	Text of the Provision	Other Agencies	Deadlines for Rules
Section 1088(a) (amending the Fair Credit Reporting Act (15 U.S.C. 1681 et seq.))	Prohibits the treatment of information as a consumer report if it is disclosed as "…determined to be necessary and appropriate, by regulation or order, by the Bureau or the applicable State insurance authority (with respect to any person engaged in providing insurance or annuities)."	Rule to be issued by the Bureau or applicable state insurance authorities	None
Section 1088(a)(4)(B) (amending the Fair Credit Reporting Act (15 U.S.C. 1681 et seq.))	"…may, after notice and opportunity for comment, prescribe regulations that permit transactions under paragraph (2) that are determined to be necessary and appropriate to protect legitimate operational, transactional, risk, consumer, and other needs…."	None	None
Section 1088(a)(10)(E) (amending the Fair Credit Reporting Act (15 U.S.C. 1681 et seq.))	"…shall prescribe such regulations as are necessary to carry out the purposes of this title, except with respect to sections 615(e) and 628. The Bureau may prescribe regulations as may be necessary or appropriate to administer and carry out the purposes and objectives of this title, and to prevent evasions thereof or to facilitate compliance therewith."	None	None
Section 1089(4) (amending the Fair Debt Collection Practices Act (15 U.S.C. 1692 et seq.))	"Except as provided in section 1029(a) of the Consumer Financial Protection Act of 2010, the Bureau may prescribe rules with respect to the collection of debts by debt collectors, as defined in this title."	None	None

Section	Text of the Provision	Other Agencies	Deadlines for Rules
Section 1093 (amending Title V of the Gramm-Leach-Bliley Act (15 U.S.C. 6801 et seq.))	"…shall have authority to prescribe such regulations as may be necessary to carry out the purposes of this subtitle with respect to financial institutions and other persons subject to their respective jurisdiction under section 505 (and notwithstanding subtitle B of the Consumer Financial Protection Act of 2010), except that the Bureau of Consumer Financial Protection shall not have authority to prescribe regulations with respect to the standards under section 501."	Bureau and the Securities and Exchange Commission authorized to issue rules	None
Section 1094 (amending the Home Mortgage Disclosure Act of 1975 (12 U.S.C. 2801 et seq.))	"…may, by regulation, exempt from the requirements of this title any State-chartered repository institution within any State or subdivision thereof, if the agency determines that, under the law of such State or subdivision, that institution is subject to requirements that are substantially similar to those imposed under this title, and that such law contains adequate provisions for enforcement."	None	None
Section 1097(1) (amending Section 626 of the Omnibus Appropriations Act, 2009 (15 U.S.C. 1638 note)).	"…shall have authority to prescribe rules with respect to mortgage loans in accordance with section 553 of title 5, United States Code. Such rulemaking shall relate to unfair or deceptive acts or practices regarding mortgage loans, which may include unfair or deceptive acts or practices involving loan modification and foreclosure rescue services."	None	None
Section 1100(6)(B) (amending the S.A.F.E. Mortgage Licensing Act of 2008 (12 U.S.C. 5101 et seq.))	"…is authorized to promulgate regulations setting minimum net worth or surety bond requirements for residential mortgage loan originators and minimum requirements for recovery funds paid into by loan originators."	None	None

Appendix. (Continued).

Section	Text of the Provision	Other Agencies	Deadlines for Rules
Section 1472(a) (amending Chapter 2 of the Truth in Lending Act (15 U.S.C. 1631 et seq.))	"…may jointly issue rules, interpretive guidelines, and general statements of policy with respect to acts or practices that violate appraisal independence in the provision of mortgage lending services for a consumer credit transaction secured by the principal dwelling of the consumer and mortgage brokerage services for such a transaction, within the meaning of subsections (a), (b), (c), (d), (e), (f), (h), and (i)."	Rule to be issued jointly with the Board of Governors, the Comptroller of the Currency, the Federal Deposit Insurance Corporation, the National Credit Union Administration Board, and the Federal Housing Finance Agency.	Per Section 1400(c), final rule to be published within 18 months after designated transfer date, and to take effect within 12 months after issuance.
Section 1472(a) (amending Chapter 2 of the Truth in Lending Act (15 U.S.C. 1631 et seq.))	"…may jointly issue regulations that address the issue of appraisal report portability, including regulations that ensure the portability of the appraisal report between lenders for a consumer credit transaction secured by a 1-4 unit single family residence that is the principal dwelling of the consumer, or mortgage brokerage services for such a transaction."	Rule to be issued jointly with the Board of Governors, the Comptroller of the Currency, the Federal Deposit Insurance Corporation, the National Credit Union Administration Board, and the Federal Housing Finance Agency.	Per Section 1400(c), final rule to be published within 18 months after designated transfer date, and to take effect within 12 months after issuance.

Source: CRS.

Regulations to be Issued by the Consumer Financial Protection Bureau

End Notes

[1] For more information on the Dodd-Frank Act, see CRS Report R41350, The Dodd-Frank Wall Street Reform and Consumer Protection Act: Issues and Summary, coordinated by Baird Webel.

[2] For more information, see CRS Report R41338, The Dodd-Frank Wall Street Reform and Consumer Protection Act: Title X, The Consumer Financial Protection Bureau, by David H. Carpenter.

[3] Section 1001.

[4] For more detailed information on Title X of the act, see CRS Report R41338, The Dodd-Frank Wall Street Reform and Consumer Protection Act: Title X, The Consumer Financial Protection Bureau, by David H. Carpenter.

[5] The relevant categories include "larger depositories" (those with more than $10 billion in assets), "smaller depositories (those with $10 billion or less in assets), and certain covered "nondepositories."

[6] For example, the CFPB will not have primary supervisory and enforcement powers over smaller depositories, but will be able to participate in examinations conducted by the institutions' prudential regulators, and can refer potential enforcement actions to their prudential regulators.

[7] Section 1100D. This section amended a statutory listing of independent regulatory agencies (44 U.S.C. 3502(5)), which includes such financial regulatory agencies as the Board of Governors of the Federal Reserve System, the Commodity Futures Trading Commission, and the Securities and Exchange Commission.

[8] See, for example, Paul R. Verkuil, "The Purposes and Limits of Independent Agencies," Duke Law Journal, vol. 37 (April-June 1988), pp. 257-279; and Marshall J. Breger and Gary J. Edles, "Established by Practice: The Theory and Operation of Independent Federal Agencies," Administrative Law Review, vol. 52 (2000), pp. 1111-1294.

[9] Section 1011(c).

[10] Section 1017.

[11] See Section 1062 for more information on the designated transfer date. The Secretary is required to determine the transfer date "in consultation with the Chairman of the Board of Governors, the Chairperson of the Corporation, the Chairman of the Federal Trade Commission, the Chairman of the National Credit Union Administration Board, the Comptroller of the Currency, the Director of the Office of Thrift Supervision, the Secretary of the Department of Housing and Urban Development, and the Director of the Office of Management and Budget."

[12] Section 1062(c). The Secretary can designate a transfer date later than 12 months after the date of enactment if Congress is provided a written notice and explanation, but in no case can the date be later than 18 months after the date of enactment.

[13] Section 1017(a)(3). As noted later in this report, Section 1002(14) of the Dodd-Frank Act defines "Federal consumer financial law" as "the provisions of this title, the enumerated consumer laws, the laws for which authorities are transferred under subtitles F and H, and any rule or order prescribed by the Bureau under this title, an enumerated consumer law, or pursuant to the authorities transferred under subtitles F and H. The term does not include the Federal Trade Commission Act." The "enumerated consumer laws" are defined in subsection (12) as including the Alternative Mortgage Transaction Parity Act of 1982 (12 U.S.C. 3801 et seq.); the Consumer Leasing Act of 1976 (15 U.S.C. 1667 et seq.); the Electronic Fund Transfer Act (15 U.S.C. 1693 et seq.), except with respect to section 920 of that act; the Equal Credit Opportunity Act (15 U.S.C. 1691 et seq.); the Fair Credit Billing Act (15 U.S.C. 1666 et seq.); the Fair Credit Reporting Act (15 U.S.C. 1681 et seq.), except with respect to sections 615(e) and 628 of that act (15 U.S.C. 1681m(e), 1681w); the Home Owners Protection Act of 1998 (12 U.S.C. 4901 et seq.); and the Fair Debt Collection Practices Act (15 U.S.C. 1692 et seq.).

[14] Interim final rulemaking is a particular application of the "good cause" exception to the notice-and-comment requirements in the Administrative Procedure Act (5 U.S.C. 553) in which an agency publishes a final rule without a previous proposed rule, but with a post-promulgation opportunity for comment.

[15] Section 1400(a).

[16] See, for example, David Cho, "Geithner's Realm Grows as Overhaul Nears Finish," Washington Post, July 17, 2010, p. A1; Lorraine Mirabella, "Lawyers Await Regulations to Spring from Financial Reform," McClatchy-Tribune Business News, July 27, 2010; and Eric Lichtblau, "Ex-Regulators Lobby to Shape Overhaul," New York Times, July 28, 2010, p. B1.

[17] See, for example, Jim Puzzanghera, "Wall Street Nervous About Watchdog's Bite; A Leading Candidate to Head a New Consumer Protection Agency Has Powerful Enemies," Los Angeles Times, p. A1; and Eileen Mozinski Schmidt, "Finance Leaders Wary of New Law," Telegraph-Herald, July 29, 2010, p. A-1, which said that "top of mind for many is how the new federal consumer-protection agency will develop and who will run it."

[18] Davis Polk & Wardwell, LLP, "Summary of the Dodd-Frank Wall Street Reform and Consumer Protection Act, Enacted into Law on July 21, 2010," available at http://www.davispolk.com/files/Publication/7084f9fe-6580-413bb870-b7c025ed2ecf/Presentation/PublicationAttachment/1d4495c7-0be0-4e9a-ba77-f786fb90464a/070910_Financial_Reform_Summary.pdf.

[19] For example, the Chamber of Commerce's Center for Capital Markets Competitiveness said that the Dodd-Frank Act "will lead to 520 rulemakings." See Thomas Quaadman, "Dodd-Frank: Governance Issues Galore and Not Limited to Financial Institutions, the Metropolitan Corporate Counsel, August 2010, p. 18, available at http://www.metrocorpcounsel.com/current.php?artType=view&artMonth=August&artYear=2010&EntryNo=11258.

[20] Titles X and XIV also require other agencies to issue regulations.

[21] Section 1002(14).

[22] The definition of "enumerated consumer laws" is in Section 1002(12).

[23] Section 1022(b)(2)(A).

[24] Section 1022(b)(2)(B) and (C).

[25] The exception is in Section 1061(b)(5), involving the authority of the Federal Trade Commission under the Federal Trade Commission Act.

[26] Section 1022(b)(4).

[27] Section 1022(c).

[28] Section 1022(c)(4)(B)(ii).

[29] Section 1022(c)(5). If these reports or answers meet the definition of a "collection of information" in the Paperwork Reduction Act (PRA), then they will have to be reviewed by the Office of Management and Budget before the information can be collected. The PRA (44 U.S.C. 3502(3)) defines "collection of information" as "the obtaining, causing to be obtained, soliciting, or requiring the disclosure to third parties or the public, of facts or opinions by or for an agency, regardless of form or format, calling for...answers to identical questions posed to, or identical reporting or recordkeeping requirements imposed on, ten or more persons, other than agencies, instrumentalities, or employees of the United States." For more information, see CRS Report R40636, Paperwork Reduction Act (PRA): OMB and Agency Responsibilities and Burden Estimates, by Curtis W. Copeland and Vanessa K. Burrows.

[30] These registration and disclosures may also be covered by the PRA's information collection and dissemination requirements. See 44 U.S.C. 3506(c) (for agency information collection requirements) and 44 U.S.C. 3506(d) (for agency information dissemination requirements).

[31] Section 1022(c)(3)(A).

[32] Section 1022(c)(6)(A) requires the Bureau to "prescribe rules regarding the confidential treatment of information obtained from persons in connection with the exercise of its authorities under Federal consumer financial law."

[33] The public may also be informed of upcoming rules through advance notices of proposed rulemaking, and through entries in the Unified Agenda of Federal Regulatory and Deregulatory Actions.

[34] The act does not specify what types of rules are to be considered "significant," presumably leaving these determinations to the Bureau.

[35] Section 553 of Title 5 generally requires federal agencies to publish a notice of proposed rulemaking, take comments on the proposed rule, develop a final rule taking those comments into consideration, and publish a final rule that cannot take effect until 30 days after the rule is published in the Federal Register. Even in the absence of this provision, these "notice and comment" requirements would generally apply to most of the rules that the Bureau is required or authorized to issue.

[36] 15 U.S.C. 1681m(h)(6)(B).

[37] Section 1041(c)(3).

[38] The only Title XIV provision that does not require that regulations be jointly issued is in Section 1463(a) (amending Section 6 of the Real Estate Settlement Procedures Act of 1974 (12 U.S.C. 2605)).

[39] Section 1011.

[40] For more information on these and other rulemaking statutes, see CRS Report RL32240, The Federal Rulemaking Process: An Overview, by Curtis W. Copeland.

[41] For more information on the operation of the Congressional Review Act, see CRS Report RL30116, Congressional Review of Agency Rulemaking: An Update and Assessment of The Congressional Review Act after a Decade, by Morton Rosenberg. See also CRS Report RL31160, Disapproval of Regulations by Congress: Procedure Under the Congressional Review Act, by Richard S. Beth.

[42] See CRS Report RL 34354, Congressional Influence on Rulemaking and Regulation Through Appropriations Restrictions, by Curtis W. Copeland.

[43] The President, Executive Order 12866, "Regulatory Planning and Review," 58 Federal Register51735, October 4, 1993, Section 6(a). A "significant" regulatory action is defined in Section 3(f) as "Any regulatory action that is likely to result in a rule that may (1) have an annual effect on the economy of $100 million or more or adversely affect in a material way the economy, a sector of the economy, productivity, competition, jobs, the environment, public health or safety, or State, local, or tribal governments or communities; (2) create a serious inconsistency or otherwise interfere with an action taken or planned by another agency; (3) materially alter the budgetary impact of entitlements, grants, user fees, or loan programs or the rights and obligations of recipients thereof; or (4) raise novel legal or policy issues arising out of legal mandates, the President's priorities, or the principles set forth in the Executive order." For more information on OIRA and its review process, see CRS Report RL32397, Federal Rulemaking: The Role of the Office of Information and Regulatory Affairs, by Curtis W. Copeland.

[44] Section 1(b)(6) of Executive Order 12866. As the executive order and OMB Circular A-4 make clear, even under this standard, the monetized benefits of a rule are not required to exceed the monetized costs of the rule before the agency can issue the rule, only that the costs of the rule be "justified" by the benefits (quantitative or non-quantitative).

[45] Section 6(a)(3)(C) of Executive Order 12866.

[46] Section 6(a)(3)(C)(iii) of Executive Order 12866.

[47] 44 U.S.C. 3508.

[48] 5 U.S.C. 553.

[49] 5 U.S.C. 553(b)(3(B). These requirements also do not apply to interpretative rules, general statements of policy, or rules of agency organization, procedure, or practice (5 U.S.C. 553(b)(A).

[50] 5 U.S.C. 553(d).

[51] For more information on the RFA, see CRS Report RL34355, The Regulatory Flexibility Act: Implementation Issues and Proposed Reforms, by Curtis W. Copeland.

[52] Agencies' interpretations of these phrases are, however, subject to judicial review (5 U.S.C. 611).

[53] See 5 U.S.C. 603(a), which states that agencies must prepare initial regulatory flexibility analyses "whenever an agency is required...to publish a general notice of proposed rulemaking for any proposed rule." See also 5 U.S.C. 604(a), which requires agencies to prepare a final regulatory flexibility analysis when an agency publishes a final rule "after being required...to publish a general notice of proposed rulemaking."

[54] Certain planning requirements in Section 4(b) and Section 4(c) regarding the "unified regulatory agenda" and the "regulatory plan" apply to independent regulatory agencies. Generally, however, the executive order does not apply to independent regulatory agencies.

[55] 44 U.S.C. 3507(f)(1).

[56] See, for example, U.S. General Accounting Office, Unfunded Mandates: Analysis of Reform Act Coverage, GAO-04-637, May 12, 2004.

[57] Section 1017. However, if the director of the CFPB determines that these unappropriated funds are insufficient, the Dodd-Frank Act authorizes appropriations of up to $200 million per year for FY2010 through FY2014. Appropriations restrictions could be added to any such appropriated funds.

[58] 5 U.S.C. 609.

[59] Section 1023(a).

[60] The Office of Financial Research was established by Section 152 of the Dodd-Frank Act.

[61] The Federal Insurance Office was established by Section 502 of the Dodd-Frank Act.

[62] Because only agencies who are "represented by members of the Council" can file petitions to stay or set aside rules, the member appointed by the President does not appear able to file a petition, since this member is supposed to be "independent" and does not represent an agency on the Council.

[63] Section 1023(c)(1). Section 102(a)(3) defines a "member agency" as a voting member of the Council

[64] Section 1023(c)(3).

[65] Section 1023(c)(4).

[66] Section 1023(c)(8).

[67] For more information on the operation of the Congressional Review Act, see CRS Report RL30116, Congressional Review of Agency Rulemaking: An Update and Assessment of The Congressional Review Act after a Decade, by Morton Rosenberg.

[68] The recent experience of rules issued pursuant to the recent health care reform legislation is instructive in this regard. The Patient Protection and Affordable Care Act (PPACA, P.L. 111-148, March 23, 2010) contained more than 40 provisions that required, permitted, or otherwise mentioned rulemaking. However, of the 10 final rules issued during the first four months of PPACA's implementation, 7 of them were not specifically required

or mentioned in the act. See CRS Report R41346, PPACA Regulations Issued During the First Four Months of the Act's Implementation, by Curtis W. Copeland.

[69] In Sierra Club v. Costle (657 F.2d 298, D.C. Cir. 1981), the D.C. Circuit concluded (at 409) that it was "entirely proper for congressional representatives vigorously to represent the interests of their constituents before administrative agencies engaged in informal, general policy rulemaking, so long as the individual Members of Congress do not frustrate the intent of Congress as a whole as expressed in statute, nor undermine applicable rules of procedure."

[70] Dominique Custos, "The Rulemaking Power of Independent Regulatory Agencies," The American Journal of Comparative Law, vol. 54 (Fall 2006), p. 633.

[71] Joint statement of House and Senate Sponsors, 142 Cong. Rec. E571, at E571 (daily ed. April 19, 1996); 142 Cong. Rec. S3683, at S3683 (daily ed. April 18, 1996).

[72] If a rule is considered "major" (e.g., has a $100 million annual effect on the economy), then the CRA generally prohibits it from taking effect until 60 days after the date that it is submitted to Congress.

[73] For a detailed discussion of CRA procedures, see CRS Report RL31160, Disapproval of Regulations by Congress: Procedure Under the Congressional Review Act, by Richard S. Beth.

[74] For more on the potential scope of the definition of a "rule" under the CRA, see CRS Report RL30116, Congressional Review of Agency Rulemaking: An Update and Assessment of The Congressional Review Act after a Decade, by Morton Rosenberg.

[75] The rule overturned in March 2001 was the Occupational Safety and Health Administration's ergonomics standard. This reversal was the result of a unique set of circumstances in which the incoming President (George W. Bush) did not veto the resolution disapproving the outgoing President's (William J. Clinton's) rule. See CRS Report RL30116, Congressional Review of Agency Rulemaking: An Update and Assessment of The Congressional Review Act after a Decade, by Morton Rosenberg, for a description of several possible factors affecting the CRA's use, and for other effects that the act may have on agency rulemaking.

[76] See CRS Report RL30116, Congressional Review of Agency Rulemaking: An Update and Assessment of The Congressional Review Act after a Decade, by Morton Rosenberg, for a description of instances in which the filing of a resolution of disapproval had an effect on agencies' decisions.

In: The Dodd-Frank Wall Street Reform...
Editors: Nathan L. Morris and Philip O. Price

ISBN: 978-1-61324-101-1
© 2011 Nova Science Publishers, Inc.

Chapter 7

THE DODD-FRANK WALL STREET REFORM AND CONSUMER PROTECTION ACT: TITLE VII, DERIVATIVES[*]

Mark Jickling and Kathleen Ann Ruane

SUMMARY

The financial crisis implicated the unregulated over-the-counter (OTC) derivatives market as a major source of systemic risk. A number of firms used derivatives to construct highly leveraged speculative positions, which generated enormous losses that threatened to bankrupt not only the firms themselves but also their creditors and trading partners. Hundreds of billions of dollars in government credit were needed to prevent such losses from cascading throughout the system. AIG was the best-known example, but by no means the only one.

Equally troublesome was the fact that the OTC market depended on the financial stability of a dozen or so major dealers. Failure of a dealer would have resulted in the nullification of trillions of dollars worth of contracts and would have exposed derivatives counterparties to sudden risk and loss, exacerbating the cycle of deleveraging and withholding of credit that characterized the crisis. During the crisis, all the major dealers came under stress, and even though derivatives dealing was not generally the direct source of financial weakness, a collapse of the $600 trillion OTC derivatives market was imminent absent federal intervention. The first group of Troubled Asset Relief Program (TARP) recipients included nearly all the large derivatives dealers.

The Dodd-Frank Act (P.L. 111-203) sought to remake the OTC market in the image of the regulated futures exchanges. Crucial reforms include a requirement that swap contracts be cleared through a central counterparty regulated by one or more federal agencies. Clearinghouses require traders to put down cash (called initial margin) at the time they open a contract to cover potential losses, and require subsequent deposits

---

[*] This is an edited, reformatted and augmented version of a Congressional Research Services publication, dated August 30, 2010.

(called maintenance margin) to cover actual losses to the position. The intended effect of margin requirements is to eliminate the possibility that any firm can build up an uncapitalized exposure so large that default would have systemic consequences (again, the AIG situation). The size of a cleared position is limited by the firm's ability to post capital to cover its losses. That capital protects its trading partners and the system as a whole.

Swap dealers and major swap participants—firms with substantial derivatives positions—will be subject to margin and capital requirements above and beyond what the clearinghouses mandate. Swaps that are cleared will also be subject to trading on an exchange, or an exchange-like "swap execution facility," regulated by either the Commodity Futures Trading Commission (CFTC) or the Securities and Exchange Commission (SEC), in the case of security-based swaps. All trades will be reported to data repositories, so that regulators will have complete information about all derivatives positions. Data on swap prices and trading volumes will be made public.

The new law provides exceptions to the clearing and trading requirements for commercial end-users, or firms that use derivatives to hedge the risks of their nonfinancial business operations. Regulators may also provide exemptions for smaller financial institutions. Even trades that are exempt from the clearing and exchange-trading requirements, however, will have to be reported to data repositories or directly to regulators.

This report describes some of the new requirements placed on the derivatives market by the Dodd-Frank Act. It will not be updated.

INTRODUCTION

Prior to the financial crisis that began in 2007, over-the-counter (OTC) derivatives were generally regarded as a beneficial financial innovation that distributed financial risk more efficiently and made the financial system more stable, resilient, and resistant to shocks. The crisis essentially reversed this view. The Dodd-Frank Act (P.L. 111-203) attempts to address the aspect of the OTC market that appeared most troublesome in the crisis: the market permitted enormous exposure to risk to grow out of the sight of regulators and other traders. Derivatives exposures that could not be readily quantified exacerbated panic and uncertainty about the true financial condition of other market participants, contributing to the freezing of credit markets. Under Dodd-Frank, risk exposures of major financial institutions must be backed by capital, minimizing the shock to the financial system should such a firm fail. In addition, regulators will have information about the size and distribution of possible losses during periods of market volatility.

Background

Derivative contracts are an array of financial instruments with one feature in common: their value is linked to changes in some underlying variable, such as the price of a physical commodity, a stock index, or an interest rate. Derivatives contracts—futures contracts, options, and swaps[1]— gain or lose value as the underlying rates or prices change, even though the holder may not actually own the underlying asset.

Thousands of firms use derivatives to manage risk. For example, a firm can protect itself against increases in the price of a commodity that it uses in production by entering into a derivative contract that will gain value if the price of the commodity rises. A notable instance of this type of hedging strategy was Southwest Airlines' derivatives position that allowed it to buy jet fuel at a low fixed price in 2008 when energy prices reached record highs. When used to hedge risk, derivatives can protect businesses (and sometimes their customers as well) from unfavorable price shocks.

Others use derivatives to seek profits by betting on which way prices will move. Such speculators provide liquidity to the market—they assume the risks that hedgers wish to avoid. The combined trading activity of hedgers and speculators provides another public benefit: price discovery. By incorporating all known information and expectations about future prices, derivatives markets generate prices that often serve as a reference point for transactions in the underlying cash markets.

Although derivatives trading had its origins in agriculture, today most derivatives are linked to financial variables, such as interest rates, foreign exchange, stock prices and indices, and the creditworthiness of issuers of bonds. The market is measured in the hundreds of trillions of dollars, and billions of contracts are traded annually.

Derivatives have also played a part in the development of complex financial instruments, such as bonds backed by pools of other assets. They can be used to create "synthetic" securities—contracts structured to replicate the returns on individual securities or portfolios of stocks, bonds, or other derivatives. Although the basic concepts of derivative finance are neither new nor particularly difficult, much of the most sophisticated financial engineering of the past few decades has involved the construction of increasingly complex mathematical models of how markets move and how different financial variables interact. Derivatives trading is often a primary path through which such research reaches the marketplace.

Since 2000, growth in derivatives markets has been explosive (although the financial crisis has caused some retrenchment since 2008). Between 2000 and the end of 2008, the volume of derivatives contracts traded on exchanges,[2] such as futures exchanges, and the notional value of total contracts traded in the over-the-counter (OTC) market[3] grew by 475% and 522%, respectively. By contrast, during the credit and housing booms that occurred over the same period, the value of corporate bonds and home mortgage debt outstanding grew by only 95% and 115%, respectively.[4]

Pre-Dodd-Frank Act Market Structure and Regulation

The various types of derivatives are used for the same purposes—avoiding business risk, or hedging, and taking on risk in search of speculative profits. Prior to the Dodd-Frank Act, however, the instruments were traded on different types of markets. Futures contracts are traded on exchanges regulated by the Commodity Futures Trading Commission (CFTC); stock options on exchanges under the Securities and Exchange Commission (SEC); and all swaps (and security-based swaps, as well as some options) were traded OTC, and were not regulated by anyone.

Exchanges are centralized markets where all the buying and selling interest comes together. Traders who want to buy (or take a long position) interact with those who want to sell (or go short), and deals are made and prices reported throughout the day. In the OTC market, contracts are made bilaterally, typically between a dealer and an end user, and there was generally no requirement that the price, the terms, or even the existence of the contract be disclosed to a regulator or to the public.

Derivatives can be volatile contracts, and the normal expectation is that there will be big gains and losses among traders. As a result, there is an issue of market integrity. How do the longs know that the shorts will be able to meet their obligations, and vice versa? A market where billions of contracts change hands is impossible if all traders must investigate the creditworthiness of the other trader, or counterparty. The exchange market deals with this credit risk problem in one way, the OTC market in another way. How this risk—often called counterparty risk—must be managed was a key element of the reforms implemented by the Dodd-Frank Act.

Market Structure for Cleared and Exchange-Traded Derivatives

The exchanges deal with the issue of credit risk with a clearinghouse.[5] The process is shown in **Figure 1** below: (1) two traders agree on a transaction on the exchange floor or on an electronic platform. (2) Once the trade is made, it goes to the clearinghouse, which guarantees payment to both parties. (3) In effect, the original contract between long and short traders is now two contracts, one between each trader and the clearinghouse. Traders then do not have to worry about counterparty default because the clearinghouse stands behind all trades.

But the credit risk remains: how does the clearinghouse ensure that it can meet its obligations? Clearing depends on a system of margin, or collateral. Before the trade, both the long and short traders have to deposit an initial margin payment with the clearinghouse to cover potential losses. Then at the end of each trading day, all contracts are repriced, or "marked to market," and all those who have lost money (because prices moved against them) must post additional margin (called variation or maintenance margin) to cover those losses before the next trading session. This is known as a margin call: traders must make good on their losses immediately, or their broker may close out their positions when trading opens the next day. The effect of the margin system is that no one can build up a large paper loss that could damage the clearinghouse in case of default: it is certainly possible to lose large amounts of money trading on the futures exchanges, but only on a "pay as you go" basis.

Market Structure for OTC Derivatives

In the OTC market, as shown on the right side of Figure 1, the long and short traders do not interact directly. Instead of a centralized marketplace, there is a network of dealers who stand ready to take either long or short positions, and make money on spreads and fees. The dealer absorbs the credit risk of customer default, while the customer faces the risk of dealer default. In this kind of market, one would expect the dealers to be the most solid and creditworthy financial institutions, and in fact the OTC market that emerged was dominated by two or three dozen firms—very large institutions like JP Morgan Chase, Goldman Sachs, Citigroup, and their foreign counterparts. Before 2007, such firms were generally viewed as too well diversified or too well managed to fail; in 2008, their fallibility was well established, and the pertinent question now is whether the government would still consider them to be too big to fail. (Title II of Dodd-Frank seeks to ensure that it will not.[6])

In the OTC market, some contracts required collateral or margin, but not all. There was no standard practice: all contract terms were negotiable. A trade group, the International

Swaps and Derivatives Association (ISDA), published best practice standards for use of collateral, but compliance was voluntary.

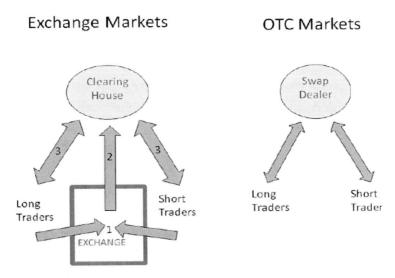

Source: CRS.

Figure 1. Pre-Dodd-Frank Act Derivatives Market Structures: Exchange and Over-the-Counter (OTC).

Because there was no universal, mandatory system of margin, large uncollateralized losses could (and did) build up in the OTC market. Perhaps the best-known example in the crisis was AIG, which wrote about $1.8 trillion worth of credit default swaps guaranteeing payment if certain mortgage-backed securities defaulted or experienced other "credit events."[7] Many of AIG's contracts required it to post collateral as the credit quality of the underlying referenced securities (or AIG's own credit rating) deteriorated, but AIG did not post initial margin, as this was deemed unnecessary because of the firm's triple-A rating. As the subprime crisis worsened, AIG faced margin calls that it could not meet. To avert bankruptcy, with the risk of global financial chaos, the Federal Reserve and the Treasury put tens of billions of dollars into AIG, the bulk of which went to its derivatives counterparties.[8]

A key reform in Dodd-Frank is a mandate that many OTC swaps be cleared, which means that they will be subject to margin requirements. This will have the effect of combining features of the two market structures shown in Figure 1.

THE DODD-FRANK ACT'S CLEARING AND REPORTING REQUIREMENTS

In order to provide more stability to the OTC derivatives market, the Dodd-Frank Act requires that most derivatives contracts formerly traded exclusively in the OTC market be cleared and traded on exchanges. Thus, traders in these previously unregulated products will be required to post margin in the fashion described above and have their contracts repriced at the close of each trading day. This system likely will have the effect of regulating trade in these contracts more closely and providing greater transparency to the participants in the market and to the government regulators. Furthermore, the Dodd-Frank Act presumes that some derivatives contracts will still be traded in the OTC market; however, it grants regulators broader powers to obtain information about these derivatives and impose margin and capital requirements on them as well.

Clearing Requirement

Title VII of the Dodd-Frank Act creates largely parallel clearing and exchange trading requirements for swaps and security-based swaps as those terms are defined by Title VII and will be further defined by the CFTC and the SEC. Section 723 creates the clearing and exchange trading requirements for swaps over which the CFTC has jurisdiction.[9] Section 763 creates largely parallel requirements for security-based swaps over which the SEC has authority.[10]

If a swap or security-based swap is required to be cleared, the final version of the Dodd-Frank Act makes it unlawful for parties to enter into swaps or security-based swaps unless the transaction has been submitted for clearing.[11] There are two ways in which a swap or security-based swap may become subject to the clearing requirement.[12] In the first way, the agency of jurisdiction is required to engage in an ongoing review of the products it has jurisdiction over to determine whether a particular swap, security-based swap, group, or class of such contracts should be subject to the clearing requirement. In the House-passed version of the clearing requirement, determinations made by the agency in this manner would not have resulted in those transactions becoming subject to the clearing requirement, because in order to be subject to the clearing requirement, the agency had to make its determination pursuant to a submission of the transaction by a derivatives clearing organization or a clearing agency.[13] The Senate-passed version was more similar to the eventual statutory language in that determinations made by the agency of its own initiative regarding transactions required to be cleared may have been subject to the clearing requirement, without having to first be submitted to the agency as a transaction that a derivatives clearing organization or clearing agency intended to offer for clearing.[14] Determinations made on the initiative of the commissions will be discussed further in the "Prevention of Evasion" section below.

The second way in which a swap or security-based swap may become subject to the clearing requirement under the Dodd-Frank Act is upon submission to the CFTC or the SEC. When a derivatives clearing organization[15] (swaps) or clearing agency[16] (security-based swaps) decides to accept a swap or security-based swap for clearing, the act requires the organization to submit the transactions to the relevant commission for a determination as to whether the transactions should be required to be cleared. Furthermore, upon enactment of the Dodd-Frank Act, all swaps and security-based swaps that were listed for clearing by derivatives clearing organizations and clearing agencies at the time of passage were deemed submitted to the SEC and the CFTC for a determination of whether the clearing requirement should apply.

Following submission to the agencies, the agencies have 90 days to determine whether the swaps or security-based swaps are subject to the clearing requirement, unless the submitting organization agrees to an extension. When making that determination, the agencies must consider (1) "the existence of significant outstanding notional exposures, trading liquidity, and adequate pricing data"; (2) "the availability of rule framework, capacity, operational expertise and resources, and credit support infrastructure to clear the contract on terms consistent with material terms and trading conventions on which the contract is then traded"; (3) "the effect on the mitigation of systemic risk ... "; (4) "the effect on competition, including appropriate fees and charges ... "; and (5) "the existence of reasonable legal certainty in the event of the insolvency of the relevant derivatives clearing organization or 1 or more of its clearing members with regard to the treatment of customer and swap counterparty positions, funds, and property."[17] In the process of making these determinations, the agencies are also required to allow the public to comment on whether the clearing requirement should apply.

Should the CFTC or the SEC determine that a particular swap or security-based swap is required to be cleared, counterparties to that type of transaction may apply to stay the clearing requirement until the relevant agency "completes a review of the terms" of the swap or security-based swap and the clearing requirement.[18] Under the act, upon completing the review, the relevant agency may require the swap or security-based swap to be cleared, either unconditionally or subject to appropriate conditions. The relevant agency may also determine that the swap or security-based swap is not required to be cleared.

With certain exceptions, counterparties to swaps and security-based swaps that are required to be cleared must either execute the transactions on exchanges or specialized execution facilities.[19]

The Exchange-Trading Requirement

With certain exceptions, swaps and security-based swaps that are required to be cleared must also be executed on a regulated exchange or on a trading platform defined in the act as a swaps execution facility (SEF) or a security-based swaps execution facility (SBSEF). Such facilities must permit multiple market participants to trade by accepting bids or offers made by multiple participants in the facility.

The goal of the trading requirement is "to promote pre-trade price transparency in the swaps market."[20] Because the old OTC market was notably opaque, with complete price information available only to dealers, swaps customers were limited in their ability to shop for the best price or rate. The expectation is that as price information becomes more widely available, competition will produce narrower spreads and better prices.

SEFs and SBSEFs must comply with a number of core principles set out in the act. While these are somewhat less prescriptive than the regulation of exchanges where public customers are allowed to trade,[21] the new trading facilities have regulatory and administrative responsibilities far beyond what applied to OTC trading desks in the past. Among other things, SEFs and SBSEFs must

- establish and enforce rules to prevent trading abuses and to provide impartial access to the trading facility;
- ensure that swap contracts are not readily susceptible to manipulation;
- monitor trading to prevent manipulation, price distortion, and disruptions in the underlying cash market;
- set position limits;

- maintain adequate financial and managerial resources, including safeguards against operational risk;
- maintain an audit trail of all transactions;
- publish timely data on prices and trading volume;
- adopt emergency rules governing liquidation or transfer of trading positions as well as trading halts; and
- employ a chief compliance officer, who will submit an annual report to regulators.

During consideration of Dodd-Frank, a central issue of debate was the extent to which existing OTC derivatives trading platforms and mechanisms could be accommodated under the new regulatory regime. OTC trading practices ranged from individual telephone negotiations to electronic systems accessible to multiple participants. One concern was that if SEFs were too much like exchanges, the existing futures and securities exchanges would monopolize trading. On the other hand, if the SEF definition were too vague or general, the OTC market might remain opaque.

The bill reported by the Senate Banking Committee defined SEF as "an electronic trading system with pre-trade and post-trade transparency."[22] The explicit reference to "pre-trade" transparency does not appear in the final legislation, in part because of concerns that such a requirement was not compatible with the business models of a number of intermediaries, such as interdealer swap brokers providing anonymous execution services.[23]

As is the case with the clearing requirement, Dodd-Frank provides exceptions to the exchange-trading mandate. If no exchange or SEF or SBSEF makes a swap available for trading, the contract may be traded OTC. A swap that meets the end-user clearing exemption is likewise exempt from the trading requirement. We now discuss the end-user exemption.

End-User Exemption

Sections 723 and 763 of the Dodd-Frank Act provide exceptions to the clearing requirement for swaps and security-based swaps when one of the counterparties to the transaction is not a financial entity, is using the transaction to hedge or mitigate its own commercial risk, and notifies the relevant agency "how it generally meets its financial obligations associated with entering into non-cleared swaps."[24] This has been widely referred to as the end-user exemption because it applies only to transactions where at least one counterparty is "not a financial entity."[25] A financial entity for the purposes of this section is defined as a swap dealer, a security-based swap dealer, a major swap participant (MSP), a major security-based swap participant, a commodity pool, a private fund, an employee benefit plan, or a person predominantly engaged in activities that are in the business of banking, or in activities that are financial in nature.[26] Who is and who is not a financial entity is discussed further in the section describing MSPs.

The definition of who is eligible for the exception is more similar here to the House-passed version than to the Senate-passed version. However, one important change was made. The House-passed version allowed any parties who were not swap dealers or MSPs, who were using the transaction to hedge commercial risk, and who notified the relevant agency properly to qualify for the exemption.[27] The final version narrowed the availability of the exemption to parties who were not financial entities, as defined above, and the definition of financial entities arguably includes more parties than only those who are not dealers or MSPs. Furthermore, the definition of "financial entity" in the act appears to be more narrow than the definition of "financial entity" contained in the Senate-passed version, because the Senate bill's definition would have included "a person that is registered or required to be registered with the Commission."[28] Moreover, the act allows regulators to exclude depository institutions, farm credit institutions, and credit unions with $10 billion or less in assets from the definition of "financial entity." Thus, the final definition of end-users represented by the act appears to fall somewhere between the House and Senate definitions in the number of entities that may qualify.

The application of the clearing exemption provided by Sections 723 and 763 of the Dodd-Frank Act is at the discretion of the counterparty that qualifies for the exemption. Eligible counterparties may elect to clear the transaction, and may choose which derivatives clearing organization or clearing agency shall clear the transaction. Under the act, eligible counterparties may also use an affiliate ("including affiliate entities predominantly engaged in providing financing for the purchase of the merchandise or manufactured goods of the person") to engage in swaps or security-based swaps under the condition that the affiliate "act on behalf of the person [qualifying for the exemption] and as an agent, uses the swap to hedge or mitigate the commercial risk of the person or other affiliate of the person that is not a financial entity."[29] The CFTC and SEC may also prescribe rules to prevent abuse of this exception to the clearing requirement.

Prevention of Evasion

The CFTC and SEC are required by the Dodd-Frank Act to promulgate rules the commissions determined to be necessary to "prevent evasions of the mandatory clearing requirements under this Act." However, this rulemaking authority, while broad, carries additional nuance described below.

As noted above, the statutory scheme of Dodd-Frank creates two ways in which a swap or security-based swap may become subject to the clearing requirement. In one scenario, derivatives clearing organizations and clearing agencies submit the swaps and security-based swaps they intend to clear to the CFTC or SEC and the agency determines whether to apply the clearing requirement to the transactions. In the other scenario, the CFTC and SEC are required to engage in an ongoing independent review of swaps and security-based swaps under their jurisdiction to determine whether those transactions should be subject to the mandatory clearing requirement. It is thus possible that the CFTC and SEC could identify swaps and security-based swaps that "would otherwise be subject to the clearing requirement" but for the fact that no derivatives clearing organization or clearing agency accepts them for clearing.

In that event, the relevant agency (CFTC for swaps, and SEC for security-based swaps) is required to investigate the relevant facts and circumstances, issue a public report of its investigation, and "take such actions as the Commission determines to be necessary and in the public interest, which may include requiring the retaining of adequate margin or capital by parties to the swap [or security-based swap], group, category, type, or class of swaps [or security-based swaps]."[30] However, neither the CFTC nor the SEC may "adopt rules requiring a derivatives clearing organization [or clearing agency] to list for clearing a swap, group, category, type, or class of swaps if the clearing of the swap, group, category, type, or class of swaps would threaten the financial integrity of the derivatives organization."[31] Eliminated from the Dodd-Frank Act was a requirement in the Senate-passed version that the agencies exempt swaps and security-based swaps from the clearing and exchange trading requirements if no derivatives clearing organization or clearing agency accepts the transactions for clearing.[32] The removal of this proposed exemption from the act may grant the agencies more flexibility in determining how to treat transactions they identify for clearing, but that are not yet accepted for clearing by any derivatives clearing organization or clearing agency as the agencies begin to implement the clearing requirement of the Dodd-Frank Act.

Reporting of Swaps and Security-Based Swaps

Swaps must be reported to registered swap data repositories or the CFTC.[33] Security-based swaps must be reported to registered security-based swap data repositories or to the SEC.[34] The Dodd-Frank Act requires all swaps to be reported.[35] Swaps and security-based swaps entered into prior to the date of the enactment of Dodd-Frank Act are exempt from the clearing requirement if they are reported in accordance with the act. Swaps and security-based swaps entered into after the enactment of the Dodd-Frank Act, but prior to the imposition of the clearing requirement, are exempt from the clearing requirement if they are reported in accordance with the act.

Section 727 of Dodd-Frank outlines the public availability of swap transaction data.[36] The CFTC is required to promulgate rules regarding the public availability of such data. Swaps that are subject to the clearing requirement, and swaps that are not subject to the clearing requirement, but are nonetheless cleared at registered derivatives clearing organizations, must have real-time reporting for such transactions. Real-time reporting means to report data relating to a swap transaction, including price and volume, as soon as technologically practicable after the time at which the swap transaction has been executed. For swaps that are not cleared and are reported pursuant to subsection (h)(6) (requiring reporting prior to the implementation of the clearing requirement), real-time reporting is required in a manner that does not disclose the business transactions and market positions of any person. Lastly, for swaps that are determined to be required to be cleared under subsection (h)(2) (outlining the two ways, discussed above, in which swaps may become subject to the clearing requirement), but are not cleared, real-time public reporting is required as well. There is no parallel requirement in the act for security-based swaps, presumably because national securities exchanges upon which these transactions will be executed already provide comparable reporting.[37]

The act also creates reporting obligations for uncleared swaps and security-based swaps (including swaps and security-based swaps that qualify for the end-user exemption).[38] Swaps entered into prior to the enactment of the act will be subject to reporting and recordkeeping requirements for uncleared swaps and security-based swaps.[39] The purpose of these requirements, presumably, is to give the relevant commissions access to a more complete picture of the derivatives market, even for swaps that are not required to be cleared.

Major Swap Participant Definition

A basic theme in Dodd-Frank is that systemically important financial institutions should maintain capital cushions above and beyond what specific regulations require in order to compensate for the risk that their failure would pose to the financial system and the economy. In addition to the margin requirements that apply to individual derivatives contracts, major participants in derivatives markets will become subject to prudential regulation in Title VII. Two categories of regulated market participants are enumerated: swap dealers and major swap participants (together with the security-based swap equivalents).

Since the OTC dealer market is highly concentrated, the proposal that swap dealers be subject to additional prudential regulation was not controversial. Only a few dozen of the largest financial institutions will be affected. The question of how many firms should be included in the definition of major swap participant (MSP), however, was contentious. How many non-dealer and non-bank firms should become subject to prudential regulation?

Several MSP definitions were considered in the House; the version of H.R. 4173 that passed the House in December 2009 defined an MSP as a non-dealer holding a "substantial net position" in swaps, excluding positions held to hedge commercial risk, or whose counterparties would suffer "significant credit losses" in the event of an MSP default.[40] Neither "substantial net position," "significant loss," nor "commercial risk" was defined in the bill. However, the bill provided guidance to regulators: the first two terms were linked to "systemically important entities" that can "significantly impact the financial system through counterparty credit risk."

The MSP definition in the bill that passed the House in December 2009 sought to prevent regulators from defining the key terms ("substantial position, "significant loss," etc.) in a way that imposed prudential regulation on most firms that used derivatives to hedge risk. In addition, MSPs are required to clear their swap contracts, and the cost of clearing was regarded as burdensome for end-users. Under the House definition, it seemed plausible that relatively few firms would be defined as MSPs—Fannie Mae and Freddie Mac, a few large non-dealer banks and insurance companies, and perhaps a few large hedge funds.

There was an opposite concern: that if the end-user exemption were too broad, and the MSP definition too narrow, significant volumes of OTC trading might escape the new regulatory scheme. Figure 2 above suggests that if mandatory clearing were applied only to inter-dealer trades, two-thirds of the market would be unaffected. Nearly 60% of OTC contracts were between a dealer and another financial institution: how many of these would be covered? While less than 10% of transactions involved nonfinancial counterparties, was it possible that risky trading activities could migrate from banks to nonfinancial firms if the exemption for hedging commercial risk were not in some way circumscribed?

Two versions of the MSP definition were considered in the Senate. The Banking Committee approved S. 3217 on April 15, 2010, including an MSP definition without the references to systemic importance that appeared in the House bill.[41] In other words, the regulators were given wide discretion to designate as MSPs firms that were not systemically important. The Senate Agriculture Committee produced another MSP definition, which was included in the bill that passed the Senate. It included "systemically significant" language generally similar to the House's, but added new prongs to the definition: an MSP would be any financial institution with a substantial position in any major swap category, or any financial entity that was highly leveraged.[42] This approach (together with changes to the clearing exemption limiting the exemption to nonfinancial entities) appeared likely to capture many swaps between dealers and other financial institutions, which make up more than half of the swap market.

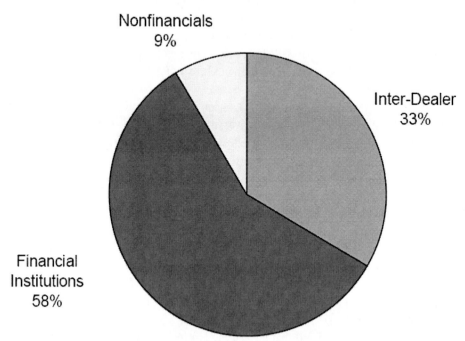

Source: Bank for International Settlements, *Regular OTC Derivatives Market Statistics*, May 2010.
Notes: Includes interest rate, foreign exchange, equity, and credit default swaps.

Figure 2. OTC Derivatives Contracts by Type of Counterparty; (Based on notional value of contracts as of December 2009).

Eliminating the clearing exemption for financial entities and bringing more financial firms under the MSP definition, as the Senate-passed bill did, had the virtue of bringing nearly all of the swaps trading under the new regulatory regime—the 33% of trades between dealers and the 58% between dealers and other financial institutions. This approach did raise questions of equity, that is, should a small community bank or credit union be subject to more stringent regulation than a giant nonfinancial corporation with a much greater volume of swaps outstanding?

The final version of the legislation made several changes to the MSP definition and the clearing requirement. The "highly leveraged" prong of the MSP definition was amended to clarify that it did not apply to regulated depository institutions, which are normally highly leveraged. In addition, as noted above, regulators were given discretion to exempt certain financial institutions with less than $10 billion in assets from the mandatory clearing requirement. The precise number of firms that are named MSPs (and the proportion of swaps that is ultimately cleared) depends on the SEC and CFTC rulemakings required by the act.

SECTION 716—PROHIBITION ON FEDERAL ASSISTANCE TO SWAPS ENTITIES

Section 716 originated in the Senate Agriculture Committee and was included in the bill that passed the Senate in May 2010. The section prohibited federal assistance, defined as the use of any funds to loan money to, buy the securities or other assets of, or to enter into "any assistance arrangement" with, a "swaps entity." Swaps entities included swap dealers and major swap participants (and the equivalents in security-based swaps), securities and futures exchanges, SEFs, and clearing organizations registered with the CFTC, the SEC, or any other federal or state agency.

The intent of the provision was to ensure that taxpayers would not have to bail out financial institutions engaged in risky derivatives trading. Such activity was deemed too risky to be under the federal safety net that covers insured depository institutions. Agriculture Committee Chairwoman Lincoln explained it this way:

> This provision seeks to ensure that banks get back to the business of banking. Under our current system, there are a handful of big banks that are simply no longer acting like banks.... In my view, banks were never intended to perform these [derivatives] activities, which have been the single largest factor to these institutions growing so large that taxpayers had no choice but to bail them out in order to prevent total economic ruin.[43]

Supporters of the original version of Section 716 described it as an appropriate means to compel banks to spin off their swap dealings, or to "push them out" into separately capitalized affiliates. Opponents of the measure argued that the definitions of federal assistance and swaps entity were so broadly drafted that there might be unanticipated consequences. For example, if Citigroup sold off its swap dealer operations, it would still have hundreds of billions of loans and other risky assets on its balance sheet, which it would need to hedge with interest rate swaps and other derivatives. This hedging activity would likely put the bank into the major swap participant category, and thus foreclose access to the discount window, FDIC insurance, and other features of the safety net. Similarly, if the Federal Reserve were supplying liquidity to the financial system during a future crisis, would it be prudent to deny such support to clearinghouses which represent concentrations of risk?

The conference committee adopted a modified version of Section 716, which narrowed the definitions of swaps entity and permitted banks to act as swap dealers under some circumstances. In the final legislation, exchanges, SEFs, and clearing organizations are not swaps entities. In addition, the term "swaps entity" does not include a major swap participant or major security-based swap participant that is an insured depository institution.

The final version clarifies that the prohibition on aid does not prevent a bank from creating an affiliate that is a swaps entity, provided that the affiliate complies with sections 23A and 23B of the Federal Reserve Act and other requirements of the Fed, the SEC, and the CFTC. Moreover, the bank itself may continue to act as a swaps dealer for contracts involving rates or reference assets that are permissible for investment by a national bank. This means that banks can continue as dealers in swaps linked to interest rates, currencies, government securities, and precious metals, but not other commodities or equities. Credit default swaps are treated as a special category: banks may deal in them if they are cleared by a derivatives clearing organization regulated by the SEC or CFTC. Dealing in uncleared credit default swaps, however, is not deemed to be a permissible bank activity.

Finally, Section 716 mandates that no taxpayer funds may be used to prevent the liquidation of a swaps entity. Any funds expended in such a liquidation proceeding, and not covered by the swaps entity's assets, may be recouped through assessments on the financial sector.

ENHANCED CFTC AUTHORITY OVER COMMODITIES MARKETS

In 2008, as energy and grain prices set new records, speculators in derivatives were blamed by some for price volatility and for price levels that many observers believed were not justified by the underlying economic fundamentals. Although the CFTC maintained that markets were functioning normally and that the price discovery process was not being distorted, the 110th Congress considered legislation intended to insulate commodity prices from the impact of excessive speculation and manipulation. Title VII includes a number of the specific provisions that appeared in those bills:

- **Margin**. The CFTC is given authority to set margin levels on the futures exchanges. (Previously, CFTC could change margins only in emergencies.) *Section 736.*
- **Position Limits**. The CFTC is directed to establish position limits for both swaps and futures. (CFTC has long had authority to set limits on the size of futures positions, but has generally delegated this function to the exchanges.) *Section 737.*
- **Anti-manipulation Authority**. New prohibitions against manipulation by means of false reporting or false information. *Section 753.*
- **Foreign Boards of Trade**. Foreign futures exchanges offering direct electronic access to their trading systems to U.S. persons must maintain rules regarding manipulation and excessive speculation comparable to those in U.S. law and regulation and must provide the CFTC with full market information.

Beyond these specific provisions, the increased transparency Dodd-Frank will bring to the OTC markets responds to a frequently heard criticism of the regulatory regime in 2008: that regulators could not be sure that price manipulation was not occurring because they lacked information about the volume of OTC trades and the identities of the big players in that market.

ACKNOWLEDGMENTS

Parts of the introductory material in this report are adapted from CRS Report R40965, *Key Issues in Derivatives Reform,* by Rena S. Miller.

End Notes

[1] For a description of the mechanics of these contracts, see CRS Report R40646, *Derivatives Regulation in the 111*[th] *Congress*, by Mark Jickling and Rena S. Miller.

[2] See Bank for International Settlements (BIS), Table 23B, for year 2000 turnover for derivative financial instruments traded on organized exchanges, available at http://www.bis.org/publ/qtrpdf/r_qa0206.pdf. For December 2008 figures for derivatives traded on organized exchanges, see BIS Quarterly Review, September 2009, International Banking and Financial Market Developments, available at http://www.bis.org/publ/qtrpdf/r_qt0909.pdf.

[3] See Bank for International Settlements (BIS), Statistical Annex, Table 19, December, 2000 figure for notional amount of total OTC contracts, available at http://www.bis.org/publ/qtrpdf/r_qa0206.pdf. See Bank for International Settlements (BIS), BIS Quarterly Review, September 2009, Statistical Annex, Table 19, for December 2008 figure for notional amount of total OTC contracts, available at http://www.bis.org/publ/qtrpdf/r_qa0909.pdf.

[4] Federal Reserve, *Flow of Funds Accounts of the United States*, September 17, 2009, accessible at http://www.federalreserve.gov/releases/z1/Current/z1r-1.pdf.

[5] Also referred to as a central counterparty or as a derivatives clearing organization (DCO).

[6] See CRS Report R41350, *The Dodd-Frank Wall Street Reform and Consumer Protection Act: Issues and Summary*, coordinated by Baird Webel.

[7] The credit events that trigger credit swap payments may include ratings downgrades, debt restructuring, late payment of interest or principal, as well as default.

[8] For an account of this process, see Office of the Special Inspector General for the Troubled Asset Relief Program ("SIGTARP"), *Factors Affecting Efforts to Limit Payments to AIG Counterparties*, November 17, 2009.

[9] Section 723 of the Dodd-Frank Act (to be codified at 7 U.S.C. §2).

[10] Section 763(a) of the Dodd-Frank Act (to be codified at 15 U.S.C. § 78a *et seq.*).

[11] Section 723(a)(3) of the Dodd-Frank Act (to be codified at 7 U.S.C. §2(h)(1)) (swaps); Section 763(a) of the Dodd-Frank Act (to be codified at 15 U.S.C. § 78a *et seq.*)(security-based swaps).

[12] Section 723(a)(3) of the Dodd-Frank Act (to be codified at 7 U.S.C. §2(h)(2)) (swaps); Section 763(a) of the Dodd-Frank Act (to be codified at 15 U.S.C. § 78a *et seq.*)(security-based swaps).

[13] Sections 3103 and 3203 of H.R. 4173 (as passed by the House).

[14] Sections 723(a) and 763 of H.R. 4173 (as passed by the Senate).

[15] Rules for the registration and regulation of derivatives clearing organizations are enacted by Section 725 of the Dodd-Frank Act (to be codified at 7 U.S.C. §7a-1).

[16] Rules for the registration and regulation of clearing agencies were enacted by Section 763(b) of the Dodd-Frank Act (to be codified at 15 U.S.C. §78a-1).

[17] Section 723(a)(3) of the Dodd-Frank Act (to be codified at 7 U.S.C. §2(h)) (swaps); Section 763(a) of the Dodd-Frank Act (to be codified at 15 U.S.C. § 78a *et seq.*)(security-based swaps). Similar considerations were mandated by the Senate passed version of the bill, but those considerations were to be applied to the agencies' rulemakings to identify other classes of transactions that should be subject to the clearing requirement that had not been submitted to the agency. Section 723(a) of H.R. 4173 (as passed by the Senate).

[18] Section 723(a)(3) of the Dodd-Frank Act (to be codified at 7 U.S.C. §2(h)(3)) (swaps); Section 763(a) of the Dodd-Frank Act (to be codified at 15 U.S.C. § 78a *et seq.*)(security-based swaps).

[19] Section 723(a)(3) of the Dodd-Frank Act (to be codified at 7 U.S.C. §2(h)(8)); Section 763(a) of the Dodd-Frank Act (to be codified at 15 U.S.C. § 78a *et seq.*)(security-based swaps).

[20] Section 723 of the Dodd-Frank Act (new section 5h(e) of the Commodity Exchange Act to be codified after 7 U.S.C. §7b-2).

[21] Only eligible contract participants will be able to trade on SEFs and SBSEFs.

[22] Section 720 of S. 3217, as reported by the Senate Committee on Banking, Housing, and Urban Affairs, Apr. 15, 2010.

[23] Section 720 of the Dodd-Frank Act, P.L. 111-203.

[24] Section 723(a)(3) of the Dodd-Frank Act (to be codified at 7 U.S.C. §2(h)(7)) (swaps); Section 763(a) of the Dodd-Frank Act (to be codified at 15 U.S.C. § 78a *et seq.*)(security-based swaps).

[25] *Id.*

[26] The CFTC and SEC must consider whether to exempt small banks, savings associations, farm credit systems institutions, and credit unions from the definition of financial entity in this section. Such a determination could make the end-user exemption available to these entities. Section 723(a)(3) of the Dodd-Frank Act (to be

codified at 7 U.S.C. §2(h)(7)) (swaps); Section 763(a) of the Dodd-Frank Act (to be codified at 15 U.S.C. § 78a *et seq.*)(security-based swaps). (page 822 and 1060).

[27] Sections 3103 and 3203 of H.R. 4173 (as passed by the House).

[28] Sections 723(a) and 763 of H.R. 4173 (as passed by the Senate).

[29] Affiliates of persons qualifying for the end user exception are not eligible to engage in swaps or security-based swaps on the behalf of qualifying persons if the affiliate is a swap dealer, security-based swap dealer, major swap participant, major security-based swap participant, companies that would be investment companies under section 3 of the Investment Company Act of 1940 but for the exceptions provided in subparagraphs (c)(1) or (c)(7) of that section (15 U.S.C. §80a-3), a commodity pool, or a bank holding company with over $50,000,000,000 in consolidated assets. Section 723(a)(3) of the Dodd-Frank Act (to be codified at 7 U.S.C. §2(h)(3)) (swaps); Section 763(a) of the Dodd-Frank Act (to be codified at 15 U.S.C. § 78a *et seq.*)(security-based swaps).

[30] Section 723(a)(3) of the Dodd-Frank Act (to be codified at 7 U.S.C. §2(h)(4)) (swaps); Section 763(a) of the Dodd-Frank Act (to be codified at 15 U.S.C. § 78a *et seq.*)(security-based swaps).

[31] Section 723(a)(3) of the Dodd-Frank Act (to be codified at 7 U.S.C. §2(h)(4)) (swaps); Section 763(a) of the Dodd-Frank Act (to be codified at 15 U.S.C. § 78a *et seq.*)(security-based swaps).

[32] Sections 723(a) and 763 of H.R. 4173 (as passed by the Senate).

[33] Section 723(a)(3) of the Dodd-Frank Act (to be codified at 7 U.S.C. §2(h)(5)).

[34] Section 763(a) of the Dodd-Frank Act (to be codified at 15 U.S.C. § 78a *et seq.*).

[35] Sections 3103 and 3203 of H.R. 4173 (as passed); Sections 723(a) and 763 of S. 3217 (as passed).

[36] Section 725 of the Dodd-Frank Act (to be codified at 7 U.S.C. §2(a)).

[37] *See* 15 U.S.C. § 78f.

[38] Section 729 of the Dodd-Frank Act (to be codified at 7 U.S.C. §6o-1) and Section 766 of the Dodd-Frank Act (to be codified at 15 U.S.C. §78a *et seq.*).

[39] *Id.*

[40] Section 3101 of H.R. 4173, as passed the House of Representatives, Dec. 11, 2009.

[41] Section 711 of S. 3217, as reported by the Senate Committee on Banking, Housing, and Urban Affairs, Apr. 15, 2010.

[42] This was not a "net" position, and applied to individual categories of swaps, as opposed to the institutions aggregate swaps book.

[43] Remarks of Senator Blanche Lincoln, *Congressional Record*, May 5, 2010, p. S3140.

In: The Dodd-Frank Wall Street Reform…
Editors: Nathan L. Morris and Philip O. Price

ISBN: 978-1-61324-101-1
© 2011 Nova Science Publishers, Inc.

Chapter 8

DODD-FRANK ACT, TITLE VIII: SUPERVISION OF PAYMENT, CLEARING, AND SETTLEMENT ACTIVITIES[*]

Donna Nordenberg and Marc Labonte

SUMMARY

The U.S. financial system processes millions of transactions each day representing daily transfers of trillions of dollars, securities, and other assets to facilitate purchases and payments. Concerns had been raised, even prior to the recent financial crisis, about the vulnerability of the U.S. financial system to infrastructure failure. These concerns about the "plumbing" of the financial system were heightened following the market disruptions of the recent crisis.

The financial market infrastructure consists of the various systems, networks, and technological processes that are necessary for conducting and completing financial transactions. Title VIII of the Dodd-Frank Act, P.L. 111-203, the *Payment, Clearing, and Settlement Supervision Act of 2010*, introduces the term "financial market utility" (FMU or utility) for those multilateral systems that transfer, clear, or settle payments, securities, or other financial transactions among financial institutions (FI) or between an FMU and a financial institution. Utilities and FIs transfer funds and settle accounts with other financial institutions to facilitate normal day-to-day transactions occurring in the U.S. economy. Those transfers include payroll and mortgage payments, foreign currency exchanges, purchases of U.S. treasury bonds and corporate securities, and derivatives trades. Further, financial institutions engage in commercial paper and securities repurchase agreements (repo) markets that contribute to liquidity in the U.S. economy. In the United States, some of the key payment, clearing, and settlement (PCS) systems are operated by the Federal Reserve, and other systems are operated by private sector organizations.

In Title VIII of the Dodd-Frank Act, which was enacted on July 21, 2010, Congress added a new regulatory framework for the FMUs and PCS activities (of FIs) designated by the Financial Stability Oversight Council as systemically important. Title VIII

---

[*] This is an edited, reformatted and augmented version of a Congressional Research Services publication, dated December 10, 2010.

expands the Federal Reserve's role, in coordination with those of other prudential regulators, in the supervision, examination, and rule enforcement with respect to those FMUs and PCS activities of financial institutions. Additionally, FMUs may borrow from the discount window of the Federal Reserve in certain unusual and exigent circumstances.

Although Title VIII primarily affects the scope of regulatory powers, certain provisions directly affect a utility's business operations. For example, Title VIII allows FMUs to maintain accounts at a Federal Reserve Bank and requires FMUs to provide governmental supervisors with advance notice of changes to their rules or operations. In addition, Title VII of the Dodd-Frank Act imposes requirements that will significantly affect the business of clearinghouses in the over-the-counter (OTC) derivatives (swaps) market. In Title VII, the *Wall Street Transparency and Accountability Act of 2010*, Congress established a new regulatory framework for the previously unregulated market of swap transactions. By requiring clearing of certain swap transactions through central counterparties (CCPs or clearinghouses), Title VII is expected to increase the volume of transactions processed by clearing systems subject to Title VIII.

This report outlines the changes to the supervision of key market infrastructure that are embodied in the Dodd-Frank Act. It is intended to be used as a reference document for persons interested in different parts of the financial system "plumbing," and how these systems are overseen and regulated following the recent enactment of the Dodd-Frank Act. It will not be updated.

LIST OF ACRONYMS OF SELECTED TERMS

ACH	Automated clearing house
ANPR	Advance Notice of Proposed Rulemaking
BIS	Bank for International Settlements
CA	Clearing agency
CCP	Central counterparty
CDS	Credit default swap
CFTC	U.S. Commodity Futures Trading Commission
Council	Financial Stability Oversight Council
CPSS	Committee on Payment and Settlement Systems
DCO	Derivatives clearing organization
Dodd-Frank Act	Dodd-Frank Wall Street Reform and Consumer Protection Act
EFT	Electronic funds transfer
FFIEC	Federal Financial Institutions Examination Council
Fed	Federal Reserve System
FI	Financial institution
FMU	Financial market utility
FSA	United Kingdom Financial Services Authority
IOSCO	International Organization of Securities Commissions
MOU	Memorandum of Understanding
OTC	Over-the-counter
PCS	Payment, clearing, and settlement
PSR Policy	Federal Reserve Policy on Payment System Risk
Repo	Repurchase agreement

RTGS	Real-time gross settlement
SEC	U.S. Securities and Exchange Commission
Title VII	Wall Street Transparency and Accountability Act of 2010
Title VIII	Payment, Clearing, and Settlement Supervision Act of 2010

INTRODUCTION

On July 21, 2010, Title VIII of the Dodd-Frank Act,[1] the *Payment, Clearing, and Settlement Supervision Act of 2010*, became effective upon enactment. Title VIII authorizes the Federal Reserve, in coordination with other federal agencies, to supervise and regulate the infrastructure that enables financial intermediaries to process and complete financial transactions.

Payment, clearing, and settlement (PCS) activities facilitate a variety of financial transactions such as transferring payments for and completing retail purchases, foreign exchange transactions, securities transactions, and derivatives trades. Prior to the Dodd-Frank Act, various federal regulatory authorities had oversight responsibilities for certain systems or entities engaged in processing those financial transactions. Some key systems in the United States have been operated by the Federal Reserve Banks and others by the private sector. PCS systems serve a critical role in the financial services sector and the broader economy. In the United States, payment and settlement systems on a typical business day settle transactions valued at over $13 trillion, according to a 2008 report by the U.S. Department of the Treasury.[2]

Events during 2008, including the failures of Lehman Brothers and Washington Mutual in September 2008 and the subsequent rescue of AIG drew attention to the functioning of the U.S. financial system during periods of stress. The interconnectedness of large financial intermediaries deemed "too-big-to-fail" heightened concerns about systemic risk, which can be understood as the failure of one firm leading to system-wide disruptions. The channel through which systemic risk can spread, as discussed in this report, is a disruption such as the failure of a "too-big-to-fail" institution cascading through PCS systems or activities.

The failure of Lehman Brothers seriously shocked domestic and global financial markets and severely strained interbank lending markets. Many investors were unable to access their funds held by Lehman and are pursuing those funds through bankruptcy proceedings in multiple jurisdictions.[3] Lehman Brothers' default on its commercial paper (similar to short-term loans) caused a severe disruption in that market, which prevented many corporate issuers from rolling over their commercial paper debt as it matured.[4]

AIG, a major insurance company, experienced a crisis stemming from a subsidiary that was a leading underwriter of credit default swaps (CDS), a type of over-the-counter derivative.[5] CDS provide protection to buyers against credit events such as an issuer's default on corporate debt obligations and structured securities. CDS had been traded bilaterally between institutions through an over-the-counter market system that regulatory authorities had criticized for its inefficiencies and lack of transparency. The Federal Reserve Bank of New York undertook efforts to encourage industry participants to voluntarily improve the infrastructure of the OTC derivatives market in recent years. In 2006, Alan Greenspan, then-Chairman of the Federal Reserve, reportedly said that he was appalled that people were relying on scraps of paper to record transactions, a practice which some blamed for causing a backlog of unconfirmed contracts.[6]

Title VIII reflects recommendations by the previous and current administrations to give the Federal Reserve explicit statutory oversight authority with respect to elements of the financial infrastructure in the United States. Title VIII introduces the term "financial market utility" (FMU or utility) for those multilateral systems that transfer, clear, or settle payments, securities, or other financial transactions among financial institutions (FI) or between a FMU and a financial institution. Title VIII addresses the federal regulatory oversight of systemically important payment, clearing, and settlement (PCS) systems and PCS activities of financial institutions that facilitate various financial transactions. Financial transactions processed daily in the U.S. economy include payment transfers ranging from small-dollar retail purchase transactions to large-value purchases of securities; clearing transactions for derivatives trading; and securities settlement.

Title VIII primarily addresses the regulatory framework rather than affecting the flows of funds through existing payment and settlement systems. With regard to clearing, however, there are some changes as Title VII of the Dodd-Frank Act, the *Wall Street Transparency and Accountability Act of 2010*, directly affects the business of clearing of OTC derivatives instruments known as swaps. In Title VII, Congress established new regulatory requirements specifically applicable to the derivatives clearing systems and activities for OTC swap transactions.[7]

Title VIII regulatory powers apply specifically to those financial market utilities and PCS activities (of financial institutions) that are systemically important. Prior to the enactment of Title VIII, the Federal Reserve derived its oversight responsibilities for payment and settlement systems from a range of statutory responsibilities for monetary policy, banking supervision, lender of last resort, and provision of payment and settlement services.[8]

Some Representatives opposed Title VIII and struck the title governing PCS supervision from the financial reform bill that the House of Representatives passed in December 2009. Concerns held by some opponents of the title may have included a sense that the U.S. financial infrastructure was adequately supervised, or that the title might have given too much discretionary authority to the Federal Reserve. Other reservations may have included the view that Title VIII was unnecessary in light of the Federal Reserve's efforts to encourage firms to voluntarily strengthen infrastructure procedures in various markets, and the absence of a PCS-related breakdown in September 2008.

This report begins by introducing the basics of PCS systems and activities and presents the major systems operating in the United States. The report then describes the different risks, including systemic risk, that are commonly associated with PCS systems and activities. The next part of the report discusses the oversight authority of the FMU and FI regulators that was in place prior to the enactment of the Dodd-Frank Act, after which the report summarizes the changes made by Title VIII, including the new regulatory oversight authority of the Fed. The final part of the report addresses implementation of Title VIII by relevant agencies and the impact of Title VIII on FMUs and FIs.

BASICS OF PAYMENT, CLEARING, AND SETTLEMENT

Title VIII expands Federal Reserve authority with respect to firms conducting one or more of the three named activities, payment, clearing, or settlement, where the Financial Stability Oversight Council (Council) designates the firms or the activities (when conducted by financial institutions) as systemically important. The existing infrastructure in the United States for those activities consists of systems operated by the Federal Reserve through the Federal Reserve Banks, and by the private sector. This section describes the definitions and functions of these systems and activities that may partly overlap.

The following types of systems and activities are covered by Title VIII:

- payment systems, which transfer funds electronically from one institution to another;
- clearing systems (or clearinghouses), which in the derivatives market often transfer credit risk to a central counterparty (CCP) (clearinghouse) from each counterparty to a trade; and
- settlement systems, which complete transactions such as securities trades.

Payment Systems

In general terms, a payment system consists of the means for transferring money between suppliers and users of funds through the use of cash substitutes such as checks, drafts, and electronic funds transfers. The Committee on Payment and Settlement Systems (CPSS), consisting of representatives from several international regulatory authorities, has developed generally accepted definitions of standard payment system terminology.[9] As defined by the CPSS, a payment system is a system that consists of a set of instruments, banking procedures, and, typically, interbank funds transfer systems that ensure the circulation of money.

In the United States, the Federal Reserve Banks and the private sector operate payment systems that process retail or wholesale transactions.[10] Retail payment systems facilitate a consumer's ability to purchase goods and services, pay bills, obtain cash through withdrawals and advances, and make person-to-person payments. Retail payments tend to generate a large number of transactions that have relatively small value per transaction and are processed through electronic funds transfer systems, including automated clearing house (ACH) transactions and debit and credit card transactions at the point of sale.[11]

The ACH is an electronic funds transfer (EFT) system that processes credit and debit transactions such as direct deposit payroll and consumer bill payments. ACH is the primary EFT system used by federal governmental agencies to make payments, according to the Financial Management Service (FMS), a bureau of the United States Department of the Treasury.[12] Providers of ACH services include the Federal Reserve Banks through the FedACH Service and The Electronic Payments Network, which is the only private-sector ACH operator in the United States.[13] Rules governing the ACH system for participating financial institutions are established by NACHA – The Electronic Payments Association, a trade association,[14] which oversees the ACH Network, and by the Federal Reserve.[15] NACHA reports that more than 18.7 billion ACH payments were made in 2009.[16]

Wholesale payment systems generally support domestic and international commercial activities and financial market related activities. Large-value, wholesale funds transfer systems are used for purchasing, selling, or financing securities transactions; disbursing or repaying loans; settling real estate transactions; and making large-value, time-critical payments (e.g., settling interbank purchases, Federal funds sales, or foreign exchange transactions).[17] Wholesale payments tend to have a large per-transaction value and a relatively small number of transactions generated daily and are processed through payment systems such as the Fedwire Funds Service (Fedwire)[18] and The Clearing House Interbank Payments System (CHIPS).[19] Wholesale payment systems also provide final clearing and settlement for a variety of retail payment systems at the end of the business day. Financial institutions use intra-bank systems to initiate, process, and transmit large-value payment orders internally and to interface with Fedwire and CHIPS.

Clearing Systems

Clearing systems conduct various activities related to payment, currency, securities or derivatives transactions. The CPSS defines a clearing system as a set of procedures whereby financial institutions present and exchange data or documents relating to funds or securities transfers to other financial institutions at a single location (clearing house). The procedures often include a mechanism to facilitate the establishment of net positions of participant obligations for settlement, a process known as netting.[20] A clearing house is a central location or central processing mechanism through which financial institutions agree to exchange payment instructions or other financial obligations such as securities. The term clearing, which is the process of transmitting, reconciling and possibly confirming payment orders or security transfer instructions prior to settlement, sometimes is used imprecisely to include settlement.

Two of the major types of clearing houses in the United States process securities and derivatives transactions. For securities transactions, a clearing corporation or a depository must register with the Securities and Exchange Commission (SEC) as a clearing agency (CA).[21] Clearing corporations clear member transactions, enable automated settlement of those trades, and often act as intermediaries in making settlements. A clearing corporation guarantees the completion of all transactions and interposes itself as a party to both sides of a transaction.[22]

Depositories maintain ownership records of securities on the books of the depository, hold securities certificates (physical securities are held in vaults), and make securities deliveries for settlements requiring delivery. Currently, the Depository Trust Company (DTC) is the primary U.S. securities depository.[23] The DTC is a subsidiary of The Depository & Clearing Corporation (DTCC),[24] which also operates the Fixed Income Clearing Corporation (FICC). FICC clears government and mortgage-backed securities through its clearing corporation divisions known as the Government Securities Division (GSD) and the Mortgage-Backed Securities Division (MBSD). In addition, the National Securities Clearing Corporation (NSCC), which is a subsidiary of DTCC, is a registered clearing corporation regulated by the SEC that provides clearing and settlement services for corporate and municipal securities.

In the futures and options markets, a clearing house, known as a derivatives clearing organization (DCO), must register with the Commodity Futures Trading Commission (CFTC) to provide clearing services with respect to futures contracts and options on those futures contracts traded on a designated contract market and swap transactions traded over-the-counter.[25] A DCO enables the parties to a derivatives transaction (counterparties) to transfer credit risk to the clearing house, for example, through novation. Novation occurs when a single derivatives contract between two counterparties becomes two separate contracts: one between the clearing house and each counterparty. Currently, there are 19 DCOs registered with the CFTC.[26]

Settlement Systems

The CPSS defines settlement, in part, as the completion of a transaction wherein the seller transfers securities or financial instruments to the buyer and the buyer transfers money to the seller. A settlement may be final or provisional. A settlement system is used to facilitate the settlement of transfers of funds or financial instruments. In a real-time gross settlement system (RTGS), processing and settling occur on an order-by-order basis in real time instead of through netting of transaction positions. A securities settlement system is a particular kind of settlement system that consists of the full set of institutional arrangements for confirmation, clearance and settlement of securities trades and safekeeping of securities.

In the United States, the Federal Reserve Banks and the private sector operate different settlement systems for securities transactions. Securities processing within financial institutions and the major markets accounts for the majority of large-value payments.[27]

The major securities markets in the United States include the markets for government securities, corporate equities and bonds, money market instruments, and municipal bonds. Those instruments are generally traded through organized exchanges or through over-the-counter dealer markets.[28] Depository institutions play several important roles in securities clearing and settlement. In addition to participating in clearing and settlement transactions, depository institutions act as custodians, issuing and paying agents, and settling banks for their customers.

The U.S. government securities market includes all primary and secondary market transactions in securities issued by the U.S. Treasury, certain federal government agencies, and federal government-sponsored enterprises.[29] Trading in government securities is conducted over-the-counter between brokers, dealers, and investors, which means that parties trade on a bilateral basis with one another rather than on an organized exchange. The Federal Reserve operates a book-entry system known as the National Book-Entry System, or the Fedwire Securities Service, through which nearly all U.S. government securities are issued and transferred.[30] The Fixed Income Clearing Corporation (FICC) also supports the selling and trading of U.S. government securities.

Corporations and municipal governments also issue various types of securities, including corporate equities and bonds, commercial paper,[31] and municipal bonds. Various securities are traded on established U.S. exchanges, including the New York Stock Exchange, the American Stock Exchange, and the NASDAQ system, and on over-the-counter markets. The National Securities Clearing Corporation (NSCC) provides clearing, settlement, and other services for virtually all broker-to-broker trades involving equities, corporate and municipal debt, and certain other instruments traded on over-the-counter markets and exchanges.[32]

MAJOR PAYMENT, CLEARING, AND SETTLEMENT SYSTEMS IN THE UNITED STATES

The Federal Reserve and the private sector operate the systems that constitute the infrastructure for the processing and completion of financial transactions in the United States. Listed below are some of the major systems currently operating in the United States. Additional information regarding selected systems, including recent volume levels, is set forth in an Appendix to this report. In the future, new and evolving types of financial products, transactions and instruments could lead to new payment, clearing, and settlement systems and activities. It is notable that Title VIII does not consolidate or centralize authority for the approval of the formation of new utilities or PCS activities with the Federal Reserve or any single regulatory agency.

Systems Operated by the Federal Reserve

The Federal Reserve Banks operate the following three wholesale payment services and an electronic payment system providing ACH services to depository institutions:

- Fedwire® Funds Service
- Fedwire Securities Service, also known as the National Book-Entry System (NBES)
- National Settlement Service (NSS)
- FedACH® Service

The Federal Reserve Banks began providing services using telecommunications in the early 1900s to transfer funds between accounts maintained in different Federal Reserve Districts.[33] In 1981, the Federal Reserve was required by law to price most of the Federal Reserve Bank financial services, including funds transfers and securities safekeeping, and to give nonmember depository institutions direct access to those services.[34] The Fedwire services enable depository institutions, the U.S. Treasury and other government agencies to transfer funds and book-entry securities nationwide. The Fedwire Funds Services is a real-time gross settlement (RTGS) system to settle funds electronically between banks; the Fedwire Securities Service provides issuance, settlement, and transfer services for U.S. Treasury securities and other government-related securities; and the National Settlement Service, which is a multilateral settlement service, is used by clearinghouses, financial exchanges, and other clearing and settlement groups. The Fedwire funds and securities transactions are processed in real time when received and are final and irrevocable when settled. By increasing the efficiency of Federal Reserve open market operations and helping to keep the market for government securities liquid, the Fedwire Securities Service plays a significant role in how the Federal Reserve conducts monetary policy,[35] which is commonly understood as the regulation of the money supply and interest rates by central banks. Open market operations, which are purchases and sales of U.S. Treasury and federal agency securities, are the Federal Reserve's principal tool for implementing monetary policy.[36]

Systems Operated by the Private Sector

Key private-sector systems in the United States include those operated by The Clearing House and The Depository Trust & Clearing Corporation (DTCC). The Clearing House operates an interbank funds transfer system known as CHIPS and an ACH system known as EPN. DTCC operates the Depository Trust Company (DTC), the major U.S. depository, and clearing corporations for government, mortgage-backed, and corporate and municipal securities. These three DTCC entities provide the primary infrastructure for the clearance, settlement, and custody of the vast majority of transactions in the United States involving equities, corporate debt, municipal bonds, money market instruments, and government securities.[37] The major components of the United States financial infrastructure include the following systems:

- Clearing House Interbank Payments System (CHIPS), owned by The Clearing House
- Electronic Payments Network, ACH operator owned by The Clearing House
- The Depository Trust & Clearing Corporation (DTCC) and subsidiaries:
  - o Depository Trust Company (DTC)
  - o National Securities Clearing Corporation (NSCC)
  - o Fixed Income Clearing Corporation operating the Government Securities Division (GSD) and the Mortgage-Backed Securities Division (MBSD)
- CLS Bank (foreign exchange)
- The Options Clearing Corporation (equity derivatives)
- Chicago Mercantile Exchange (CME) Clearing (credit default and interest rate swaps)
- ICE Trust (credit default swaps)
- Society for Worldwide Interbank Financial Telecommunication (SWIFT), an international financial messaging system headquartered in Belgium with U.S. operations

The Appendix to this report provides additional information regarding these systems.

RISKS OF PAYMENT, CLEARING, AND SETTLEMENT SYSTEMS AND ACTIVITIES

Section 802 of the Dodd-Frank Act reflects concern about risks related to PCS systems and activities. For example, the proper functioning of the financial markets is considered dependent upon safe and efficient arrangements for the clearing and settlement of payment, securities, and other financial transactions. Although financial market utilities that conduct or support multilateral PCS activities may reduce risks for their participants and the broader financial system, such utilities may also concentrate and create new risks. Congress also found that PCS activities conducted by financial institutions present risks to the participating financial institutions and to the financial system. Congress found it necessary to enhance the regulation and supervision of utilities and PCS activities that are systemically important, in part, to reduce systemic risk and to promote safety and soundness.

Further, both the Bush and Obama Administrations addressed the risks arising from payment and settlement systems in proposing financial regulatory reforms. In those proposals for heightened supervision by the Federal Reserve, the U.S. Department of the Treasury noted concerns about the ability of payment and settlement systems to contribute to financial crises, rather than reduce them, potentially threatening the stability of U.S. and foreign financial markets.[38]

Systemic Risk

There is no single definition of systemic risk. The Federal Reserve Bank of Cleveland has indicated that a firm is considered systemically important if its failure would have economically significant spillover effects which, if left unchecked, could destabilize the financial system and have a negative impact on the real economy.[39] In order to provide more guidance in practice, however, the Cleveland Fed proposes using the following four factors, other than size, for designating firms as systemically important: contagion, correlation, concentration, and conditions (context). The International Monetary Fund summarizes systemic risk as the large losses to other financial institutions induced by the failure of a particular interconnected institution.[40] Congress has addressed systemic risk in a number of provisions of the Dodd-Frank Act, in part, through the establishment of the Financial Stability Oversight Council and the regulation of systemically significant firms.[41]

Systemic risk can be increased by the transmission of financial system disruptions through payment and settlement systems. The global payment and settlement infrastructure consists of a network of domestic and cross-border systems that are increasingly connected through a wide array of complex interrelationships.[42] Financial market utilities, financial institutions, and other system participants are increasingly connected as operators of and participants in such systems.

Payment and settlement risks have the potential to impose losses on the entity at the source of a disruption as well as on its direct counterparties or customers, and in some circumstances, their counterparties or customers.[43] Financial institutions engage in a range of financial activities that require the settlement of obligations and transfer of assets, which can lead to principal credit losses or replacement costs when these transfers do not occur as expected.[44] The entity that is the source of an initial credit, liquidity or operational disruption, such as a failed securities trade or operational outage, may face lost revenue. That entity's customers and counterparties may face replacement costs from the purchase of additional funds or securities at a potentially higher market price to complete their own obligations. A settlement institution may also redistribute payment and settlement risks back to its participants through loss-sharing arrangements that may apply to participants that had no transactions with the failing entity. Further, some types of interdependencies among systems can allow an initial disruption to activate a chain of different risks and transmit an initial disruption through multiple systems.

The interdependencies of financial intermediaries thus increase the potential for disruptions to spread quickly and widely, including across multiple systems. Several factors over the past few decades have contributed to the development of such interdependencies.[45] These factors include the globalization and regional integration of the financial sector, consolidation of financial institutions, and advances in computer and telecommunications technology.

Events during the financial crisis of 2008 included the transmission of disruptions arising from the failure of large, interconnected financial institutions through payment, clearing, and settlement systems. In the view of some international banking regulators, the financial market infrastructures generally performed well during the recent financial crisis and did much to help prevent the crisis from becoming even more serious.[46] Those regulators have argued that when robust financial market infrastructures can enable settlement to take place without significant counterparty risk, such systems help markets to remain liquid even during times of financial stress.[47]

Some observers argue that another source of systemic risk could be the clearing house that functions as a central counterparty, i.e., the buyer to every seller and the seller to every buyer, in derivatives transactions.[48] That risk arguably could increase because of the Title VII provisions requiring the clearing of swaps transactions under certain circumstances. In addition, academics are studying whether the use of central clearing counterparties actually reduces counterparty risk.[49] In Title VIII, Congress indicated that financial market utilities may also concentrate and create new risks and stated that such utilities must be well designed and operated in a safe and sound manner.[50]

Other Risks

In addition to systemic risk, the Federal Reserve has identified the following four basic risks in payment and settlement systems:

- **credit risk**, which is the risk that a counterparty will not settle an obligation for full value either when due, or anytime thereafter;
- **liquidity risk**, which is the risk that a counterparty will not settle an obligation for full value when due;
- **operational risk**, which is the risk of loss resulting from inadequate or failed
- internal processes, people, and systems, or from external events, and which includes various physical and information security risks; and
- **legal risk**, which is the risk of loss because of the unexpected application of a law or regulation or because a contract cannot be enforced.[51]

These risks can, but need not, lead to systemic risk. Due to the potential for significant loss resulting from the large dollar value of wholesale payments, regulators expect financial institutions to implement effective and appropriate risk management policies, procedures, and controls to protect against such risks as well as reputation and strategic risk.[52] Institutions involved with wholesale payments must also manage legal and compliance risk under laws administered by the Office of Foreign Assets Control imposing economic sanctions against specified foreign countries and individuals and by the record-keeping and reporting requirements of the Bank Secrecy Act, as amended by the USA PATRIOT Act.[53]

Operational risks arising from wholesale payments include risks relating to internal and operational controls, audit, information security, business continuity planning, and vendor and third-party management. Security risk may arise from intra-bank funds transfers. A financial institution's funds transfer operation, often known as "the wire room," is responsible for originating, transmitting, and receiving payment orders. Financial institutions must establish the authenticity of incoming and outgoing funds transfer messages and the time of receipt of incoming payment orders.[54]

REGULATORY OVERSIGHT PRIOR TO TITLE VIII

Recommendations to Strengthen Oversight

Prior to the enactment of Title VIII, United States and international regulatory authorities called for the strengthening of the supervisory oversight of the financial infrastructure for payment and settlement systems. The U.S. Department of the Treasury issued reports during both the Bush and Obama Administrations recommending that oversight of systemically important payment and settlement systems should be given to the Federal Reserve.[55]

Prior to Title VIII, an entity's supervisory agencies, and for certain entities, the Federal Reserve, conducted prudential oversight of payment, clearing, and settlement systems and activities of financial institutions.[56] The Federal Reserve relied on "a patchwork of authorities, largely derived from [its] role as a banking supervisor, as well as on moral suasion" as a means to help ensure that payment and settlement systems had necessary procedures and controls in place to manage their risks.[57] In 2008, the Chairman of the Federal Reserve System asked Congress for authority to oversee systemically important payment and settlement systems, noting that many major central banks around the world have that explicit statutory authority.[58] In that testimony,

Chairman Bernanke stated that "the stability of the broader financial system requires key payment and settlement systems to operate smoothly under stress and to effectively manage counterparty risk."[59]

The Federal Reserve, together with other regulators and the private sector, was also engaged in efforts to strengthen various financial infrastructures prior to the Dodd-Frank Act. In 2005, the Federal Reserve Bank of New York began leading an initiative with industry participants to strengthen clearing and settling of credit default swaps and other OTC derivatives.[60] In addition, the Federal Reserve Bank of New York has worked with the private sector to enhance the oversight of tri-party repurchase agreements (repos).[61] A repo transaction is an agreement between two parties on the sale and subsequent repurchase of securities at an agreed price.[62] In economic terms, a repo transaction is equivalent to a loan backed by collateral consisting of the securities.

Prudential Regulators

Prior to the Dodd-Frank Act, the Federal Reserve had prudential oversight responsibilities for key private-sector infrastructure systems, including CHIPS, CLS, DTCC (and its three primary subsidiaries, DTC, NSCC, and FICC), ICE Trust, and SWIFT.[63] The Federal Reserve had authority to oversee certain firms or their PCS activities under its statutory authority to conduct monetary policy and banking supervision, to act as the lender of last resort, and to supervise the Federal Reserve Banks' provision of payment and settlement services.[64] Other federal and state regulatory agencies also exercised prudential oversight of PCS systems and activities within their supervisory jurisdiction. For example, DTC was supervised by the New York State Banking Department based on its charter as a limited-purpose trust company under New York law. In addition, DTC was regulated by the Federal Reserve as a Fed member institution and by the SEC as a registered clearing agency.

The prudential regulators include the CFTC for derivatives clearing organizations, the SEC for clearing agencies, and the federal bank regulatory agencies for depository institutions as follows: the Office of the Comptroller of the Currency for national banks and federal savings and loan associations;[65] the Federal Deposit Insurance Corporation for state nonmember banks and state savings associations; and the Federal Reserve for state member banks and Edge Act Corporations, which are bank subsidiaries that conduct international banking and financial operations under a special charter.

The Federal Reserve also has supervisory authority (under the Federal Reserve Act) with respect to the Federal Reserve Banks' operation of key payment and settlement systems, including the Fedwire Funds Service and the Fedwire Securities Service. The Federal Reserve Board sets policy and is responsible for general supervision and oversight of the Federal Reserve Banks, including the provision of payment services.[66] Under such authority, the Federal Reserve conducts regular reviews of these systems and periodic assessments of the Fedwire Services against the relevant international standards.

Supervisory Policies

The Federal Reserve Policy on Payment System Risk (PSR Policy) addresses the risks that payment and settlement activity present to the financial system and the Federal Reserve Banks.[67] The PSR Policy sets out the Board's views, principles and minimum standards applicable to risk management for private-sector and Federal Reserve Bank payment and settlement systems.[68] In addition, the Federal Reserve's Regulation F requires insured depository institutions to establish policies and procedures to avoid excessive exposures to any other depository institutions, including those created through the clearing and settlement of payments.[69]

Bank supervision guidelines include the 2003 *Interagency Paper on Sound Practices to Strengthen the Resilience of the U.S. Financial System* adopted by the Federal Reserve, SEC and OCC to improve the resilience of the private-sector clearing and settlement infrastructure following the events of September 11, 2001.[70] The goal of the Interagency Paper was to ensure the smooth operation of the financial system in the event of a wide-scale disruption. The sound practices for organizations that are systemically important for U.S. financial markets include consideration of the back-up capacity for operations sites and data centers in the wholesale markets of federal funds, foreign exchange, commercial paper, corporate equities and bonds, and government, agency, and mortgage-backed securities.

A 2008 interagency agreement among the Federal Reserve, the CFTC, and the SEC reflects the agencies' intent to cooperate and share information in carrying out their respective regulatory and supervisory responsibilities with regard to central counterparties for credit default swaps.[71]

The CFTC has also entered into an international interagency agreement with the United Kingdom Financial Services Authority (FSA) regarding derivatives clearing organizations and clearing houses based in the UK. In 2009, the CFTC and FSA signed a memorandum of understanding (MOU) that establishes a framework expressing their willingness to cooperate with each other in the interest of fulfilling their statutory functions.[72] Under the MOU, the agencies intend to consult, cooperate, and exchange information with respect to the clearing organizations. The MOU also addresses conducting on-site visits of respective clearing organizations.

International Regulatory Standards

International banking regulators have also taken actions to identify risks related to PCS systems and to strengthen the financial infrastructure. The Committee for Payments and Settlement Systems (CPSS) was set up in 1990 by the central banks of the Group of 10[73] countries. In 2009, the CPSS enlarged its membership to include many other important central banks. The CPSS meets three times annually and promotes sound and efficient payment and settlement systems. The CPSS acts as an international standard-setting body for payment and securities settlement systems and as a forum for central banks to monitor and analyze developments in domestic PCS systems and cross-border and multicurrency settlement systems.[74]

The standards consist of the Core Principles for Systemically Important Payment Systems (January 2001)[75] and two sets of recommendations published together with IOSCO (International Organization of Securities Commissions),[76] the Recommendations for Securities Settlement Systems (November 2001)[77] and the Recommendations for Central Counterparties (May 2004).[78] In February 2010, the CPSS and IOSCO launched a comprehensive review of the three sets of standards for financial market infrastructures with a view to strengthening them where appropriate.[79]

The CPSS also publishes policy reports analyzing issues related to large-value payment systems, retail payment instruments and systems, settlement mechanisms for foreign exchange transactions, and clearing and settlement of securities and derivatives transactions.[80]

A CPSS report from May 2005 expressed the view that a core responsibility of central banks is the oversight function with respect to payment and settlement systems.[81] The report indicates that central banks have traditionally influenced payment and settlement systems primarily by acting as banks providing a variety of such services to other banks. Further, central bank oversight of such systems has developed recently and rapidly into a more formal and systematic function. Various central banks monitor existing and planned systems, assessing them against the objectives of safety and efficiency and, where necessary, inducing change to the systems.

In September 2010, the CPSS published a report entitled *Strengthening Repo Clearing and Settlement Arrangements* after the repo markets proved to be a less reliable source of funding liquidity than expected in some countries during the recent financial crisis.[82] The report examines the extent to which the market infrastructures (i.e., the practices, procedures and systems used for clearing and settling repos and liquidating a defaulting cash borrower's collateral) added to uncertainty in repo markets, and presents options to strengthen the repo clearing and settlement infrastructure.

TITLE VIII OF THE DODD-FRANK ACT

Title VIII of the *Dodd-Frank Wall Street Reform and Consumer Protection Act*, P.L. 111-203 establishes a regulatory framework for systemically important utilities and systemically important PCS activities conducted by financial institutions. It provides explicit statutory oversight authority to the Federal Reserve (Fed) in coordination with an entity's chartering and supervisory authority.

The Dodd-Frank Act also affects PCS systems and activities through Title VII, the *Wall Street Transparency and Accountability Act of 2010*, which establishes a comprehensive regulatory framework in regard to the over-the-counter (OTC) derivatives market and swap transactions.[83] Title VII establishes requirements for the clearing of certain bilateral swap transactions through derivatives clearinghouses. Title VII also strengthens regulatory oversight of designated clearing entities (registered derivatives clearing organizations and clearing agencies) by the CFTC and the SEC, which are subject to the regulatory framework established in Title VIII.

The Senate, but not the House of Representatives, passed a version of the financial reform bill containing a title similar to Title VIII.[84] The House Financial Services Committee considered but struck by amendment a similar title prior to the House of Representatives' floor consideration of the financial reform bill, H.R. 4173. Both the version of Title VIII in the Senate's bill and the version offered in the Conference Committee were modeled on proposed legislation released by the Obama Administration in 2009.[85] During the Conference Committee, participants agreed to changes that enhanced the authority of the CFTC and SEC with respect to their supervised entities. The changes to the relevant title gave the CFTC and the SEC rule-writing authority for risk management standards and excluded some of their supervised entities from definitions and Federal Reserve oversight.

Purpose

Section 802 sets forth the purpose of Title VIII, which is "to mitigate systemic risk in the financial system and promote financial stability" by providing the Federal Reserve with additional powers. Section 802 authorizes the Fed to promote uniform standards for risk management and conduct and provide the Fed with an enhanced supervisory role for systemically important utilities and PCS activities by financial institutions. Another statutory purpose is strengthening the liquidity of systemically important financial market utilities.

Definitions and Exclusions

Section 803 defines the term payment, clearing, or settlement activity to mean an activity carried out by one or more financial institutions to facilitate the completion of financial transactions. The term financial transaction includes, among other things, funds transfers, securities and futures contracts, repurchase agreements, foreign exchange contracts, financial derivatives contracts, and swaps. A PCS activity does not include any offer or sale of a security or any pre-trade or execution activity such as a quotation or order entry.

Title VIII's regulatory framework distinguishes between financial market utilities and payment, clearing, or settlement activities of financial institutions. It is possible that the regulatory differences simply recognize the existing oversight authority of the federal banking agencies. Another rationale may be an intent to avoid a loophole for systemically important PCS activities conducted by financial institutions that are not financial market utilities as defined in Title VIII. A financial market utility (FMU) means any person that manages or operates a multilateral system for the purpose of transferring, clearing, or settling payments, securities, or other financial transactions among financial institutions or between financial institutions and the person.

Section 803 excludes from the FMU definition specified registered trading entities (exchanges) and data repositories registered and subject to CFTC oversight, including designated contract markets and swap data repositories, or registered and subject to SEC oversight, including national securities exchanges and swap execution facilities. Those exclusions are limited to the activities that require the entities to be registered.

Other exclusions from the FMU definition apply to various parties that act as intermediaries, including any broker, dealer, transfer agent, investment company, futures commission merchant, introducing broker, commodity trading advisor, or commodity pool operator. Such exclusions are limited to functions performed as part of the institution's named business. Also excluded are activities conducted by such institutions on behalf of a FMU or an FMU participant so long as the activities are not part of the FMU's critical risk management or processing functions.

A financial institution (FI) means any institution on a list of specified entities as defined in various other statutes, including a depository institution, a branch or agency of a foreign bank, a broker or dealer, a futures commission merchant, and any company engaged in activities that are financial in nature or incidental to a financial activity.

Section 803 excludes from the FI definition *designated clearing entities*, which are the systemically important DCOs and CAs subject to oversight by the CFTC and the SEC, respectively. The exclusion applies to the activities that require the entity to be registered. Thus, Title VIII regulation could apply to those entities only as FMUs rather than FIs.

Section 803 also excludes from the FI definition those registered trading entities (exchanges) and data repositories subject to CFTC or SEC oversight that are excluded from the definition of an FMU, such as designated contract markets, swap data repositories, and swap execution facilities, and additionally other entities, including securities information processors. The exclusion applies to the activities that require the entity to be registered.

A designated activity or designated financial market utility means a PCS activity or utility that the Financial Stability Oversight Council has designated as systemically important under section 804 of the Dodd-Frank Act discussed in this section below. A designated clearing entity means a designated financial market utility that is either a registered derivatives clearing organization or registered clearing agency.

The terms systemically important and systemic importance apply to a situation where the failure of or a disruption to the functioning of a financial market utility or the conduct of a PCS activity could create or increase the risk of significant liquidity or credit problems spreading among financial institutions or markets and thereby threaten the stability of the financial system of the United States.

In general, a supervisory agency means the federal agency that has primary jurisdiction over a designated financial market utility under federal banking, securities, or commodity futures laws and means the SEC with respect to a registered clearing agency, the CFTC with respect to a registered derivatives clearing organization, the appropriate federal banking agency with respect to an institution described in section 3(q) of the Federal Deposit Insurance Act, and the Federal Reserve Board with respect to any other type of designated financial market utility.

Designation of Systemic Importance
by the Financial Stability Oversight Council

Congress provides a role to the newly created Financial Stability Oversight Council (Council) in the enhanced regulatory oversight framework in Title VIII. The members of the Council include the Secretary of the Treasury as Chairperson of the Council, the Chair of the Federal Reserve Board, and the heads of certain other agencies. The agencies with a role in Title VIII (the CFTC, SEC, and the federal banking agencies) are members of the Council.

Section 804 authorizes the Council to designate by at least a 2/3 vote, including the Chairperson (Secretary of the Treasury), those financial market utilities or PCS activities that the Council determines are, or are likely to become, systemically important. Prior to such determination, the Council shall consult with the relevant Supervisory Agency and the Federal Reserve Board.[86] The Council may similarly rescind a designation of systemic importance.

The Council has broad authority to determine systemic importance. In addition to four listed factors, Congress provides that the Council shall consider any other factor that the Council deems appropriate. The Council must consider the following statutory factors:

- first, the aggregate monetary value of transactions processed by the utility or carried out through the PCS activity;
- second, the aggregate exposure of the utility or financial institution to its counterparties;
- third, the relationship, interdependencies, or other interactions of the utility or PCS activity with other financial market utilities or PCS activities; and,
- fourth, the effect that the failure of or a disruption to the utility or PCS activity would have on critical markets, financial institutions, or the broader financial system.

The Council must give advance notice of the proposed determination and opportunity for a written or oral hearing before the Council to the utility or financial institution. The Council may waive or modify those procedural safeguards, however, upon 2/3 vote, including the Chairperson, if necessary to prevent or mitigate an immediate threat to the financial system posed by the utility or PCS activity. The Council's final determination must be made within 60 days of any hearing or 30 days after the expiration of the opportunity to request a hearing, and the Council may extend the time periods affecting the consultation, notice, and hearing process.

In connection with assessing systemic importance, the Council may require any utility or financial institution to submit information as the Council may require if the Council has reasonable cause to believe that the utility or PCS activity meets the standards for systemic importance.[87]

Risk Management Standards

Except with respect to designated clearing entities, section 805 of Title VIII authorizes the Fed to prescribe risk management standards, in consultation with the Council and Supervisory Agencies, governing the operations related to PCS activities of systemically important financial market utilities and the conduct of systemically important PCS activities by financial institutions. The Fed may prescribe such standards by rule or order and must take into consideration relevant international standards and existing prudential requirements.

The CFTC and the SEC may each prescribe regulations, in consultation with the Council and the Fed, containing risk management standards of similar scope for systemically important DCOs and CAs, respectively, and supervised financial institutions (for example, a futures commission merchant supervised by the CFTC) that engage in systemically important PCS activities. Those regulations, like the Fed's standards, must take into consideration relevant international standards and existing prudential requirements.

If the Fed determines that CFTC or SEC rules are insufficient to prevent or mitigate certain risks to the financial markets or to the financial stability of the United States, the Fed may impose risk management standards on an SEC- or CFTC-regulated entity. If the CFTC or the SEC objects within 60 days of the Fed's determination, then the Council would decide with a 2/3 vote which agency's risk management standards would apply.

The standards of the Fed, the CFTC, and the SEC may address areas such as risk management policies and procedures, margin and collateral requirements, participant or counterparty default policies and procedures, the ability to complete timely clearing and settlement of financial transactions, and capital and financial resource requirements for designated financial market utilities.[88] The agencies' standards must, where appropriate, establish a threshold of the amount (level or significance) of an institution's activity that will cause the standards to apply to the institution.

The Fed and the Council may not impose standards with respect to certain specified areas under CFTC or SEC authority, including the approval of clearing requirements, transaction reporting, or trade execution.[89] Further, pursuant to section 811, Title VIII in general does not divest any federal or state agency of any authority derived from any other applicable law. However, any standards prescribed by the Federal Reserve Board under section 805 shall supersede any less stringent requirements established under other authority.

Operations of Designated Financial Market Utilities

Section 806 authorizes the Federal Reserve to provide to systemically important financial market utilities the Federal Reserve Bank services that are available to depository institutions. There are four such services. First, designated utilities may have certain accounts and deposit accounts at Federal Reserve Banks provided to depository institutions. Second, Federal Reserve Banks may pay earnings on balances maintained by a designated utility to the same extent paid to depository institutions. Third, the Fed may exempt a designated utility from reserve requirements or modify any applicable reserve requirement. Lastly, the Fed may authorize a Federal Reserve Bank to provide discount and borrowing privileges to a designated utility, but only in unusual or exigent circumstances and upon majority vote of the Fed after consultation with the Secretary of the Treasury. The utility would have to show that it is unable to secure adequate credit accommodations from other banking institutions.

Title VIII also establishes procedures that a systemically important financial market utility must follow when proposing changes to its rules, procedures, or operations. The designated utility must provide its Supervisory Agency with 60 days' advance notice of a proposed change that could materially affect the nature or level of risks presented by the utility. If the agency objects within 60 days, the utility may not implement the change. However, a designated utility may implement changes on an emergency basis in order for the utility to provide its services in a safe and sound manner.

Examination and Enforcement

In addition to standard-setting authority, Congress gives the Fed a role in examinations conducted by prudential regulators and enforcement for compliance with Title VIII. The Fed may, at its discretion, participate in an examination of a systemically important utility and may exercise back-up examination authority of a financial institution in certain circumstances. Title VIII also enables the Fed to take enforcement actions directly when necessary and with the Council's approval.

Section 807 requires a Supervisory Agency to conduct examinations at least annually of a systemically important financial market utility to assess compliance with Title VIII.[90] The Supervisory Agency must consult with the Fed at least annually regarding the scope of such examinations. The Fed in its discretion may participate in such examinations led by the Supervisory Agency. After consulting with the Council and Supervisory Agency, the Fed may at any time recommend that the agency take enforcement action to prevent risks to the financial markets or the financial stability of the United States. In the event of imminent risk of substantial harm to financial institutions, critical markets, or the U.S. financial system, the Fed with the affirmative vote of the Council may take enforcement action against the designated utility.

Section 808 authorizes the appropriate financial regulator of a financial institution to examine such institution with respect to a systemically important PCS activity for compliance with Title VIII. The Fed may consult with, and provide technical assistance to, the appropriate financial regulator, and the regulator may ask the Fed to conduct or participate in such examination or enforce Title VIII against the financial institution. Title VIII also gives the Fed back-up examination and enforcement authority, which the Fed may exercise with the

Council's approval under certain conditions, including having reasonable cause to believe that a financial institution is not in compliance with Title VIII.

Title VIII extends certain enforcement provisions of section 8 of the Federal Deposit Insurance Act[91] to a systemically important financial market utility to the same extent as if the utility were an insured depository institution and to a financial institution subject to standards for a systemically important PCS activity.

Regulatory Coordination

As described in the purposes of Title VIII in Section 802, Congress is trying to mitigate systemic risk in the financial system and promote financial stability by authorizing the Board to promote uniform risk management standards for relevant institutions and providing the Board an enhanced role in the supervision of such standards. Title VIII, however, in general maintains certain regulatory and supervisory authority of the CFTC and SEC with respect to designated clearing entities. Further, Title VIII establishes various limitations requiring the Fed to consult with or act in coordination with the primary supervisor of a utility or financial institution and to obtain approval of the Council to exercise certain authority. The Council similarly must consult with or act in coordination with other agencies in certain circumstances.

Title VIII does not remove prudential oversight by federal and state regulatory and supervisory agencies of their supervised institutions. In general, the Federal Reserve must exercise its new authority and responsibilities in coordination with prudential regulators. In some circumstances, however, the Federal Reserve may take actions, or seek approval of the Financial Stability Oversight Council to take actions, without the agreement of the primary supervisory agency.

The following provisions illustrate examples of required regulatory coordination under Title VIII:

- the Council must consult with the Fed and Supervisory Agencies in making systemic importance determinations under Section 804;
- the Fed or the Council must coordinate with a utility's Supervisory Agency or a financial institution's supervisor to request material information from or impose reporting or recordkeeping requirements on the entity under Section 809;
- the Fed, Council, Supervisory Agency, and appropriate financial regulator are authorized to promptly notify each other of material concerns about a designated utility or financial institution engaged in designated activities and share appropriate reports, information, or data relating to such concerns under Section 809(e); and
- coordination of examination and enforcement authority under Sections 807 and 808 is required, except to the extent that the Fed may exercise back-up or independent authority in limited circumstances.

Under Section 811, Title VIII does not divest agencies of existing authority derived from other applicable law except that standards prescribed by the Fed supersede any less stringent requirements established under other authority to the extent of a conflict.

The Conference Committee added certain provisions that limit the role of the Federal Reserve with respect to entities supervised by the CFTC and SEC. For example, Section 805 authorizes the CFTC and SEC to prescribe risk management standards for designated clearing entities (registered derivatives clearing organizations and registered clearing agencies), which the Fed can potentially override with the approval of the Council.

Title VIII also requires the CFTC and SEC to exercise certain authority in coordination with the Fed. Section 812 requires the CFTC and SEC to consult with the Fed prior to exercising authorities, including rulemaking authorities, under various provisions of law as amended by Title VIII. Section 813 requires the CFTC and the SEC to coordinate with the Fed to jointly develop risk management supervision programs for designated clearing entities.

TITLE VIII IMPLEMENTATION

Financial Stability Oversight Council

On November 23, 2010, the Council released an advance notice of proposed rulemaking (ANPR) regarding the Council's authority to designate financial market utilities as systemically important.[92] The ANPR raises various questions for commenters. The Council is seeking information that it may use to develop the specific criteria and analytical framework for systemic importance designations under Title VIII. The Council will consider separately the designation criteria and analytical framework for PCS activities carried out by financial institutions.

Federal Reserve

The statutory changes made by Title VIII are consistent with the view of international banking authorities that the oversight of payment and settlement systems is a core responsibility of central banks. Section 805 of the Dodd-Frank Act provides that, except for certain entities supervised by the CFTC and SEC, the Federal Reserve by rule or order shall prescribe risk management standards governing operations of systemically important utilities and the conduct of systemically important activities by financial institutions. As of November 30, 2010, the Federal Reserve had not issued any proposed rulemakings related to its Title VIII authority.

CFTC and SEC

Title VIII provides the CFTC and the SEC, respectively, with additional authority to supervise and regulate those systemically important utilities that are derivatives clearing organizations (DCOs) and clearing agencies (CAs), which together are called designated clearing entities.

Section 805 of the Dodd-Frank Act authorizes the CFTC and SEC to prescribe regulations containing risk management standards governing the operations of designated clearing entities or the conduct of designated activities by financial institutions that each agency supervises. Although the Fed may challenge such rules as insufficient, the CFTC and SEC may object to the Council regarding the Fed's determination. The Council would make the final decision upon the affirmative 2/3 vote of its members.

On October 14, 2010, the CFTC proposed regulations to establish requirements applicable to DCOs for the purpose of ensuring that DCOs maintain sufficient financial resources to enable them to perform their functions under the Commodity Exchange Act and the Dodd-Frank Act.[93] Comments on the proposed rule are due December 13, 2010.

As of November 30, 2010, the SEC had not issued any proposed rulemakings under its Title VIII authority, but has issued timelines for the upcoming release of implementing regulatory proposals.[94] For example, the SEC plans to issue proposed rules regarding standards for clearing agencies designated as systemically important in December 2010 as well as during April-July 2011.

The scope of Title VIII encompasses the infrastructure for the clearing of OTC derivatives, which is governed by the regulatory framework established in Title VII of the Dodd-Frank Act. Title VII requires firms to clear certain OTC derivatives, including credit default swaps, through central counterparties. Both the CFTC and the SEC must write various rules to implement Title VII, which will apply to derivatives clearing organizations and clearing agencies supervised by those agencies.[95] The clearing requirements in Title VII could increase the likelihood of a systemic importance designation under Title VIII for financial market utilities that engage in clearing OTC derivatives.

Impact on Payment, Clearing, and Settlement Systems and Activities

Those financial market utilities and PCS activities conducted by financial institutions that are designated as systemically important will be affected by additional supervision and requirements to comply with newly adopted risk management and conduct standards. Further, those designated firms could potentially be subject to increased oversight through the Federal Reserve's enhanced examination authority and role in enforcing compliance with applicable rules.

Certain payment system infrastructures were previously subject to Federal Reserve or other agency oversight. Newer systems and technologies may be developed in the future to process financial transactions via the Internet and by other means. The impact on evolving technologies would depend upon the extent to which their activities fall within the scope of the supervisory framework established under the Dodd-Frank Act and whether newer systems become systemically important.

The impact of Title VIII on a particular entity is likely to vary depending upon whether a financial market utility or financial institution is currently subject to Federal Reserve supervision, whether a system or institution has operated previously outside the scope of bank regulatory or other federal agency oversight, and whether the utility or institution will also be subject to requirements and potentially increased clearing transaction volume under Title VII requirements.

The impact of Title VIII will also depend upon the actions of various regulators such as how broadly the Financial Stability Oversight Council applies the designation of systemic importance to financial market utilities and PCS activities of financial institutions and how stringently the Fed, CFTC and SEC decide to set risk management rules and standards.

APPENDIX. SELECTED PAYMENT, CLEARING, AND SETTLEMENT SYSTEMS IN THE UNITED STATES

Name	Type/Regulator	Owners/Operators	Users/Participants	Uses/Functions	Transactions	Volume/Value
Fedwire Funds Service	Real-time gross settlement system (RGSS). Payments are continuously settled on an individual, order-by-order basis without netting. Transfer of funds is final and irrevocable when settled.	Federal Reserve/Federal Reserve Banks	Depository institutions, U.S. Treasury, Federal government agencies. In 2008, there were 5,458 participants (excluding the U.S. Treasury and certain other domestic and foreign entities), a decrease from the 6,388 participants in 2007.	Sending funds to other institutions, including for customers. Payment orders by depository institutions are processed individually and settled in central bank money upon receipt. The U.S. Treasury and other federal agencies use this service to disburse and receive funds.	Purchase and sale of federal funds (depository institutions lend balances at the Federal Reserve to other depository institutions overnight); purchase, sale, and financing of securities transactions; disbursement or repayment of loans; settlement of cross-border U.S. dollar commercial transactions; settlement of real estate transactions and other high-value, time-critical payments.	In 2009, there were 124.7 million transfers originated (a 5.0% decrease from 2008), valued at $631 trillion. The average value per transfer was $5.1 million. In 2010 (Q2), the average daily volume of transfers (for business days) was 488 thousand with an average daily value of $2.4 trillion.

Name	Type/Regulator	Owners/Operators	Users/Participants	Uses/Functions	Transactions	Volume/Value
Fedwire Securities Service (National Book-Entry System)	Real-time transfers on individual or gross basis. Transfer of securities and related funds, if any, is final and irrevocable when made. Most securities transfers involve the simultaneous exchange of payment known as delivery versus payment (DVP), which ensures that the final transfer of securities occurs if and only if the final transfer of payment occurs.	Federal Reserve/Federal Reserve Banks. The Federal Reserve Banks act as fiscal agents to facilitate the issuance of book-entry securities to participants.	Limited to depository institutions and a few other entities, including the U.S. Treasury, government-sponsored enterprises, state treasurers, and limited-purpose trust companies that are members of the Federal Reserve System. Nonbank broker-dealers typically hold and transfer their Fedwire securities through depository institution participants. In 2008, there were 1,203 participants in NBES.	Issuance, transfer, and settlement for all marketable Treasury securities, for many federal government agency and government-sponsored enterprise securities, and for certain international organizations' securities. There is a safekeeping function (electronic storage of securities holding records in custody accounts) and a transfer and settlement function (electronic transfer of securities between parties with or without a settlement payment).	Transfer of securities – for example, to settle secondary market trades, including open market operations; to move collateral used to secure obligations; and to facilitate repurchase (repo) agreement transactions.	In 2009, there were 21.1 million transfers originated (a 15.7% decrease from 2008), valued at $295.7 trillion. The average value per transfer was $14.0 million. In 2010 (Q2), the average daily volume of transfers (for business days) was 77 thousand with an average daily value of $1.3 trillion. Securities held in custody at end of 2nd quarter 2010 were $54.8 trillion.
National Settlement Service (NSS)	Multilateral settlement service implemented in March 1999. Settlement finality occurs on day of settlement.	Federal Reserve/Federal Reserve Banks	Depository institutions that settle for participants in clearinghouses, financial exchanges, and other clearing and settlement groups. Key private-sector system users include DTC and NSCC for end-of-day cash settlement; FICC for funds-only settlement; EPN; The Options Clearing Corp; and several large and regional check clearinghouses.	Settlement agents acting on behalf of depository institution participants in a settlement arrangement electronically submit settlement files to the Federal Reserve Banks. The files are processed upon receipt, and entries are automatically posted to a depository institution's Federal Reserve account.	Currently, there are approximately 40 NSS arrangements establishes by financial market utilities, check clearinghouse associations, and automated clearinghouse networks.	In 2009, processed about 469,000 transfers valued at about $16.5 trillion. In 2010 (Q2), the average daily volume of entries processed was 2,050 with an average daily settlement value of $59.6 billion.

Appendix. (Continued).

Name	Type/Regulator	Owners/Operators	Users/Participants	Uses/Functions	Transactions	Volume/Value
FedACH Service	Electronic payment system providing automated clearing house (ACH) services.	Federal Reserve/Federal Reserve Banks	Depository institutions	The ACH system exchanges batched debit and credit payments among business, consumer, and government accounts.	Pre-authorized recurring payments such as payroll, Social Security, mortgage, and utility payments. Non-recurring payments such as telephone-initiated payments and the conversion of checks into ACH payments at lockboxes and points of sale. Also outbound cross-border ACH payments through FedGlobal service.	In 2009, originated 11.4 billion transactions with a value of $19.8 trillion.
Clearing House Interbank Payments System (CHIPS)	Large-value payment system with real-time final settlement of payments. Payments become final on completion of settlement, which occurs throughout the day.	The Clearing House, which is owned by the largest U.S. banks or the U.S. branches or affiliates of major foreign banks.	In 2008, CHIPS had 47 total participants.	CHIPS payment instructions are settled against a positive current position in its account at the Federal Reserve Bank of New York (FRBNY) or simultaneously offset by incoming payments or both. At the end of the day, remaining payment instructions are netted on a multilateral basis.		In 2008, processed 92 million transactions, a 5.4% increase from 2007, valued at $508.8 billion. The average value per transaction was $5.5 million.

Name	Type/Regulator	Owners/Operators	Users/Participants	Uses/Functions	Transactions	Volume/Value
				CHIPS participants in a net debit position fund their residual net positions through Fedwire funds transfers to the CHIPS account at the FRBNY.		
Electronic Payments Network (EPN)	ACH operator	The Clearing House, which is owned by the largest U.S. banks or the U.S. branches or affiliates of major foreign banks.	Over 1350 financial institutions. Approximately 53% of customers are credit unions, 36% commercial, 9% savings, and 2% savings and loan institutions.	Payment system handling credit transfers such as payroll and dividends and debit transfers such as loan and bill payments and insurance premiums.	Processes 48% of all commercial ACH volume in the U.S.	Processes over 8 billion transactions annually.
The Depository Trust Company	Central securities depository. DTC is a member of the Federal Reserve System, a limited-purpose trust company under New York State banking law supervised by the New York State Banking Department, and a registered clearing agency with the SEC.	The Depository Trust & Clearing Corporation (DTCC). DTCC is owned by its users, including major banks, broker-dealers, and other financial institutions.	Banks and broker-dealers. In 2008, there were 413 participants.	Settling trades in corporate, municipal, and mortgage-backed securities.	DTC moves securities for net settlements of the NSCC, which is also owned by DTCC, and settlement for institutional trades typically involving money and securities transfers between custodian banks and broker-dealers as well as money market instruments.	In 2008, processed 316.6 million transactions, a 2.6% decrease from 2007, valued at $182 trillion. The average value per transaction was $575 thousand. In 2009, settled transactions worth more than $299 trillion and processed 299.5 million book-entry deliveries.

Appendix. (Continued).

Name	Type/Regulator	Owners/Operators	Users/Participants	Uses/Functions	Transactions	Volume/Value
						DTC retains custody of more than 3.5 million securities issues in the U.S. and more than 120 foreign countries and territories worth almost $34 trillion. (As of 10/29/10 system website.)
National Securities Clearing Corporation (NSCC)	Regulated by the SEC	DTCC, which is owned by its users, including major banks, broker-dealers, and other financial institutions.	Brokers. In 2008, there were 221 participants.	Clearing, settlement, and central counterparty services for virtually all broker-to-broker trades in the U.S. involving equities and corporate and municipal debt.		In 2008, cleared 21.9 billion transactions, a 61.6% increase from 2007, valued at $315.5 billion. The average value per transaction was $14 thousand.

Name	Type/Regulator	Owners/Operators	Users/Participants	Uses/Functions	Transactions	Volume/Value
ICE Trust	Limited purpose New York trust company (New York State Banking Department). Member of the Federal Reserve System. Operates under an exemption from the SEC and the U.S. Treasury Department.	Operated by Intercontinental Exchange, a publicly listed company, which operates three regulated futures exchanges, trading platforms, clearinghouses, and over-the-counter markets.	14 clearing firm members. Customers of ICE are commercial hedgers, traders, brokers, risk managers, futures commission merchants, and portfolio managers.	Central credit facility for credit default swaps (CDS). Began clearing CDS contracts in March 2009.	Offers CDS clearing for 89 single-name and 38 index contracts.	From launch in March 2009 through 11/15/10, cleared approximately 72 thousand single-name CDS trades (with a gross notional cleared value of $541 billion) and 95 thousand index CDS trades (with a gross notional cleared value of $7.7 trillion).
CLS Bank	Multi-currency cash settlement system founded in 1997	Financial services institutions in the foreign exchange business.	Settlement members and user members.	Settles payment instructions related to trades executed in six traded instruments and in 17 major currencies. Eliminates risk associated with foreign exchange settlement across time zones.	Foreign exchange	Over half of the world's foreign exchange payment instructions. In April 2010,

Appendix. (Continued).

Name	Type/Regulator	Owners/Operators	Users/Participants	Uses/Functions	Transactions	Volume/Value
Society for Worldwide Interbank Financial Telecommunication (SWIFT)	Financial messaging service	User-owned, limited liability cooperative organized under Belgian law headquartered in Belgium with operational centers in the Netherlands and the United States.	More than 9,000 banking organizations, securities institutions, and corporate customers in 209 countries. U.S. financial intermediaries are among the heaviest users of SWIFT services for correspondent banking communications.	Provides secure, standardized financial messages and related services to its member financial institutions, their market infrastructures, and their end-users.		As of September 2010, processed 2.98 trillion messages year-to-date, averaging 15.8 million messages per business day.

Source: CPSS Publication No 88, Red Book Statistical Update, Statistics on payment and settlement systems in selected countries, December 2009, available at http://www.bis.org/publ/cpss88.htm; U.S. Department of the Treasury, Blueprint for a Modernized Financial Regulatory Structure, March 2008; Federal Reserve website at http://www.federalreserve.gov/paymentsystems/fedfunds_data.htm, and http://www.federalreserve.gov/paymentsystems/fedsecs_data.htm; and websites of selected systems.

End Notes

[1] P.L. 111-203, the Dodd-Frank Wall Street Reform and Consumer Protection Act.

[2] U.S. Department of the Treasury, Blueprint for a Modernized Financial Regulatory Structure, Washington, DC, March 2008, p. 102. Hereafter cited as 2008 Blueprint.

[3] Financial Crisis Inquiry Commission, Governmental Rescues of "Too-Big-To-Fail" Financial Institutions, Preliminary Staff Report, August 31, 2010, p. 24, http://fcic.gov/reports/pdfs/2010-0831-Governmental-Rescues.pdf.

[4] Ibid., p. 25.

[5] Ibid. AIG was also exposed to significant losses from its securities lending operation.

[6] John Glover and Hamish Risk, "Exchange-Traded Credit Derivatives Poised to Curb Bank Monopoly," Bloomberg, December 11, 2006.

[7] See CRS Report R41398, The Dodd-Frank Wall Street Reform and Consumer Protection Act: Title VII, Derivatives, by Mark Jickling and Kathleen Ann Ruane.

[8] Bank for International Settlements, Committee on Payment and Settlement Systems, Central Bank Oversight of Payment and Settlement Systems, CPSS Publications No. 68, Basel, Switzerland, May 2005, p. 13, http://www.bis.org/ publ/cpss68.pdf. Hereafter cited as BIS, Central Bank Oversight.

[9] Bank for International Settlements, Committee for Payment and Settlement Systems, A Glossary of Terms Used in Payments and Settlement Systems, Basel, Switzerland, March 2003, http://www.bis.org/publ/cpss00b.pdf. Hereafter cited as BIS, Glossary.

[10] For background information on retail and wholesale payment systems, see Federal Financial Institutions Examination Council, Retail Payment Systems, IT Examination Handbook, Washington, DC, February 2010, http://www.ffiec.gov/ffiecinfobase/booklets/Retail/retail.pdf, hereafter cited as FFIEC, Retail Handbook; and Federal Financial Institutions Examination Council, Wholesale Payment Systems, IT Examination Handbook, Washington, DC, July 2004, http://www.ffiec.gov/ffiecinfobase/booklets/Wholesale/whole.pdf, hereafter cited as FFIEC, Wholesale Handbook.

[11] FFIEC, Retail Handbook, p. 4. Retail payment instruments include check-based payments, card-based and other electronic payments such as electronic cash and electronic benefits transfer, and ACH transactions.

[12] See Financial Management Service website, http://www.fms.treas.gov/ach/index.html.

[13] See Electronic Payments Network website, http://www.epaynetwork.com/cms/services

[14] The trade association was formerly known as the National Automated Clearing House Association.

[15] ACH transfers between financial institutions are not considered check transactions, and thus are not subject to laws governing check processing. FFIEC, Retail Handbook, p. 10.

[16] NACHA—The Electronic Payments Association, ACH Network Statistics, Herndon, VA, 2010, http://www.nacha.org/c/ACHntwkstats.cfm, visited December 8, 2010.

[17] FFIEC, Wholesale Handbook, p. 3.

[18] Fedwire participants maintain a reserve or securities account with a Federal Reserve Bank. Direct access to Federal Reserve payment services is generally limited to deposit-taking institutions; however, non-depository institutions may indirectly use those services as customers of Federal Reserve payment services participants. Ibid, p.4.

[19] CHIPS is operated by The Clearing House, which also operates the Electronic Payments Network, a private-sector provider of ACH services. CHIPS' website is http://www.chips.org/home.php.

[20] The Committee on Payment and Settlement Services defines netting as an agreed offsetting of positions or obligations by trading partners or participants. Netting reduces a large number of individual positions or obligations to a smaller number and may take several forms that have varying degrees of legal enforceability in the event of default of one of the parties. BIS, Glossary.

[21] U.S. Securities and Exchange Commission, Clearing Agencies, Washington, DC, http://www.sec.gov/divisions/marketreg/mrclearing.shtml.

[22] Ibid.

[23] Ibid.

[24] The Depository Trust & Clearing Corporation, About DTCC, Our Structure, New York, New York, http://www.dtcc.com/about/subs/.

[25] U.S. Commodity Futures Trading Commission, Clearing Organizations, Derivatives Clearing Organizations, Washington, DC, http://www.cftc.gov/IndustryOversight/ClearingOrganizations/index.htm.

[26] Ibid.

[27] Federal Financial Institutions Examination Council, Wholesale Payment Systems, IT Examination Handbook Presentations, Washington, DC, July 2004, p. 3, http://www.ffiec.gov/ffiecinfobase/presentations/whole_presntation.pdf.

[28] FFIEC, Wholesale Handbook, p. 11.

[29] Ibid.

[30] Ibid. The Federal Reserve Banks in their capacity as fiscal agents facilitate the issuance of book-entry securities to the Fedwire Securities Service participants. The Fedwire Securities system maintains in electronic form all marketable U.S. Treasury securities as well as many federal government agency, GSE, and certain international organizations' securities. See Federal Reserve Bank Services, Fedwire Securities Service, http://www.frbservices.org/serviceofferings/fedwire/fedwire_security_service.html.

[31] Commercial paper is a money market instrument issued by prime-rated non-financial and financial companies with maturities ranging from one to 270 days. Commercial paper is issued through dealer placements or direct placements with investors. Commercial paper is an important source of short-term funding for financial corporations and municipal governments and secondary market trading is limited. FFIEC, Wholesale Handbook, p. 14.

[32] The Depository Trust & Clearing Corporation, About DTCC, National Securities Clearing Corporation (NSCC), New York, New York, http://www.dtcc.com/about/subs/nscc.php.

[33] Federal Reserve Bank of New York, Fedwire and National Settlement Services, New York, New York. http://www.newyorkfed.org/aboutthefed/fedpoint/fed43.html.

[34] The relevant law is the Depository Institutions Deregulation and Monetary Control Act of 1980, P.L. 96-221, enacted on March 31, 1980.

[35] Federal Reserve Bank of New York, Fedwire and National Settlement Services, New York, New York, http://www.newyorkfed.org/aboutthefed/fedpoint/fed43.html.

[36] Board of Governors of the Federal Reserve System, Open Market Operations, Washington, DC, January 26, 2010, http://www.federalreserve.gov/monetarypolicy/openmarket.htm.

[37] 2008 Blueprint, p. 211.

[38] See 2008 Blueprint, p. 101; U.S. Department of the Treasury, Financial Regulatory Reform, A New Foundation: Rebuilding Financial Supervision and Regulation, Washington, DC, June 2009, p. 52, http://www.financialstability.gov/docs/regs/FinalReport_web. Hereafter cited as 2009 New Foundation.

[39] James B. Thomson, On Systemically Important Financial Institutions and Progressive Systemic Mitigation, Federal Reserve Bank of Cleveland, Policy Discussion Paper Number 27, August 2009, p. 1, http://www.clevelandfed.org/ research/policydis/pdp27.pdf.

[40] International Monetary Fund, Meeting New Challenges to Stability and Building a Safer System, Global Financial Stability Report, April 2010, p. 2, http://www.imf.org/external/pubs/ft/gfsr/2010/01/index.htm.

[41] For a discussion of provisions addressing systemic risk, see CRS Report R41384, The Dodd-Frank Wall Street Reform and Consumer Protection Act: Systemic Risk and the Federal Reserve, by Marc Labonte.

[42] Bank for International Settlements, Committee on Payment and Settlement Systems, The Interdependencies of Payment and Settlement Systems, CPSS Publications No. 84, Basel, Switzerland, June 2008, p. iii, http://www.bis.org/publ/cpss84.pdf.

[43] Ibid., p. 27.

[44] Ibid.

[45] Ibid., p. 14.

[46] Bank for International Settlements, "Standards for Payment, Clearing, and Settlement Systems: Review by CPSS-IOSCO," Basel, Switzerland, press release, February 2, 2010, http://www.bis.org/press/p100202.htm. Hereafter cited as BIS, Standards Review Press Release.

[47] Ibid.

[48] See, e.g., Elena Logutenkova and Fabio Benedetti-Valentini, "Blankfein Says Clearinghouses May Increase Risks in Crisis," Bloomberg Businessweek, September 29, 2010, http://www.businessweek.com/news/2010-09-29/blankfein-says-clearinghouses-may-increase-risks-in-crisis.html.

[49] Darrell Duffie and Haoxiang Zhu, "Does a Central Clearing Counterparty Reduce Counterparty Risk?," Graduate School of Business, Stanford University, Updated March 6, 2010, p. http://www.stanford.edu/~duffie/DuffieZhu.pdf.

[50] Section 802(a)(2) of the Dodd-Frank Act, P.L. 111-203.

[51] Board of Governors of the Federal Reserve System, Policy on Payment System Risk, Washington, DC, as amended effective June 16, 2010, http://federalreserve.gov/paymentsystems/psr_policy

[52] See FFIEC, Wholesale Handbook, p. 21.

[53] Ibid., p. 27.

[54] Ibid., p. 18.

[55] 2008 Blueprint; 2009 New Foundation.

[56] See Prudential Regulators in the next section of this report.

[57] Statement of Ben S. Bernanke, Chairman, Board of Governors of the Federal Reserve System, in U.S. Congress, House Committee on Financial Services, Systemic Risk and the Financial Markets, 110th Cong., 2nd sess., July 10, 2008, H.Hrg., p. 65 (Washington: GPO, 2008).

[58] Ibid.

[59] Ibid.

[60] Federal Reserve Bank of New York, "Statement Regarding Meeting on Credit Derivatives," press release, New York, New York, September 15, 2005, http://www.newyorkfed.org/newsevents/news_archive/markets/2005/an050915.html. For information on developments from this initiative, see Federal Reserve Bank of New York, OTC Derivatives Market Infrastructure, New York, New York, http://www.newyorkfed.org/newsevents/ otc_derivative.html.

[61] The Payments Risk Committee is a private sector group representing various U.S. banks. The Payments Risk Committee is sponsored by the Federal Reserve Bank of New York. See Federal Reserve Bank of New York, Payments Risk Committee, New York, New York, http://www.newyorkfed.org/prc/. In May 2010, the Federal Reserve Bank of New York released a white paper on Tri-Party Repurchase Agreement (Repo) Reform. Federal Reserve Bank of New York, Tri-Party Repo Infrastructure Reform, White Paper, New York, New York, May 17, 2010, http://www.newyorkfed.org/banking

[62] Bank for International Settlements, Committee on Payment and Settlement Systems, Strengthening Repo Clearing and Settlement Arrangements, CPSS Publications No. 91, Basel, Switzerland, September 2010, p. 5, http://www.bis.org/publ/cpss91.pdf. Hereafter cited as BIS, Strengthening Repo.

[63] See Board of Governors of the Federal Reserve System, Oversight of Key Financial Market Infrastructures, Private-Sector Systems, Washington, DC, http://www.federalreserve.gov/paymentsystems/over_pssystems.htm.

[64] BIS, Central Bank Oversight, p. 13.

[65] Title III of the Dodd-Frank Act provides for the transfer of powers to supervise federal savings associations to the OCC and state savings associations to the FDIC from the Office of Thrift Supervision.

[66] Board of Governors of the Federal Reserve System, Oversight of Key Financial Market Infrastructures, Reserve Bank Systems, Washington, DC, http://www.federalreserve.gov/paymentsystems/over_rbsystems.htm.

[67] The current PSR Policy, as amended effective June 16, 2010, is effective through March 23, 2011 and is accessible at http://www.federalreserve.gov/paymentsystems/psr_policy. The PSR Policy that will become effective on March 24, 2011 is accessible at http://www.federalreserve.gov/payment systems/2011_psr_policy.htm.

[68] The PSR Policy also governs the provision of intraday or "daylight" credit provided by Federal Reserve Banks, including policies regarding overdrafts in accounts at Federal Reserve Banks, net debit caps, and daylight overdraft fees.

[69] 12 C.F.R. Part 206.

[70] Dated April 7, 2003. Issued with Board of Governors of the Federal Reserve System, Federal Reserve Supervisory Letter SR 03-9, Washington, DC, May 28, 2003, http://www.federalreserve.gov/boarddocs/srletters/2003/sr0309.htm.

[71] U.S. Department of the Treasury, "Memorandum of Understanding Between the Board, the CFTC, and the SEC Regarding Central Counterparties for Credit Default Swaps," press release, Washington, DC, November 14, 2008, http://www.ustreas.gov/press/releases/hp1272.htm.

[72] U.S. Commodity Futures Trading Commission, Memorandum of Understanding Concerning Cooperation and the Exchange of Information Related to the Supervision of Cross-Border Clearing Organizations, Washington, DC, September 14, 2009, http://www.cftc.gov/ucm/groups/public/ @internationalaffairs/ documents/file/ukfsa09.pdf.

[73] The Group of 10 or G10 includes the United States, the United Kingdom, Germany, France, Canada, Japan, Sweden, Italy, Switzerland, the Netherlands and Belgium (11 countries).

[74] Bank for International Settlements, Committee on Payment and Settlement Systems, CPSS Publications, Basel, Switzerland, http://www.bis.org/cpss/index.htm. The current chairman of the CPSS is William C. Dudley, President of the Federal Reserve Bank of New York. Timothy Geithner, then-President and Chief Executive Officer of the Federal Reserve Bank of New York, chaired the CPSS from 2005 to 2009. See Bank for International Settlements, CPSS History, Organisation, Cooperation, Basel, Switzerland, http://www.bis.org/cpss/cpssinfo01.htm.

[75] Bank for International Settlements, Committee on Payment and Settlement Systems, CPSS Publications No. 43, Basel, Switzerland, http://www.bis.org/publ/cpss43.pdf.

[76] IOSCO is a policy forum for securities regulators whose membership regulates more than 95% of the world's securities markets in over 100 jurisdictions.

[77] Bank for International Settlements, Committee on Payment and Settlement Systems, CPSS Publications No. 46, Basel, Switzerland, http://www.bis.org/publ/cpss46.pdf.

[78] Bank for International Settlements, Committee on Payment and Settlement Systems, CPSS Publications No. 64, Basel, Switzerland, http://www.bis.org/publ/cpss64.pdf.

[79] BIS, Standards Review Press Release. The CPSS expects to issue draft revised standards by early 2011. The International Monetary Fund and the World Bank are also participating in the CPSS-IOSCO standards review, which is part of the Financial Stability Board's work to reduce the risks that arise from interconnectedness in the financial system.

[80] See Bank for International Settlements, Committee on Payment and Settlement Systems, CPSS Publications, http://www.bis.org/cpss/index.htm.

[81] BIS, Central Bank Oversight, p. iii.

[82] BIS, Strengthening Repo.

[83] See CRS Report R41398, The Dodd-Frank Wall Street Reform and Consumer Protection Act: Title VII, Derivatives, by Mark Jickling and Kathleen Ann Ruane.

[84] S. 3217 contained the language of the Senate version of the financial reform bill. The Senate passed H.R. 4173, with an amendment in the nature of a substitute, replacing the House language with the text of S. 3217.

[85] U.S. Department of the Treasury, Title VIII, Washington, DC, http://www.financialstability.gov/docs/regulatoryreform/title-VIIIjayments_072209.pdf. For information on all of the proposed titles, see U.S. Department of the Treasury, http://www.financialstability.gov/roadtostability/timeline.html.

[86] By referring to the defined term "Supervisory Agency," this provision apparently does not require the Council to consult with a Federal banking regulator with respect to a financial institution that conducts a PCS activity but that is not a utility regardless of whether the PCS activity is determined to be systemically important.

[87] Because Title VIII does not set forth standards for systemic importance, this text apparently refers to statutory considerations rather than standards.

[88] Congress did not authorize regulators under Title VIII to modify existing prudential capital and financial resource requirements that apply to financial institutions conducting systemically important PCS activities.

[89] The Fed's enforcement authority under Section 807(e) and (f), however, is not subject to the same limitations.

[90] A Supervisory Agency also may examine services integral to the operation of the utility by a third-party service provider.

[91] 12 U.S.C. Section 1818(i).

[92] U.S. Department of the Treasury, Financial Stability Oversight Council, Advance Notice of Proposed Rulemaking Regarding Authority to Designate Financial Market Utilities and Systemically Important, Washington, DC, November 23, 2010, http://www.treasury.gov/initiatives/Documents/VIII%20-%20ANPR%20on%20FMU%20Designations%20111910.pdf.

[93] 75 Federal Register 63113, October 14, 2010. For information on rulemakings under Title VIII, see U.S. Commodity Futures Trading Commission, Dodd-Frank Act, Systemically Important DCO Rules Authorized Under Title VIII, Washington, DC, http://www.cftc.gov/LawRegulation/DoddFrankAct/ OTC_10_SystemicDCO.html.

[94] U.S. Securities and Exchange Commission, Clearing and Settlement, Washington, DC, http://www.sec.gov/spotlight/dodd-frank/clearing-settlement.shtml.

[95] International standards applicable to clearing organizations are also undergoing revision. In May 2010, the CPSS and IOSCO released guidance with respect to how the 2004 Recommendations for central counterparties should be applied to the handling of OTC derivatives by central counterparties. Bank for International Settlements, Committee on Payment and Settlement Systems, Guidance on the Application of the 2004 CPSS-IOSCO Recommendations for Central Counterparties to OTC Derivatives CCPs – Consultative Report, CPSS Publications No. 89, Basel, Switzerland, May 2010, http://www.bis.org/publ/cpss89.pdf. In November 2010, the CPSS released a report entitled, Market Structure Developments in the Clearing Industry: Implications for Financial Stability. Bank for International Settlements, Committee on Payment and Settlement Systems, CPSS Publications No. 92, Basel, Switzerland, http://www.bis.org/publ/cpss92.pdf.

In: The Dodd-Frank Wall Street Reform...
Editors: Nathan L. Morris and Philip O. Price

ISBN: 978-1-61324-101-1
© 2011 Nova Science Publishers, Inc.

Chapter 9

THE DODD-FRANK WALL STREET REFORM AND CONSUMER PROTECTION ACT: TITLE IX, INVESTOR PROTECTION[*]

Mark Jickling

SUMMARY

Title IX of the Dodd-Frank Wall Street Reform and Consumer Protection Act (P.L. 111-203) contains 10 subtitles and 113 separate sections amending federal securities laws intended to improve investor protection. The range of Title IX's provisions is very broad: some sections will bring significant changes to the securities business, while others are little more than technical clarifications of the Securities and Exchange Commission's (SEC's) authority. This report provides brief summaries of those provisions that create new SEC authority, that were controversial during the legislative process, or that appear likely to have far-reaching consequences.

Some of the most noteworthy sections of Title IX address issues viewed as central to the financial crisis that erupted in 2007. These include:

- enhanced regulation of credit rating agencies, whose triple-A ratings of "toxic" mortgage-backed bonds set the stage for panic;
- more stringent regulation of asset-backed securities, including a "skin in the game" requirement that issuers of such securities retain some of the risk; and
- a number of provisions relating to executive compensation, including authority to prohibit pay structures that create inappropriate risk in financial institutions.

Another driving force behind Title IX was the Bernard Madoff Ponzi scheme, which repeated SEC examinations and investigations failed to detect. Many sections seek to improve the SEC's performance, including

- creation of an Investor Advocate and Investor Advisory Committee within the SEC;
- establishment of a whistleblower program to produce tips about securities fraud;

---

[*] This is an edited, reformatted and augmented version of a Congressional Research Services publication, dated November 24, 2010.

- various measures to improve SEC management, including a wide-ranging outside consultant study and various Government Accountability Office audits; and
- more budget flexibility and authorization for higher appropriations levels.

Another group of provisions addresses the rights of investors and shareholders:

- the SEC may impose a fiduciary duty on broker-dealers who give investment advice, similar to the duty that already applies to investment advisers;
- municipal financial advisors must register with the SEC, and a majority of the Municipal Securities Rulemaking Board must be independent of the industry; and
- new disclosures and shareholder votes relating to executive compensation and corporate performance and governance, including SEC authority to allow certain shareholders to nominate candidates for the board of directors.

Because of the diversity of these and other provisions, it is difficult to characterize the scope and thrust of Title IX in its entirety. Some observers, however, describe it as the most significant change to securities law since the enactment of the original federal statutes in the 1930s. This report provides a selective overview, and will not be updated.

INTRODUCTION

Title IX of the Dodd-Frank Wall Street Reform and Consumer Protection Act deals with investor protection and securities regulation. Within that general rubric, the title contains a very broad range of provisions. Parts of Title IX address aspects of the securities markets that are commonly viewed as directly involved in the financial crisis, such as credit ratings and securitization. In developing the legislation, however, Congress also addressed issues not directly related to the financial crisis. In particular, the Madoff and Stanford Ponzi schemes, discovered in late 2008 and early 2009, raised questions about the quality of regulation by the Securities and Exchange Commission (SEC). As a result, numerous provisions in Title IX address the SEC's performance and resources. Other key provisions deal with the duty of care that investment industry professionals owe to their clients and mechanisms by which shareholders can exert more effective control over corporate management.

This report provides brief summaries of selected provisions in Title IX. It attempts to include those provisions that create new SEC authority, that were controversial during the legislative process, or that appear likely to have far-reaching consequences for the regulation of securities markets. Among the provisions omitted are sections making marginal enhancements to SEC authority in particular areas of securities law.[1] Numerous such provisions, which were generally included at the request of the SEC and appear to make incremental changes in law and regulation, are not included in the interest of flow and brevity.

SUBTITLE A: INCREASING INVESTOR PROTECTION

The Investor Advocate and Investor Advisory Committee

Sections 911 and 915 of Dodd-Frank create two entities within the SEC: an Investor Advisory Committee (IAC) and an Office of the Investor Advocate (IA). Section 911 establishes a statutory mandate for the IAC, which was created by the SEC in 2009 using its existing authority. The IAC is to advise and consult with the SEC on (1) regulatory priorities of the Commission; (2) the regulation of securities products, trading strategies, and fee structures, and the effectiveness of disclosure; (3) initiatives to protect investors; and (4) initiatives to promote investor confidence and market integrity. Members of the IAC will include the Investor Advocate, a representative of state securities commissions, and a representative of the interests of senior citizens. In addition, the SEC will appoint between 10 and 20 individuals, including individuals representing the interests of individual equity and debt investors (including investors in mutual funds) and the interests of institutional investors (including the interests of pension funds and registered investment companies). IAC members must be knowledgeable about investment issues and decisions and have reputations of integrity. The SEC is not bound to follow the IAC's recommendations, but it must issue a public statement assessing such recommendations and stating whether it intends to implement them.

Section 915 creates a new Office of the Investor Advocate. The IA, who is appointed by and reports to the Chairman of the SEC, will assist retail investors in resolving significant problems investors may have with the SEC or with self-regulatory organizations (SROs); identify areas in which investors would benefit from changes in the rules of the SEC or the SROs; identify problems that investors have with financial service providers and investment products; analyze the potential impact on investors of proposed SEC and SRO regulations; and (to the extent practicable) propose to the SEC and to Congress any changes that may be appropriate to mitigate problems and to promote the interests of investors.

Section 919D creates an Ombudsman position in the Office of the Investor Advocate, to act as a liaison between the SEC and retail investors in resolving problems that retail investors may have with the SEC or SROs and to make recommendations regarding policies and procedures to encourage persons to present questions to the IA regarding compliance with the securities laws. The Ombudsman will be appointed by the IA.

Fiduciary Duty for Providers of Investment Advice

Both SEC-registered broker-dealers and investment advisers frequently give their customers advice regarding securities investments. Under federal securities law, however, the two classes of investment professionals are held to different standards as to the quality of advice they must provide. Investment advisers are under a fiduciary duty as defined in the Investment Advisers Act of 1940 and the associated jurisprudence. The essence of the fiduciary duty is that investment advice must be in the best interest of the customer. Broker-dealers, under the Securities Exchange Act of 1934, must meet a standard of suitability: their recommendations must not be unsuitable to the needs of a particular customer.

Since many securities firms employ both brokers and advisers—and many individuals are registered in both capacities—there is the possibility that customers may not understand the difference. When a customer is advised to buy a certain mutual fund, for example, is the advice influenced by the compensation that the seller receives? If the adviser is under a fiduciary duty, the answer should be no, even though the recommended fund may be a suitable investment for the customer.

Section 913 deals with the issue of a fiduciary duty that would apply to broker-dealers and investment advisers alike.[2] The House and Senate took different approaches: the House-passed version of H.R. 4173 directed the SEC to create a single fiduciary standard by regulation, while the Senate-passed version called for a study of the issue. The conference version adopted both approaches: the SEC is to study the fiduciary duty question and report to Congress within six months of enactment. At the same time the legislation gives the SEC authority to establish a uniform fiduciary duty by rule. The SEC is not required to issue such a rule.

Streamlined SRO Rule Approval

The SEC has the right of approval over all proposed rules of self-regulatory organizations (SROs) in the securities industry—the stock and options exchanges and (the Financial Industry Regulatory Authority (FINRA, formerly the National Association of Securities Dealers), which registers brokers and handles many customer complaints. Section 916 responds to industry concerns that the SEC has not always approved (or disapproved) proposed rules in a timely manner. The section sets timetables for SEC consideration of proposed SRO rules: generally, the SEC must act within 45 days, but extensions are possible, particularly for rule proposals that are lengthy or complex or raise novel regulatory issues.

Financial Planners Study

Section 919C calls for a Government Accountability Office (GAO) study of the financial planning industry and the use of the "financial planner" designation. The study is to consider, among other things, the possible risk posed to investors and other consumers by individuals who otherwise use titles, designations, or marketing materials in a misleading way in connection with the delivery of financial advice; the ability of investors to understand licensing requirements and standards of care that apply to those who hold themselves out as financial planners; and the possible benefits of enhanced regulation and professional oversight of financial planners. The Senate Banking Committee considered provisions that would have created an SRO for individuals who called themselves financial planners, but the bill reported out of committee included the study, as did the version that passed the House.

Title IX, Investor Protection

SUBTITLE B: INCREASING REGULATORY ENFORCEMENT AND REMEDIES

SEC Whistleblower Program

Section 922 seeks to create a robust whistleblower program within the SEC to encourage individuals with knowledge of securities fraud to come forward. The program is modeled on the Internal Revenue Service whistleblower program. A key element is the establishment of minimum awards—whistleblowers whose tips result in successful enforcement actions shall receive not less than 10% of the monetary sanctions collected in the action. SEC, SRO and other law enforcement personnel are not eligible, nor are auditors or persons convicted of criminal charges in the case where they brought forward information. The section also provides appeal rights in cases where the SEC decides not to make an award and confidentiality protections for whistleblowers.

Mandatory Arbitration of Securities Disputes

Section 921 addresses a controversial practice in securities markets—customers opening brokerage accounts often must agree to submit disputes to arbitration, waiving their right to take their broker to court.[3] Critics of mandatory arbitration characterize features of the process as unfair to investors. For example, the securities industry controls the pools of individuals from which arbitrators are selected, and customers bringing complaints are limited in their ability to compel brokerage firms to produce documents. On the other hand, defenders of arbitration point to cost savings that benefit investors and argue that the results of arbitration cases do not show any pro-industry bias.

The legislation amends the Securities Exchange Act of 1934 and the Investment Advisers Act of 1940 to authorize the SEC to issue rules that prohibit or restrict the use of agreements that require customers or clients of any broker, dealer, adviser, or municipal securities dealer to arbitrate any future dispute between them arising under federal securities law or regulation, or SRO rules, if the SEC finds that such action is in the public interest and for the protection of investors.

Regulation D Offerings

Regulation D permits private offerings of securities, where issuers are not required to make the financial disclosures required of publicly traded companies. To qualify for Regulation D, issuers must abide by certain conditions and restrictions: generally, they may sell only to accredited investors,[4] they may not advertise their offerings to the general public, and there are restrictions on the resale of private securities. Under the SEC's Rule 506, issuers may sell an unlimited amount of securities without registering or filing reports with the SEC.[5]

Section 926 of Dodd-Frank prohibits "bad actors"—persons who have been convicted of violating securities law or been subject to certain enforcement actions by federal or state financial regulators—from issuing securities using the exemptions provided under Rule 506. (Similar prohibitions already applied to other forms of Regulation D offerings.)

Other Provisions

Subtitle B includes 35 separate sections, most of which provide enhancement or clarification of SEC enforcement authority or resources. These provisions include

- clarifying SEC authority over unlawful margin lending (Sec. 929);
- amendments to Fair Fund procedures, whereby defrauded investors may recover some of their losses (Sec. 929B);
- giving the SEC authority to serve subpoenas nationwide, regardless of where a particular case is filed (Sec. 929E);
- expanding the SEC's authority to punish aiders and abettors of securities fraud (Secs. 929M and 929N); and
- various amendments to the Securities Investor Protection Act (which reimburses investors when their brokers fail), including an increase in the minimum assessment paid into the insurance fund by broker-dealers and an increase in cash advances available to customers of failed brokerages from $100,000 to $250,000, which amount may be adjusted annually for inflation beginning 2011. (Secs. 929H and 929V.)

SUBTITLE C: CREDIT RATING AGENCIES

Credit rating agencies took a large share of the blame for the financial crisis. They assigned triple-A ratings to thousands of complex subprime mortgage-backed bonds that plunged in value when the housing boom stalled, triggering uncertainty about the true value of those securities and contributing to market-wide panic. Several distinct approaches to rating agency reform were considered:

- stricter regulation by the SEC, to ensure that conflicts of interest (e.g., between the rating and sales operations of the businesses) did not compromise the integrity or accuracy of ratings;
- enhanced accountability through private litigation, by lowering the pleading standard for damage claims against rating agencies based on losses attributable to faulty ratings;
- reducing the significance of ratings in the securities marketplace by removing references to ratings in law and regulation, in order to remove any hint of government imprimatur; and
- increasing transparency, by requiring rating agencies to disclose information about their methods and models, and about the facts underlying the rating, to allow investors to perform independent evaluations of securities.

The first two approaches are somewhat at odds with the third—the first two implicitly assume that ratings will remain a critical tool for investment decisions and seek to improve their accuracy, while the third considers them inherently fallible, and views any implicit or explicit government endorsement of ratings as undermining market discipline. The fourth approach in a sense bridges the gaps between the others. In Dodd-Frank, Congress adopted all these approaches.

Enhanced Regulation and Accountability

Subtitle C includes provisions enhancing the SEC regulatory scheme for "nationally recognized statistical rating organizations" (NRSROs) that was created by the Credit Rating Agency Reform Act of 2006 (P.L. 109-291). Dodd-Frank follows the 2006 act in that it does not permit the SEC to regulate or evaluate rating methodologies or models, but it does seek to ensure that ratings are actually based on an objective application of those methodologies, and that commercial considerations do not influence rating decisions.

Section 932 creates an Office of Credit Ratings in the SEC, imposes more stringent conflict-ofinterest regulation (for example, the act includes "revolving door" restrictions on rating agency employees who go to work for companies whose securities they rated), and gives rating agency compliance officers additional responsibilities, including an annual report to the SEC. Section 936 requires rating analysts to meet standards of training, experience, and competence necessary to produce accurate ratings, and to be tested for knowledge of the credit rating process.

Section 932 also requires NRSROs to have boards of directors with at least half the members independent of the NRSRO.

Section 939F addresses what many observers believe to be the central conflict of interest in the ratings business: the "issuer pays" model, where companies not only compensate the rating agency but also choose the agency that will perform the rating. Section 939F directs the SEC to study the issue and create by rule a mechanism whereby the selection of an NRSRO to rate an asset-backed security issue is made on a random or semi-random basis. The mechanism is to be that set out in Section 939D of the Senate-passed version of H.R. 4173 (the Franken amendment), unless the SEC determines that an alternative mechanism would better serve the public interest and protect investors. Under the Franken amendment, the SEC is to define a pool of "qualified" NRSROs, and establish a board to assign initial credit ratings for certain complex securities and to determine rating agency compensation for performing such ratings.

Section 933 increases legal liability by lowering the pleading standard in private lawsuits seeking money damages from a credit rating agency. Under the new standard, it shall be sufficient, for purposes of pleading any required state of mind in relation to such action, that the complaint state with particularity facts giving rise to a strong inference that the credit rating agency knowingly or recklessly failed (1) to conduct a reasonable investigation of the rated security with respect to the factual elements relied upon by its own methodology for evaluating credit risk; or (2) to obtain reasonable verification of such factual elements (which verification may be based on a sampling technique that does not amount to an audit) from other sources that the credit rating agency considered to be competent and that were independent of the issuer and underwriter of the security.

Section 933 also states that credit ratings are not to be considered "forward-looking statements" for the purposes of Section 21E of the Securities Exchange Act, which provides a safe harbor for certain corporate disclosures (such as estimates of future earnings) from private lawsuits alleging untrue statements of material fact.

De-emphasizing Ratings

Dodd-Frank also contains provisions intended to reduce market reliance on ratings. Section 939 repeals several statutory provisions that make reference to credit ratings—including, for example, the provision in the Federal Deposit Insurance Act that prohibits federally insured thrift institutions from holding bonds that are rated below-investment-grade by a nationally recognized statistical rating organization (NRSRO). As a substitute for ratings, the FDIC (and other federal agencies) are directed to establish their own standards of credit-worthiness.

In addition, Section 939A requires each federal agency to review its regulations, identify any references to credit ratings, and remove any reference to or requirement of reliance on credit ratings. In substitution, each agency is to establish standards of credit-worthiness that are appropriate for the purposes of the regulations. The intent of removing references to credit ratings from law and regulation is to eliminate any sense that ratings carry a government imprimatur, and to encourage investors to perform their own analyses.

Section 939B removes rating agencies' exemption from the SEC's fair disclosure rules (Regulation FD). This means that corporations can no longer provide the agencies rating their securities with proprietary, non-public financial information (a common practice in the past) unless such information is simultaneously made public. As a result, investors should no longer believe that ratings are based on information superior to what they themselves can obtain.

Section 939G nullifies Rule 436(g) under the Securities Act of 1933, which exempted NRSROs from certain liability when ratings are included in an SEC registration statement or a securities offering prospectus. In the absence of Rule 436(g), an issuer that includes a credit rating issued by an NRSRO in a registration statement would be required to obtain the consent of the rating agency. As a result, the rating agency would be subject to potential Securities Act liability for false or incomplete disclosure. Since NRSROs receive no benefit from the inclusion of ratings, it might be expected that they would refuse to consent and that ratings would appear less frequently in offering materials.

Transparency and Disclosure

Section 932 includes extensive disclosure requirements. Each NRSRO rating must be accompanied by a form (in paper or electronic form, at the SEC's discretion) that contains information that can be used by investors and other users of credit ratings to better understand ratings, including the assumptions underlying the credit rating procedures and methodologies, the data that were relied on to determine the credit rating, and any problems or limitations with those data. Specific disclosure requirements apply to ratings of asset-backed securities—rating agencies must provide data on the underlying assets, as well as (if applicable) how and with what frequency the agency uses servicer or remittance reports to conduct surveillance of the credit rating. The nature and results of any due diligence investigation of the facts underlying a rating must also be disclosed.

Section 938 deals with universal rating symbols and addresses concerns that rating symbols can mean different things in different classes of securities. For example, the probability of default for a municipal bond rated AA might be significantly lower than for a corporate bond with the same rating. Section 938 requires NRSROs to apply any symbol used in a manner that is consistent for all types of securities for which the symbol is used. The section does not, however, prohibit an NRSRO from using distinct sets of symbols to denote credit ratings for different types of securities.

SUBTITLE D: IMPROVEMENTS TO THE ASSET-BACKED SECURITIZATION PROCESS

The asset securitization process, where home mortgages or other loans are sold by the original lenders, pooled, and resold to bond investors, produced the assets that came to be called "toxic" during the crisis. Losses in value accruing to mortgage-backed securities, together with uncertainty as to the true value of such securities, were a key factor in the freezing of interbank credit flows, as market participants came to doubt the credit-worthiness of banks and the reliability of balance sheets.

Subtitle D addresses the asset-backed securities (ABS) market by imposing new obligations on "securitizers"—issuers of an ABS, or persons who organize and initiate ABS transactions by selling or transferring assets to an issuer—and (in some cases) on "originators," those who, through an extension of credit or otherwise, create a financial asset that collateralizes an asset-backed security and sell that asset directly or indirectly to a securitizer.

Risk Retention or "Skin in the Game"

The basic approach of Subtitle D is to require securitizers to have "skin in the game," that is, to retain a material portion of the credit risk in any ABS that they sell. By aligning the interests of sellers and buyers of ABS, the intent is to create incentives such that securitizers will take more care in selecting assets of good quality and that they will be less likely to create securities of such complexity that valuation is difficult in normal times and impossible when markets are under stress.

Section 941 directs the SEC and the banking regulators (Fed, OCC, and FDIC) to write rules that require any securitizer to retain an economic interest in a portion of the credit risk for any asset that the securitizer, through the issuance of an asset-backed security, transfers, sells, or conveys to a third party. With regard to securitization of residential mortgages, the Secretary of HUD and the director of the Federal Housing Finance Agency (FHFA) will also participate in the rulemaking. The rules will address classes of securitized assets separately—individual risk retention requirements will be tailored to securitizations of home mortgages, commercial mortgages, commercial loans, auto loans, and any other asset class that the regulators deem appropriate.

Securitizers must retain at least 5% of the total credit risk, unless the securitized assets meet standards of low credit risk to be established by the regulators for each asset class. In such cases, the amount of risk retained may be below 5%. Regulators must further define "qualified residential mortgages," taking into consideration underwriting and product features that historical loan performance data indicate result in a lower risk of default. Securitizations where all assets are qualified residential mortgages will be exempt from risk retention requirements.

Risk retention requirements may be divided between securitizers and originators, but only if the SEC and banking regulators jointly consider (1) whether the assets sold to the securitizer have terms, conditions, and characteristics that reflect low credit risk; (2) whether the form or volume of transactions in securitization markets creates incentives for imprudent origination of the type of loan or asset to be sold to the securitizer; and (3) the potential impact of the risk retention obligations on the access of consumers and businesses to credit on reasonable terms.

Section 941 gives regulators broad authority to exempt any securitization from the risk retention rules, provided that such exemptions help ensure high quality underwriting standards, encourage appropriate risk management practices by the securitizers and originators, improve the access of consumers and businesses to credit on reasonable terms, or otherwise are in the public interest and protect investors. Several types of securitizers are automatically exempt: Farm Credit System institutions, municipal issuers, and securitizations of certain assets insured or guaranteed by the United States or an agency of the United States. For purposes of this section, Fannie Mae, Freddie Mac, and the Federal Home Loan Banks are not considered to be agencies of the United States, although the regulators may, at their discretion, exempt securities issued by those government-sponsored enterprises.

Section 941 authorizes the regulators to craft risk retention rules that are appropriate to second-degree securitizations, where the assets being pooled and securitized are themselves ABS. Such complex securities, known as collateralized debt obligations (CDOs), or "CDO-squared," were among the instruments that lost the most value during the crisis. The exemption for qualified residential mortgages does not apply to second-degree securitizations.

Enhanced Disclosure

Section 942 directs the SEC to adopt regulations governing disclosure of information about the assets underlying any ABS. Such disclosures shall include asset-level or loan-level data, if such data are necessary for investors to independently perform due diligence, including data having unique identifiers relating to loan brokers or originators; the nature and extent of the compensation of the broker or originator of the assets backing the security; and the amount of risk retention by the originators and the securitizer of such assets. To the extent feasible, the disclosures should permit investors to compare the performance of different ABS. The SEC has authority to exempt any issuers from the disclosure requirements.

Representations and Warranties

Section 943 deals with representations and warranties, which are essentially promises by originators to securitizers that assets meet certain credit standards. When rating an ABS, NRSROs must describe the representations, warranties, and enforcement mechanisms available to investors in the particular security and how they differ from the representations, warranties, and enforcement mechanisms in similar ABS. With regard to problem loans in the asset pool, securitizers must disclose fulfilled and unfulfilled repurchase requests across all trusts aggregated by the securitizer, so that investors may identify asset originators with clear underwriting deficiencies.

Issuer Due Diligence

Section 945 directs the SEC to write rules that require issuers of ABS to perform a due diligence review of the underlying assets and to disclose the nature of that review.

SUBTITLE E: ACCOUNTABILITY AND EXECUTIVE COMPENSATION

Many analyses of the causes of the financial crisis assign a role to flawed compensation structures: when executives and traders receive much of their pay in the form of a bonus that reflects a single year's results, they may have an incentive to take long-term risks that boost short-term earnings. In most years, they profit, and when the rare loss comes, they keep their past bonuses. Subtitle E contains a number of provisions intended to align the incentives and interests of long-term shareholders and employees.

Say-on-Pay Vote

Section 951 gives shareholders a "say-on-pay" vote, to approve or disapprove the compensation of executives. The vote will occur every one, two, or three years, at the shareholders' option. Another shareholder resolution vote will involve "golden parachute" payments, or severance pay received by executives in the event of a merger or takeover. Neither resolution will be binding on the company or its board of directors.

Independent Compensation Committee

Section 952 requires each stock exchange to adopt listing standards that require all listed companies to have a compensation committee of the board made up entirely of directors who are independent of the company. The listing standards shall permit compensation committees to hire compensation consultants (after taking into consideration SEC rules regarding compensation consultant independence) and to hire outside legal counsel.

Pay Versus Performance

Section 953 requires companies to include in their annual proxy statements disclosures that permit shareholders to compare executive compensation actually paid to the financial performance of the issuer. The disclosures shall include a comparison of the compensation of the CEO with the median pay of all employees of the company.

Clawback of Erroneously Awarded Compensation

Section 954 requires the stock exchanges to adopt listing standards that require executives to repay erroneously awarded compensation under certain circumstances. If a company files an accounting restatement due to "material noncompliance" with any financial reporting requirement, the company will recover from any current or former executive officer who received incentive-based compensation (including stock options awarded as compensation) during the three-year period preceding the date on which the issuer is required to prepare the restatement, the difference between the amount that was actually paid and what would have been paid to the executive officer had the original financial statement been accurate.

Pay Structures that Encourage Inappropriate Risks

Section 956 gives regulators broad authority to deal with the types of incentive-based compensation structures that some observers identify as a cause of the crisis. The banking regulators (the Fed, OCC, FDIC, and NCUA), the FHFA, and the SEC are directed to jointly issue regulations or guidelines to require covered financial institutions to disclose information about compensation structures (not individual pay packages) sufficient to allow regulators to determine whether an institution's pay structure provides compensation, fees, or benefits that (1) are excessive, or (2) could lead to material financial loss to the covered financial institution. The regulators are directed to prohibit incentive-based compensation structures that encourage inappropriate risks by covered financial institutions.

A "covered financial institution," for purposes of Section 956, means

- a depository institution or depository institution holding company, as such terms are defined in section 3 of the Federal Deposit Insurance Act (12 U.S.C. 1813);
- a broker-dealer registered with the SEC;
- an investment adviser, as such term is defined in section 202(a)(11) of the Investment Advisers Act of 1940 (15 U.S.C. 80b-2(a)(11));
- a credit union, as described in section 19(b)(1)(A)(iv) of the Federal Reserve Act;
- Fannie Mae or Freddie Mac; and
- any other financial institution that the appropriate federal regulators, jointly, by rule, determine should be treated as a covered financial institution for purposes of this section.

This section does not apply to financial institutions with less than $1 billion in assets.

Subtitle F: Improvements to the Management of the Securities and Exchange Commission

Subtitle F is in significant part a response to perceived failures at the SEC. The Bernard Madoff Ponzi scheme, which was investigated several times by the SEC but not detected, raised questions about the competence of some SEC employees and about managerial and organizational weaknesses. Specifically, some of the SEC staff assigned to inspect Madoff's firm were inexperienced and took Madoff's false assertions at face value. Others failed to take simple steps, such as making a phone call or sending a letter to verify accounts where Madoff claimed to hold customer securities, that would have brought the fraud to light much earlier. There was little or no communication between divisions of the SEC: in one case, a team of investigators did not realize that another SEC investigation of Madoff had recently concluded. SEC supervisors did not support the efforts of front-line staff, in some cases transferring them to other projects before their Madoff inspections had reached a conclusion.

Certification of Internal Supervisory Controls

Section 961, modeled after the Sarbanes-Oxley Act, requires the SEC to submit an annual report to Congress containing an assessment of the effectiveness of the Commission's internal supervisory controls and procedures applicable to SEC staff who perform examinations of registered entities, enforcement investigations, or reviews of corporate financial filings. The report shall include a certification, signed by the directors of the Division of Enforcement, the Division of Corporation Finance, and the Office of Compliance Inspections and Examinations, that the SEC has adequate internal supervisory controls to carry out its duties. In addition, at least once every three years, the GAO shall review the adequacy and effectiveness of the internal supervisory control structure, and furnish Congress with a summary of that review.

GAO Evaluation of Personnel Management

Section 962 mandates that the GAO submit to Congress every three years an evaluation of the effectiveness of personnel management at the SEC. The GAO shall consider

- the effectiveness of supervisors in using the skills, talents, and motivation of SEC employees;
- the criteria for promoting employees to supervisory positions;
- the fairness of the application of the promotion criteria;
- the competence of the professional staff of the Commission;
- the efficiency of communication between the units of the SEC regarding the work of the Commission and efforts to promote such communication;
- the turnover within subunits of the SEC, including the consideration of supervisors whose subordinates have an unusually high rate of turnover;

- whether there are excessive numbers of low-level, mid-level, or senior-level managers;
- any initiatives that increase the competence of the staff of the Commission;
- actions taken regarding employees who have failed to perform their duties and circumstances under which the SEC has issued to employees a notice of termination; and
- such other factors relating to the management of the SEC as the Comptroller General determines are appropriate.

Annual GAO Audit of SEC Financial Controls

Section 963 requires the GAO to submit annually to Congress a report that describes the responsibility of the management of the SEC for establishing and maintaining an adequate internal control structure and procedures for financial reporting, and contains an assessment of the effectiveness of that internal control structure and the procedures for financial reporting of the SEC during the previous fiscal year.

GAO Review of SEC Oversight of National Securities Associations

Federal securities law provides for the existence of a national securities association to play a self-regulatory role in the securities industry, under the oversight of the SEC. The only national securities association now extant is FINRA. Section 964 requires GAO to submit to Congress every three years an evaluation of SEC oversight of national securities associations. The GAO shall consider the governance of such national securities associations; examinations carried out, including the expertise of the examiners; executive compensation practices; arbitration services; regulation of advertising; cooperation with state securities administrators by the national securities associations to promote investor protection; funding; and other matters.

SEC Compliance Examiners

SEC compliance examiners work in the Office of Compliance, Inspections, and Examinations (OCIE). Section 965 of Dodd-Frank requires that the SEC's Division of Trading and Markets (which regulates broker-dealers and securities exchanges) and Division of Investment Management (which oversees investment advisers and mutual funds) also employ compliance examiners. The intent of the provision is to ensure that SEC examiners have expertise regarding the business of the entity they are examining.

SEC Organizational Study and Reform

Section 967 calls for the SEC to hire an independent consultant of high caliber and with expertise in organizational restructuring and the operations of capital markets to examine the internal operations, structure, funding, and the need for comprehensive reform of the SEC, as well as the SEC's relationship with and the reliance on self-regulatory organizations and other entities relevant to the regulation of securities and the protection of securities investors that are under the SEC's oversight. Specific areas of study shall include

- possible elimination of unnecessary or redundant units at the SEC;
- improving communications between SEC offices and divisions;
- the need to put in place a clear chain-of-command structure, particularly for enforcement examinations and compliance inspections;
- the effect of high-frequency trading and other technological advances on the market and what the SEC requires to monitor the effect of such trading and advances on the market;
- the SEC's hiring authorities, workplace policies, and personal practices; and
- whether the SEC's oversight and reliance on self-regulatory organizations promotes efficient and effective governance for the securities markets.

SUBTITLE G: STRENGTHENING CORPORATE GOVERNANCE

Proxy Access

Shareholder groups have for many years sought legislation or regulations that allow shareholders to nominate candidates for a company's board of directors, and to have those candidates included next to management's candidates on the company's proxy materials that are mailed to shareholders each year before the annual meeting. Section 971 clarifies the SEC's authority to issue rules permitting the use by a shareholder of proxy solicitation materials supplied by an issuer of securities for the purpose of nominating individuals to membership on the board of directors of the issuer, under such terms and conditions as the Commission determines are in the interests of shareholders and for the protection of investors.

On August 25, 2010, the SEC adopted a final rule allowing holders of 3% of a company's stock who have held the shares for three years to place a nominee for director in the company's proxy materials.[6]

DISCLOSURES REGARDING CHAIRMAN AND CEO STRUCTURES

Section 972 requires companies to disclose in their annual proxy report the reasons why the issuer has chosen the same person to serve as chairman of the board of directors and CEO or why the company has chosen to have different individuals fill those two positions.

SUBTITLE H: MUNICIPAL SECURITIES

The financial crisis raised a number of concerns about municipal securities markets. A number of towns and counties were sold complex derivatives contracts that proved very costly, and concerns persisted about "pay-to-play" abuses by politically connected intermediaries. Subtitle H makes a number of significant changes to the regulation of municipal markets.

Regulation of Municipal Advisors

Section 975 creates a new class of registrants under federal securities law. "Municipal advisors" are defined as persons who are not employees of a municipal entity but who provide advice to a municipal entity with respect to municipal financial products or the issuance of municipal securities, including advice relating to the structure, timing, and terms of securities offerings, or who undertake solicitations of a municipal entity. Municipal advisors include financial advisors, guaranteed investment contract brokers, third-party marketers, placement agents, solicitors, finders, and swap advisors, but do *not* include broker-dealers or municipal securities dealers serving as an underwriter (as defined in section 2(a)(11) of the Securities Act of 1933), SEC-registered investment advisers, or CFTC-registered commodity trading advisors. Municipal advisors must register with the Municipal Securities Rulemaking Board (MSRB), which is directed to make rules governing the business conduct of municipal advisors, and the SEC shall enforce those rules.

Majority of MSRB Members to be Independent

Section 975 also amends the composition of the Municipal Securities Rulemaking Board—the board will now have 15 members, eight of whom shall be public members, independent of the industry. That is, the majority of the board will consist of members not associated with any municipal securities broker, municipal securities dealer, or municipal advisor. The eight independent board members shall include at least one representative of investors in municipal securities, one representative of municipal entities, and at least one shall be a member of the public with knowledge of or experience in the municipal securities industry. The seven board members from the industry shall include representatives of bank and non-bank municipal securities dealers and at least one individual who is associated with a municipal advisor. Each member of the board shall be knowledgeable of matters related to the municipal securities markets.

GAO Studies

Sections 976 and 977 call for GAO to conduct (1) a study of the adequacy of disclosures made to investors in municipal securities, and (2) a broad review of the market, including an analysis of trading mechanisms; the needs of the markets and investors and the impact of recent innovations; recommendations for how to improve the transparency, efficiency, fairness, and liquidity of trading in the municipal securities markets; and potential uses of derivatives in the municipal securities markets.

GASB Funding

Section 978 establishes a source of funding for the Government Accounting Standards Board (GASB), which formulates accounting standards for the voluntary use of state and local governments. The section authorizes to SEC to require FINRA to collect reasonable accounting support fees from its members (who are broker-dealers and other securities professionals) and to remit such fees to the Financial Accounting Foundation (GASB's parent organization).

Office of Municipal Securities within the SEC

Responding to concerns that in recent years the SEC has devoted fewer resources to the oversight of municipal markets, Section 979 establishes the Office of Municipal Securities within the SEC. The Office shall be staffed sufficiently to carry out the requirements of this section, and must include individuals with knowledge of and expertise in municipal finance.

SUBTITLE I: PUBLIC COMPANY ACCOUNTING OVERSIGHT BOARD, PORTFOLIO MARGINING, AND OTHER MATTERS

Subtitle I contains 19 sections dealing with a range of different topics.

PCAOB and Foreign Auditor Oversight Authorities

Section 981 deals with the authority of the Public Company Accounting Oversight Board (PCAOB) to exchange information with foreign regulatory bodies. If the PCAOB determines that it is appropriate and necessary to protect investors, it may share confidential and privileged information gathered in the course of its oversight of U.S. auditing firms with a foreign auditor oversight authority, provided that the foreign agency supplies (1) such assurances of confidentiality as the PCAOB may request; (2) a description of the applicable information systems and controls of the foreign auditor oversight authority; and (3) a description of the laws and regulations of the foreign government of the foreign auditor oversight authority that are relevant to information access.

PCAOB Authority Over Auditors of Broker-Dealers

Section 982 requires that all auditors of registered broker-dealers be regulated and examined by the PCAOB, whether or not the broker-dealer is a public company. (In general, PCAOB oversees only auditors of publicly traded firms.) This provision is related to the Madoff Ponzi scheme case—Madoff's broker-dealer was audited by an unregulated accounting firm with only two employees.

Portfolio Margining in SIPC Accounts

Section 983 amends the Securities Investor Protection Act of 1970 (SIPA), which protects customers from certain losses caused by the insolvency of their broker-dealer. Customers of failed broker-dealers may be reimbursed up to $500,000. Under previous law, the protections of SIPA did not extend to futures contracts (other than security futures). As a result, customers who used futures to hedge against drops in securities prices were not afforded SPIA protection across their entire portfolio.

Section 983 will enable customers to include both securities and related futures products in a single "portfolio margining account." SIPA protection will be based upon the net risk of the positions in the account.

Material Loan Loss Reviews

When insured depository institutions fail, and there is a material loss to the FDIC's deposit insurance fund, the Inspector General of the primary federal regulator of the failed institution is required to review the agency's supervision of the failed institution, including the agency's implementation of Prompt Corrective Action; ascertain why the institution's problems resulted in a material loss to the deposit insurance fund; and make recommendations for preventing any such loss in the future.

Before Dodd-Frank, the threshold for a material loan loss review was a loss of $25 million. Section 987 raises the threshold of "material loss" to $200 million for losses that occur in 2010 and 2011, to $150 million for losses in 2012 and 2013, and $50 million thereafter. The purpose of this section is to eliminate duplicative and repetitive reviews of many bank failures experienced in the crisis that are generally attributable to the same causes.

In addition, Section 987 directs the Inspectors General to prepare a semi-annual report on nonmaterial losses to determine if there were cases with unusual features that might justify a full loan loss review even though the materiality threshold was not reached. Those reports shall be made available upon request to any member of Congress.

Senior Investor Protections

Section 989A directs the Bureau of Consumer Financial Protection to establish a program to provide grants of up to $500,000 per fiscal year to individual states to investigate and

Title IX, Investor Protection   199

prosecute misleading and fraudulent marketing practices or to develop educational materials and training to reduce misleading and fraudulent marketing of financial products toward seniors. States may use the grants for staff, technology, equipment, training and educational materials. To receive these grants, states must adopt rules on the use of designations in the offer or sale of securities, insurance products, or investment advice; on fiduciary or suitability requirements in the sale of securities; and on the sale of annuity products by insurers. The section authorizes $8 million to be appropriated for these purposes for fiscal years 2011 through 2015.

Inspector General Provisions

Section 989B amends Section 8G of the Inspector General Act of 1978 to clarify the delegation of authority to the Inspectors General of the Federal Labor Relations Authority, the National Archives and Records Administration, the National Credit Union Administration, the National Endowment for the Arts, the National Endowment for the Humanities and the Peace Corps.

Section 989C provides for a more transparent peer review process among federal inspectors general to increase accountability.

Section 989D provides that, in federal agencies for which a board or commission is the head of the entity, an inspector general may be removed only with the written concurrence of two-thirds of the board or commission.

Section 989E establishes a Council of Inspectors General on Financial Oversight, made up of the inspectors general of the banking agencies, the SEC, the CFTC, the Departments of Treasury and HUD, and the FHFA. The Council shall meet quarterly to discuss the ongoing work of each inspector general, with a focus on concerns that may apply to the broader financial sector and ways to improve financial oversight.

Section 989H requires the Chairmen of the Federal Reserve, the CFTC, the SEC, the NCUA, and the Director of the Pension Benefit Guaranty Corporation (PBGC) to take action to address deficiencies identified by a report or investigation of the Inspector General of the establishment concerned, or to certify to Congress that no action is necessary or appropriate in connection with such deficiency.

Exemption from Section 404(b) of the Sarbanes-Oxley Act

Section 989G provides an exemption from Section 404(b) of the Sarbanes-Oxley Act for public companies with a market capitalization of less than $75 million. Section 404(b) requires that a company's internal accounting controls be audited by the firm's outside accountant.[7] Section 404(a), which requires management to certify its responsibility for establishing and maintaining adequate internal controls, remains in force for all public companies.

In addition, the SEC is directed to study and report to Congress on the effect of extending the 404(b) exemption to companies with market capitalization below $250 million. Section 989I directs the GAO to study the impact of Section 989G, in terms of number of accounting restatements, cost of capital, investor confidence, and voluntary compliance.

Regulation of Fixed Index Annuities

Section 989J states that certain insurance or endowment policy or annuity contracts, the values of which do not vary according to the performance of a separate account, shall be treated as exempt securities under the Securities Act of 1933. This means that the sale of such contracts will be regulated by state insurance commissions rather than by the SEC. The exemption will only apply in states that adopt suitability or fiduciary standards that meet or exceed model codes developed by the National Association of Insurance Commissioners (NAIC).

SUBTITLE J: SEC FUNDING

Subtitle J changes the way the SEC is funded. Since its creation in the 1930s, the SEC has collected fees on a variety of securities market transactions. Usually, the amount of such fee collections has exceeded the SEC's budget. Since 2000, the excess has gone not to the Treasury general fund, but rather to a special account available only to appropriators to fund the SEC. Under Dodd-Frank, one of the two major fees (a percentage of the proceeds from all sales of corporate stock) will be adjusted periodically so that the amount collected is approximately equal to the SEC's annual appropriation. The other major fee (a percentage of the value of all new securities registered for public sale) will go to the Treasury general fund. Target collection amounts are set out through FY2020.

Subtitle J establishes a Reserve Fund in the SEC which may hold up to $100 million in excess fee collections. The Fund may be used to achieve flexibility and continuity in spending, in order that delays in enacting appropriations bills do not impede multi-year spending projects.

In addition, the law provides for the SEC to submit its budget request directly to Congress, rather than through the Office of Management and Budget. Appropriations for the SEC are authorized through FY2015, when the amount will be $2.25 billion, about double the SEC's 2010 budget.

End Notes

[1] For example, under Section 929T, where it was previously a violation of law to offer an investor a securities contract that waived investor rights contained in SEC regulations, it is now also a violation to offer a contract that waives rights guaranteed by the rules of a securities exchange or a national securities association.

[2] See CRS Report R41381, *The Dodd-Frank Wall Street Reform and Consumer Protection Act: Standards of Conduct of Brokers, Dealers, and Investment Advisers*, by Michael V. Seitzinger.

[3] For more information, see CRS Report RS22127, *Securities Arbitration: Background and Questions of Fairness*, by Gary Shorter.

[4] "Accredited investors" must meet certain asset and income tests, which are modified by Section 413 of Dodd-Frank. They are presumed to be sophisticated investors, able to understand and bear investment risks, and thus less in need of government protection than general public investors.

[5] For a summary of the terms of Rule 506 offerings, see http://www.sec.gov/answers/rule506.htm.

[6] Securities and Exchange Commission, "FACILITATING SHAREHOLDER DIRECTOR NOMINATIONS," Final Rule: Release Nos. 33-9136; 34-62764; IC-29384; File No. S7-10-09, Aug 25, 2010.

Title IX, Investor Protection   201

[7] See CRS Report RS22482, *Section 404 of the Sarbanes-Oxley Act of 2002 (Management Assessment of Internal Controls): Current Regulation and Congressional Concerns*, by Michael V. Seitzinger.

In: The Dodd-Frank Wall Street Reform... ISBN: 978-1-61324-101-1
Editors: Nathan L. Morris and Philip O. Price © 2011 Nova Science Publishers, Inc.

Chapter 10

THE DODD-FRANK WALL STREET REFORM AND CONSUMER PROTECTION ACT: EXECUTIVE COMPENSATION[*]

Michael V. Seitzinger

SUMMARY

As part of their financial regulatory reform legislation, both the House and the Senate passed bills with provisions applying to executive compensation. The House- and Senate-passed executive compensation provisions differed, in some cases significantly.

The House and Senate conferees on Wall Street reform passed an executive compensation subtitle. On June 30, 2010, the House agreed to the conference report for H.R. 4173, now referred to as the Dodd-Frank Wall Street Reform and Consumer Protection Act. The Senate agreed to the conference report on July 15, 2010. The President signed the bill into law as P.L. 111-203 on July 21, 2010.

Among the provisions of the bill are say-on-pay requirements, the establishing of independent compensation committees, the clawback of unwarranted excessive compensation, and requirements on the executive compensation at financial institutions.

On October 18, 2010, the Securities and Exchange Commission (SEC or Commission) proposed rules to implement Dodd-Frank's executive compensation provisions.

INTRODUCTION

Concern about shareholder value, corporate governance, and the economic and social impact of escalating pay for corporate executives has led to discussions, particularly over the past few years, regarding the practices of paying these executives. Since the economic downturn, Congress has considered various proposals to address the concerns relating to

---

[*] This is an edited, reformatted and augmented version of a Congressional Research Services publication, dated November 9, 2010.

executive compensation. As part of their financial regulatory reform legislation, both the House[1] and the Senate[2] passed bills with provisions applying to executive compensation.[3] The House- and Senate-passed executive compensation provisions differed, in some cases significantly, but both required a nonbinding shareholder vote on approval of the executives' compensation packages.

The House and Senate conferees on Wall Street reform passed an executive compensation subtitle; subtitle E of Title IX of the bill is titled Accountability and Executive Compensation. On June 30, 2010, the House agreed to the conference report[4] for H.R. 4173, now referred to as the Dodd-Frank Wall Street Reform and Consumer Protection Act. On July 15, 2010, the Senate agreed to the conference report. The President signed the bill into law as P.L. 111-203 on July 21, 2010.

SECTION 951. SHAREHOLDER VOTE ON EXECUTIVE COMPENSATION DISCLOSURES

This section amends section 14[5] of the Securities Exchange Act of 1934[6] to require that, not less frequently than every three years at any annual or other meeting of shareholders, companies must provide their shareholders with a nonbinding vote to approve executive compensation, pursuant to federal regulations. Shareholders must also be provided with a nonbinding vote at least every six years to determine whether the shareholder approval vote shall occur every one, two, or three years. If a company asks voters to approve an acquisition, merger, consolidation, or proposed sale or other disposition of all or substantially all of the assets of the company, the company must disclose any compensation arrangements to be paid to the company's executive officers (golden parachutes) and provide shareholders with a nonbinding approval vote on these arrangements. An institutional investment manager must disclose at least annually how it voted on say-on-pay and golden parachutes. The Securities and Exchange Commission (SEC or Commission) may exempt an issuer from the voting requirements and must, among other considerations, take into account in its exemption decisions whether the voting requirements disproportionately burden small issuers.

SECTION 952. COMPENSATION COMMITTEE INDEPENDENCE

According to requirements of the bill, the SEC must by rule require the national securities exchanges and associations to prohibit the listing of equity securities of an issuer unless each member of the compensation committee of the board of directors of the issuer is an actual member of the board and independent. In determining the definition of "independence," the national securities exchanges and associations must consider relevant factors, such as the source of compensation of a board member, and whether the board member is affiliated with the issuer, a subsidiary of the issuer, or an affiliate of a subsidiary of the issuer. The independence requirement shall not apply to a controlled company, limited partnership, company in bankruptcy, open-ended management investment company, or a foreign private issuer. Only an issuer's compensation committee may select a compensation consultant, legal counsel, or other adviser to the compensation committee, and must take into consideration the factors identified by the Commission as affecting the independence of the consultant, counsel, or other adviser. The SEC's rules must provide for appropriate procedures for an issuer to cure any defects concerning the independence of compensation committees before the SEC prohibits the selling of the issuer's stock. The SEC may allow an exchange or association to provide for independent compensation committee exemptions, taking into account the impact of the independence requirements upon smaller reporting issuers. Controlled companies, as defined, are not covered by the independent compensation committee requirements.

SECTION 953. EXECUTIVE COMPENSATION DISCLOSURES

This section amends section 14 of the Securities Exchange Act of 1934 to require that the SEC must by rule require each issuer to disclose in annual meeting materials a clear description of executive compensation, including information showing the relationship between executive compensation actually paid and the financial performance of the issuer, taking into account any change in the value of the issuer's shares of stock, dividends, and distributions. The SEC shall require each issuer to disclose the median of the annual total compensation of all employees of the issuer, except the chief executive officer; the annual total compensation of the chief executive officer (CEO); and the ratio of the employees' median salary to the CEO.

SECTION 954. RECOVERY OF ERRONEOUSLY AWARDED COMPENSATION

The Commission must issue rules which direct the national securities exchanges and associations to prohibit the listing of a security of any issuer that does not have a policy providing for (1) the disclosure of the issuer's policy on incentive-based compensation and (2) clawback policies which recover incentive-based compensation after an accounting restatement. The clawback trigger is based upon the material noncompliance of the issuer with any financial reporting requirement which leads to the accounting restatement. The amount to be clawed back is the excess of what would have been paid to the executive under the accounting restatement.

SECTION 955. DISCLOSURE REGARDING EMPLOYEE AND DIRECTOR HEDGING

The provision amends section 14 of the Securities Exchange Act of 1934 to require the Commission by rule to require each issuer to disclose in annual meeting materials whether any employee or member of the board of directors is permitted to purchase financial instruments designed to hedge or offset any decrease in the market value of equity securities.

SECTION 956. ENHANCED COMPENSATION STRUCTURE REPORTING

According to the bill, the appropriate federal regulators[7] shall jointly prescribe regulations requiring each covered financial institution[8] to disclose the structures of all incentive-based compensation structures which it offers to an executive officer, employee, director, or principal shareholder so as to determine whether excessive compensation is provided or whether the compensation could lead to material financial loss to the covered financial institution. The appropriate federal regulators shall jointly prescribe regulations which prohibit incentive-based compensation that is excessive or that couldlead to material financial loss. The standards for compensation shall be comparable to the standards for insured depository institutions under the Federal Deposit Insurance Act.[9]

Section 957. Voting by Brokers. This section amends section 6(b)[10] of the Securities Exchange Act of 1934 to prohibit a broker from voting a shareholder's proxy without authorization from the beneficial owner of the security.

On October 18, 2010, the SEC proposed rules to implement Dodd-Frank's executive compensation provisions.[11] The proposed rules would require public companies to give shareholders an advisory vote on executive compensation and an opportunity to decide how often—every year, every other year, or every three years—they wish to have a vote on executive compensation. Shareholders would be able to revisit every six years how often they want to have an advisory vote on say on pay.

End Notes

[1] H.R. 4173, Title II.

[2] S. 3217, Title IX, Subtitle E.

[3] For additional information about Securities and Exchange Commission and congressional executive compensation proposals, see CRS Report RS22583, *Executive Compensation: SEC Regulations and Congressional Proposals*, by Michael V. Seitzinger.

[4] H.Rept. 111-517.

[5] 15 U.S.C. § 78n.

[6] 15 U.S.C. §§ 78a *et seq*.

[7] Federal Reserve, Comptroller of the Currency, Federal Deposit Insurance Corporation, Office of Thrift Supervision, National Credit Union Administration Board, Securities and Exchange Commission, and Federal Housing Finance Agency.

[8] Depository institution, depository institution holding company, registered broker-dealer, credit union, investment adviser, Federal National Mortgage Association, Federal Home Loan Mortgage Corporation, and any other institution which the regulators determine should be covered.

[9] 12 U.S.C. § 1831p-1 (standards of safety and soundness).

[10] 15 U.S.C. § 78f(b).

[11] http://www.sec.gov/rules

In: The Dodd-Frank Wall Street Reform...
Editors: Nathan L. Morris and Philip O. Price

ISBN: 978-1-61324-101-1
© 2011 Nova Science Publishers, Inc.

Chapter 11

THE DODD-FRANK WALL STREET REFORM AND CONSUMER PROTECTION ACT: TITLE X, THE CONSUMER FINANCIAL PROTECTION BUREAU[*]

David H. Carpenter

SUMMARY

In the wake of what many believe is the worst U.S. financial crisis since the Great Depression, the Obama Administration proposed sweeping reforms of the financial services regulatory system— including the creation of an executive agency with authority over consumer financial issues, the broad outline of which has been encompassed in a document called the Administration's White Paper (the White Paper). The House of Representatives began consideration of bills seeking similar reform, which in large part were shepherded by Representative Barney Frank, Chairman of the Committee on Financial Services. On December 11, 2009, the House approved H.R. 4173, the Wall Street Reform and Consumer Protection Act of 2009. On May 20, 2010, the Senate approved its own financial reform measure, H.R. 4173, the Restoring American Financial Stability Act of 2010. (For an analysis of the consumer protection provisions of these proposals and how they varied, see CRS Report R40696, *Financial Regulatory Reform: Consumer Financial Protection Proposals*, by David H. Carpenter and Mark Jickling; for an overview of the overall financial reform proposals, see CRS Report R40975, *Financial Regulatory Reform and the 111th Congress*, coordinated by Baird Webel.)

A conference committee, chaired by Representative Frank and Senator Christopher Dodd, Chairman of the Senate Committee on Banking, Housing, and Urban Affairs, was formed to reconcile the two bills. On June 25, 2010, the conference committee agreed to file a conference report for H.R. 4173, renamed the Dodd-Frank Wall Street Reform and Consumer Protection Act (Dodd-Frank Act). On June 30, 2010, the House approved the conference report. The Senate approved the measure on July 15, 2010. The bill was signed into law on July 21, 2010, by President Obama as P.L. 111-203.

Title X of the Dodd-Frank Act is entitled the Consumer Financial Protection Act of 2010 (CFP Act). The CFP Act establishes a Bureau of Consumer Financial Protection

---

[*] This is an edited, reformatted and augmented version of a Congressional Research Services publication, dated July 21, 2010.

(CFPB or Bureau) within the Federal Reserve System with rulemaking, enforcement, and supervisory powers over many consumer financial products and services and the entities that sell them. The law also transfers to the Bureau the primary rulemaking and enforcement authority over many federal consumer protection laws enacted prior to the Dodd-Frank Act (the "enumerated consumer laws"), such as the Truth in Lending Act and the Real Estate Settlement Procedures Act.

This report provides a legal overview of the regulatory structure of consumer finance under existing federal law, which is followed by an analysis of how the CFP Act will change this legal structure, with a focus on the Bureau's organization and funding; the entities and activities that fall (and do not fall) under the Bureau's supervisory, enforcement, and rulemaking authority; the Bureau's general and specific rulemaking powers and procedures; and an analysis of the act's preemption standards over state consumer protection laws as they apply to national banks and thrifts.

INTRODUCTION

In the wake of what many believe is the worst U.S. financial crisis since the Great Depression, the Obama Administration proposed sweeping reforms of the financial services regulatory system— including the creation of an executive agency with authority over consumer financial issues, the broad outline of which has been encompassed in a document called the Administration's White Paper (the White Paper).[1] The House of Representatives began consideration of bills seeking similar reform, which in large part were shepherded by Representative Barney Frank, Chairman of the Committee on Financial Services. On December 11, 2009, the House approved H.R. 4173, the Wall Street Reform and Consumer Protection Act of 2009. On May 20, 2010, the Senate approved its own financial reform measure, H.R. 4173, the Restoring American Financial Stability Act of 2010. (For an analysis of the consumer protection provisions of these proposals and how they varied, see CRS Report R40696, *Financial Regulatory Reform: Consumer Financial Protection Proposals*, by David H. Carpenter and Mark Jickling; for an overview of the overall financial reform proposals, see CRS Report R40975, *Financial Regulatory Reform and the 111th Congress*, coordinated by Baird Webel.)

A conference committee, chaired by Representative Frank and Senator Christopher Dodd, Chairman of the Senate Committee on Banking, Housing, and Urban Affairs, was formed to reconcile the two bills. On June 25, 2010, the conference committee agreed to file a conference report for H.R. 4173, renamed the Dodd-Frank Wall Street Reform and Consumer Protection Act (Dodd-Frank Act). On June 30, 2010, the House approved the conference report. The Senate approved the measure on July 15, 2010. The bill was signed into law on July 21, 2010, by President Obama as P.L. 111-203.

Title X of the Dodd-Frank Act is entitled the Consumer Financial Protection Act of 2010 (CFP Act). The CFP Act establishes a Bureau of Consumer Financial Protection (CFPB or Bureau) within the Federal Reserve System with rulemaking, enforcement, and supervisory powers over many consumer financial products and services and the entities that sell them. The law also transfers to the Bureau the primary rulemaking and enforcement authority over many federal consumer protection laws enacted prior to the Dodd-Frank Act (the "enumerated consumer laws"), such as the Truth in Lending Act and the Real Estate Settlement Procedures Act.

This report provides a legal overview of the regulatory structure of consumer finance under existing federal law, which is followed by an analysis of how the CFP Act will change this legal structure, with a focus on the Bureau's organization and funding; the entities and activities that fall (and do not fall) under the Bureau's supervisory, enforcement, and rulemaking authority; the Bureau's general and specific rulemaking powers and procedures; and an analysis of the act's preemption standards over state consumer protection laws as they apply to national banks and thrifts.

FEDERAL CONSUMER FINANCIAL PROTECTION IN ABSENCE OF THE CFPB

Until the CFP Act goes into effect, which will largely occur at some point six to 18 months after enactment (called the "designated transfer date"), the Board of Governors of the Federal Reserve System (FRB) retains its authority to write rules to implement the majority of the consumer financial protection laws. Enforcement of these laws and the supervisory powers over the individuals and companies offering and selling consumer financial products and services will continue to be shared by a number of different federal agencies until the CFPB takes over.

Until the Bureau's powers take effect, the federal bank regulators are the primary consumer protection enforcers and supervisors for the institutions under their jurisdictions. These regulators include the Office of the Comptroller of the Currency (OCC) for national banks; the FRB for domestic operations of foreign banks and for state-chartered banks that are members of the Federal Reserve System (FRS); the Federal Deposit Insurance Corporation (FDIC) for state-chartered banks and other state-chartered banking institutions that are not members of the FRS;[2] the National Credit Union Administration (NCUA) for federally insured credit unions; and the Office of Thrift Supervision (OTS)[3] for federal savings and loan associations and thrifts. Banks, credit unions, and thrifts (which this report will collectively refer to as "depository institutions" or "depositories") are subject to regular examinations to ensure they are complying with consumer protection and other laws, being managed well, and conducting business in a safe and sound fashion. All depositories generally must be examined at least once every 18 months, but the largest depositories have examiners on-site on a near-constant basis.[4] Additionally, federal regulators of depository institutions have a full range of strong and flexible enforcement tools, such as prompt corrective action powers, to rectify any problems that are found during examinations.[5]

The Federal Trade Commission (FTC) is the primary federal regulator for non-depository financial institutions, such as payday lenders and mortgage brokers, in addition to many other non-financial commercial enterprises. However, the FTC's powers generally are limited to enforcement. Unlike the federal depository regulators, the FTC has little up front supervisory authority over non-depository financial institutions. Thus, the FTC does not regularly examine businesses or impose reporting requirements on them. Instead, these non-depository institutions are primarily supervised by state regulators. The powers granted to state regulators and the level of supervision these regulators provide varies considerably from state-to-state, but in most cases, non-depositories have not been as rigorously regulated as depository institutions.

OVERVIEW OF THE BUREAU

The CFP Act establishes a Bureau of Consumer Financial Protection that brings the consumer protection regulation of depository and non-depository financial institutions into closer, but not complete, alignment. As proposals that ultimately resulted in Title X of the Dodd-Frank Act were moving through Congress, a couple of fundamental policy questions seemed to arise consistently during debate, which seemed in large part to account for the remaining disparities.

One policy question is how best to balance the safety and soundness regulation of depositories with that of consumer compliance. Although a loan that cannot be repaid is typically bad for both the borrower and the lender, there are some areas in which there can be a conflict between safety and soundness regulation and consumer protection. When a banking activity is profitable, safety and soundness regulators tend to look upon it favorably, since it enables the bank to meet capital requirements and withstand financial shocks. A consumer protection regulator, however, may look at such activity less favorably, especially if the profit is seen to have been gained unfairly at the expense of consumers. Removing consumer compliance authority from the federal bank regulators may weaken the safety and soundness regulation of banks if, for example, the separation results in a less complete picture of bank operations for the prudential regulator. The Fed has argued that its role in consumer protection aids its other authorities, including bank supervision and systemic risk. On the other hand, some, including the Obama Administration, have argued that professional bank examiners are trained "to see the world through the lenses of institutions and markets, not consumers,"[6] and separating compliance and safety and soundness authorities among different regulators is the best way to protect both consumers and financial institutions.

A related question that surfaced frequently during the debate is the extent to which large and small financial institutions should be treated differently in the proposed regulatory structure. Whereas the largest depository institutions are accustomed to having examiners on-site constantly, examinations are far more disruptive for smaller depositories. Enhanced compliance costs also are likely to hit smaller depositories, with their lower aggregate revenues, more than larger depositories. Similar arguments could be made for large versus small non-depository financial institutions. Additionally, when assessing the causes of the Great Recession, many tend to place much more blame on this country's large financial institutions than on smaller ones. Thus, one could argue that the larger institutions should be subject to greater, more-costly regulation than smaller institutions. On the other hand, the goal of the Dodd-Frank Act appears to be geared not just towards eliminating the exact causes of the Great Recession, but also towards preventing future crises.

The CFP Act establishes the Bureau within the FRS to have authority over an array of consumer financial products and services (including deposit taking, mortgages, credit cards and other extensions of credit, loan servicing, check guaranteeing, collection of consumer report data, debt collection, real estate settlement, money transmitting, and financial data processing). It will also serve as the primary federal consumer financial protection supervisor and enforcer of federal consumer protection laws over many of the institutions that offer these products and services.

However, apparently as a result of the policy considerations outlined above, the act's allocation of regulatory authority among the prudential regulators and the CFPB varies based

Title X, The Consumer Financial Protection Bureau

on institution size and type. Regulatory authority differs for (1) depository institutions with more than $10 billion in assets (i.e., "larger depositories"); (2) depository institutions with $10 billion or less in assets (i.e., "smaller depositories"); and (3) non-depositories. The Dodd-Frank Act also explicitly exempts a number of different entities and consumer financial activities from the CFPA's supervisory and enforcement authority.

Consequently, compliance costs and the extent to which the cost and availability of credit will be affected by the new regulator will depend on the type of institution that is providing consumer financial products and services, as well as exactly what rules the Bureau prescribes and how aggressively it and the other regulators enforce consumer protection laws and regulations.

BUREAU STRUCTURE AND FUNDING

The stated goal of the Bureau is to

> implement and, where applicable, enforce Federal consumer financial law consistently for the purpose of ensuring that all consumers have access to markets for consumer financial products and services and that markets for consumer financial products and services are fair, transparent, and competitive.[7]

The Bureau is established within the Federal Reserve System, but it has some measure of independence from the FRB. For instance, the FRB does not have the formal authority to stop, delay, or disapprove of a Bureau regulation, nor can it

A. intervene in any matter or proceeding before the Director [of the CFPB], including examinations or enforcement actions, unless otherwise specifically provided by law;
B. appoint, direct, or remove any officer or employee of the Bureau; or
C. merge or consolidate the Bureau, or any of the functions or responsibilities of the Bureau, with any division or office of the Board of Governors or the Federal reserve banks.[8]

However, the Bureau is not completely independent of the FRB. As an example, the act allows, but does not require, the FRB to "delegate to the Bureau the authorities to examine persons subject to the jurisdiction of the [Board] for compliance with the Federal consumer financial laws."[9]

The Bureau is to be headed by a director appointed by the President, subject to the advice and consent of the Senate, to serve for a five-year term from which s/he could only be removed for "inefficiency, neglect of duty or malfeasance in office."[10] Until the director is confirmed, the Secretary of the Treasury will have the power to perform the Bureau's functions.[11] The director has authority to hire the employees necessary to carry out the duties of the Bureau. The act establishes a procedure by which the FRS, OCC, OTS, NCUA, FDIC, and the Department of Housing and Urban Development will transfer employees to the Bureau as necessary to perform the consumer financial protection functions that are transferred from those agencies to the Bureau.[12]

The law requires the director to establish units within the Bureau to focus on consumer financial research; providing guidance and technical assistance to traditionally underserved areas and individuals; and monitoring and responding to consumer complaints. The act also requires the establishment of an Office of Fair Lending and Equal Opportunity; an Office of Financial Education; an Office of Service Member Affairs directed towards members of the military and their families; an Office of Financial Protection for Older Americans to, among other things, "facilitate the financial literacy of individuals who have attained the age of 62 years or more ... on protection from unfair, deceptive, and abusive practices on current and future financial choices";[13] and a Private Education Loan Ombudsman to, among other things, attempt to settle and study private education loan borrower complaints.[14]

The Bureau will be funded "from the combined earnings of the Federal Reserve System [in an] amount determined by the Director to be reasonably necessary to carry out the authorities of the Bureau" subject to specified caps. The cap will be 10% of the total operating expenses of the FRS for FY2011, 11% for FY2012, and 12% thereafter.[15] As a gauge of how much money this will be, the FRS's total operating expenses for FY2009 were $4.98 billion, 10% of which is just under $500 million.[16] These funds are not reviewable by either the House or Senate Committees on Appropriations. The act also authorizes appropriations if the director "determine[s] that sums available to the Bureau [as specified by the caps] under this section will not be sufficient to carry out the authorities of the Bureau under Federal consumer financial law for the upcoming year." Upon making such a finding and submitting a report to both the House and Senate Committees on Appropriations, the CFP Act provides authorization for an appropriation of $200 million per year for FY2010-FY2014.[17]

The act also establishes a Consumer Financial Civil Penalty Fund for civil penalties obtained by the Bureau for violations of consumer financial protection laws. The fund is to be used to pay victims of such violations, as well as for financial literacy and consumer education programs.[18]

GENERAL POWERS

The authorities of the Bureau fall into three different categories: supervisory, which includes the power to examine and require reports; enforcement of various consumer protection laws and regulations; and rulemaking. Some of these powers are newly created by the Dodd-Frank Act.

Some are to be transferred from other regulators to the Bureau, including the primary rulemaking and enforcement authority of many existing consumer protection laws. These "enumerated consumer laws" are the Alternative Mortgage Transaction Parity Act;[19] the Consumer Leasing Act of 1976;[20] the Electronic Funds Transfer Act[21] except with respect to section 920 of that act;[22] the Equal Credit Opportunity Act;[23] the Fair Credit Billing Act;[24] the Fair Credit Reporting Act,[25] except with respect to sections 615(e) and 628 of that act;[26] the Home Owners Protection Act of 1998;[27] the Fair Debt Collection Practices Act;[28] subsections (b) through (f) of section 43 of the Federal Deposit Insurance Act;[29] sections 502 through 509 of the Gramm-Leach-Bliley Act,[30] except for section 505 as it applies to section 501(b);[31] the Home Mortgage Disclosure Act of 1975;[32] the Home Ownership and Equity Protection Act of 1994;[33] the Real Estate Settlement Procedures Act of 1974;[34] the S.A.F.E. Mortgage Licensing Act of 2008;[35] the Truth in Lending Act (TILA);[36] the Truth in Savings Act;[37]

section 626 of the Omnibus Appropriations Act, 2009;[38] the Interstate Land Sales Full Disclosure Act;[39] and most provisions of the Mortgage Reform and Anti-Predatory Lending Act.[40]

The powers under these consumer laws will be transferred to the Bureau within six to 18 months after enactment, as determined by the Secretary of the Treasury in consultation with other federal agency heads.[41] The act refers to this date as the "designated transfer date."

Other authorities became effective on the date of enactment. It is unclear exactly how the powers that are effective immediately will be utilized by the new Bureau, which cannot be fully established overnight. Because the Secretary of the Treasury acquires all powers of the director until a director is confirmed, the Secretary is likely to prescribe regulations to outline how he will utilize these powers while the Bureau gets up and running.

COVERED ENTITIES AND ACTIVITIES

Under the CFP Act, the Bureau has authority over an array of consumer financial products and services, including deposit taking, mortgages, credit cards and other extensions of credit, loan servicing, check guaranteeing, collection of consumer report data, debt collection, real estate settlement, money transmitting, financial data processing, and others.[42] The CFPA does not have authority over most insurance activities[43] nor most activities conducted by firms regulated by the Securities and Exchange Commission (SEC) or the Commodity Futures Trading Commission (CFTC). The Bureau also does not have authority under the CFP Act to impose interest rate caps (a.k.a., usury limits) on any loan or other extension of credit.[44] While the breadth of the products and services that fall within the Bureau's jurisdiction is considerable, the CFP Act imposes some important exceptions on the types of entities and activities that are subject to the CFPB's rulemaking, enforcement, and supervisory powers.

Non-Depositories

For instance, the CFP Act imposes limitations on the Bureau's supervisory and enforcement powers over non-depository institutions. The Bureau is the primary supervisor and enforcer of non-depository entities that

- are engaged in consumer mortgage related activities (i.e., mortgage origination, brokerage, or servicing activities; mortgage modification or foreclosure relief activities);
- are non-mortgage related consumer financial entities that are "larger participant[s] in a market" as determined by the Bureau in regulations and after consultation with the FTC;
- the Bureau has reasonable cause to believe are "engaging, or ha[ve] engaged, in conduct that poses risks to consumers with regard to the offering or provision of consumer financial products or services";
- provide or offer to provide private student loans; or
- provide or offer to provide payday loans.[45]

Even for a company that falls into one of these categories (a "covered non-depository"), the Bureau must rely on existing reports required by prudential regulators "to the fullest extent possible" and must coordinate examinations with the company's primary regulator (state or federal). The Bureau generally will be the primary enforcer of federal consumer financial laws with respect to covered non-depositories and will have primary rulemaking authority over such entities. Finally, the Bureau has the authority to require covered non-depositories to register with the Bureau, submit to background checks, and adhere to other measures "to ensure that such persons are legitimate entities and are able to perform their obligations to consumers."[46]

The Bureau's authority over covered non-depositories became effective on the date of enactment, except for those powers stemming from the enumerated consumer laws, which will become effective on the designated transfer date.[47]

Depositories with More than $10 Billion in Assets

The Bureau will be the primary rule maker, supervisor, and enforcer of consumer protection laws and regulations over depository institutions holding more than $10 billion in assets. The CFP Act requires the Bureau to coordinate examinations and other supervisory activities with large depositories' state and federal prudential regulators and establishes a procedure by which conflicts between the Bureau and a prudential regulator could be resolved.[48] The Bureau acquired its examination powers over these institutions on the date of enactment. However, most of its remaining powers over larger depositories will take effect on the designated transfer date.[49]

Depositories with $10 Billion or Less in Assets

The primary consumer protection supervisory and enforcement powers over banks, thrifts, and credit unions with $10 billion or less in assets (smaller depository institutions) largely remain in those institutions' prudential regulators. The CFP Act does not provide a process by which the Bureau may acquire enforcement powers over these institutions. However, the Bureau, "on a sampling basis," may participate in examinations of these smaller depository institutions that are conducted by the prudential regulator. The new law also establishes a procedure by which the Bureau can refer potential enforcement actions against smaller depository institutions to their prudential regulators. The Bureau generally will have access to examination reports prepared by prudential regulators of these smaller depository institutions and will have the authority to require reports directly from these depositories, although the Bureau will have to rely on existing reports "to the fullest extent possible."[50] These smaller depositories generally will be subject to the rulemaking powers of the Bureau. The Bureau's authority over smaller depositories generally will take effect on the designated transfer date.[51]

Entities and Activities with Explicit Exemptions

The Dodd-Frank Act explicitly exempts a number of entities and activities from the CFPB's jurisdictional reach. However, each of these exemptions is subject to certain limitations that, while spelled out in the act, are subject to interpretation. How the Bureau interprets these limited exemptions could significantly impact the scope of the Bureau's reach.

Merchants, Retailers, and Sellers of Nonfinancial Goods and Services

The act significantly limits the Bureau's supervisory, enforcement, and rulemaking powers over a

> merchant, retailer, or seller of nonfinancial goods or services ... to the extent that such person (i) extends credit directly to a consumer ... exclusively for the purpose of enabling that consumer to purchase such nonfinancial good or service directly from the merchant, retailer, or seller; (ii) ... collects debt arising from [such] credit ... or (iii) sells or conveys [such] debt ... that is delinquent or otherwise in default.[52]

In spite of these restrictions, the CFPB does have authority over a merchant, retailer, and seller of nonfinancial goods or services if such an entity "regularly extends credit and the credit is subject to a finance charge" and is "engaged significantly in offering or providing consumer financial products or services"; or if such entity either (1) "assigns, sells or otherwise conveys to another person such [nondelinquent] debt owed by a consumer," or (2) extends credit that "significantly exceeds the market value of the nonfinancial good or service provided" or otherwise evades the CFP Act. The Bureau will also have authority over merchants, retailers, and sellers of nonfinancial goods or services to the extent that they fall within the ambit of an enumerated consumer law.[53] The Bureau's rulemaking, supervisory, and enforcement authorities are further restricted against certain small businesses that otherwise would only fall under the Bureau's jurisdiction because they "regularly extend[] credit and the credit is subject to a finance charge."[54]

Automobile Dealers

The Bureau generally does not have supervisory, rulemaking, or enforcement powers over automobile dealers engaged in leasing, selling, or servicing automobiles except to the extent that such dealers (1) engage in activities related to either commercial or residential mortgages; (2) engage in the extension of credit or leases directly to consumers that are "not routinely assigned to an unaffiliated third party finance or leasing source"; or (3) sell or offer to sell consumer financial products or services unrelated "to the sale, financing, leasing, rental, repair, refurbishment, maintenance, or other servicing of motor vehicles, motor vehicle parts, or any related or ancillary product or services."[55]

However, the CFP Act does provide the FTC the authority to prescribe unfair or deceptive trade practice rules against automobile dealers in accordance with the standard informal rulemaking procedures of the Administrative Procedure Act[56] rather than having to adhere to the much more rigorous procedures of the Magnuson-Moss Act[57] that normally apply when the FTC promulgates rules declaring unfair or deceptive acts or practices pursuant to section 5 of the Federal Trade Commission Act.[58] Thus, while auto dealers generally are outside of the Bureau's authority, the CFP Act makes it somewhat easier for the FTC to regulate them.

Other Entities

The CFP Act also generally excludes from the Bureau's rulemaking, supervisory, and enforcement authority real estate brokers,[59] real estate agents,[60] sellers of manufactured and mobile homes,[61] income tax preparers,[62] and accountants[63] to the extent that they are acting in their normal capacity (e.g., a real estate broker is exempt to the extent that s/he brings parties together to purchase a property). However, the CFP Act authorizes some authority for the Bureau to regulate these entities if they engage in the extension of credit or otherwise sell or offer to sell a consumer financial product or service or if they otherwise engage in an activity that makes them subject to an enumerated consumer law.

Attorneys generally are exempt from the Bureau's supervisory and enforcement authority (although, the act does not explicitly exempt attorneys from the Bureau's rulemaking authority) when they are practicing law. However, this exemption would not apply to the extent that an attorney sells or offers to sell "a consumer financial product or service ... that is not offered or provided as part of, or incidental to, the practice of law, occurring exclusively within the scope of the attorney-client relationship; or that is otherwise offered or provided by the attorney in question with respect to any consumer who is not receiving legal advice or services from the attorney in connection with such financial product or service." The CFPB could still exert control over attorneys to the extent that they are subject to an enumerated consumer law.[64]

Other entities and activities that generally fall outside of the Bureau's jurisdictional reach include insurance companies;[65] employee benefit plans;[66] entities that are regulated by state securities commissions;[67] those regulated by the Farm Credit Administration;[68] and donations to tax-exempt charities.[69]

Rulemaking Procedures

The Dodd-Frank Act establishes procedures that the Bureau must follow when proposing and prescribing rules, generally, which are in addition to the notice of proposed rulemaking and comment period procedures required for informal rulemakings under the Administrative Procedure Act.[70] The act also imposes additional procedures for specific types of rulemaking (e.g., when declaring certain acts or practices to be unfair or abusive), which are discussed below.

General Rulemaking Powers
The CFP Act authorizes the Bureau to "prescribe rules and issue orders and guidance, as may be necessary or appropriate to enable the Bureau to administer and carry out the purposes and objectives of the Federal consumer financial laws, and to prevent evasions thereof."[71] Before proposing a rule and during the comment period of a proposed rule, the CFPB is required to consult with the "appropriate" financial regulators. The Bureau must address any written objections by the federal prudential regulators when issuing final regulations. Additionally, the CFPB must consider "the potential benefits and costs to consumers and covered persons, including the potential reduction of access by consumers to consumer financial products and services resulting from such rule," as well as the impact the rule would have on smaller depositories and "consumers in rural areas."[72] These general rulemaking powers became effective on the date of enactment.[73]

Within five years of any CFPB "significant rule or order" becoming effective and after a public comment period, the Bureau must publish a report assessing the effectiveness of the rule or order.[74] The act does not specify what is to be considered "significant," presumably leaving these determinations to the Bureau.

On the designated transfer date, the CFP Act will also transfer to the CFPB rulemaking authority under the enumerated consumer laws. In some instances, the Bureau will share rulemaking powers under the enumerated consumer laws with other financial regulators.[75]

Although previous iterations of H.R. 4173 modified the FTC's rulemaking procedures for declaring unfair or abusive trade practices under the FTC Act, those changes were not included in the Dodd-Frank Act.[76] On a related issue that is outside the scope of the FTC Act, the CFP Act provides the Bureau new authority to prescribe rules declaring acts or practices to be unlawful because they are unfair or abusive (discussed in the next section).

As a check on the Bureau's rulemaking powers, the Financial Stability Oversight Council—which is established under Title III of the Dodd-Frank Act and mainly composed of the federal financial regulators, including the director of the Bureau[77]—has the ability to set aside or stay a regulation prescribed by the Bureau if the regulation "would put the safety and soundness of the United States banking system or the stability of the financial system of the United States at risk." These powers are in addition to the Financial Stability Oversight Council's authority to settle jurisdictional disputes among the federal financial regulators.[78] The Council's power to stay and set aside Bureau rules does not appear to be limited to the new rulemaking powers established by the CFP Act, which means the power also may extend to rules prescribed under the authority of an enumerated consumer law.

Specific Rulemaking Powers

The following specific rulemaking powers will take effect on the designated transfer date.

Unfair or Abusive Acts or Practices

The CFP Act will provide the Bureau the authority to prescribe rules declaring acts or practices pertaining to covered consumer financial products or services to be unlawful because they are unfair or abusive. This is a similar mandate to that provided to the FTC under the FTC Act, except that the Bureau's authority is limited to consumer financial issues and to those entities that fall under the Bureau's rulemaking jurisdiction. When prescribing such rules, the Bureau must consult with the other federal financial regulators, as appropriate.

In order to declare an act or practice unlawful because it is *unfair*, the CFPB must have "a reasonable basis to conclude that the act or practices causes or is likely to cause substantial injury to consumers, which is not reasonably avoidable by consumers; and such substantial injury is not outweighed by countervailing benefits to consumers or competition."

An abusive act or practice may only be deemed unlawful by regulation if it

> materially interferes with the ability of a consumer to understand a term or condition of a consumer financial product or service; or takes unreasonable advantage of (a) a lack of understanding on the part of the consumer ...; (b) the inability of the consumer to protect the interests of the consumer in selecting or using a consumer financial product or service; or (c) the reasonable reliance by the consumer on a covered person to act in the interests of the consumer.[79]

Disclosure Requirements

The Bureau will also have the authority to prescribe rules imposing disclosure requirements to help consumers understand the terms, benefits, costs, and risks of financial products and services. When prescribing these rules, the CFPB is to "consider the available evidence about consumer awareness, understanding of, and responses to disclosures or communications about the risks, costs, and benefits of consumer financial products or services."[80]

Rulemakings Initiated by the States

When a majority of states adopt a resolution requesting a new consumer protection regulation under the CFPB's jurisdiction or a change in an existing rule, the Bureau must submit a notice of proposed rulemaking on the subject. Before finalizing such a rule, the Bureau must address in the final rule notice whether or not the final rule will (1) increase consumer protection; (2) create more benefits than costs for consumers; (3) unfairly discriminate against a group of consumers; and (4) "likely [] present an unacceptable safety and soundness risk to insured depository institutions," if such a concern is raised by a prudential regulator. If the Bureau decides not to finalize such a rule, it will have to justify why a final regulation was not prescribed.[81]

Preemption of State Laws

Preemption Standards for National Banks in Absence of the Dodd-Frank Act

The federal government derives much of its power to regulate banks through the Commerce Clause of Article I, clause 8 of the U.S. Constitution. The 10th Amendment of the Constitution reserves the right of states to legislate all matters neither prohibited by the Constitution nor delegated to federal government. At the same time, the Supremacy Clause of Article VI, clause 2 of the Constitution[82] provides that the U.S. Constitution and the laws enacted under it are preeminent to state laws. Although the federal government has extensively regulated depository institutions pursuant to the Commerce Clause, federal law does leave some room for states to regulate national banks and thrifts on consumer financial protection issues. In some cases, it is clear when a state law is preempted by federal law. In many cases, however, preemption is not so clear.[83]

The courts have recognized three different types of preemption: express, field, and conflict. Express preemption involves an explicit preemption statement in a piece of legislation. Conflict preemption occurs either when it is not possible to comply with both federal and state law at the same time or when state law imposes an obstacle to the achievement of a federal law's purpose.

Field preemption, which is a subset of conflict preemption, arises when federal preemption in a legislative field is so pervasive that it can be reasonably inferred that Congress left no room for states to add to it.[84]

There is a large body of Supreme Court precedent analyzing conflict preemption as it applies to national banks dating all the way back to the 1819 decision in *McCulloch vs. Maryland*,[85] in which the Court expressed its broad interpretation of the Supremacy Clause by stating that "the States have no power, by taxation or otherwise, to retard, impede, burden, or in any manner control, the operations of the constitutional laws enacted by Congress to carry into execution the powers vested in the general government." More recently, the Court in a 2007 decision, *Watters v. Wachovia N.A.*,[86] explained that federal laws protect national banks "from unduly burdensome and duplicative [state] regulation."[87] The *Watters* Court went on to reiterate the preemption standard expressed in the Court's 1996 opinion of *Barnett Bank of Marion County, N.A. v. Nelson*[88] by stating the following:

> States are permitted to regulate the activities of national banks where doing so does not prevent or significantly interfere with the national bank's or the national bank regulator's exercise of its powers. But when state prescriptions significantly impair the exercise of authority, enumerated or incidental under the [National Bank Act[89]], the State's regulations must give way.[90]

CFP Act

Generally, state consumer protection laws are only to be preempted by the provisions of the CFP Act and the regulations prescribed under the authority of the act to the extent of their inconsistency. A state law is not to be considered inconsistent with a federal law if the Bureau determines that the state law provides greater protection to consumers. With some exceptions,[91] the Dodd-Frank Act does not alter the express preemption provisions of the existing enumerated consumer protection laws.

In addition to these more general preemption principles, the act establishes preemption standards specific to national banks and thrifts. The CFP Act will restrict the ability of the OCC to preempt state consumer financial laws as they apply to national banks by imposing procedural standards that the agency must follow when making such determinations. The same standards will apply for federal thrifts. The act also clarifies and expands the rights of state attorneys general to bring civil claims against national banks and thrifts.

Under the act, consumer financial protection laws as they apply to national banks and thrifts are preempted only if (1) the state law "would have a discriminatory effect on national banks" or thrifts as compared to state banks or thrifts; (2) the OCC or a court, on a case-by-case basis, determines by regulation or order that the state law, "in accordance with the legal standard for preemption in the decision ... in *Barnett* ... prevents or significantly interferes with the exercise by the national bank of its powers"; or (3) the state law is preempted by another federal law.[92]

The Dodd-Frank Act establishes standards that the OCC and courts must follow when making case-by-case preemption decisions. The OCC will have to consult with the Bureau before making a determination that a state law that the OCC has determined to be preempted is "substantively equivalent" to another consumer financial law in a different state. In order to preempt such "substantively equivalent" state statutes, the OCC must support its decision with "substantial evidence, on the record of the proceeding" that the preemption decision meets the legal standards of the *Barnett* opinion. When reviewing an OCC preemption decision,[93] a court

> shall assess the validity of such determinations, depending upon the thoroughness evident in the consideration of the agency, the validity of the reasoning of the agency, the consistency with other valid determinations made by the agency, and other factors which the court finds persuasive and relevant to its decision.[94]

The act's preemption standards for depositories do not apply to the non-depository subsidiaries or affiliates of federally chartered banks or thrifts.[95] The CFP Act requires the OCC to review preemption determinations periodically (at least once every five years) and to publicly list each preemption decision "that identifies the activities and practices covered by each determination and the requirements and constraints determined to be preempted."[96]

The CFP Act also places in statute the standard of the U.S. Supreme Court's decision in *Cuomo v. Clearing House Association*,[97] which pertains to the limitations of state regulators' visitorial[98] rights over federally chartered banks. The 2009 opinion confirms the ability of state regulators to enforce non-preempted state laws against national banks. The CFP Act extends these same powers to cover federal thrifts.[99]

Finally, the act creates a right of action for state attorneys general to enforce the substantive provisions of the CFP Act against all covered persons other than national banks and thrifts. State attorneys general are provided the authority to enforce *regulations* prescribed by the Bureau under the authority of the CFP Act against all covered persons, including national banks and thrifts. However, a state attorney general generally must provide advance notice of an enforcement action to the Bureau, which will then have the right to intervene in the matter.[100]

These preemption standards will take effect on the designated transfer date.[101]

Miscellaneous Provisions

The CFP Act addresses additional issues including imposing disclosure requirements on remittance transfers;[102] providing the Bureau the authority to curb pre-dispute arbitration clauses;[103] requiring studies on reverse mortgages[104] and credit scores;[105] and requiring the FRB to prescribe rules on debit card interchange fees.[106]

End Notes

[1] Financial Regulatory Reform, Obama Administration White Paper, June 19, 2009, available at http://www.financialstability.gov/docs/regs/FinalReport_web (hereinafter, White Paper).

[2] The FDIC, which administers the Deposit Insurance Fund, also has certain regulatory powers over state and national banks holding FDIC insured deposits; however, these authorities generally are secondary to the institution's primary federal regulator.

[3] The Dodd-Frank Act will eliminate the OTS and transfer much of its power to the OCC.

[4] See, e.g., 12 U.S.C. § 1820(d).

[5] 12 U.S.C. § 1831o; 12 U.S.C. § 1818.

[6] U.S. Department of the Treasury, *Financial Regulatory Reform: A New Foundation*, June 2009, p. 56, available at http://www.financialstability.gov/docs/regs/FinalReport_web

[7] Dodd-Frank Act § 1021.

[8] Dodd-Frank Act § 1012.

[9] Dodd-Frank Act § 1012.

[10] Dodd-Frank Act § 1011.

[11] Dodd-Frank Act § 1066.

[12] Dodd-Frank Act § 1064.

[13] Dodd-Frank Act § 1013.

[14] Dodd-Frank Act § 1035.

[15] Dodd-Frank Act § 1017. According to the act, this cap is to be adjusted for inflation.

[16] Federal Reserve 2009 Annual Report, available at http://www.federalreserve.gov/boarddocs/ rptcongress/annual09/ sec6/c3.htm.

[17] Dodd-Frank Act § 1017.

Title X, The Consumer Financial Protection Bureau
221

[18] Dodd-Frank Act § 1017.

[19] 12 U.S.C. §§ 3801 *et seq.*

[20] 15 U.S.C. §§ 1667 *et seq.*

[21] 15 U.S.C. §§ 1693 *et seq.*

[22] Section 920 of the Electronic Funds Transfer Act (15 U.S.C. § 1693q) delineates the interaction between the EFTA and state laws.

[23] 15 U.S.C. §§ 1691 *et seq.*

[24] 15 U.S.C. §§ 1666-1666j.

[25] 15 U.S.C. §§ 1681 *et seq.*

[26] 15 U.S.C. §§ 1681m(e) and 1681w. These provisions primarily pertain to "red flag" identity theft prevention measures for federal financial institutions and credit report record retention by federal financial institutions.

[27] 12 U.S.C. §§ 4901 *et seq.*

[28] 15 U.S.C. §§ 1692 *et seq.*

[29] 12 U.S.C. § 1831t(c)-(f). These provisions pertain to disclosure requirements for depository institutions that do not hold federal deposit insurance.

[30] 15 U.S.C. §§ 6802-6809. These provisions deal with financial institutions' use and protection of nonpublic consumer information.

[31] This provision pertains to federal banking agency rulemaking applicable to the safeguarding of nonpublic personal information by banking concerns.

[32] 12 U.S.C. §§ 2801 *et seq.*

[33] 15 U.S.C. § 1639.

[34] 12 U.S.C. §§ 2601-2610.

[35] 12 U.S.C. §§ 5101-5116.

[36] 15 U.S.C. §§ 1601 *et seq.*

[37] 12 U.S.C. §§ 4301 *et seq.*

[38] P.L. 111-8 § 626. This provision pertains to a regulation under which states may bring actions to enforce certain Truth in Lending Act requirements regarding mortgage loans.

[39] 15 U.S.C. §§ 1701 *et seq.*

[40] Dodd-Frank Act, Title XIV, Subtitles A, B, C, and E, and §§ 1471, 1472, 1475, and 1476. See Dodd-Frank Act § 1400.

[41] Dodd-Frank Act § 1062.

[42] Dodd-Frank Act § 1002(15). The Bureau also has authority over "service providers," which generally includes individuals that provide "a material service to a covered person in connection with the offering or provision of a consumer financial product or service" (Dodd-Frank Act § 1002(26)).

[43] Dodd-Frank Act § 1002(15).

[44] Dodd-Frank Act § 1027(o).

[45] Dodd-Frank Act § 1024. While the Bureau has authority to regulate payday lenders, the Bureau does not have authority to set usury limits. Dodd-Frank Act § 1027(o). Some consumer advocates have argued that interest rate caps are the only proven way to effectively curb predatory practices of payday lenders. Center for Responsible Lending, *Issue Brief: Payday Loans Put Families in the Red*, Feb. 2009, available at http://www.responsiblelending.org/payday-lending/research-analysis/payday-puts-families-in-the-red-final.pdf ("Payday lending industry representatives have lobbied for other reforms, such as payment plans and renewal bans, because they understand that these measures have done nothing to slow the rate at which they can flip loans to the same borrowers. But an interest rate cap is the only measure that has proven effective.").

[46] Dodd-Frank Act § 1024.

[47] Dodd-Frank Act § 1029A.

[48] Dodd-Frank Act § 1025.

[49] Dodd-Frank Act § 1029A.

[50] Dodd-Frank Act § 1026.

[51] Dodd-Frank Act § 1029A.

[52] Dodd-Frank Act § 1027(a).

[53] Dodd-Frank Act § 1027(a). Certain small businesses that would only fall within the CFPB's authority because they "regularly extend[] credit" subject to finance charges would not be considered to be engaged significantly in offering or providing consumer financial products or services if they only offer credit for nonfinancial goods or services, keep ownership of such nondelinquent credit, and meet the size threshold under the Small Business Act. Dodd-Frank Act § 1027(a).

[54] Dodd-Frank Act § 1027(a)(D).

[55] Dodd-Frank Act § 1029.

[56] 5 U.S.C. § 553.

[57] 15 U.S.C. § 57a.

[58] 15 U.S.C. § 45.

[59] Dodd-Frank Act § 1027(b).

[60] Dodd-Frank Act § 1027(b).

[61] Dodd-Frank Act § 1027(c).

[62] Dodd-Frank Act § 1027(d).

[63] Dodd-Frank Act § 1027(d).

[64] Dodd-Frank Act § 1027(e).

[65] Dodd-Frank Act § 1027(f).

[66] Dodd-Frank Act § 1027(g).

[67] Dodd-Frank Act § 1027(h).

[68] Dodd-Frank Act § 1027(k).

[69] Dodd-Frank Act § 1027(l).

[70] 5 U.S.C. § 553.

[71] Dodd-Frank Act § 1022.

[72] Dodd-Frank Act § 1022.

[73] Dodd-Frank Act § 1029A.

[74] Dodd-Frank Act § 1023(d).

[75] Dodd-Frank Act Title X, Subtitle H.

[76] The FTC's rulemaking procedures under the FTC Act (15 U.S.C. § 18b), commonly referred to as "Magnuson-Moss rulemaking procedures," are far more onerous than standard Administrative Procedure Act (5 U.S.C. § 553) informal rulemaking procedures.

[77] The director also will serve as an ex-officio member of the FDIC board (Dodd-Frank Act § 336).

[78] Dodd-Frank Act § 1023.

[79] Dodd-Frank Act § 1031.

[80] Dodd-Frank Act § 1032.

[81] Dodd-Frank Act § 1041(e).

[82] U.S. Const., Art. VI, cl. 2, declaring that the Constitution and "the laws of the United States which shall be made in Pursuance thereof ... shall be the supreme Law of the Land ... any Thing in the Constitution or Laws of the any State to the Contrary notwithstanding."

[83] The OCC and the OTS (until that agency is abolished pursuant to Title III of the Dodd-Frank Act) as the primary prudential regulators of national banks and thrifts generally would weigh in on preemption questions, which often arise in disputes between a depository and a state regulator. In such instances, courts are likely to give deference to reasonable agency interpretations of federal banking and consumer protection laws.

[84] CRS Report 97-589, *Statutory Interpretation: General Principles and Recent Trends*, by Larry M. Eig and Yule Kim.

[85] 17 U.S. (4 Wheat.) 316, 436 (1819).

[86] 550 U.S. 1 (2007).

[87] *Watters*, 550 U.S. at 11.

[88] 517 U.S. 25 (1996).

[89] 12 U.S.C. §§ 1, *et seq.*

[90] *Watters*, 550 U.S. at 12, *citing Barnett*, 517 U.S. at 32-34.

[91] Dodd-Frank Act § 1090.

[92] Dodd-Frank Act §§ 1044 [for banks] and 1046 [for thrifts].

[93] Preemption decisions under the CFP Act or under the authority of 12 U.S.C. § 371, which governs the power of national banks to engage in real estate lending.

[94] Dodd-Frank Act §§ 1044 [for banks] and 1046 [for thrifts].

[95] Dodd-Frank Act §§ 1044 [for banks] and 1046 [for thrifts].

[96] Dodd-Frank Act §§ 1044 [for banks] and 1046 [for thrifts].

[97] 129 S.Ct. 2710 (2009).

[98] "Visitation, in law, is the act of a superior or superintending officer, who visits a corporation to examine into its manner of conducting business, and enforce an observance of its laws and regulations. [Alexander M.] Burrill defines the word to mean 'inspection; superintendence; direction; regulation.'" Guthrie v. Harkness, 199 U.S. 148, 158 (1905). Burrill authored legal dictionaries often used at the time of the case.

[99] Dodd-Frank Act § 1047. For more information on the *Cuomo* decision, see CRS Report R40595, *Cuomo v. The Clearing House Association, L.L.C: National Banks Are Subject to State Lawsuits to Enforce Non-Preempted State Laws*, by M. Maureen Murphy.

[100] Dodd-Frank Act § 1042.

[101] Dodd-Frank Act § 1048.

[102] Dodd-Frank Act § 1073.

[103] Dodd-Frank Act § 1028.

[104] Dodd-Frank Act § 1076.

[105] Dodd-Frank Act § 1078.

[106] Dodd-Frank Act § 1075.

In: The Dodd-Frank Wall Street Reform...
Editors: Nathan L. Morris and Philip O. Price

ISBN: 978-1-61324-101-1
© 2011 Nova Science Publishers, Inc.

Chapter 12

THE DODD-FRANK WALL STREET REFORM AND CONSUMER PROTECTION ACT: STANDARDS OF CONDUCT OF BROKERS, DEALERS, AND INVESTMENT ADVISERS[*]

Michael V. Seitzinger

SUMMARY

Brokers and dealers and investment advisers have been held to different standards of conduct in their dealings with investors. In very general terms, a broker-dealer is held to a suitability standard, and an investment adviser is held to a fiduciary duty standard. With passage of the Dodd-Frank Wall Street Reform and Consumer Protection Act (P.L. 111-203), which tasks the Securities and Exchange Commission (SEC) with issuing rules concerning the standards of conduct for brokers, dealers, and investment advisers, the current standards may be changed.

The Financial Industry Regulatory Authority, a self-regulatory organization that oversees securities firms doing business in the United States and issues rules that the Securities and Exchange Commission may oversee, enforces a suitability standard for brokers and dealers. The standard requires that brokers and dealers assess their customers' knowledge of securities and their financial situations and recommend securities that are suitable for their customers.

An individual investor wishing to pursue action against a broker-dealer for recommending an unsuitable investment will often have to allege the violation of the general anti-fraud provision of the Securities Exchange Act, section 10(b), and the SEC rule issued to implement the statute, Rule 10b-5. To pursue a section 10(b) violation, an individual plaintiff must allege that, in connection with the purchase or sale of securities, he relied on a misstatement or omission of a material fact made with scienter by the defendant and that this reliance caused his injury. Investors seeking to sue a broker-dealer for violation of the suitability rule may also have to comply with the requirements of the Private Securities Litigation Reform Act.

---

[*] This is an edited, reformatted and augmented version of a Congressional Research Services publication, dated August 19, 2010.

In contrast to the suitability standard, which is most often applied to broker-dealers, investment advisers usually have a fiduciary duty with respect to investors. An investment adviser comes within the requirements of the Investment Advisers Act. Although the Investment Advisers Act does not use the word "fiduciary" to apply to the standard of conduct to which an investment adviser is held in managing a client's account, court cases have interpreted that an investment adviser has a fiduciary duty.

Changes to the standards of conduct applied to broker-dealers and investment advisers were present in both the House and the Senate versions of financial regulatory reform. However, the House and the Senate had different approaches to this issue. The House approach was to harmonize the fiduciary standard for brokers, dealers, and investment advisers. The Senate approach was to have the SEC conduct a study to evaluate the effectiveness of existing standards of conduct for brokers, dealers, and investment advisers. The House and Senate conferees on Wall Street reform approved a financial regulatory reform bill, called the Dodd-Frank Wall Street Reform and Consumer Protection Act. Dodd-Frank forged a kind of compromise between the House and Senate approaches. Section 913 of the legislation, titled "Study and Rulemaking regarding Obligations of Brokers, Dealers, and Investment Advisers," is the major provision setting out the new approach toward defining standards of conduct for these financial industry professionals. It requires the SEC to conduct a study to evaluate the effectiveness of the current legal or regulatory standards of care for brokers, dealers, and investment advisers and whether there are legal gaps, shortcomings, or overlaps in the standards. Criteria that the SEC must consider are set out. The SEC may issue new rules concerning the standards of conduct to be applied to brokers, dealers, and investment advisers. This report will be updated as warranted.

INTRODUCTION

Brokers and dealers[1] and investment advisers[2] have been held to different standards of conduct in their dealings with investors. In very general terms, a broker-dealer is held to a suitability standard, and an investment adviser is held to a fiduciary duty standard.[3] With passage of the Dodd-Frank Wall Street Reform and Consumer Protection Act,[4] which tasks the Securities and Exchange Commission (SEC) with issuing rules concerning the standards of conduct for brokers, dealers, and investment advisers, the current standards may be changed.

STANDARD OF CONDUCT FOR BROKER-DEALERS

The Financial Industry Regulatory Authority (FINRA) was created in 2007 through the consolidation of the National Association of Securities Dealers (NASD) and the member regulation, enforcement, and arbitration functions of the New York Stock Exchange. FINRA is a self-regulatory organization, "the largest independent regulator for all securities firms doing business in the United States,"[5] and issues rules that the SEC may oversee. With respect to the required standard of conduct to that brokers and dealers are held, FINRA, adopting NASD Rule 2310, enforces a "suitability" standard. The rule states:

> a. In recommending to a customer the purchase, sale or exchange of any security, a member shall have reasonable grounds for believing that the recommendation

Standards of Conduct of Brokers, Dealers, and Investment Advisers   227

is suitable for such customer upon the basis of the facts, if any, disclosed by such customer as to his other security holdings and as to his financial situation and needs.

b. Prior to the execution of a transaction recommended to a non-institutional customer, other than transactions with customers where investments are limited to money market mutual funds, a member shall make reasonable efforts to obtain information concerning:

1. the customer's financial status;
2. the customer's tax status;
3. the customer's investment objectives; and
4. such other information used or considered to be reasonable by such member or registered representative in making recommendations to the customer.[6]

An individual investor wishing to pursue action against a broker-dealer for recommending an unsuitable investment will often have to allege the violation of the general anti-fraud provision of the Securities Exchange Act, section 10(b),[7] and the SEC rule issued to implement the statute, Rule 10b-5.[8] To pursue a section 10(b) violation, an individual plaintiff must allege that, in connection with the purchase or sale of securities, he relied on a misstatement or omission of a material fact made with scienter[9] by the defendant and that this reliance caused his injury. Investors seeking to sue a broker-dealer for violation of the suitability rule may also have to comply with the requirements of the Private Securities Litigation Reform Act (PSLRA).[10] The PSLRA is very specific about what the plaintiff must show concerning the defendant's state of mind when he committed an allegedly illegal act and requires that:

In any private action arising under this chapter in which the plaintiff may recover money damages only on proof that the defendant acted with a particular state of mind, the complaint shall, with respect to each act or omission alleged to violate this chapter, state with particularity facts giving rise to a strong inference that the defendant acted with the required state of mind.[11]

Although the fiduciary duty standard does not generally apply to broker-dealers, there are instances in which courts have in fact applied a fiduciary duty standard to actions by a broker-dealer. For example, a broker-dealer who handles a discretionary account[12] for a customer has often been held to a fiduciary duty standard.[13]

STANDARD OF CONDUCT FOR INVESTMENT ADVISERS

In contrast to the suitability standard, which is most often applied to broker-dealers, investment advisers usually have a fiduciary duty with respect to investors. As referenced in footnote 2, a person who for compensation advises others about purchasing securities (i.e., an investment adviser) comes within the requirements of the Investment Advisers Act. Unless registered with the SEC, an investment adviser may not make use of the mails or any means or instrumentality of interstate commerce in connection with his business as an investment adviser.[14] An investment adviser may register by filing specified information with the SEC.[15]

Although the Investment Advisers Act does not use the word "fiduciary" to apply to the standard of conduct to which an investment adviser is held in managing a client's account,[16] court cases have interpreted that an investment adviser has a fiduciary duty. In 1963 a United States Supreme Court case, *Securities and Exchange Commission v. Capital Gains Research Bureau, Inc.*,[17] stated that an investment adviser owes a fiduciary duty to a client. The SEC brought suit in this case to obtain an injunction requiring a registered investment adviser to disclose to clients that he often purchased securities for his own account before recommending those securities to his clients and then sold those securities at a profit when the market price rose after the recommendation. The Court held for the SEC and in its decision examined the legislative history, including congressional reports and hearings, of the Investment Advisers Act. From its examination of this legislative history, the Court concluded that an investment adviser has a fiduciary duty to a client that includes disclosing his practice of selling securities shortly after recommending them in order to make a profit. At the beginning of its analysis, the Court discussed the basic purpose behind the major federal securities laws.

> The Investment Advisers Act of 1940 was the last in a series of Acts designed to eliminate certain abuses in the securities industry, abuses which were found to have contributed to the stock market crash of 1929 and the depression of the 1930's It was preceded by the Securities Act of 1933, the Securities Exchange Act of 1934, the Public Utility Holding Company Act of 1935, the Trust Indenture Act of 1939, and the Investment Company Act of 1940. A fundamental purpose, common to these statutes, was to substitute a philosophy of full disclosure for the philosophy of *caveat emptor* and thus to achieve a high standard of business ethics in the securities industry. As we recently said in a related context, "It requires but little appreciation ... of what happened in this country during the 1920's and 1930's to realize how essential it is that the highest ethical standards prevail" in every facet of the securities industry [footnotes and citations omitted].[18]

After examining the history of the Act, the Court discussed Congress's philosophy concerning the investment adviser's relationship with a client.

> The Investment Advisers Act of 1940 thus reflects a congressional recognition "of the delicate fiduciary nature of an investment advisory relationship," as well as a congressional intent to eliminate, or at least to expose, all conflicts of interest which might incline an investment adviser—consciously or unconsciously—to render advice which was not disinterested. It would defeat the manifest purpose of the Investment Advisers Act of 1940 for us to hold, therefore, that Congress, in empowering the courts to enjoin any practice which operates "as a fraud or deceit," intended to require proof of intent to injure and actual injury to clients.[19]

The Court went on to emphasize the fiduciary nature of an investment adviser's relationship to his client.

> Nor is it necessary in a suit against a fiduciary, which Congress recognized the investment adviser to be, to establish all the elements required in a suit against a party to an arm's-length transaction. Courts have imposed on a fiduciary an affirmative duty of "utmost good faith, and full and fair disclosure of all material facts," as well as an affirmative obligation "to employ reasonable care to avoid misleading" his clients.[20]

Congressional Action on Standard of Conduct for Broker-Dealers and Investment Advisers

A broker-dealer, traditionally acting upon the orders of a client with respect to a non-discretionary account, is thereby excluded from the requirements of the Investment Advisers Act; an investment adviser, as defined by that Act, is one who is paid for giving investment advice concerning investments in securities. There has been criticism over the years that this traditional distinction has become blurred and that, because of this blurring, the same standard of conduct should be applied to both broker-dealers and investment advisers. Critics point, for example, to the increase of discretionary accounts in which a broker-dealer has at least some control over the buying and selling of securities without always informing the client of each action. Critics also point to other kinds of accounts that broker-dealers have come to offer in addition to the transaction-based account, such as fee-based accounts and wrap accounts.[21]

Changes to the standards of conduct applied to broker-dealers and investment advisers were present in both the House and the Senate versions of financial regulatory reform. However, the House and the Senate had different approaches to this issue. The House approach was to harmonize the fiduciary standard for brokers, dealers, and investment advisers.[22] The Senate approach was to have the SEC conduct a study to evaluate the effectiveness of existing standards of conduct for brokers, dealers, and investment advisers; submit a report of the study, with conclusions and recommendations, to the Senate Committee on Banking, Housing, and Urban Affairs and the House Committee on Financial Services; and begin rulemaking concerning any gaps or overlaps found by the study.[23]

The House and Senate conferees on Wall Street reform approved a financial regulatory reform bill. On June 30, 2010, the House agreed to the conference report[24] for H.R. 4173, now referred to as the Dodd-Frank Wall Street Reform and Consumer Protection Act. On July 15, 2010, the Senate agreed to the conference report. The President signed the bill into law as P.L. 111-203 on July 21, 2010.

Dodd-Frank forged a kind of compromise between the House and Senate approaches. Section 913 of the legislation, titled "Study and Rulemaking regarding Obligations of Brokers, Dealers, and Investment Advisers," is the major provision setting out the new approach toward defining standards of conduct for these financial industry professionals.

Section 913 of Dodd-Frank

Subsection (a) sets out the definition of "retail customer" as:

a natural person, or the legal representative of such natural person, who—

1. receives personalized investment advice about securities from a broker or dealer or investment adviser; and
2. uses such advice primarily for personal, household, or family purposes.

Subsection (b) requires the SEC to conduct a study to evaluate the effectiveness of the current legal or regulatory standards of care for brokers, dealers, and investment advisers and those associated with them and whether there are legal gaps, shortcomings, or overlaps in the legal or regulatory standards for the protection of retail customers that should be addressed by rule or statute.

Subsection (c) sets out what the SEC is required to consider in conducting the study: (1) the effectiveness of current legal or regulatory standards of care which have been imposed by the SEC or a national securities association and other federal and state legal or regulatory standards; (2) whether there are legal or regulatory gaps, shortcomings, or overlaps in the standards of conduct for protecting retail customers that should be addressed by rule or statute; (3) whether retail customers understand that there are different standards of care applicable to brokers, dealers, and investment advisers in the provision of personalized investment advice about securities to retail customers; (4) whether the existence of different standards of care concerning the quality of personalized investment advice that retail customers receive is confusing to them; (5) the resources and activities of the SEC, the states, and a national securities association to enforce the standards of care, including the effectiveness of examinations of brokers, dealers, and investment advisers in determining compliance with regulations, the frequency of examinations, and the length of time of the examinations; (6) the substantive differences in regulating brokers, dealers, and investment advisers in their providing personalized investment advice and recommendations about securities to retail customers; (7) specific instances concerning personalized investment advice about securities in which regulation and oversight of investment advisers provide greater protection than regulation and oversight of brokers and dealers and instances in which regulation and oversight of brokers and dealers provide greater protection than regulation and oversight of investment advisers; (8) existing legal or regulatory standards of state securities regulators and other regulators intended to protect retail customers; (9) the potential impact on retail customers of imposing upon brokers and dealers the standard of care applied under the Investment Advisers Act; (10) the potential impact of eliminating the broker and dealer exclusion from the definition of "investment adviser" in the Investment Advisers Act; (11) the varying level of services provided by brokers, dealers, and investment advisers to retail customers; (12) the potential impact on retail customers that could result from changing the regulatory requirements or legal standards of care affecting brokers, dealers, and investment advisers concerning their obligations to retail customers about investment advice; (13) the potential additional costs to retail customers concerning the potential impact on the profitability of their investment decisions and to brokers, dealers, and investment advisers resulting from changes to the regulatory requirements or legal standards affecting brokers, dealers, or investment advisers; and (14) any other consideration that the SEC considers necessary and appropriate in determining whether to conduct a rulemaking.

Subsection (d) requires the SEC not later than six months after the date of enactment of Dodd-Frank to submit a report on the study to the Senate Committee on Banking, Housing, and Urban Affairs and to the House Committee on Financial Services. The report must describe the findings, conclusions, and recommendations of the SEC from the study.

Subsection (e) requires the SEC to seek public comments in preparing the report.

Subsection (f) allows the SEC to begin rulemaking to address the legal or regulatory standards of care for brokers, dealers, and investment advisers for providing personalized investment advice about securities to retail customers.

Subsection (g) amends section 15 of the Securities Exchange Act[25] to add a provision allowing the SEC to issue rules to provide that, with respect to a broker's or dealer's providing personalized investment advice about securities to a retail customer, the standard of conduct for the broker or dealer shall be the same as the standard of conduct applicable to an investment adviser under section 211 of the Investment Advisers Act.[26] The broker or dealer shall not be required to have a continuing duty or loyalty to the customer after providing personalized investment advice about securities. If a broker or dealer sells only a limited range of products, the SEC may require by rule that the broker or dealer provide notice to each retail customer and obtain the consent or acknowledgment of the customer. The SEC is required to facilitate providing simple and clear disclosures to investors concerning the terms of their relationships with brokers, dealers, and investment advisers, including any material conflicts of interest and issue appropriate rules prohibiting or restricting certain sales practices, conflicts of interest, and compensation schemes for brokers, dealers, and investment advisers.

Subsection (g) also amends section 211 of the Investment Advisers Act to allow the SEC to issue rules to provide that the standard of conduct for all brokers, dealers, and investment advisers shall be to act in the best interests of the customer without regard to the financial or other interest of the broker, dealer, or investment adviser providing the advice. Any material conflicts of interest must be disclosed and may be consented to by the customer. The rules must provide that the standard of conduct shall be no less stringent than the antifraud standard applied to investment advisers under section 206(1) and (2) of the Investment Advisers Act.[27] As with the amendment to section 15 of the Securities Exchange Act, the SEC must with respect to the Investment Advisers Act facilitate providing simple and clear disclosures to investors concerning the terms of their relationships with brokers, dealers, and investment advisers, including any material conflicts of interest. The SEC shall issue rules prohibiting or restricting certain sales practices, conflicts of interest, and compensation schemes for brokers, dealers, and investment advisers that the SEC has decided to be contrary to the public interest and the protection of investors.

Subsection (h) amends section 15 of the Securities Exchange Act and section 211 of the Investment Advisers Act to provide for harmonization of enforcement by the SEC with respect to violations by brokers, dealers, and investment advisers in their providing personalized investment advice about securities to retail customers.

At this time any statements as to what the SEC study might find and whether there will be new rules concerning the standards of conduct for brokers, dealers, and investment advisers are completely speculative. Nevertheless, it is interesting to note what the Chair of the SEC, Mary Schapiro, stated in 2009:

> When a retail investor turns to a financial professional for investment advice or assistance in accessing the securities markets, there is an array of choices. There are broker-dealers, investment advisers, financial advisors, financial consultants and financial planners to name just a few.
>
> When assessing these financial service providers, there is a commonality of names in certain cases—and an apparent commonality of function and service provided.
>
> However, the types of financial service providers I just mentioned are subject to very different regulatory regimes. And the standards of conduct and legal duties owed to investors under those regimes are not consistent.

I believe that, when investors receive similar services from similar financial service providers, they should be subject to the same standard of conduct—regardless of the label applied to that financial service provider. I therefore believe that all financial service providers that provide personalized investment advice about securities should owe a fiduciary duty to their customers or clients.

The fiduciary duty means that the financial service provider must at all times act in the best interest of customers or clients. In addition, a fiduciary must avoid conflicts of interest that impair its capacity to act for the benefit of its customers or clients. And if such conflicts cannot be avoided, a fiduciary must provide full and fair disclosure of the conflicts and obtain informed consent to the conflict.

A fiduciary owes its customers and clients more than mere honesty and good faith alone. A fiduciary must put its clients' and customers' interests before its own, absent disclosure of, and consent to, conflicts of interest.[28]

Congress may closely examine the report which the SEC must issue and any rules and regulations which the SEC issues concerning the standards of conduct for brokers, dealers, and investment advisers.

End Notes

[1] The Securities Exchange Act of 1934, 15 U.S.C. sections 78a *et seq.*, defines a "broker" as "any person engaged in the business of effecting transactions in securities for the account of others." 15 U.S.C. § 78c(4)(A). A "dealer" is defined as "any person engaged in the business of buying and selling securities for such person's own account through a broker or otherwise." However, a "dealer does not include a person that buys or sells securities for such person's account, either individually or in a fiduciary capacity, but not as a part of a regular business." 15 U.S.C. § 78c(5)(A) and (B). The term "broker-dealer" is often used because of the frequent overlap of their duties.

[2] The Investment Advisers Act, 15 U.S.C. sections 80b-1 *et seq.*, defines an "investment adviser" as: any person who, for compensation, engages in the business of advising others, either directly or through publications or writings, as to the value of securities or as to the advisability of investing in, purchasing, or selling securities, or who, for compensation and as part of a regular business, issues or promulgates analyses or reports concerning securities; but does not include (A) a bank, or any bank holding company ... ; (B) any lawyer, accountant, engineer, or teacher whose performance of such services is solely incidental to the practice of his profession; (C) any broker or dealer whose performance of such services is solely incidental to the conduct of his business as a broker or dealer and who receives no special compensation therefor; (D) the publisher of any bona fide newspaper, news magazine or business or financial publication of general and regular circulation; (E) any person whose advice, analyses, or reports relate to no securities other than securities which are direct obligations of or obligations guaranteed as to principal or interest by the United States.... 15 U.S.C. § 80b-2(11).

[3] Fiduciary is defined as "a person or institution who manages money or property for another and who must exercise a standard of care in such management activity imposed by law or contract." BLACK'S LAW DICTIONARY (5th ed. 1979).

[4] P.L. 111-203.

[5] http://www.finra.org.

[6] http://finra.complinet.com/en/display/display_main.html?rbid=2403&element_id=3638.

[7] 15 U.S.C. § 78j(b). The provision states: It shall be unlawful for any person, directly or indirectly, by the use of any means or instrumentality of interstate commerce or of the mails, or of any facility of any national securities exchange— (b) To use or employ, in connection with the purchase or sale of any security registered on a national securities exchange or any security not so registered, or any securities-based swap agreement (as defined in section 206B of the Gramm-Leach-Bliley Act), any manipulative or deceptive device or contrivance in contravention of such rules and regulations as the Commission may prescribe as necessary or appropriate in the public interest or for the protection of investors.

Standards of Conduct of Brokers, Dealers, and Investment Advisers   233

[8] 17 C.F.R. § 240.10b-5.

[9] Scienter is defined as a "Latin term for a person's guilty knowledge; i.e., knowing that a person's actions are wrong." MODERN DICTIONARY FOR THE LEGAL PROFESSION (3d 2d. 2001).

[10] 15 U.S.C. § 78u-4.

[11] 15 U.S.C. § 78u-4(b)(2).

[12] A discretionary account is one in which an investor allows the broker-dealer to purchase and sell securities without having to give his consent for each transaction. In a nondiscretionary account the broker-dealer buys and sells securities only as ordered by the investor.

[13] *See, e.g., Leib v. Merrill Lynch, Pierce, Fenner & Smith, Inc.,* 461 F.Supp. 951 (E.D. Mich. 1978), in which at 953 [citations omitted] the court stated: Unlike the broker who handles a non-discretionary account, the broker handling a discretionary account becomes the fiduciary of his customer in a broad sense. Such a broker, while not needing prior authorization for each transaction, must (1) manage the account in a manner directly comporting with the needs and objectives of the customer as stated in the authorization papers or as apparent from the customer's investment and trading history; (2) keep informed regarding the changes in the market which affect his customer's interest and act responsively to protect those interests; (3) keep his customer informed as to each completed transaction; and (5) [sic] explain forthrightly the practical impact and potential risks of the course of dealing in which the broker is engaged.

[14] 15 U.S.C. § 80b-3(a).

[15] 15 U.S.C. § 80b-3(c).

[16] The SEC has used the word "fiduciary' in describing the duties of an investment adviser to his clients. *Information for Newly-Registered Investment Advisers,* prepared by the staff of the SEC's Division of Investment Management and Office of Compliance Inspections and Examinations, available at http://www.sec.gov/divisions/investment/ adoverview.htm, states: As an investment adviser, you are a "fiduciary" to your advisory clients. This means that you have a fundamental obligation to act in the best interests of your clients and to provide investment advice in your clients' best interests. You owe your clients a duty of undivided loyalty and utmost good faith. You should not engage in any activity in conflict with the interest of any client, and you should take steps reasonably necessary to fulfill your obligations. You must employ reasonable care to avoid misleading clients and you must provide full and fair disclosure of all material facts to your clients and prospective clients. Generally, facts are "material" if a reasonable investor would consider them to be important. You must eliminate, or at least disclose, all conflicts of interest that might incline you—consciously or unconsciously—to render advice that is not disinterested. If you do not avoid a conflict of interest that could impact the partiality of your advice, you must make full and frank disclosure of the conflict. You cannot use your clients' assets for your own benefit or the benefit of other clients, at least without client consent. Departure from this fiduciary standard may constitute "fraud" upon your clients (under Section 206 of the Advisers Act). It should be noted that section 206 of the Investment Advisers Act, 15 U.S.C. section 80b-6, states in part: It shall be unlawful for any investment adviser, by the use of the mails or any means or instrumentality of interstate commerce, directly or indirectly— (1) to employ any device, scheme, or artifice to defraud any client or prospective client; (2) to engage in any transaction, practice, or course of business which operates as a fraud or deceit upon any client or prospective client....

[17] 375 U.S. 180 (1963).

[18] *Capital Gains Research Bureau*, at 186-187.

[19] *Capital Gains Research Bureau*, at 191-192.

[20] *Capital Gains Research Bureau*, at 194 [footnotes omitted].

[21] A wrap account is one "in which a brokerage manages an investor's portfolio for a flat quarterly or annual fee. This fee covers all administrative, commission, and management expenses. Sometimes this also includes funds of funds." Available at http://www.investopedia.com/terms/w/wrapaccount.asp.

[22] H.R. 4173, § 7103.

[23] S. 3217, as amended, § 913.

[24] H.Rept. 111-517.

[25] 15 U.S.C. § 78o.

[26] 15 U.S.C. § 80b-11. This section gives the SEC rulemaking authority over investment advisers.

[27] 15 U.S.C. § 80b-6(1) and (2).

[28] Speech by SEC Chairman: Address before the New York Financial Writers' Association Annual Awards Dinner (June 18, 2009), available at http://www.sec.gov/news/speech

In: The Dodd-Frank Wall Street Reform...   ISBN: 978-1-61324-101-1
Editors: Nathan L. Morris and Philip O. Price   © 2011 Nova Science Publishers, Inc.

Chapter 13

RULEMAKING REQUIREMENTS AND AUTHORITIES IN THE DODD-FRANK WALL STREET REFORM AND CONSUMER PROTECTION ACT[*]

Curtis W. Copeland

SUMMARY

The Dodd-Frank Wall Street Reform and Consumer Protection Act (P.L. 111-203, July 21, 2010) contains more than 300 provisions that expressly indicate in the text that rulemaking is required or permitted. However, it is unclear how many rules will ultimately be issued pursuant to the act because, among other things, (1) most of the provisions appear to be discretionary (e.g., stating that an agency "may" issue a rule); (2) individual provisions may result in multiple rules; (3) some provisions appear to provide rulemaking authorities to agencies that they already possess; and (4) rules may be issued to implement provisions that do not specifically require or permit rulemaking.

Nearly 80% of the relevant provisions in the Dodd-Frank Act assign rulemaking responsibilities or authorities to four agencies: the Securities and Exchange Commission (SEC), the Board of Governors of the Federal Reserve System, the Commodity Futures Trading Commission (CFTC), and the Consumer Financial Protection Bureau. Many of the mandatory provisions specify the details of the rules to be issued, but many of the discretionary provisions allow the agencies to issue such rules "as may be necessary." Most of the rulemaking provisions in the act do not indicate how the regulations should be developed, but some either require or prohibit notice-andcomment procedures before the final rule is issued.

Fewer than 40% of the rulemaking provisions in the Dodd-Frank Act indicate when the required or permitted rule should be issued or go into effect. Of the provisions with deadlines, four require rules to be issued within 90 days of enactment (i.e., by October 19, 2010), and five other provisions require rules within 180 days (i.e., by January 17,

---

[*] This is an edited, reformatted and augmented version of a Congressional Research Services publication, dated November 3, 2010.

2011). As of October 20, 2010, 10 final rules had been published in the *Federal Register* implementing the act, including six by the SEC and two by the CFTC.

Many of the government-wide rulemaking requirements (e.g., the Administrative Procedure Act) appear to apply to rulemaking under the Dodd-Frank Act, but the exceptions and exemptions to those requirements also apply. Other rulemaking requirements and controls (e.g., Executive Order 12866) are not applicable to the independent regulatory agencies like the SEC and the CFTC, who are responsible for issuing most of the rules under the act. Also, some of the rulemaking agencies do not receive congressionally appropriated funds, and therefore may not be subject to appropriations restrictions that Congress has used to control rulemaking.

Nevertheless, Congress has a number of oversight tools available to affect the nature of Dodd-Frank Act rulemaking, including confirmation hearings for nominees to head the agencies, oversight hearings, and letters to and meetings with agency representatives. Appropriations restrictions can be used with regard to agencies who receive appropriated funds. Congressional Review Act resolutions of disapproval can call attention to certain rules.

This report will not be updated.

INTRODUCTION

The Dodd-Frank Wall Street Reform and Consumer Protection Act (P.L. 111-203, July 21, 2010, hereafter the Dodd-Frank Act) was enacted in the wake of what many believe was the worst U.S. financial crisis since the Great Depression. Among other things, the act creates a new Financial Stability Oversight Council with the authority to designate certain financial firms as "systemically significant," thereby subjecting them to increased regulation; consolidates consumer protection responsibilities in a new Consumer Financial Protection Bureau (CFPB); consolidates bank regulation by merging the Office of Thrift Supervision into the Office of the Comptroller of the Currency; requires more derivatives to be cleared and traded through regulated exchanges; and attempts to reduce the incentives to take excessive risks by reforming executive compensation and securitization.[1]

Although the Dodd-Frank Act itself may change the financial sector landscape in some ways, many of the changes are likely to be implemented through regulations that are to be developed and issued by regulatory agencies. As one observer put it, the rules would "turn reform into reality."[2] Shortly after the legislation was enacted, another observer said, "In most pieces of legislation like this, the real teeth is in the regulations."[3] Another said that the Dodd-Frank Act "is complicated and contains substantial ambiguities, many of which will not be resolved until regulations are adopted."[4] An article in the *New York Times* stated that the legislation

> is basically a 2,000-page missive to federal agencies, instructing regulators to address subjects ranging from derivatives trading to document retention. But it is notably short on specifics, giving regulators significant power to determine its impact—and giving partisans on both sides a second chance to influence the outcome.[5]

More than two months after the Dodd-Frank Act was enacted, Jeremy J. Siegel, a professor at the University of Pennsylvania's Wharton School, said the following:

The vast majority of regulations required by the law are yet to be written. If they become burdensome, they will make our financial sector less competitive. If not, they can contribute to growth and stability. The devil of this law is not only in the details, but also in the regulators who enforce them.[6]

Although it is clear that rulemaking will be important to the implementation of the Dodd-Frank Act, the number and nature of the rules that will be issued is less clear—in part because it is difficult to determine which provisions to include as "rulemaking" provisions, and whether those provisions will ultimately result in rules. The law firm of Davis Polk & Wardwell has estimated that the law will require at least 243 rules to be issued by 10 different federal agencies.[7] Others, like the U.S. Chamber of Commerce, have put the number of rules to be issued even higher.[8]

THIS REPORT

In a previous report, CRS identified several dozen provisions in Title X and Title XIV of the Dodd-Frank Act that require or permit the CFPB (either individually or with other agencies) to issue rules.[9] This report takes a broader view, and identifies provisions in the act as a whole that either require or permit rulemaking by any federal agency, including the Board of Governors of the Federal Reserve System (hereafter, the Board of Governors), the Securities and Exchange Commission (SEC), the Commodity Futures Trading Commission (CFTC), and the CFPB. The list of mandatory rulemaking provisions identified in the act is provided in Appendix A of this report, and the list of discretionary rulemaking provisions is provided in Appendix B. Most of these provisions amended statutes that were first enacted decades earlier (e.g., the Securities and Exchange Act of 1934, the Commodity Exchange Act, the Investment Advisers Act of 1940, and the Truth in Lending Act). As used in this report, the term "rulemaking" includes all agency actions that may result in rules, including any amendments to existing regulations and rules that are issued without notice and comment. The section numbers referred to in this report and the appendices refer to sections in the Dodd-Frank Act, not to the underlying statutes that are often amended by the act.

Methodology

To develop the lists of rulemaking provisions in the Dodd-Frank Act, CRS searched the text of the act in the enrolled version of H.R. 4173 as passed by the House of Representatives and the Senate (since the text of the public law was not then available) using the words "regulation" and "rule." Mandatory rulemaking was indicated by such phrases as "shall establish, by regulation," "shall promulgate regulations," "shall issue regulations," "shall issue final rules," "shall prescribe regulations," and "shall amend regulations." Phrases such as "may prescribe regulations," "may issue regulations," "may, by rule or regulation," and "shall prescribe such regulations as are necessary" were treated as discretionary rulemaking provisions. Certain other phrases were also considered to be discretionary rulemaking authority. For example, Section 165(g)(3) states that the term "short-term debt" means "such liabilities with short-dated maturity that the Board of Governors identifies, by regulation."

Because the act appears to authorize, but not require, the issuance of rules on this point, the provision was treated as a discretionary rulemaking provision.

The lists of regulatory provisions do not include provisions that limit (rather than require or allow) agency rulemaking activity. For example, the mandatory rulemaking list does not include Section 153(c)(1) of the act, which states that the Office of Financial Research within the Financial Stability Oversight Council "shall issue rules, regulations, and orders only to the extent necessary to carry out the purposes and duties prescribed in (previous paragraphs)." Also not included are provisions that require the implementation, rather than the promulgation, of rules (e.g., Section 153(c)(2) of the act, which requires member agencies to implement certain rules). Neither do the lists include provisions that require or allow entities to establish internal rules of procedure. For example, not included is Section 210(A)(16)(d)(i), which states that "The [Federal Deposit Insurance] Corporation shall prescribe such regulations and establish such retention schedules as are necessary to maintain the documents and records of the Corporation generated in exercising the authorities of this title."

Also, if one rulemaking requirement was clearly a subset of another requirement, only the larger requirement was included. For example:

- Section 165(e)(1) requires the Board of Governors of the Federal Reserve System to issue regulations limiting the risks that "the failure of any individual company could pose to a nonbank financial company supervised by the Board." The next paragraph states that "The regulations prescribed by the Board of Governors under paragraph (1) shall" contain certain prohibitions. In this case, the second set of requirements appears to be a subset of the first, and therefore was not included in the list of mandatory rulemaking provisions.
- Section 619 amends the Bank Holding Company Act of 1956 (12 U.S.C. § 1841 *et seq.*), and subsection (b)(2) of those amendments requires various agencies to "adopt rules to carry out this section." Later in Section 619, the act requires "the appropriate Federal banking agencies," the CFTC, and the SEC to "issue regulations to implement subparagraph (A) (limitation on certain transactions or activities being deemed a permitted activity), as part of the regulations issued under subsection (b)(2)." As a result of this construction, this and several other rulemaking requirements in Section 619 were considered to be part of the rules required under subsection (b)(2).

If it was unclear whether one provision was a subset of another, or if a provision could result in the issuance of two or more sets of regulations, the provisions were counted separately. For example:

- Section 210(c) of the act ("Provisions Relating to Contracts Entered Into Before Appointment of Receiver") contains several provisions permitting the Federal Deposit Insurance Corporation (FDIC) to issue regulations on a variety of subjects. Although FDIC may ultimately issue one regulation covering all of the provisions, there is no requirement that the agency do so. Therefore, the provisions were treated separately in this report.

- Section 358(2) states that "the Comptroller of the Currency shall prescribe regulations applicable to savings associations and the Board of Governors shall prescribe regulations applicable to insured State member banks, bank holding companies and savings and loan holding companies." Because each organization may issue separate regulations to satisfy this requirement, it was treated as two rulemaking provisions.

NUMBER OF DODD-FRANK ACT RULES IS UNKNOWABLE

CRS searches of the Dodd-Frank Act identified a total of 330 provisions that expressly indicated in the text that rulemaking is required or permitted. For a variety of reasons, however, the number of final rules that will be ultimately issued pursuant to the act is unknowable. First of all, 182 of the 330 rulemaking provisions (55.2%) appear to be discretionary in nature, stating that certain agencies "may" issue rules to implement particular provisions, or that the agencies shall issue such rules as they "determine are necessary and appropriate." Therefore, the agencies may decide to promulgate rules regarding all, some, or none of these provisions.

Also, as indicated previously, an agency may issue one rule that covers multiple rulemaking requirements, or may decide to issue more than one rule under a single requirement. For example, Section 922(a) of the Dodd-Frank Act (amending the Securities Exchange Act of 1934 (15 U.S.C. § 78a *et seq.*)) states that "the term 'whistleblower' means any individual who provides ... information relating to a violation of the securities laws to the (Securities and Exchange) Commission, in a manner established, by rule or regulation, by the Commission." Another provision states that awards are to be paid to whistleblowers "under regulations prescribed by the Commission." The SEC is also given the authority to issue "such rules and regulations as may be necessary or appropriate to implement the provisions of this section consistent with the purposes of this section." The agency may issue one rule covering all of these provisions, or may issue separate rules under each rulemaking authority.[10]

A number of Dodd-Frank Act provisions state that the responsible agency shall or may establish certain requirements "by rule, regulation, or order."[11] Therefore, the agencies may take action pursuant to those provisions by issuing rules or regulations, or by issuing orders that are not promulgated through the rulemaking process.

Some individual provisions appear to contemplate that multiple agencies will issue multiple rules, but even there, the eventual outcome is not clear. For example, Section 165(i)(2)(C) of the act requires "each Federal primary financial regulatory agency" to issue "consistent and comparable regulations to implement this paragraph." While each agency may issue separate rules after ensuring that they are "consistent" and "comparable," the agencies may also decide to accomplish that goal by issuing a single joint rule.

Some Rulemaking Authorities May Have Existed Previously

Some sections of the Dodd-Frank Act provide financial regulatory agencies with new statutory authority to issue rules.[12] Other sections, however, arguably provide rulemaking authority that the designated agency already possessed. For example, Section 411 of the act amended the Investment Advisers Act of 1940 (15 U.S.C. § 80b-1 *et seq.*) and states that a registered investment advisor "shall take such steps to safeguard client assets over which such advisor has custody...as the Commission may, by rule, prescribe." The SEC appears to have had this authority before the Dodd-Frank Act was enacted. Because the agency's rulemaking authority in this area has not changed, the SEC may decide not to issue any new rules. On the other hand, the agency may decide to issue new rules in the context of the reforms enacted through the Dodd-Frank Act that are the same as, or similar to, rules that the agency would have issued even if the Dodd-Frank Act had not been enacted.

Other provisions in the Dodd-Frank Act appear to transfer rulemaking authority from one agency (or set of agencies) to another agency. For example, one provision in Section 1088(a) of the act amends Section 604(g) of the Fair Credit Reporting Act (at 15 U.S.C. § 1681b(g)) to say that 15 U.S.C. § 1681a(d)(3) must not be construed so as to treat information or any communication of information as a consumer report if the information or communication is disclosed in a manner "determined to be necessary and appropriate, by regulation or order, by the [Consumer Financial Protection] Bureau or the applicable State insurance authority (with respect to any person engaged in providing insurance or annuities)." Prior to this amendment, that authority had been given to the "[Federal Trade] Commission, any Federal banking agency or the National Credit Union Administration (with respect to any financial institution subject to the jurisdiction of such agency or Administration under paragraph (1), (2), or (3) of section 1681s(b) of this title, or the applicable State insurance authority (with respect to any person engaged in providing insurance or annuities)."

Non-rulemaking Provisions May Result in Rules

In addition to the provisions in the Dodd-Frank Act that explicitly require or permit rulemaking, there are numerous other provisions in the act that may ultimately lead to regulations. For example, Section 120 of the act states that the Financial Stability Oversight Council "may provide for more stringent regulation of a financial activity by issuing recommendations to the primary financial regulatory agencies to apply new or heightened standards and safeguards." The primary regulatory agencies are required to "impose the standards recommended by the Council" or "explain in writing to the Council, not later than 90 days after the date on which the Council issues the recommendation, why the agency has determined not to follow the recommendation of the Council." If those "new or heightened standards and safeguards" are intended to be binding on regulated entities, then it is possible that the council's recommendations could lead to new regulations.[13]

Other provisions in the Dodd-Frank Act also require regulatory agencies to take certain actions, but do not specifically mention "regulations" or "rules." For example, Section 732 of the act amended Section 4d of the Commodity Exchange Act (7 U.S.C. § 6d), and states that the CFTC shall require that futures commission merchants and introducing brokers implement conflictof-interest systems and procedures that (1) establish structural and institutional safeguards to ensure that the activities of any person within the firm relating to research or analysis of the price or market for any commodity are separated by appropriate informational partitions within the firm from the review, pressure, or oversight of persons whose involvement in trading or clearing activities might potentially bias the judgment or supervision of the persons; and (2) address such other issues as the Commission determines to be appropriate.

It is possible that many of these kinds of provisions will, either by the agencies' choice or by legal necessity, be implemented through the rulemaking process. This has been the case in the implementation of other statutes. For example, of the first 10 final rules that were issued pursuant to the health care reforms in the Patient Protection and Affordable Care Act (P.L. 111-148), only three were specifically required or permitted in the legislation.[14]

Various Agencies Are Required or Permitted to Issue Rules

As **Table 1** below indicates, nearly 80% of the relevant provisions in the Dodd-Frank Act (258 of 330) assign rulemaking authorities or responsibilities to four agencies: the SEC, the Board of Governors, the CFTC, and the CFPB. In addition to the rules they may promulgate independently, these four agencies are also required or permitted to issue rules with one or more other agencies. For example, of the 25 provisions that give rulemaking responsibilities to three or more agencies, at least seven of them specifically involve the Board of Governors and the CFPB.[15]

Some of the Dodd-Frank Act rulemaking provisions require multiple agencies to issue certain rules jointly, other provisions require multiple agencies to issue rules separately, and some provisions involve a mix of these approaches. For example, Section 619 of the act (amending the Bank Holding Company Act of 1956 (12 U.S.C. § 1841 *et seq.*)) requires that certain rules be issued jointly by the "appropriate Federal banking agencies," while other rules required under this section are to be issued individually by the Board of Governors, the Commodity Futures Trading Commission, and the Securities and Exchange Commission. Section 623(a) of the act assigns rulemaking responsibilities to the Office of Thrift Supervision before the date that certain responsibilities are to be transferred to the CFPB, and to the Comptroller of the Currency after that date.[16] Section 1088(a) permits certain rules to be issued by the CFPB "or the applicable State insurance authority."

Several Dodd-Frank Act provisions require that rules be issued by one agency, in consultation with another agency. For example:

- Section 166(a) requires the Board of Governors to prescribe certain regulations, in consultation with the Financial Stability Oversight Council and the FDIC.
- Section 205(h) requires the SEC and the FDIC to issue certain rules after consulting with the Securities Investor Protection Corporation.
- Section 210(o)(6)(A) requires the FDIC to consult with the Secretary of the Treasury before issuing certain rules.

242   Curtis W. Copeland

- Section 1024(a)(2) requires the CFPB to consult with the FTC before issuing certain rules.
- Section 1094(3)(B) (amending the Home Mortgage Disclosure Act of 1975 (12 U.S.C. § 2801 *et seq.*)) requires the CFPB to issue certain rules after consulting with "appropriate banking agencies," the FDIC, the National Credit Union Administration Board, and the Secretary of Housing and Urban Development.

Because these provisions only require the rulemaking agency to consult with other parties, they were each counted in this report as requiring the issuance of rules by a single agency. However, the agencies may ultimately decide to issue these rules jointly with the consulted agency.

Table 1. Provisions in the Dodd-Frank Act That Expressly Reference Rulemaking, by Agency.

Agency or Agencies	Mandatory	Discretionary	Total
SEC	46	51	97
Board of Governors	25	42	67
CFTC	21	31	52
CFPB	17	25	42
FDIC	7	8	15
Other individual agencies	4	10	14
Two agencies	8	10	18
Three or more agencies	20	5	25
Total	148	182	330

Source: CRS.

Note: The "other individual agencies" include the Secretary of the Treasury, the Federal Trade Commission, and the Comptroller of the Currency. The "two agencies" provisions include rules to be issued by the CFTC and the SEC, and by the FDIC and the Board of Governors. Provisions requiring rules to be issued by "all primary financial regulatory agencies," "each federal primary financial regulatory agency," "the appropriate federal banking agencies," or "the prudential regulators" were treated as issued by three or more agencies. Other "three or more agencies" provisions listed the agencies required or permitted to issue rules (e.g., "Board of Governors of the Federal Reserve System, the Comptroller of the Currency, the Federal Deposit Insurance Corporation, the National Credit Union Administration Board, the Federal Housing Finance Agency, and the Bureau of Consumer Financial Protection").

Other provisions appear to establish a stricter standard, and require the "concurrence" or "approval" of at least one other agency before a rule can be issued. For example, Section 152(g) requires the Secretary of the Treasury to obtain the concurrence of the Office of Government Ethics before issuing certain conflict-of-interest regulations. Also, Section 155(d) requires the Secretary of the Treasury to receive the approval of the Financial Stability Oversight Council before issuing certain rules. Each of these provisions was counted in this report as requiring the issuance of rules by two agencies. However, the agencies may ultimately decide not to issue these rules jointly.

Rulemaking Agency Discretion

In many of the mandatory rulemaking provisions, the Dodd-Frank Act specifies the details of the required regulations. For example, Section 165(e)(1) of the act requires the Board of Governors to prescribe standards in regulation limiting the risks that the failure of any individual company could pose to a nonbank financial company supervised by the board. Subsection (e)(2) requires that the regulation

> shall prohibit each nonbank financial company supervised by the Board of Governors and bank holding company described in subsection (a) from having credit exposure to any unaffiliated company that exceeds 25 percent of the capital stock and surplus (or such lower amount as the Board of Governors may determine by regulation to be necessary to mitigate risks to the financial stability of the United States) of the company.

The provision goes on to provide five categories of definition for the term "credit exposure," as well as "any other similar transactions that the Board of Governors, by regulation, determines to be a credit exposure for purposes of this section." Other provisions in the act are even more detailed.

Many of the discretionary rulemaking provisions, on the other hand, give the rulemaking agencies substantial leeway to decide not only whether to issue rules, but also the content of those rules. For example:

- Section 355 of the act (amending Section 106(b)(1) of the Bank Holding Company Act Amendments of 1970 (12 U.S.C. § 1972(1))) states that Board of Governors may "issue such regulations as are necessary to carry out this section."
- Section 369(4) (amending the Home Owners' Loan Act (12 U.S.C. § 1461 *et seq.*)) states that the Comptroller of the Currency "may prescribe regulations with respect to savings associations, as the Comptroller determines to be appropriate to carry out the purposes of this Act."
- Section 1093(3)(A) (amending Title V of the Gramm-Leach-Bliley Act (15 U.S.C. § 6801 *et seq.*)) states that the CFTC "shall have authority to prescribe such regulations as may be necessary to carry out the purposes of this subtitle with respect to financial institutions and other persons subject to the jurisdiction of the Commodity Futures Trading Commission under section 5g of the Commodity Exchange Act."

These kinds of broad delegations of rulemaking authority to the agencies may be chosen because of the technical expertise needed to craft detailed legislation, or because Congress cannot reach consensus on how particular issues should be resolved. Nevertheless, when Congress permits agencies to prescribe "such regulations as are necessary," it grants substantial policymaking discretion to rulemaking agencies. On the other hand, when Congress requires that a regulation contain certain elements, Congress retains a measure of control over (and responsibility for) the subsequent policymaking process.

Methods of Rulemaking

Most federal rulemaking is governed by the Administrative Procedure Act (5 U.S.C. § 551 *et seq.*), which generally requires that agencies (1) publish a notice of proposed rulemaking (NPRM) in the *Federal Register,* (2) take comments from "interested persons" on the proposed rule, (3) publish a final rule in the *Federal Register* after considering those comments, and (4) make the rule effective not less than 30 days after it is published. There are, however, numerous exceptions to these general requirements. For example, an agency may dispense with notice and comment and issue a final rule without a prior proposed rule when the agency concludes that there is "good cause" to do so.[17] A procedure known as "interim final rulemaking" is a particular application of this "good cause" exception in which an agency issues a final rule without an NPRM that is often effective immediately, but with a post-promulgation opportunity for the public to comment.[18]

Most of the rulemaking provisions in the Dodd-Frank Act do not specify the method by which the agencies should issue the required or permitted rules. In a few cases, however, the act stipulates that the agencies issue rules through notice-and-comment rulemaking processes. For example:

- Section 332(1)(B) requires the FDIC to "prescribe, by regulation, after notice and opportunity for comment, the method for the declaration, calculation, distribution, and payment of dividends under this paragraph."
- Section 413(b)(1)(B) permits the SEC to "make such adjustments to the definition of the term 'accredited investor' ... as the Commission may deem appropriate for the protection of investors, in the public interest, and in light of the economy." If the SEC does make those adjustments, it is required to use "notice and comment rulemaking."
- Section 982(e) states that the Public Company Accounting Oversight Board "may, by rule, conduct and require a program of inspection in accordance with paragraph (1), on a basis to be determined by the Board, of registered public accounting firms that provide one or more audit reports for a broker or dealer." It goes on to say that "Any rules of the Board pursuant to this paragraph shall be subject to prior approval by the Commission pursuant to section 107(b) before the rules become effective, including an opportunity for public notice and comment."
- Section 1088(a)(4)(B) (amending the Fair Credit Reporting Act (15 U.S.C. § 1681 *et seq.*)) states that the CFPB "may, after notice and opportunity for comment, prescribe regulations that permit transactions under paragraph (2) that are determined to be necessary and appropriate to protect legitimate operational, transactional, risk, consumer, and other needs."
- Section 1473(d) (amending Section 1106 of the Financial Institutions Reform, Recovery, and Enforcement Act of 1989 (12 U.S.C. § 3335)) permits the appraisal subcommittee to "prescribe regulations in accordance with [the Administrative Procedure Act] after notice and opportunity for comment" regarding certain issues.

Several other provisions, most of which require rules to be issued relatively quickly, require or permit the agencies to issue interim final rules without prior notice and comment. For example:

- Section 729 (amending the Commodity Exchange Act after section 4q (7 U.S.C. § 60-1)) requires the CFTC to "promulgate an interim final rule... providing for the reporting of each swap entered into before the date of enactment as referenced in subparagraph (A)." The interim final rule is required by October 19, 2010, 90 days after the date of enactment.
- Section 766(a) (amending the Securities Exchange Act of 1934 (15 U.S.C. § 78a *et seq.*)) requires the SEC to "promulgate an interim final rule... providing for the reporting of each security-based swap entered into before the date of enactment," the terms of which had not expired as of that date. The interim final rule is required by October 19, 2010, 90 days after the date of enactment.
- Section 1472(a) (amending Chapter 2 of the Truth in Lending Act (15 U.S.C. § 1631 *et seq.*)) requires the Board of Governors to "prescribe interim final regulations defining with specificity acts or practices that violate appraisal independence in the provision of mortgage lending services for a consumer credit transaction secured by the principal dwelling of the consumer or mortgage brokerage services for such a transaction and defining any terms in this section or such regulations." This rule is also required by October 19, 2010.

One provision stipulates that notice and comment not be provided, but does not require interim final rulemaking. Section 916(a) (amending Section 19(b) of the Securities Exchange Act of 1934 (15 U.S.C. § 78s(b))) requires the SEC to "promulgate rules setting forth the procedural requirements of the proceedings required under this paragraph," and says that the rules "are not required to include republication of proposed rule changes or solicitation of public comment."

Additional Comment Opportunities and Transparency

The agencies that are expected to issue most of the rules under the Dodd-Frank Act have indicated that they will offer the public enhanced and expanded opportunities to track and participate in the rulemaking process. For example, both the FDIC and the SEC said they will allow the public to participate in the process before the rules are drafted, and will attempt to meet with any interested parties who want to discuss pending rules.[19] The FDIC said it will hold a series of roundtable discussions with external parties on implementation issues, and the CFTC and the SEC said they have created a series of e-mail inboxes, organized by topic, to facilitate participation and commenting.[20] The Federal Reserve reportedly plans to require all staff members to keep track of all meetings with private sector representatives about the rules being developed under the Dodd-Frank Act, and summaries of those meetings are to be placed on the agency's website. However, not all agencies intend to expand commenting and transparency. For example, both the Office of the Comptroller of the Currency and the Office of Thrift Supervision indicated that they plan no changes in their rulemaking practices.[21]

It appears that some individuals and organizations are using these new opportunities for public participation. A study by the Sunlight Foundation reportedly showed that the CFTC had 192 meetings with outside groups from July 26, 2010, to October 4, 2010.[22] The two most frequent visitors were officials from the firms Morgan Stanley and Goldman Sachs, each of which met with the agency 16 times during that period.

MOST RULEMAKING PROVISIONS HAVE NO DEADLINES

In addition to specifying the content of rules and the methods by which they are to be promulgated, Congress has also attempted to control and expedite agency rulemaking by establishing deadlines for the issuance or implementation of rules. Although the Administrative Conference of the United States has questioned the value of statutory rulemaking deadlines,[23] Congress has continued to use them, and they are regularly cited in litigation in an effort to force agencies to either initiate or complete regulatory actions.[24]

As shown in Table 2 below, 208 of the 330 rulemaking provisions in the Dodd-Frank Act (63.0%) did not expressly provide a deadline for when the required or permitted rule should be issued. As one might expect, a higher percentage of the discretionary rulemaking provisions had no specified deadline (157 of 182, or 86.3%) than the mandatory provisions (51 of 148, or 34.0%).

Table 2. Deadlines for Issuing Rules Pursuant to the Dodd-Frank Act.

Deadline	Mandatory Rulemaking Provisions	Discretionary Rulemaking Provisions	Total
No deadline	51	157	208
Less than 360 days after enactment	22	4	26
By 360 days of enactment (i.e., by July 16, 2011)	27	2	29
Within one year of enactment (i.e., by July 21, 2011)	17	1	18
One to two years after enactment (i.e., by July 21, 2012)	15	16	31
More than two years after enactment (i.e., after July 21, 2012)	16	2	18
Total	148	182	330

Source: CRS.

Notes: The category "less than 360 days after enactment" includes provisions in which rules were required to be issued "as soon as is practicable," within 90 days, within 180 days, within six months, within 270 days, and within nine months after the date of enactment. The "more than two years after enactment" category includes all deadlines after July 21, 2012.

Although most of the Dodd-Frank Act provisions establishing rulemaking deadlines do not provide consequences if those deadlines are not met, at least one provision appears to do so. Section 210(c)(8)(H)(iii) of the act (entitled "Back-Up Rulemaking Authority") states that if the "primary financial regulatory agencies" do not jointly prescribe certain rules on records maintenance within 24 months after the date of enactment (i.e., by July 21, 2012), the chairperson of the Financial Stability Oversight Council (the Secretary of the Treasury, per Section 111(b)(1)(A)) is required to issue the rules.

How Rulemaking Deadlines Are Established

Most of the 122 rulemaking deadlines in the Dodd-Frank Act are keyed to the date that the legislation was enacted (July 21, 2010). In most of these cases, the act requires the rule to be issued within a specified period of time after that date. Therefore, agencies appear to be able to satisfy these deadlines at any point prior to the specified date. For example, Section 924(a) states that the SEC is to issue certain regulations "not later than 270 days after the date of enactment of this Act," or by April 17, 2011. The SEC could satisfy the requirement by issuing the regulations on that date, or months earlier than that date.

In a few cases, however, the act does not permit the required rule to be issued or made effective before the deadline. For example:

- Section 155(d) of the act states that, "beginning 2 years after the date of enactment," the Secretary of the Treasury must establish certain requirements "by regulation." Therefore, it does not appear that the required rule can be made effective before July 21, 2012.
- Section 1083(a) of the act (amending the Alternative Mortgage Transaction Parity Act of 1982 (12 U.S.C. § 3801 *et seq.*)) states that a required rule to be issued by the CFPB applies to transactions "after the designated transfer date." The "transfer date" is the date that certain functions are required to be transferred from the existing prudential regulators to the CFPB, and has been established as July 21, 2011 (the one-year anniversary of the date of enactment).[25] Therefore, it does not appear that the rule required by this section can take effect until at least July 22, 2011.

Other deadlines are based not on the date of enactment, but on the act's effective date (which Section 4 of the Dodd-Frank Act says is July 22, 2010, unless otherwise specified). For example, Section 168 of the act states that, except as otherwise specified in subtitles A or C, the Board of Governors is required to issue final regulations in those subtitles "not later than 18 months after the effective date of this Act." Therefore, these rules are required to be issued by January 22, 2012.

As noted previously, other rulemaking deadlines are based on the transfer date. For example, Section 1402(a) of the Dodd-Frank Act (amending Chapter 2 of the Truth in Lending Act (15 U.S.C. § 1631 *et seq.*)) requires that the Board of Governors

> prescribe regulations requiring depository institutions to establish and maintain procedures reasonably designed to assure and monitor the compliance of such depository institutions, the subsidiaries of such institutions, and the employees of such institutions or subsidiaries with the requirements of this section and the registration procedures established under section 1507 of the Secure and Fair Enforcement for Mortgage Licensing Act of 2008.

Although this provision does not specify when the regulations are to be issued, Section 1400(c) of the act requires that all mandatory Title XIV rules be issued within 18 months after the transfer date, and be effective within 12 months after issuance. Because the transfer date is July 21, 2011, these rules (and all other mandatory Title XIV rules) must be issued by January 21, 2013.

Several other provisions in the Dodd-Frank Act also require that all rules within a particular title or subtitle must be promulgated or made effective by a certain date. For example:

- Section 168 states that, except as otherwise specified in subtitles A or C, the Board of Governors is required to issue final regulations in those subtitles "not later than 18 months after the effective date of this Act." As noted previously, the effective date of the act was July 22, 2010. Therefore, all final regulations under subtitles A and C are required to be issued by January 22, 2012.

- Section 712(e) requires that all Title VII CFTC and SEC rules (other than those issued jointly) be promulgated within 360 days after the date of enactment, unless another provision states otherwise.
- Section 937 states that, unless otherwise specified, the SEC "shall issue final regulations, as required by this subtitle and the amendments made by this subtitle (subtitle C on 'Improvements to the Regulation of Credit Rating Agencies'), not later than 1 year after the date of enactment of this Act."

The deadlines for several other rules required in the act are contingent upon other actions. For example:

- Section 619 (amending the Bank Holding Company Act of 1956 (12 U.S.C. § 1841 *et seq.*)) states that the agencies responsible for issuing rules "shall consider the findings of the study under paragraph (1) and adopt rules to carry out this section." The referenced study is required to be completed within six months of enactment, and the rules are required within nine months of the completion of the study. Therefore, the rules are required no later than 15 months after the date of enactment (i.e., by October 21, 2011).
- Section 809(b)(3) states that the Board of Governors "may, upon an affirmative vote of the [Financial Stability Oversight] Council, prescribe regulations under this section that impose a recordkeeping or reporting requirement on designated clearing entities or financial institutions engaged in designated activities that are subject to standards that have been prescribed under section 805(a)(2)." Therefore, the rules cannot be issued unless the council gives its approval.

In a few cases, the deadlines appear to be flexible. For example, Section 626 of the act (amending Home Owners' Loan Act (12 U.S.C. § 1461 *et seq.*)) states that, under certain conditions, the Board of Governors may require companies "to establish and conduct all or a portion of such financial activities in or through an intermediate holding company, which

Rulemaking Requirements and Authorities... 249

shall be a savings and loan holding company, established pursuant to regulations of the Board." The provision goes on to say that the regulations must be issued within 90 days of the transfer date, "or such longer period as the Board may deem appropriate."

Some Early Deadlines

Of the 122 provisions in the Dodd-Frank Act with a deadline, 73 (59.8%) fall on or before the one-year anniversary date of the enactment of the legislation (i.e., by July 21, 2011). Some of the earliest deadlines (those within the first six months after enactment) are discussed below.

As Soon as Practicable

Two provisions require that rules be issued "as soon as is practicable after the date of enactment."

- Section1101(a)(6) of the act (amending Section 13 of the Federal Reserve Act (12 U.S.C. § 343)) states that the Board of Governors "shall establish, by regulation, in consultation with the Secretary of the Treasury, the policies and procedures governing emergency lending under this paragraph."
- Section 1105(b)(1) states that the FDIC "shall establish, by regulation, and in consultation with the Secretary, policies and procedures governing the issuance of guarantees authorized by this section" (on "emergency financial stabilization").

Within 90 Days

Four provisions in the act require rules to be issued within 90 days of the date of enactment (i.e., by October 19, 2010):

- Section 729 (amending the Commodity Exchange Act (at 7 U.S.C. § 6o-1)) requires the CFTC to "promulgate an interim final rule ... providing for the reporting of each swap entered into before the date of enactment," the terms of which had not expired as of that date.[26]
- Section 766(a) (amending the Securities Exchange Act of 1934 (15 U.S.C. § 78a *et seq.*)) requires the SEC to "promulgate an interim final rule ... providing for the reporting of each security-based swap entered into before the date of enactment," the terms of which had not expired as of that date.[27]
- Section 939B requires the SEC to "revise Regulation FD (17 C.F.R. 243.100) to remove from such regulation the exemption for entities whose primary business is the issuance of credit ratings (17 C.F.R. 243.100(b)(2)(iii))."[28]
- Section 1472(a) of the Dodd-Frank Act (amending Chapter 2 of the Truth in Lending Act (15 U.S.C. § 1631 *et seq.*)) requires the Board of Governors to "prescribe interim final regulations defining with specificity acts or practices that violate appraisal independence in the provision of mortgage lending services for a consumer credit transaction secured by the principal dwelling of the consumer or mortgage brokerage

services for such a transaction and defining any terms in this section or such regulations."[29]

Within 180 Days

Five other Dodd-Frank Act provisions require that rules be issued within 180 days of enactment (i.e., by January 17, 2011):

- Section 726(a) states that the CFTC, "in order to mitigate conflicts of interest ...shall adopt rules which may include numerical limits on the control of, or the voting rights with respect to, any derivatives clearing organization that clears swaps, or swap execution facility or board of trade designated as a contract market that posts swaps or makes swaps available for trading, by a bank holding company ... with total consolidated assets of $50,000,000,000 or more, a nonbank financial company ... supervised by the Board, an affiliate of such a bank holding company or nonbank financial company, a swap dealer, major swap participant, or associated person of a swap dealer or major swap participant."
- Section 916(a) (amending Section 19(b) of the Securities Exchange Act of 1934 (15 U.S.C. § 78s(b))) states that the SEC (after consulting with other regulatory agencies) "shall promulgate rules setting forth the procedural requirements of the proceedings required under this paragraph."
- Section 943 requires the SEC to "prescribe regulations on the use of representations and warranties in the market for asset-backed securities."
- Section 945 (amending Section 7 of the Securities Act of 1933 (15 U.S.C. § 77g)) states that the SEC "shall issue rules relating to the registration statement required to be filed by any issuer of an asset-backed security (as that term is defined in section 3(a)(77) of the Securities Exchange Act of 1934) that require any issuer of an asset-backed security—(1) to perform a review of the assets underlying the asset-backed security; and (2) to disclose the nature of the review under paragraph (1)."
- Section 972 (amending the Securities Exchange Act of 1934 (15 U.S. C. § 78a *et seq.*), creating a new Section 14B) states that the SEC "shall issue rules that require an issuer to disclose in the annual proxy sent to investors the reasons why the issuer has chosen—(1) the same person to serve as chairman of the board of directors and chief executive officer (or in equivalent positions); or (2) different individuals to serve as chairman of the board of directors and chief executive officer (or in equivalent positions of the issuer)."

Within Six Months

Two provisions require rules to be issued within six months of enactment (i.e., by January 21, 2011):

- Section 619 (amending the Bank Holding Company Act of 1956 (12 U.S.C. § 1841 *et seq.*)) requires that the Board of Governors issue rules to implement provisions on "conformance period for divestiture" and "extended transition for illiquid funds."
- Section 951 (amending the Securities Exchange Act of 1934 (15 U.S.C. § 78a *et seq.*)) requires the SEC to issue rules regarding the disclosure of "agreements and

understandings" (in proxy or consent solicitation materials by those making those solicitations) or "related to the compensation of executives where a corporation is acquired through tender offer."

An "Obligation of Speed"

Although some rules are not required to be issued until much later than these early deadlines, it is possible that they could be issued more quickly. Secretary of the Treasury Timothy F. Geithner has indicated that federal financial agencies "have an obligation of speed" when it comes to issuing rules under the Dodd-Frank Act, and said "We will move as quickly as possible to bring clarity to the new rules of finance. The rule writing process traditionally has moved at a frustrating, glacial pace. We must change that."[30] Others, however, have questioned how the rules can be written quickly in light of the complexities of the legislation and the requirements for public participation.[31]

Ten Dodd-Frank Act Final Rules Have Been Published

As of October 20, 2010, 10 final rules implementing provisions in the Dodd-Frank Act had been published in the *Federal Register*:

- an August 13, 2010, FDIC final rule implementing Section 335 of the act, which made permanent the standard maximum share insurance amount of $250,000;[32]
- a September 2, 2010, final rule issued by the National Credit Union Administration implementing Section 335 of the act, which made permanent the standard maximum share insurance amount of $250,000;[33]
- a September 8, 2010, SEC "interim final temporary rule" to implement changes made by Section 975 of the act to Section 15B(a) of the Securities and Exchange Act (which made it unlawful for municipal advisors to provide certain advice or solicit municipal entities or certain other persons without registering with the SEC);[34]
- a September 10, 2010, CFTC final rule implementing Section 742 of the act regarding off-exchange transactions in foreign currency with members of the retail public;[35]
- a September 21, 2010, SEC final rule implementing changes made by Section 989G of the act, which added a new Section 404(c) to the Sarbanes-Oxley Act of 2002;[36]
- a September 21, 2010, SEC final rule rescinding then-existing rules under a statutory requirement that was rescinded by Section 922 of the act;[37]
- an October 4, 2010, SEC final rule implementing Section 939B of the act removing the specific exemption for disclosures made to nationally recognized statistical rating organizations and credit rating agencies for the purpose of determining or monitoring credit ratings;[38]
- an October 12, 2010, SEC final rule implementing changes made by Section 916 of the act regarding new deadlines by which the SEC must act upon proposed rule changes submitted by self-regulatory organizations;[39]

- an October 14, 2010, CFTC interim final rule implementing Section 729 of the act for the reporting of swap transactions entered into before the date of enactment whose terms had not expired;[40] and
- an October 20, 2010, SEC "interim final temporary rule" implementing Section 766 of the act on reporting of security-based swaps entered into before July 21, 2010.[41]

Also, the Board of Governors posted on its website and requested comments on an interim final rule implementing Section 1472(a) of the Dodd-Frank Act.[42] As of October 20, 2010, however, this rule had not been published in the *Federal Register*. Several other final rules that were published in the *Federal Register* mentioned the Dodd-Frank Act, but did not implement its provisions.[43] Also, federal agencies have issued several proposed rules pursuant to the act.[44]

SOME FEDERAL RULEMAKING REQUIREMENTS ARE NOT APPLICABLE TO DODD-FRANK RULES

During the past 65 years, Congress and various presidents have developed an elaborate set of procedures and requirements to guide and oversee the federal rulemaking process. Statutory requirements include the Administrative Procedure Act, the Regulatory Flexibility Act, the Paperwork Reduction Act, the Unfunded Mandates Reform Act, and the Congressional Review Act—each of which states that certain procedural or analytical requirements be addressed before the agencies' rules can be published and take effect.[45] Presidential review of agency rulemaking is currently centered in Executive Order 12866, which requires covered agencies to submit their "significant" regulatory actions to the Office of Information and Regulatory Affairs (OIRA) within the Office of Management and Budget (OMB) before they are published in the *Federal Register*.[46] OIRA reviews the rules to determine their consistency with the analytic requirements in the executive order, the statutes under which they are issued, the President's priorities, and the rules issued by other agencies. The executive order states that the agencies are to "propose or adopt a regulation only upon a reasoned determination that the benefits of the intended regulation justify its costs."[47] Covered agencies are required to estimate the costs and benefits of their "significant" rules, and to conduct a full cost-benefit analysis before issuing any "economically significant" rule (e.g., one that is expected to have a $100 million annual impact on the economy).[48] That analysis is required to include an assessment of not only the underlying benefits and costs, but also the costs and benefits of "potentially effective and reasonably feasible alternatives to the planned regulation."[49]

OIRA also plays a key role in implementing the requirements of the Paperwork Reduction Act (PRA, 44 U.S.C. §§ 3501-3520). The PRA created OIRA, and generally requires that federal agencies receive OIRA approval for certain information collection requests before they are conducted. Before approving a proposed collection of information, OIRA must determine whether the collection is "necessary for the proper performance of the functions of the agency."[50] OIRA's information collection approvals must be renewed at least every three years if the agency wishes to continue collecting the information.

Many Rulemaking Requirements, and Exceptions, Apply to Dodd-Frank Act Rules

Many of the government-wide rulemaking requirements appear to apply to rulemaking under the Dodd-Frank Act, but the exceptions and exemptions to those requirements also apply.

Administrative Procedure Act

For example, as noted earlier in this report, the Administrative Procedure Act (APA) generally requires that federal agencies publish a notice of proposed rulemaking in the *Federal Register*, give "interested persons" an opportunity to comment on the rule, consider those comments and publish a final rule with a general statement of its basis and purpose, and make the final rule effective no less than 30 days after its publication.[51] However, the APA also says that these "notice and comment" procedures do not apply when the agency finds, for "good cause," that those procedures are "impracticable, unnecessary, or contrary to the public interest."[52] Also, agencies can make their rules take effect less than 30 days after they are published if there is "good cause."[53] Therefore, the agencies issuing rules under the Dodd-Frank Act can publish final rules without allowing the public to comment on prior proposed rules, and can make those final rules effective immediately, if they conclude that there is "good cause" to do so. Agencies' use of the APA's good cause exceptions are subject to judicial review.

Of the 10 Dodd-Frank Act final rules that had been published in the *Federal Register* as of October 20, 2010, the issuing agencies invoked the "good cause" exception in eight rules,[54] and the agency said notice and comment was not required in one other rule because it only involved agency organization and procedure.[55] The remaining rule was preceded by a notice of proposed rulemaking, but that notice was published on January 20, 2010, more than six months before the Dodd-Frank Act was enacted.[56]

Regulatory Flexibility Act

The Regulatory Flexibility Act (RFA, 5 U.S.C. §§ 601-612) requires federal agencies to assess the impact of their forthcoming rules on "small entities," which includes small businesses, small governmental jurisdictions, and small not-for-profit organizations.[57] Under the RFA, federal agencies must prepare a regulatory flexibility analysis at the time that proposed and certain final rules are published in the *Federal Register*. The act requires the analyses to describe, among other things, (1) why the regulatory action is being considered and its objectives; (2) the small entities to which the rule will apply and, where feasible, an estimate of their number; (3) the projected reporting, recordkeeping, and other compliance requirements of the rule; and, for final rules, (4) steps the agency has taken to minimize the impact of the rule on small entities. However, these requirements are not triggered if the head of the issuing agency certifies that the rule would not have a "significant economic impact on a substantial number of small entities." The RFA does not define "significant economic impact" or "substantial number of small entities," thereby giving federal agencies substantial discretion regarding when the act's analytical requirements apply.[58] Also, the RFA's analytical requirements do not apply when an agency is not required to publish a notice of proposed rulemaking.[59] Therefore, if an agency publishes a final rule implementing the Dodd-

Frank Act without a prior proposed rule (e.g., using the "good cause exception), then the RFA's analytical requirements do not apply.

Of the 10 Dodd-Frank Act final rules that had been published as of October 20, 2010, the issuing agencies certified that four of them did not have a "significant economic impact" on a "substantial number of small entities,"[60] and said that four other rules were not covered by the RFA because there was no prior proposed rule.[61] Another rule did not mention the RFA.[62] In the remaining rule, the agency did a regulatory flexibility analysis even though the final rule had been published without a prior proposed rule.[63]

Some Rulemaking Requirements and Controls Are Not Applicable to Certain Agencies

In addition to these exceptions and exclusions, some notable regulatory oversight mechanisms (e.g., Executive Order 12866) do not apply to the independent regulatory agencies that are required or permitted to issue most of the rules under the Dodd-Frank Act— the SEC, the Board of Governors, the CFTC, the CFPB, and the FDIC.[64] Also, those agencies may be able to void certain other rulemaking requirements. (These inapplicable requirements were also not applicable to most, if not all, of the independent regulatory agencies before the Dodd-Frank Act was enacted.)

Executive Order 12866

Most of the requirements in Executive Order 12866 do not apply to independent regulatory agencies.[65] Therefore, the independent regulatory agencies that are expected to issue most of the rules under the Dodd-Frank Act do not have to submit their proposed or final significant rules to OIRA for review before they are published. Also, these independent regulatory agencies do not have to conduct cost-benefit analyses for their economically significant rules, and do not have to show that the benefits of their significant rules "justify" the costs. Although certain sections of the Dodd-Frank Act (e.g., Sections 1022 and 1041(c)(1)) require that certain agencies "consider" and "take into account" the potential benefits and costs of their rules, these provisions may be interpreted to establish somewhat less stringent analytical thresholds than the general requirement in Executive Order 12866 that the benefits of agencies' rules "justify" the costs.[66]

Paperwork Reduction Act

Also, although the Paperwork Reduction Act covers independent regulatory agencies, and permits OIRA to disapprove their proposed collections of information, the agencies may be able to collect information even if OIRA objects. The PRA states that

> An independent regulatory agency which is administered by 2 or more members of a commission, board, or similar body, may by majority vote void (A) any disapproval by the Director [of OMB], in whole or in part, of a proposed collection of information of that agency; or (B) an exercise of authority under subsection (d) of section 3507 concerning that agency (regarding information collections that are part of a proposed rule).[67]

Therefore, for example, if OIRA denies a request to collect information by the SEC, the Board of Governors, or the CFTC, those agencies can, by a majority vote, void that disapproval. Although the CFPB is an independent regulatory agency, it is headed by a single director, not a multimember body. Therefore, this PRA authority would not appear to apply to the bureau. However, Section 1100D(c) of the Dodd-Frank Act amended the PRA, and states that

> Notwithstanding any other provision of law, the Director (of OMB) shall treat or review a rule or order prescribed or proposed by the Director of the Bureau of Consumer Financial Protection on the same terms and conditions as apply to any rule or order prescribed or proposed by the Board of Governors of the Federal Reserve System.

Applying this subsection, because the Board of Governors, a multi-member board, is authorized to void OIRA disapprovals of its information collections, the director of the CFPB may arguably be authorized to do so as well.

Unfunded Mandates Reform Act

The Unfunded Mandates Reform Act (UMRA) of 1995 was enacted in an effort to reduce the costs associated with federal imposition of responsibilities, duties, and regulations upon state, local, and tribal governments and the private sector without providing the funding appropriate to the costs imposed by those responsibilities. Title II of UMRA (2 U.S.C. §§ 1532-1538) generally requires Cabinet departments and other agencies to prepare a written statement containing specific descriptions and estimates for any proposed rule that is expected to result in the expenditure of $100 million or more in any year to state, local, or tribal governments, or to the private sector.

However, UMRA does not apply to independent regulatory agencies, and therefore does not apply to many of the rules to be issued pursuant to the Dodd-Frank Act. Even if UMRA did apply to these agencies, UMRA contains numerous other exceptions and exclusions that may exempt their rules from its requirements.[68]

Appropriations Restrictions

In recent years, Congress has added provisions to agency appropriations bills that restrict federal rulemaking or regulatory activity, including provisions that (1) prevent the finalization of particular proposed rules, (2) restrict regulatory activity within certain areas, (3) inhibit the implementation or enforcement of certain rules, and (4) employ condition restrictions (e.g., preventing the implementation of a rule until certain actions are taken).[69] Appropriations restrictions have been advocated by representatives of virtually all political parties and interest groups, and some of these restrictions have been repeated year after year.

It should be noted that several of the agencies required or authorized to issue rules under the Dodd-Frank Act do not receive appropriated funds. As a result, Congress arguably may not be able to use appropriations restrictions to control their rulemaking actions.[70] For example, the Federal Reserve System, of which the Board of Governors is a part, receives income primarily from the interest on U.S. government securities that it has acquired through open market operations.[71] The CFPB is funded (up to certain caps) using money from the combined earnings of the Federal Reserve System, and the Dodd-Frank Act states that those funds are not reviewable by either the House or the Senate appropriations committees.[72]

However, the SEC, the CFTC, and several other agencies issuing rules under the Dodd-Frank Act receive appropriations, so Congress can place restrictions on those agencies' appropriations to control their rulemaking actions.[73]

Depending on how they are written, appropriations restrictions to affect rulemaking may have certain limitations. In general, they do not nullify existing regulations (i.e., remove them from the *Code of Federal Regulations*) or permanently prevent the agencies from issuing the same or similar regulations. As a result, any final rule that has taken effect and been codified in the *Code of Federal Regulations* will continue to be binding—even if language in the relevant regulatory agency's appropriations act prohibits the use of funds to enforce the rule. Regulated entities may still be required to adhere to applicable requirements (e.g., installation of pollution control devices, submission of relevant paperwork), even if violations are unlikely to be detected and enforcement actions cannot be taken by federal agencies. Also, unless otherwise indicated, regulatory restrictions in appropriations acts are generally binding only for the period of time covered by the legislation (i.e., a fiscal year or a portion of a fiscal year).[74] Therefore, any such restriction that is not repeated in the next relevant appropriations act or enacted in other legislation is no longer binding on the relevant agency or agencies.

CONGRESSIONAL OVERSIGHT

In order for Congress to oversee the rules implementing the Dodd-Frank Act, it must first have a sense of what rules the agencies are going to issue, and when. By identifying the provisions in the act that require or permit rulemaking, this report can help to inform Congress in this regard. As noted previously, however, many of the rules that the agencies will likely issue to implement the Dodd-Frank Act are not specifically mentioned in the act. Also, some of the rules that the agencies are permitted (but not required) to issue may never be developed.

Another way for Congress to identify upcoming rules is by reviewing the Unified Agenda of Federal Regulatory and Deregulatory Actions, which is published twice each year.[75] The Unified Agenda lists upcoming rulemaking activities, by agency, in five separate categories: (1) prerule stage (e.g., advance notices of proposed rulemaking); (2) proposed rule stage (i.e., upcoming proposed rules); (3) final rule stage (i.e., upcoming final rules); (4) long-term actions (i.e., rules that agencies do not expect to issue in the next 12 months); and (5) completed actions (i.e., final rules or rules that have been withdrawn since the last edition of the Unified Agenda). There is no penalty for issuing a rule without a prior notice in the Unified Agenda, and some prospective rules listed in the Unified Agenda never get issued. Nevertheless, the Unified Agenda can help Congress and the public know what actions are about to occur. A previous CRS report indicated that about three-fourths of the significant proposed rules published after having been reviewed by OIRA in 2008 were previously listed in the "proposed rule" section of the Unified Agenda.[76] The first edition of the Unified Agenda after the enactment of the Dodd-Frank Act is expected to be published on November 22, 2010.[77]

Options

Congress has a number of oversight tools available to affect the nature of Dodd-Frank Act rulemaking, including

- confirmation hearings for nominees to head the rulemaking agencies;
- oversight hearings on the agencies' implementation of the act; and
- letters and meetings between individual Members and representatives of the agencies regarding pending rules, and filing comments on proposed and interim final rules.[78]

As one author indicated,

[I]nvestigations conducted by congressional committees constitute another powerful device of formal political supervision.... The public legislative hearings, in which administrative action is carefully scrutinized and a commissioner or staff member is plied with questions, symbolizes the unparalleled sophistication of American congressional control over administrative action, in general and by [independent regulatory agencies], in particular. Individual oversight by representatives or senators also takes place. Through correspondence or meetings, the latter convey the concerns of their constituents.[79]

Congress, committees, and individual Members can also request that the Government Accountability Office (GAO) evaluate the agencies' actions to implement the Dodd-Frank Act. However, the act itself contains more than 40 provisions requiring GAO to conduct studies and write reports.[80] For example:

- Section 412 of the act requires GAO to examine compliance costs associated with SEC rules regarding custody of funds or securities of clients by investment advisers, and any additional costs if a portion of a rule relating to operational independence is eliminated. GAO is required to submit a report on the results of the study to the Senate Committee on Banking, Housing, and Urban Affairs and the House Committee on Financial Services not later than three years after the date of enactment (i.e., by July 21, 2013).
- Section 939E requires GAO to study the feasibility and merits of creating an independent professional organization for rating analysts employed by nationally recognized statistical rating organizations. GAO is to submit a report on the results of the study to the Senate Committee on Banking, Housing, and Urban Affairs and the House Committee on Financial Services not later than one year after the date of publication of the rules issued by the commission pursuant to Section 936 of the act.
- Section 1421 requires GAO to submit a report to Congress within one year of the date of enactment (i.e., by July 21, 2011) assessing the effects of the Dodd-Frank Act on the availability and affordability of credit for consumers, small businesses, homebuyers, and mortgage lending.

GAO has indicated that it considers congressional mandates as a top priority, followed by requests from senior congressional leaders and committee leaders, with the third priority being individual Member requests.[81]

Restrictions on the use of agencies' appropriations is also an option, at least for the agencies that receive congressionally appropriated funds (e.g., the SEC and the CFTC). As noted previously, while such restrictions can prevent agencies from using such funds to finalize or implement the rules in question, they do not eliminate published final rules, and do not relieve regulated parties from complying with their requirements. Also, unless otherwise indicated, regulatory restrictions in appropriations acts are binding only for the period of time covered by the legislation.

Congressional Review Act

Another congressional oversight option regarding agencies' rules is the Congressional Review Act (CRA, 5 U.S.C. § 801 *et seq*.), which was enacted in 1996 in an attempt to reestablish a measure of congressional authority over rulemaking "without at the same time requiring Congress to become a super regulatory agency."[82] The act generally requires all federal agencies (including independent regulatory agencies) to submit all of their covered final rules to both houses of Congress and GAO before they can take effect.[83] It also established expedited legislative procedures (primarily in the Senate) by which Congress may disapprove agencies' final rules by enacting a joint resolution of disapproval.[84] The definition of a covered rule in the CRA is quite broad, arguably including any type of document (e.g., legislative rules, policy statements, guidance, manuals, and memoranda) that the agency wishes to make binding on the affected public.[85] After a rule is submitted, Congress can use the expedited procedures specified in the CRA to disapprove of the rule. CRA resolutions of disapproval must be presented to the President for signature or veto.

For a variety of reasons, however, the CRA has been used to disapprove only one rule in the more than 14 years since it was enacted.[86] Perhaps most notably, it is likely that a President would veto a resolution of disapproval to protect rules developed under his own administration, and it may be difficult for Congress to muster the two-thirds vote in both houses needed to overturn the veto. Congress can also use regular (i.e., non-CRA) legislative procedures to disapprove agencies' rules, but such legislation may prove even more difficult to enact than a CRA resolution of disapproval (primarily because of the lack of expedited procedures in the Senate), and if enacted may also be vetoed by the President.

These difficulties notwithstanding, even if the use of the CRA does not result in the disapproval of a rule, just the threat of filing a resolution of disapproval can sometimes exert pressure on agencies to modify or withdraw their rules.[87] Also, the expedited procedures in the Senate can provide a forum to discuss concerns about a rule. After a joint resolution is introduced, it is referred to the appropriate committee of jurisdiction. If the committee does not report the resolution within a specified period, it can be discharged from committee by a petition signed by 30 Senators. After the joint resolution has been reported by the appropriate committee or discharged by petition, it is placed on the Senate calendar. At that point, it is in order to consider a motion to proceed to the consideration of the joint resolution at any time. The CRA provides that all points of order against the joint resolution (and against consideration of the joint resolution) are waived. The motion to proceed is not debatable and is also not subject to amendment, or to a motion to postpone, or to a motion to proceed to the consideration of other business. If the motion to proceed were agreed to, debate on the joint resolution would be limited to no more than 10 hours (debate may be less than 10 hours if the

Senate agrees to a non-debatable motion to limit debate). Amendments and motions to recommit are not in order. The 10 hours of debate would be divided equally between those favoring and those opposing the joint resolution. Immediately following the conclusion of debate on the joint resolution, the Senate is required to vote on final passage of the joint resolution.

APPENDIX A. MANDATORY RULEMAKING PROVISIONS

Table A-1 below lists provisions in the Dodd-Frank Act that require agencies to issue certain rules (e.g., stating that the agency or agencies "shall" establish, promulgate, or issue rules or regulations on a particular topic).

Table A-1. Mandatory Rulemaking Provisions in the Dodd-Frank Act.

Section	Text of the Provision	Agency	Deadline
Section 102(b)	"…shall establish, by regulation, the requirements for determining if a company is predominantly engaged in financial activities…."	Board of Governors	None
Section 120(e)(2)(B)	"…shall promulgate regulations to establish a procedure under which entities under its jurisdiction may appeal a determination by such agency under this paragraph that standards imposed under this section (providing more stringent regulation of a financial activity) should remain in effect."	All primary financial regulatory agencies that impose standards under this section.	January 22, 2012 (Per Section 168, unless otherwise specified, Board of Governors' final rules in subtitles A and C of this title must be issued within 18 months of the act's effective date.)
Section 152(g)	"…shall issue regulations prohibiting the Director and any employee of the Office (of Financial Research) who has had access to the transaction or position data maintained by the Data Center or other business confidential information about financial entities required to report to the Office from being employed by or providing advice or consulting services to a financial company, for a period of 1 year after last having had access in the course of official duties to such transaction or position data or business confidential information, regardless of whether that entity is required to report to the Office."	Secretary of the Treasury, with the concurrence of the Office of Government Ethics	None
Section 154(b)(1)(C)	"…shall promulgate regulations pursuant to subsections (a)(1), (a)(2), (a)(7), and (c)(1) of section 153 regarding the type and scope of the data to be collected by the Data Center under this paragraph." (Data to be used by Council to determine threats to financial stability.)	Department of the Treasury, Office of Financial Research	None

Table A-1. (Continued).

Section	Text of the Provision	Agency	Deadline
Section 155(d)	"…shall establish, by regulation … an assessment schedule and rates, applicable to bank holding companies with total consolidated assets of $50,000,000,000 or greater and nonbank financial companies supervised by the Board of Governors…."	Secretary of the Treasury, with the approval of the Financial Stability Oversight Council	July 21, 2012 (Rules can be issued starting two years after the date of enactment.)
Section 165(d)(8)	"…shall jointly issue final rules implementing this subsection" (on "Resolution Plan and Credit Exposure Reports").	Board of Governors and the Federal Deposit Insurance Corporation	January 21, 2012 (Within 18 months after the date of enactment.)
Section 165(e)(1)	"In order to limit the risks that the failure of any individual company could pose to a nonbank financial company supervised by the Board of Governors or a bank holding company described in subsection (a), the Board of Governors, by regulation, shall prescribe standards that limit such risks."	Board of Governors	January 22, 2012 (Per Section 168, unless otherwise specified, Board of Governors' final rules in subtitles A and C must be issued within 18 months of the act's effective date.)
Section 165(h)	"…shall issue final rules to carry out this subsection…" (on "Risk Committee"). Specifically required to "issue regulations requiring each bank holding company that is a publicly traded company and that has total consolidated assets of not less than $10,000,000,000 to establish a risk committee…."	Board of Governors	July 21, 2012 (Rules must be issued within one year after the transfer date, and must take effect no later than 15 months after the transfer date (i.e., by October 21, 2012).)
Section 165(i)(2)(C)	"…shall issue consistent and comparable regulations to implement this paragraph that shall—(i) define the term 'stress test' for purposes of this paragraph; (ii) establish methodologies for the conduct of stress tests required by this paragraph that shall provide for at least 3 different sets of conditions, including baseline, adverse, and severely adverse; (iii) establish the form and content of the report required by subparagraph (B); and (iv) require companies subject to this paragraph to publish a summary of the results of the required stress tests."	"Each Federal primary financial regulatory agency, in coordination with the Board of Governors and the Federal Insurance Office"	None
Section 165(j)(3)	"…shall promulgate regulations to establish procedures and timelines for complying with the requirements of this subsection" (on 'leverage limitation')."	Board of Governors	January 22, 2012 (Per Section 168, unless otherwise specified, Board of Governors' final rules in subtitles A and C must be issued within 18 months of the act's effective date.)

Section	Text of the Provision	Agency	Deadline
Section 166(a)	"…shall prescribe regulations establishing requirements to provide for the early remediation of financial distress of a nonbank financial company supervised by the Board of Governors or a bank holding company described in section 165(a)…."	Board of Governors, in consultation with the Financial Stability Oversight Council and the Federal Deposit Insurance Corporation	January 22, 2012 (Per Section 168, unless otherwise specified, Board of Governors' final rules in subtitles A and C must be issued within 18 months of the act's effective date.)
Section 170(a)	"…shall promulgate regulations…setting forth the criteria for exempting certain types or classes of U.S. nonbank financial companies or foreign nonbank financial companies from supervision by the Board of Governors."	Board of Governors, in consultation with the Financial Stability Oversight Council	January 22, 2012 (Per Section 168, unless otherwise specified, Board of Governors' final rules in subtitles A and C must be issued within 18 months of the act's effective date.)
Section 201(b)	"…shall establish, by regulation" definitional criteria to determine if the consolidated revenues of a company from certain activities constitute less than 85 percent of the total consolidated revenues of such company.	Federal Deposit Insurance Corporation, in consultation with the Secretary	None
Section 205(h)	"… shall jointly issue rules to implement this section" (on "Orderly Liquidation of Covered Brokers and Dealers").	The Securities and Exchange Commission and the Federal Deposit Insurance Corporation, after consultation with the Securities Investor Protection Corporation	None
Section 210 (c)(8)(H)(i)	"…shall jointly prescribe regulations requiring that financial companies maintain such records with respect to qualified financial contracts (including market valuations) that the Federal primary financial regulatory agencies determine to be necessary or appropriate in order to assist the Corporation as receiver for a covered financial company in being able to exercise its rights and fulfill its obligations under this paragraph or paragraph (9) or (10)." The rules issued may be "joint final or interim final regulations."	"Federal primary financial regulatory agencies" (or the chairperson of the Financial Stability Oversight Council, if the deadline is not met)	July 21, 2012 (Within 24 months of the date of enactment.)
Section 210(n)(7)	"…shall jointly … prescribe regulations governing the calculation of the maximum obligation limitation defined in this paragraph."	Federal Deposit Insurance Corporation and the Secretary of the Treasury, in consultation with the Financial Stability Oversight Council	None

Table A-1. (Continued).

Section	Text of the Provision	Agency	Deadline
Section 210(o)(6)(A)	"…shall prescribe regulations to carry out this subsection" (on assessments to pay for obligations issued by the FDIC).	Federal Deposit Insurance Corporation, in consultation with the Secretary of the Treasury	None
Section 210(r)	"…shall prescribe regulations which, at a minimum, shall prohibit the sale of assets of a covered financial company by the Corporation to … (any person who has certain characteristics)."	Federal Deposit Insurance Corporation	None
Section 210(s)(3)	"…shall promulgate regulations to implement the requirements of this subsection (on recoupment of compensation from senior executives and directors of failed financial companies), including…."	Federal Deposit Insurance Corporation	None
Section 213(d)	"…shall jointly prescribe rules or regulations to administer and carry out this section" (on banning certain activities by senior executives and directors).	Federal Deposit Insurance Corporation and the Board of Governors, in consultation with the Financial Stability Oversight Council	None
Section 331(b)	"…shall amend the regulations issued by the Corporation under section 7(b)(2) of the Federal Deposit Insurance Act (12 U.S.C. 1817(b)(2)) to define the term 'assessment base' with respect to an insured depository institution for purposes of that section 7(b)(2), as an amount equal to…."	Federal Deposit Insurance Corporation	None
Section 332(1)(B)	"…shall prescribe, by regulation, after notice and opportunity for comment, the method for the declaration, calculation, distribution, and payment of dividends under this paragraph."	Federal Deposit Insurance Corporation	None
Section 358(2) (amending Section 806 of the Community Reinvestment Act of 1977 (12 U.S.C. 2901 et seq.))	"… shall prescribe regulations applicable to savings associations …."	Comptroller of the Currency	None

Rulemaking Requirements and Authorities...

Section	Text of the Provision	Agency	Deadline
Section 358(2) (amending Section 806 of the Community Reinvestment Act of 1977 (12 U.S.C. 2901 et seq.))	"... shall prescribe regulations applicable to insured State member banks, bank holding companies and savings and loan holding companies."	Board of Governors	None
Section 404(2) (amending Section 204 of the Investment Advisers Act of 1940 (15 U.S.C. 80b-4))	"...shall issue rules requiring each investment adviser to a private fund to file reports containing such information as the Commission deems necessary and appropriate in the public interest and for the protection of investors or for the assessment of systemic risk."	Securities and Exchange Commission	None
Section 406(2) (amending Section 211 of the Investment Advisers Act of 1940 (15 U.S.C. 80b-11))	"...shall ... jointly promulgate rules to establish the form and content of the reports required to be filed with the Commission under subsection 204(b) and with the Commodity Futures Trading Commission by investment advisers that are registered both under this title and the Commodity Exchange Act (7 U.S.C. 1a et seq.)."	Securities and Exchange Commission and Commodity Futures Trading Commission	July 21, 2011 (Not later than 12 months after the date of enactment of the Private Fund Investment Advisers Registration Act of 2010, which is Title IV of the Dodd-Frank Act.)
Section 407 (amending Section 203 of the Investment Advisers Act of 1940 (15 U.S.C. 80b-3))	"...shall issue final rules to define the term 'venture capital fund' for purposes of this subsection" (on "Exemption of Venture Capital Fund Advisers").	Securities and Exchange Commission	July 21, 2011 (Not later than one year after the date of enactment.)
Section 409 (amending Section 202(a)(11) of the Investment Advisers Act of 1940 (15 U.S.C. 80b-2(a)(11)))	Requires an exemption for "any family office, as defined by rule, regulation, or order of the Commission, in accordance with the purposes of this title...." Goes on to require that the exemption meet certain criteria.	Securities and Exchange Commission	None
Section 413(a)	"...shall adjust any net worth standard for an accredited investor, as set forth in the rules of the Commission under the Securities Act of 1933...."	Securities and Exchange Commission	None
Section 616(d) (amending the Federal Deposit Insurance Act (12 U.S.C. 1811 et seq.)	"...shall jointly issue final rules to carry out this section" (which requires holding companies to serve as a "source of strength" for subsidiaries).	The "appropriate Federal banking agencies."	July 21, 2012 (Within one year after the transfer date.)

Table A-1. (Continued).

Section	Text of the Provision	Agency	Deadline
Section 618(d)(1)	"…shall, by regulation or order, prescribe capital adequacy and other risk management standards for supervised securities holding companies that are appropriate to protect the safety and soundness of the supervised securities holding companies and address the risks posed to financial stability by supervised securities holding companies."	Board of Governors	None
Section 619 (amending the Bank Holding Company Act of 1956 (12 U.S.C. 1841 et seq.))	"…shall consider the findings of the study under paragraph (1) (on implementing the provisions in this section on prohibitions on proprietary trading and relationships with hedge funds and private equity funds) and adopt rules to carry out this section…."	Certain rules are to be issued jointly by the "appropriate Federal banking agencies," while other rules are to be issued individually by the Board of Governors, the Commodity Futures Trading Commission, and the Securities and Exchange Commission	October 21, 2011 (Within 15 months of the date of enactment. Study required within six months of enactment, and rule required within nine months of enactment.)
Section 619 (amending the Bank Holding Company Act of 1956 (12 U.S.C. 1841 et seq.))	"…shall issues [sic] rules to implement paragraphs (2) and (3)" (on "Conformance Period for Divestiture" and "Extended Transition for Illiquid Funds").	Board of Governors	January 21, 2011 (Not later than six months after the date of enactment.)
Section 620(a) (amending the Securities Act of 1933 (15 U.S.C. 77a et seq.))	"…shall issue rules for the purpose of implementing subsection (a)" (on conflicts of interest relating to certain securitizations).	Securities and Exchange Commission	April 17, 2011 (Within 270 days after the date of enactment.)
Section 621 (amending the Securities Act of 1933 (15 U.S.C. 77a et seq.), new Section 27B)	"…shall issue rules for the purpose of implementing subsection (a)" (which establishes certain conflict of interest requirements).	Securities and Exchange Commission	April 17, 2011 (Within 270 days after the date of enactment.)
Section 622 (amending the Bank Holding Company Act of 1956 (12 U.S.C. 1841 et seq.))	The term "liabilities," "with respect to an insurance company or other nonbank financial company supervised by the Board, (means) such assets of the company as the Board shall specify by rule, in order to provide for consistent and equitable treatment of such companies."	Board of Governors	None

Rulemaking Requirements and Authorities...

Section	Text of the Provision	Agency	Deadline
Section 622 (amending the Bank Holding Company Act of 1956 (12 U.S.C. 1841 et seq.), new Section 14)	"…shall issue regulations implementing this section (on 'Concentration Limits on Large Financial Firms') in accordance with the recommendations of the (Financial Stability Oversight) Council…."	Board of Governors	None
Section 622 (amending the Bank Holding Company Act of 1956 (12 U.S.C. 1841 et seq.), new Section 14)	"…shall issue final regulations implementing this section, which shall reflect any recommendations by the (Financial Stability Oversight) Council under paragraph (1)(B)."	Board of Governors	October 21, 2011 (Within 15 months of the date of enactment. Study required within six months of enactment, and rule required within nine months of enactment.)
Section 626 (creating a new Section 10A on "Intermediate Holding Companies" to the Homeowners' Loan Act)	"…shall promulgate regulations to establish the criteria for determining whether to require a grandfathered unitary savings and loan holding company to establish an intermediate holding company under subsection (b)…."	Board of Governors	None
Section 712(a)(8)	"…shall jointly prescribe such regulations regarding mixed swaps, as described in section 1a(47)(D) of the Commodity Exchange Act (7 U.S.C. 1a(47)(D)) and in section 3(a)(68)(D) of the Securities Exchange Act of 1934 (15 U.S.C. 78c(a)(68)(D)), as may be necessary to carry out the purposes of this title."	Commodity Futures Trading Commission and the Securities and Exchange Commission, after consultation with the Board of Governors	July 16, 2011 (Section 712(a)(3) states that regulations "shall be prescribed in accordance with applicable requirements of title 5, United States Code, and shall be issued in final form not later than 360 days after the date of enactment of this Act.")
Section 721(a)(16) (amending Section 1a of the Commodity Exchange Act (7 U.S.C. 1a))	"…shall define by rule or regulation the term 'substantial position' at the threshold that the Commission determines to be prudent for the effective monitoring, management, and oversight of entities that are systemically important or can significantly impact the financial system of the United States."	Commodity Futures Trading Commission	July 16, 2011 (Section 712(e) requires that all mandatory Title VII CFTC and SEC rules (other than those issued jointly) be promulgated within 360 days after the date of enactment, unless another provision states otherwise.)
Section 721(a)(21) (amending Section 1a of the Commodity Exchange Act (7 U.S.C. 1a))	"The Commission shall exempt from designation as a swap dealer an entity that engages in a de minimis quantity of swap dealing in connection with transactions with or on behalf of its customers. The Commission shall promulgate regulations to establish factors with respect to the making of this determination to exempt."	Commodity Futures Trading Commission	July 16, 2011 (Section 712(e) requires that all mandatory Title VII CFTC and SEC rules (other than those issued jointly) be promulgated within 360 days after the date of enactment, unless another provision states otherwise.)

Table A-1. (Continued).

Section	Text of the Provision	Agency	Deadline
Section 721(c)	"To include transactions and entities that have been structured to evade this subtitle, (the Commission) shall adopt a rule to further define the terms 'swap,' 'swap dealer,' 'major swap participant," and 'eligible contract participant.'"	Commodity Futures Trading Commission	July 16, 2011 (Section 712(e) requires that all mandatory Title VII CFTC and SEC rules (other than those issued jointly) be promulgated within 360 days after the date of enactment, unless another provision states otherwise.)
Section 723(a)(3) (amending Section 2 of the Commodity Exchange Act (7 U.S.C. 2))	"…shall adopt rules for a derivatives clearing organization's submission for review, pursuant to this paragraph, of a swap, or a group, category, type, or class of swaps, that it seeks to accept for clearing."	Commodity Futures Trading Commission	July 21, 2011 (Within one year after the date of enactment.)
Section 723(a)(3) (amending Section 2 of the Commodity Exchange Act (7 U.S.C. 2))	"…shall adopt rules for reviewing, pursuant to this paragraph, a derivatives clearing organization's clearing of a swap, or a group, category, type, or class of swaps, that it has accepted for clearing."	Commodity Futures Trading Commission	July 21, 2011 (Within one year after the date of enactment.)
Section 725(d)	"…shall adopt rules mitigating conflicts of interest in connection with the conduct of business by a swap dealer or a major swap participant with a derivatives clearing organization, board of trade, or a swap execution facility that clears or trades swaps in which the swap dealer or major swap participant has a material debt or material equity investment."	Commodity Futures Trading Commission	July 16, 2011 (Section 712(e) requires that all mandatory Title VII CFTC and SEC rules (other than those issued jointly) be promulgated within 360 days after the date of enactment, unless another provision states otherwise.)
Section 726(a)	"…shall adopt rules which may include numerical limits on the control of, or the voting rights with respect to, any derivatives clearing organization that clears swaps, or swap execution facility or board of trade designated as a contract market that posts swaps or makes swaps available for trading, by a bank holding company … with total consolidated assets of $50,000,000,000 or more, a nonbank financial company … supervised by the Board, an affiliate of such a bank holding company or nonbank financial company, a swap dealer, major swap participant, or associated person of a swap dealer or major swap participant."	Commodity Futures Trading Commission	January 17, 2011 (Within 180 days after enactment.)

Rulemaking Requirements and Authorities...

Section	Text of the Provision	Agency	Deadline
Section 727 (amending Section 2(a) of the Commodity Exchange Act (7 U.S.C. 2(a)))	"…is authorized and required to provide by rule for the public availability of swap transaction and pricing data as follows…."	Commodity Futures Trading Commission	July 16, 2011 (Section 712(e) requires that all mandatory Title VII CFTC and SEC rules (other than those issued jointly) be promulgated within 360 days after the date of enactment, unless another provision states otherwise.)
Section 728 (amending the Commodity Exchange Act by inserting a new section after section 20 (7 U.S.C. 24))	"…shall adopt rules governing persons that are registered under this section" (on swap data repositories).	Commodity Futures Trading Commission	July 16, 2011 (Section 712(e) requires that all mandatory Title VII CFTC and SEC rules (other than those issued jointly) be promulgated within 360 days after the date of enactment, unless another provision states otherwise.)
Section 729 (amending the Commodity Exchange Act after section 4q (7 U.S.C. 6o-1))	"…shall promulgate an interim final rule … providing for the reporting of each swap entered into before the date of enactment," the terms of which were in effect as of that date.	Commodity Futures Trading Commission	October 19, 2010 (Within 90 days of the date of enactment.)
Section 731 (amending the Commodity Exchange Act (7 U.S.C. 1 et seq.))	"…shall adopt rules governing reporting and recordkeeping for swap dealers and major swap participants."	Commodity Futures Trading Commission	July 16, 2011 (Section 712(e) requires that all mandatory Title VII CFTC and SEC rules (other than those issued jointly) be promulgated within 360 days after the date of enactment, unless another provision states otherwise.)
Section 731 (amending the Commodity Exchange Act (7 U.S.C. 1 et seq.))	"…shall adopt rules for persons that are registered as swap dealers or major swap participants under this section" (on registration and regulation of swap dealers and major swap participants).	Commodity Futures Trading Commission	July 16, 2011 (Section 712(e) requires that all mandatory Title VII CFTC and SEC rules (other than those issued jointly) be promulgated within 360 days after the date of enactment, unless another provision states otherwise.)
Section 731 (amending the Commodity Exchange Act (7 U.S.C. 1 et seq.))	"… shall prescribe rules under this subsection governing business conduct standards for swap dealers and major swap participants."	Commodity Futures Trading Commission	July 16, 2011 (Section 712(e) requires that all mandatory Title VII CFTC and SEC rules (other than those issued jointly) be promulgated within 360 days after the date of enactment, unless another provision states otherwise.)

Table A-1. (Continued).

Section	Text of the Provision	Agency	Deadline
Section 731 (amending the Commodity Exchange Act (7 U.S.C. 1 et seq.))	"…shall jointly adopt rules for swap dealers and major swap participants, with respect to their activities as a swap dealer or major swap participant, for which there is a prudential regulator imposing (i) capital requirements; and (ii) both initial and variation margin requirements on all swaps that are not cleared by a registered derivatives clearing organization."	The prudential regulators, in consultation with the Commodity Futures Trading Commission and the Securities and Exchange Commission	July 16, 2011 (Section 712(e) requires that all mandatory Title VII CFTC and SEC rules (other than those issued jointly) be promulgated within 360 days after the date of enactment, unless another provision states otherwise.)
Section 731 (amending the Commodity Exchange Act (7 U.S.C. 1 et seq.))	"…shall adopt rules for swap dealers and major swap participants, with respect to their activities as a swap dealer or major swap participant, for which there is not a prudential regulator imposing (i) capital requirements; and (ii) both initial and variation margin requirements on all swaps that are not cleared by a registered derivatives clearing organization."	Commodity Futures Trading Commission	July 16, 2011 (Section 712(e) requires that all mandatory Title VII CFTC and SEC rules (other than those issued jointly) be promulgated within 360 days after the date of enactment, unless another provision states otherwise.)
Section 731 (amending the Commodity Exchange Act (7 U.S.C. 1 et seq.))	"…shall prescribe rules under this subsection governing duties of swap dealers and major swap participants."	Commodity Futures Trading Commission	July 16, 2011 (Section 712(e) requires that all mandatory Title VII CFTC and SEC rules (other than those issued jointly) be promulgated within 360 days after the date of enactment, unless another provision states otherwise.)
Section 731 (amending the Commodity Exchange Act (7 U.S.C. 1 et seq.))	"…shall adopt rules governing daily trading records for swap dealers and major swap participants."	Commodity Futures Trading Commission	July 16, 2011 (Section 712(e) requires that all mandatory Title VII CFTC and SEC rules (other than those issued jointly) be promulgated within 360 days after the date of enactment, unless another provision states otherwise.)
Section 731 (amending the Commodity Exchange Act (7 U.S.C. 1 et seq.))	"…shall prescribe rules under this subsection governing business conduct standards for swap dealers and major swap participants."	Commodity Futures Trading Commission	July 16, 2011 (Section 712(e) requires that all mandatory Title VII CFTC and SEC rules (other than those issued jointly) be promulgated within 360 days after the date of enactment, unless another provision states otherwise.)

Rulemaking Requirements and Authorities...

269

Section	Text of the Provision	Agency	Deadline
Section 731 (amending the Commodity Exchange Act (7 U.S.C. 1 et seq.))	"...shall adopt rules governing documentation standards for swap dealers and major swap participants."	Commodity Futures Trading Commission	July 16, 2011 (Section 712(e) requires that all mandatory Title VII CFTC and SEC rules (other than those issued jointly) be promulgated within 360 days after the date of enactment, unless another provision states otherwise.)
Section 733 (amending the Commodity Exchange Act by inserting after section 5g (7 U.S.C. 7b-2) a new Section 5h on "Swap Execution Facilities")	"...shall prescribe rules governing the regulation of alternative swap execution facilities under this section."	Commodity Futures Trading Commission	July 16, 2011 (Section 712(e) requires that all mandatory Title VII CFTC and SEC rules (other than those issued jointly) be promulgated within 360 days after the date of enactment, unless another provision states otherwise.)
Section 737(a)(4) (amending Section 4a(a) of the Commodity Exchange Act (7 U.S.C. 6a(a)))	"...shall by rule, regulation, or order establish limits on the amount of positions, as appropriate, other than bona fide hedge positions, that may be held by any person with respect to contracts of sale for future delivery or with respect to options on the contracts or commodities traded on or subject to the rules of a designated contract market."	Commodity Futures Trading Commission	July 16, 2011 (Section 712(e) requires that all mandatory Title VII CFTC and SEC rules (other than those issued jointly) be promulgated within 360 days after the date of enactment, unless another provision states otherwise.)
Section 737(a)(4) (amending Section 4a(a) of the Commodity Exchange Act (7 U.S.C. 6a(a)))	"...shall, by rule or regulation, establish limits (including related hedge exemption provisions) on the aggregate number or amount of positions in contracts based upon the same underlying commodity (as defined by the Commission) that may be held by any person...."	Commodity Futures Trading Commission	July 16, 2011 (Section 712(e) requires that all mandatory Title VII CFTC and SEC rules (other than those issued jointly) be promulgated within 360 days after the date of enactment, unless another provision states otherwise.)
Section 761 (amending Section 3(a) of the Securities Exchange Act of 1934, 15 U.S.C. 78c(a))	"...shall define, by rule or regulation, the term 'substantial position' at the threshold that the Commission determines to be prudent for the effective monitoring, management, and oversight of entities that are systemically important or can significantly impact the financial system of the United States."	Securities and Exchange Commission	July 16, 2011 (Section 712(e) requires that all mandatory Title VII CFTC and SEC rules (other than those issued jointly) be promulgated within 360 days after the date of enactment, unless another provision states otherwise.).

Table A-1. (Continued).

Section	Text of the Provision	Agency	Deadline
Section 761 (amending Section 3(a) of the Securities Exchange Act of 1934, 15 U.S.C. 78c(a))	"…shall exempt from designation as a security-based swap dealer an entity that engages in a de minimis quantity of security based swap dealing in connection with transactions with or on behalf of its customers. The Commission shall promulgate regulations to establish factors with respect to the making of any determination to exempt."	Securities and Exchange Commission	July 16, 2011 (Section 712(e) requires that all mandatory Title VII CFTC and SEC rules (other than those issued jointly) be promulgated within 360 days after the date of enactment, unless another provision states otherwise.)
Section 763(a) (amending the Securities Exchange Act of 1934 (15 U.S.C. 78a et seq.))	"…shall prescribe rules under this section (and issue interpretations of rules prescribed under this section), as determined by the Commission to be necessary to prevent evasions of the mandatory clearing requirements under this Act."	Securities and Exchange Commission	July 16, 2011 (Section 712(e) requires that all mandatory Title VII CFTC and SEC rules (other than those issued jointly) be promulgated within 360 days after the date of enactment, unless another provision states otherwise.)
Section 763(a) (amending the Securities Exchange Act of 1934 (15 U.S.C. 78a et seq.))	"…shall adopt rules for a clearing agency's submission for review, pursuant to this subsection, of a security-based swap, or a group, category, type, or class of security-based swaps, that it seeks to accept for clearing."	Securities and Exchange Commission	July 21, 2011 (Within one year after the date of enactment.)
Section 763(b) (amending Section 17A of the Securities Exchange Act of 1934 (15 U.S.C. 78q-1))	"…shall adopt rules governing persons that are registered as clearing agencies for security-based swaps under this title."	Securities and Exchange Commission	July 16, 2011 (Section 712(e) requires that all mandatory Title VII CFTC and SEC rules (other than those issued jointly) be promulgated within 360 days after the date of enactment, unless another provision states otherwise.)
Section 763(c) (amending the Securities Exchange Act of 1934 (15 U.S.C. 78a et seq.))	"…shall prescribe rules governing the regulation of security-based swap execution facilities under this section."	Securities and Exchange Commission	July 16, 2011 (Section 712(e) requires that all mandatory Title VII CFTC and SEC rules (other than those issued jointly) be promulgated within 360 days after the date of enactment, unless another provision states otherwise.)

Rulemaking Requirements and Authorities…

Section	Text of the Provision	Agency	Deadline
Section 763(g) (amending Section 9 of the Securities Exchange Act of 1934 (15 U.S.C. 78i))	"…shall, for the purposes of this subsection, by rules and regulations define, and prescribe means reasonably designed to prevent, such transactions, acts, practices, and courses of business as are fraudulent, deceptive, or manipulative, and such quotations as are fictitious."	Securities and Exchange Commission	July 16, 2011 (Section 712(e) requires that all mandatory Title VII CFTC and SEC rules (other than those issued jointly) be promulgated within 360 days after the date of enactment, unless another provision states otherwise.)
Section 763(i) (amending Section 13 of the Securities Exchange Act of 1934 (15 U.S.C. 78m))	"…shall adopt rules governing persons that are registered under this subsection."	Securities and Exchange Commission	July 16, 2011 (Section 712(e) requires that all mandatory Title VII CFTC and SEC rules (other than those issued jointly) be promulgated within 360 days after the date of enactment, unless another provision states otherwise.)
Section 764 (amending Securities Exchange Act of 1934 (15 U.S.C. 78a et seq.) creating a new Section 15F)	"… shall issue rules under this section to provide for the registration of security-based swap dealers and major security-based swap participants."	Securities and Exchange Commission	July 21, 2011 (Within one year after the date of enactment.)
Section 766(a) (amending the Securities Exchange Act of 1934 (15 U.S.C. 78a et seq.))	"…shall promulgate an interim final rule … providing for the reporting of each security-based swap entered into before the date of enactment," the terms of which had not expired as of that date.	Securities and Exchange Commission	October 19, 2010 (Within 90 days of the date of enactment.)
Section 805(a)1	"…by rule or order … shall prescribe risk management standards, taking into consideration relevant international standards and existing prudential requirements, governing…."	Board of Governors	None
Section 806(e)(1)(B)	"…shall prescribe regulations that define and describe the standards for determining when notice (of proposed changes to a designated financial market utility's rules, procedures or operations) is required to be provided under subparagraph (A)."	Each supervisory agency, in consultation with the Board of Governors	None
Section 915 (amending Section 4 of the Securities Exchange Act of 1934 (15 U.S.C. 78d))	"…shall, by regulation, establish procedures requiring a formal response to all recommendations submitted to the Commission by the Investor Advocate, not later than 3 months after the date of such submission."	Securities and Exchange Commission	None

Table A-1. (Continued).

Section	Text of the Provision	Agency	Deadline
Section 916(a) (amending Section 19(b) of the Securities Exchange Act of 1934 (15 U.S.C. 78s(b)))	"…shall promulgate rules setting forth the procedural requirements of the proceedings required under this paragraph."	Securities and Exchange Commission, after consultation with other regulatory agencies	January 17, 2011 (Within 180 days after enactment.)
Section 924	"…shall issue final regulations implementing the provisions of section 21F of the Securities Exchange Act of 1934, as added by this subtitle…."	Securities and Exchange Commission	April 17, 2011 (Within 270 days after the date of enactment.)
Section 926	"…shall issue rules for the disqualification of offerings and sales of securities made under section 230.506 of title 17, Code of Federal Regulations…."	Securities and Exchange Commission	July 21, 2011 (Within one year after the date of enactment.)
Section 929W (amending Section 17A of the Securities Exchange Act of 1934 (15 U.S.C. 78q-1))	"…shall revise its regulations in section 240.17Ad-17 of title 17, Code of Federal Regulations, as in effect on December 8, 1997, to extend the application of such section to brokers and dealers and to provide for the following…."	Securities and Exchange Commission	None
Section 929X(a) (amending Section 13(f) of the Securities Exchange Act of 1934 (15 U.S.C. 78m(f)))	"…shall prescribe rules providing for the public disclosure of the name of the issuer and the title, class, CUSIP number, aggregate amount of the number of short sales of each security, and any additional information determined by the Commission following the end of the reporting period. At a minimum, such public disclosure shall occur every month."	Securities and Exchange Commission	None
Section 932(a)(2)(B) (amending Section 15E of the Securities Exchange Act of 1934 (15 U.S.C. 78o-7))	"…shall prescribe rules requiring each nationally recognized statistical rating organization to submit to the Commission an annual internal controls report, which shall contain…."	Securities and Exchange Commission	July 21, 2011 (Per Section 937, within one year of the date of enactment.)
Section 932(a)(8) (amending Section 15E of the Securities Exchange Act of 1934 (15 U.S.C. 78o-7))	"…shall adopt rules requiring a nationally recognized statistical rating organization … to disclose the certification described in subparagraph (B) to the public in a manner that allows the public to determine the adequacy and level of due diligence services provided by a third party."	Securities and Exchange Commission	July 21, 2011 (Per Section 937, within one year of the date of enactment.)

Section	Text of the Provision	Agency	Deadline
Section 932(a)(4) (amending Section 15E of the Securities Exchange Act of 1934 (15 U.S.C. 78o–7))	"…shall issue rules to prevent the sales and marketing considerations of a nationally recognized statistical rating organization from influencing the production of ratings by the nationally recognized statistical rating organization." (Goes on to detail contents.)	Securities and Exchange Commission	July 21, 2011 (Per Section 937, within one year of the date of enactment.)
Section 932(a)(8) (amending Section 15E of the Securities Exchange Act of 1934 (15 U.S.C. 78o–7))	"…shall (A) establish, by rule, fines, and other penalties applicable to any nationally recognized statistical rating organization that violates the requirements of this section and the rules thereunder; and (B) issue such rules as may be necessary to carry out this section."	Securities and Exchange Commission	July 21, 2011 (Per Section 937, within one year of the date of enactment.)
Section 932(a)(8) (amending Section 15E of the Securities Exchange Act of 1934 (15 U.S.C. 78o–7))	"…shall, by rule, require that each nationally recognized statistical rating organization publicly disclose information on the initial credit ratings determined by the nationally recognized statistical rating organization for each type of obligor, security, and money market instrument, and any subsequent changes to such credit ratings…."	Securities and Exchange Commission	July 21, 2011 (Per Section 937, within one year of the date of enactment.)
Section 932(a)(8) (amending Section 15E of the Securities Exchange Act of 1934 (15 U.S.C. 78o–7))	"….shall prescribe rules, for the protection of investors and in the public interest, with respect to the procedures and methodologies, including qualitative and quantitative data and models, used by nationally recognized statistical rating organizations that require each nationally recognized statistical rating organization…."	Securities and Exchange Commission	July 21, 2011 (Per Section 937, within one year of the date of enactment.)
Section 932(a)(8) (amending Section 15E of the Securities Exchange Act of 1934 (15 U.S.C. 78o–7))	"…shall require, by rule, each nationally recognized statistical rating organization to prescribe a form to accompany the publication of each credit rating that discloses…."	Securities and Exchange Commission	July 21, 2011 (Per Section 937, within one year of the date of enactment.)
Section 936	"…shall issue rules that are reasonably designed to ensure that any person employed by a nationally recognized statistical rating organization to perform credit ratings—(1) meets standards of training, experience, and competence necessary to produce accurate ratings for the categories of issuers whose securities the person rates; and (2) is tested for knowledge of the credit rating process."	Securities and Exchange Commission	July 21, 2011 (Per Section 937, within one year of the date of enactment.)

Table A-1. (Continued).

Section	Text of the Provision	Agency	Deadline
Section 938	"…shall require, by rule, each nationally recognized statistical rating organization to establish, maintain, and enforce written policies and procedures that…."	Securities and Exchange Commission	July 21, 2011 (Per Section 937, within one year of the date of enactment.)
Section 939B	"…shall revise Regulation FD (17 C.F.R. 243.100) to remove from such regulation the exemption for entities whose primary business is the issuance of credit ratings (17 C.F.R. 243.100(b)(2)(iii))."	Securities and Exchange Commission	October 19, 2010 (Within 90 days of the date of enactment.)
Section 941(b) (amending the Securities Exchange Act of 1934 (15 U.S.C. 78a et seq.))	"…shall jointly prescribe regulations to require any securitizer to retain an economic interest in a portion of the credit risk for any asset that the securitizer, through the issuance of an asset-backed security, transfers, sells, or conveys to a third party."	Federal banking agencies and the Securities and Exchange Commission	April 17, 2011 (Within 270 days after the date of enactment.)
Section 941(b) (amending the Securities Exchange Act of 1934 (15 U.S.C. 78a et seq.))	"…shall jointly issue regulations to exempt qualified residential mortgages from the risk retention requirements of this subsection."	Federal banking agencies, the Securities and Exchange Commission, the Secretary of Housing and Urban Development, and the Director of the Federal Housing Finance Agency	None. (However, all rules under this section become effective either one year or two years after the date they are published.)
Section 942(b) (amending Section 7 of the Securities Act of 1933 (15 U.S.C. 77g))	"…shall adopt regulations under this subsection requiring each issuer of an asset-backed security to disclose, for each tranche or class of security, information regarding the assets backing that security." (Goes on to detail contents.)	Securities and Exchange Commission	None
Section 943	"…shall prescribe regulations on the use of representations and warranties in the market for asset-backed securities … that…."	Securities and Exchange Commission	January 17, 2011 (Within 180 days after enactment.)
Section 945 (amending Section 7 of the Securities Act of 1933 (15 U.S.C. 77g)	"…shall issue rules relating to the registration statement required to be filed by any issuer of an asset-backed security (as that term is defined in section 3(a)(77) of the Securities Exchange Act of 1934) that require any issuer of an asset-backed security—(1) to perform a review of the assets underlying the asset backed security; and (2) to disclose the nature of the review under paragraph (1)."	Securities and Exchange Commission	January 17, 2011 (Within 180 days after enactment.)

Rulemaking Requirements and Authorities... 275

Section	Text of the Provision	Agency	Deadline
Section 951 (amending the Securities Exchange Act of 1934 (15 U.S.C. 78a et seq.))	"...the person making such solicitation shall disclose in the proxy or consent solicitation material, in a clear and simple form in accordance with regulations to be promulgated by the Commission, any agreements or understandings that....."	Securities and Exchange Commission	January 21, 2011 (Rule must be in place six months after the date of enactment.)
Section 952(a) (amending the Securities Exchange Act of 1934 (15 U.S.C. 78 et seq.))	"...shall, by rule, direct the national securities exchanges and national securities associations to prohibit the listing of any equity security of an issuer (other than certain ones) that does not comply with the requirements of this subsection."	Securities and Exchange Commission	None
Section 952(a) (amending the Securities Exchange Act of 1934 (15 U.S.C. 78 et seq.))	"...shall, by rule, direct the national securities exchanges and national securities associations to prohibit the listing of any security of an issuer that is not in compliance with the requirements of this section."	Securities and Exchange Commission	July 16, 2011 (Within 360 days after the date of enactment.)
Section 953(a) (amending Section 14 of the Securities Exchange Act of 1934 (15 U.S.C. 78n))	"...shall, by rule, require each issuer to disclose in any proxy or consent solicitation material for an annual meeting of the shareholders of the issuer a clear description of any compensation required to be disclosed by the issuer under section 229.402 of title 17, Code of Federal Regulations...."	Securities and Exchange Commission	None
Section 953(b)	"...shall amend section 229.402 of title 17, Code of Federal Regulations, to require each issuer to disclose in any filing of the issuer ... (certain compensation levels and ratios)...."	Securities and Exchange Commission	None
Section 954 (amending the Securities Exchange Act of 1934 after section 10C)	"...shall, by rule, direct the national securities exchanges and national securities associations to prohibit the listing of any security of an issuer that does not comply with the requirements of this section."	Securities and Exchange Commission	None
Section 955 (amending Section 14 of the Securities Exchange Act of 1934 (15 U.S.C. 78n))	"...shall, by rule, require each issuer to disclose in any proxy or consent solicitation material for an annual meeting of the shareholders of the issuer whether any employee or member of the board of directors of the issuer, or any designee of such employee or member, is permitted to purchase financial instruments ... that are designed to hedge or offset any decrease in the market value of equity securities...."	Securities and Exchange Commission	None

Table A-1. (Continued).

Section	Text of the Provision	Agency	Deadline
Section 956(a)	"...shall prescribe regulations or guidelines to require each covered financial institution to disclose to the appropriate Federal regulator the structures of all incentive-based compensation arrangements offered by such covered financial institutions...."	The "appropriate Federal regulators"	April 21, 2011 (Within nine months after the date of enactment.)
Section 956(b)	"...shall jointly prescribe regulations or guidelines that prohibit any types of incentive-based payment arrangement, or any feature of any such arrangement, that the regulators determine encourages inappropriate risks by covered financial institutions...."	The "appropriate Federal regulators"	April 21, 2011 (Within nine months after the date of enactment.)
Section 972 (amending Securities Exchange Act of 1934 (15 U.S. C. 78a et seq.) creating a new Section 14B)	"...shall issue rules that require an issuer to disclose in the annual proxy sent to investors the reasons why the issuer has chosen—(1) the same person to serve as chairman of the board of directors and chief executive officer (or in equivalent positions); or (2) different individuals to serve as chairman of the board of directors and chief executive officer (or in equivalent positions of the issuer)."	Securities and Exchange Commission	January 17, 2011 (Within 180 days of the date of enactment.)
Section 984(b)	"...shall promulgate rules that are designed to increase the transparency of information available to brokers, dealers, and investors, with respect to the loan or borrowing of securities."	Securities and Exchange Commission	July 21, 2012 (Within two years after the date of enactment.)
Section 1022(c)(6)(A)	"...shall prescribe rules regarding the confidential treatment of information obtained from persons in connection with the exercise of its authorities under Federal consumer financial law."	Consumer Financial Protection Bureau	None
Section 1024(a)(2)	"...shall consult with the Federal Trade Commission prior to issuing a rule, in accordance with paragraph (1)(B), to define covered persons subject to this section..." (on "Supervision of Nondepository Covered Persons").	Consumer Financial Protection Bureau, in consultation with the Federal Trade Commission	July 21, 2012 ("Initial rule" required within one year after the designated transfer date.)
Section 1024(b)(7)(A)	" ... shall prescribe rules to facilitate supervision of persons described in subsection (a)(1) and assessment and detection of risks to consumers."	Consumer Financial Protection Bureau	None

Rulemaking Requirements and Authorities...

Section	Text of the Provision	Agency	Deadline
Section 1025(e)(4)(E)	"…shall prescribe rules to provide safeguards from retaliation against the insured depository institution, insured credit union, or other covered person described in subsection (a) instituting an appeal under this paragraph, as well as their officers and employees."	Consumer Financial Protection Bureau and the "prudential regulators."	None
Section 1033(d)	"…by rule, shall prescribe standards applicable to covered persons to promote the development and use of standardized formats for information, including through the use of machine readable files, to be made available to consumers under this section" (on "Consumer Rights to Access Information").	Consumer Financial Protection Bureau	None
Section 1035(c)	"The Ombudsman designated under this subsection (re private education loans) shall … in accordance with regulations of the Director, receive, review, and attempt to resolve informally complaints from borrowers of loans described in subsection (a)…."	Consumer Financial Protection Bureau	None
Section 1041(c)(1)	"…shall issue a notice of proposed rulemaking whenever a majority of the States has enacted a resolution in support of the establishment or modification of a consumer protection regulation by the Bureau."	Consumer Financial Protection Bureau	None
Section 1042(c)	"…shall prescribe regulations to implement the requirements of this section…" (on "Preservation of Enforcement Powers of the States").	Consumer Financial Protection Bureau	None
Section 1053(e)	"…shall prescribe rules establishing such procedures as may be necessary to carry out this section" (on "Hearings and Adjudication Proceedings").	Consumer Financial Protection Bureau	None
Section 1071(a) (amending the Equal Credit Opportunity Act (15 U.S.C. 1691 et seq.))	"Each financial institution shall compile and maintain, in accordance with regulations of the Bureau, a record of the information provided by any loan applicant pursuant to a request under subsection (b)."	Consumer Financial Protection Bureau	None

Table A-1. (Continued).

Section	Text of the Provision	Agency	Deadline
Section 1071(a) (amending the Equal Credit Opportunity Act (15 U.S.C. 1691 et seq.))	"Information compiled and maintained under this section ("Small Business Loan Data Collection") shall be—(A) retained for not less than 3 years after the date of preparation; (B) made available to any member of the public, upon request, in the form required under regulations prescribed by the Bureau; (C) annually made available to the public generally by the Bureau, in such form and in such manner as is determined by the Bureau, by regulation."	Consumer Financial Protection Bureau	None
Section 1075(a) (amending the Electronic Fund Transfer Act (15 U.S.C. 1693 et seq.))	"…shall prescribe regulations in final form … to establish standards for assessing whether the amount of any interchange transaction fee described in paragraph (2) is reasonable and proportional to the cost incurred by the issuer with respect to the transaction."	Board of Governors	April 21, 2011 (Within nine months of the date of enactment of the Consumer Financial Protection Act of 2010.)
Section 1075(a) (amending the Electronic Fund Transfer Act (15 U.S.C. 1693 et seq.))	"…shall … prescribe regulations providing that an issuer or payment card network shall not directly or through any agent, processor, or licensed member of a payment card network, by contract, requirement, condition, penalty, or otherwise, restrict the number of payment card networks on which an electronic debit transaction may be processed…."	Board of Governors	July 21, 2011 (Within one year of the date of enactment.)
Section 1079(c)	"…shall, consistent with subtitle B ("General Powers of the Bureau"), propose regulations or otherwise establish a program to protect consumers who use exchange facilitators."	Consumer Financial Protection Bureau	July 21, 2014 (Rule or program must be established within two years after the submission of a report (which is required within one year of the transfer date).)
Section 1083(a) (amending the Alternative Mortgage Transaction Parity Act of 1982 (12 U.S.C. 3801 et seq.))	Bureau is required to determine whether the existing regulations applicable under paragraphs (1) through (3) of subsection (a) are "fair and not deceptive and otherwise meet the objectives of the Consumer Financial Protection Act of 2010," and "(3) promulgate regulations under subsection (a)(4)…."	Consumer Financial Protection Bureau	July 22, 2011 (Regulations to be promulgated "after the designated transfer date.)

Rulemaking Requirements and Authorities...

Section	Text of the Provision	Agency	Deadline
Section 1084 (amending the Electronic Fund Transfer Act (15 U.S.C. 1693 et seq.)	" ... shall prescribe rules to carry out the purposes of this title" (with certain exceptions).	Consumer Financial Protection Bureau Board of Governors	None
Section 1085(3)(F) (amending the Equal Credit Opportunity Act (15 U.S.C. 1691 et seq.)	"...shall prescribe regulations to carry out the purposes of this title with respect to a person described in section 1029(a) of the Consumer Financial Protection Act of 2010."		None
Section 1088(a)(9) (amending the Fair Credit Reporting Act (15 U.S.C. 1681 et seq.)	"...shall prescribe rules to carry out this subsection" (on amendments to the Fair Credit Reporting Act).	Consumer Financial Protection Bureau	None
Section 1088(a)(11)(C) (amending the Fair Credit Reporting Act (15 U.S.C. 1681 et seq.))	"...shall ... prescribe regulations requiring ... each person that furnishes information to a consumer reporting agency to establish reasonable policies and procedures for implementing the guidelines established pursuant to subparagraph (A)."	Consumer Financial Protection Bureau	None
Section 1088(b)(3)	"Regulations to carry out section 624 of the Fair Credit Reporting Act (15 U.S.C. 1681s-3), shall be prescribed, as described in paragraph (2), by...."	Commodity Futures Trading Commission, Securities and Exchange Commission, and the Consumer Financial Protection Bureau	None
Section 1094(3)(B) (amending the Home Mortgage Disclosure Act of 1975 (12 U.S.C. 2801 et seq.))	"..., shall develop regulations that" (establish certain information collection and disclosure requirements).	Consumer Financial Protection Bureau, in consultation with "appropriate banking agencies," the Federal Deposit Insurance Corporation, the National Credit Union Administration Board, and the Secretary of Housing and Urban Development.	None

Table A-1. (Continued).

Section	Text of the Provision	Agency	Deadline
Section 1094(3)(F) (amending the Home Mortgage Disclosure Act of 1975 (12 U.S.C. 2801 et seq.))	"The data required to be disclosed under subsection (b) shall be submitted to the Bureau or to the appropriate agency for any institution reporting under this title, in accordance with regulations prescribed by the Bureau."	Consumer Financial Protection Bureau	None
Section 1101(a)(6) (amending Section 13 of the Federal Reserve Act (12 U.S.C. 343)) Section 1105(b)(1)	"... shall establish, by regulation ... the policies and procedures governing emergency lending under this paragraph." "...the Corporation shall establish, by regulation ... policies and procedures governing the issuance of guarantees authorized by this section."	Board of Governors, in consultation with the Secretary of the Treasury Federal Deposit Insurance Corporation, in consultation with the Secretary of the Treasury	As soon as is practicable after the date of enactment. As soon as is practicable after the date of enactment.
Section 1402(a) (amending Chapter 2 of the Truth in Lending Act (15 U.S.C. 1631 et seq.))	"...shall prescribe regulations requiring depository institutions to establish and maintain procedures reasonably designed to assure and monitor the compliance of such depository institutions, the subsidiaries of such institutions, and the employees of such institutions or subsidiaries with the requirements of this section and the registration procedures established under section 1507 of the Secure and Fair Enforcement for Mortgage Licensing Act of 2008."	Board of Governors	January 21, 2013 (Section 1400(c) requires that all mandatory Title XIV rules be issued within 18 months after the transfer date, and be effective within 12 months after issuance.)
Section 1403 (amending Section 129B of the Truth in Lending Act (as added by section 1402(a)))	"...shall prescribe regulations to prohibit (A) mortgage originators from steering any consumer to a residential mortgage loan that (has certain characteristics)...."	Board of Governors	January 21, 2013 (Section 1400(c) requires that all mandatory Title XIV rules be issued within 18 months after the transfer date, and be effective within 12 months after issuance.)
Section 1405(a) (amending Section 129B of the Truth in Lending Act)	"...shall, by regulations, prohibit or condition terms, acts or practices relating to residential mortgage loans that the Board finds to be abusive, unfair, deceptive, predatory, necessary or proper to ensure that responsible, affordable mortgage credit remains available to consumers...."	Board of Governors	January 21, 2013 (Section 1400(c) requires that all mandatory Title XIV rules be issued within 18 months after the transfer date, and be effective within 12 months after issuance.)

Section	Text of the Provision	Agency	Deadline
Section 1411(a)(2) (amending Chapter 2 of the Truth in Lending Act (15 U.S.C. 1631 et seq.))	"In accordance with regulations prescribed by the Board, no creditor may make a residential mortgage loan unless the creditor makes a reasonable and good faith determination based on verified and documented information that ... the consumer has a reasonable ability to repay the loan...."	Board of Governors	January 21, 2013 (Section 1400(c) requires that all mandatory Title XIV rules be issued within 18 months after the transfer date, and be effective within 12 months after issuance.)
Section 1412 (amending Section 129C of the Truth in Lending Act)	"...shall prescribe regulations to carry out the purposes of this subsection" (re "safe harbor and rebuttable presumption").	Board of Governors	January 21, 2013 (Section 1400(c) requires that all mandatory Title XIV rules be issued within 18 months after the transfer date, and be effective within 12 months after issuance.)
Section 1412 (amending Section 129C of the Truth in Lending Act)	"...shall prescribe rules adjusting the criteria under subparagraph (A)(vii) in order to permit lenders that extend smaller loans to meet the requirements of the presumption of compliance under paragraph (1)."	Board of Governors	January 21, 2013 (Section 1400(c) requires that all mandatory Title XIV rules be issued within 18 months after the transfer date, and be effective within 12 months after issuance.)
Section 1412 (amending Section 129C of the Truth in Lending Act)	"...shall ... prescribe rules defining the types of loans they insure, guarantee, or administer, as the case may be, that are qualified mortgages for purposes of paragraph (2)(A)...."	The Departments of Housing and Urban Development, Veterans Affairs, and Agriculture; and the Rural Housing Service, in consultation with the Board of Governors	January 21, 2013 (Section 1400(c) requires that all mandatory Title XIV rules be issued within 18 months after the transfer date, and be effective within 12 months after issuance.)
Section 1442 (amending Section 4 of the Department of Housing and Urban Development Act (42 U.S.C. 3533))	Office is responsible for "establishing rules necessary for (i) the counseling procedures under section 106(g)(1) of the Housing and Urban Development Act of 1968 (12 U.S.C. 1701x(h)(1)); and (ii) carrying out all other functions of the Secretary under section 106(g) of the Housing and Urban Development Act of 1968."	Office of Housing Counseling within the Department of Housing and Urban Development	January 21, 2013 (Section 1400(c) requires that all mandatory Title XIV rules be issued within 18 months after the transfer date, and be effective within 12 months after issuance.)

Table A-1. (Continued).

Section	Text of the Provision	Agency	Deadline
Section 1463(a) (amending Section 6 of the Real Estate Settlement Procedures Act of 1974 (12 U.S.C. 2605))	"A servicer of a federally related mortgage shall not ... charge fees for responding to valid qualified written requests (as defined in regulations which the Bureau of Consumer Financial Protection shall prescribe) under this section" (or) "fail to comply with any other obligation found by the Bureau of Consumer Financial Protection, by regulation, to be appropriate to carry out the consumer protection purposes of this Act."	Consumer Financial Protection Bureau	January 21, 2013 (Section 1400(c) requires that all mandatory Title XIV rules be issued within 18 months after the transfer date, and be effective within 12 months after issuance.)
Section 1471 (amending Chapter 2 of the Truth in Lending Act (15 U.S.C. 1631 et seq.))	"...shall jointly prescribe regulations to implement this section" ("Property Appraisal Requirements"). It goes on to say that the agencies "may jointly exempt, by rule, a class of loans from the requirements of this subsection or subsection (a) if the agencies determine that the exemption is in the public interest and promotes the safety and soundness of creditors."	Board of Governors, the Comptroller of the Currency, the Federal Deposit Insurance Corporation, the National Credit Union Administration Board, the Federal Housing Finance Agency, and the Consumer Financial Protection Bureau	January 21, 2013 (Section 1400(c) requires that all mandatory Title XIV rules be issued within 18 months after the transfer date, and be effective within 12 months after issuance.)
Section 1471 (amending Chapter 2 of the Truth in Lending Act (15 U.S.C. 1631 et seq.)	"...shall jointly prescribe regulations to implement this section" (on property appraisal requirements).	Board of Governors, the Comptroller of the Currency, the Federal Deposit Insurance Corporation, the National Credit Union Administration Board, the Federal Housing Finance Agency, and the Consumer Financial Protection Bureau	January 21, 2013 (Section 1400(c) requires that all mandatory Title XIV rules be issued within 18 months after the transfer date, and be effective within 12 months after issuance.)

Rulemaking Requirements and Authorities...

Section	Text of the Provision	Agency	Deadline
Section 1472(a) (amending Chapter 2 of the Truth in Lending Act (15 U.S.C. 1631 et seq.))	"...shall, for purposes of this section, prescribe interim final regulations defining with specificity acts or practices that violate appraisal independence in the provision of mortgage lending services for a consumer credit transaction secured by the principal dwelling of the consumer or mortgage brokerage services for such a transaction and defining any terms in this section or such regulations."	Board of Governors	October 19, 2010 (Rule is required "no later than 90 days after the date of enactment of this section.") Also, "Effective on the date the interim final regulations are promulgated pursuant to subsection (g), the Home Valuation Code of Conduct announced by the Federal Housing Finance Agency on December 23, 2008, shall have no force or effect."
Section 1473(f)(2) (amending Title XI of the Financial Institutions Reform, Recovery, and Enforcement Act of 1989 (12 U.S.C. 3331 et seq.))	"...shall jointly promulgate regulations for the reporting of the activities of appraisal management companies to the Appraisal Subcommittee in determining the payment of the annual registry fee."	Board of Governors, the Comptroller of the Currency, the Federal Deposit Insurance Corporation, the National Credit Union Administration Board, the Federal Housing Finance Agency, and the Consumer Financial Protection Bureau	January 21, 2013 (Section 1400(c) requires that all mandatory Title XIV rules be issued within 18 months after the transfer date, and be effective within 12 months after issuance.)
Section 1473(f)(2) (amending Title XI of the Financial Institutions Reform, Recovery, and Enforcement Act of 1989 (12 U.S.C. 3331 et seq.))	"...shall jointly, by rule, establish minimum requirements to be applied by a State in the registration of appraisal management companies."	Board of Governors, the Comptroller of the Currency, the Federal Deposit Insurance Corporation, the National Credit Union Administration Board, the Federal Housing Finance Agency, and the Consumer Financial Protection Bureau	January 21, 2013 (Section 1400(c) requires that all mandatory Title XIV rules be issued within 18 months after the transfer date, and be effective within 12 months after issuance.)
Section 1473(q) (amending Title XI of the Financial Institutions Reform, Recovery, and Enforcement Act of 1989 (12 U.S.C. 3331 et seq.))	"...shall promulgate regulations to implement the quality control standards required under this section" (on automated valuation models used to estimate collateral value for mortgage lending purposes).	Board of Governors, the Comptroller of the Currency, the Federal Deposit Insurance Corporation, the National Credit Union Administration Board, the Federal Housing Finance Agency, and the Consumer Financial Protection Bureau	January 21, 2013 (Section 1400(c) requires that all mandatory Title XIV rules be issued within 18 months after the transfer date, and be effective within 12 months after issuance.)

Table A-1. (Continued).

Section	Text of the Provision	Agency	Deadline
Section 1483(b)(2)	Secretary is required to make data tables available to the public at the individual record level, and "shall issue regulations prescribing—(A) the procedures for disclosing such data to the public; and (B) such deletions as the Secretary may determine to be appropriate to protect any privacy interest of any mortgage modification applicant, including the deletion or alteration of the applicant's name and identification number."	Secretary of the Treasury	January 21, 2013 (Section 1400(c) requires that all mandatory Title XIV rules be issued within 18 months after the transfer date, and be effective within 12 months after issuance.)
Section 1502(b) (amending Section 13 of the Securities Exchange Act of 1934 (15 U.S.C. 78m)	"…shall promulgate regulations requiring any person described in paragraph (2) to disclose annually, beginning with the person's first full fiscal year that begins after the date of promulgation of such regulations, whether conflict minerals that are necessary as described in paragraph (2)(B), in the year for which such reporting is required, did originate in the Democratic Republic of the Congo or an adjoining country…."	Securities and Exchange Commission	April 17, 2011 (Within 270 days after the date of enactment.)
Section 1504 (amending Section 13 of the Securities Exchange Act of 1934 (15 U.S.C. 78m))	"…shall issue final rules that require each resource extraction issuer to include in an annual report of the resource extraction issuer information relating to any payment made by the resource extraction issuer, a subsidiary of the resource extraction issuer, or an entity under the control of the resource extraction issuer to a foreign government or the Federal Government for the purpose of the commercial development of oil, natural gas, or minerals…."	Securities and Exchange Commission	April 17, 2011 (Within 270 days after the date of enactment.)

APPENDIX B. DISCRETIONARY RULEMAKING PROVISIONS

Table B-1 below lists provisions in the Dodd-Frank Act that permit, but do not require, agencies to issue certain rules (e.g., stating that the agency or agencies "may" establish, promulgate, or issue rules or regulations on a particular topic).

Table B-1. Discretionary Rulemaking Provisions in the Dodd-Frank Act.

Section	Text of the Provision	Agency	Deadline
Section 102(a)(7)	"The terms 'significant nonbank financial company' and 'significant bank holding company' have the meanings given those terms by rule of the Board of Governors,"	Board of Governors	None
Section 121(d)	"...may prescribe regulations regarding the application of this section ('Mitigation of Risks to Financial Stability') to foreign nonbank financial companies supervised by the Board of Governors and foreign-based bank holding companies...."	Board of Governors	January 22, 2012 (Per Section 168, unless otherwise specified, Board of Governors' final rules in subtitles A and C must be issued within 18 months of the act's effective date.)
Section 165(c)(1)	" ... may issue regulations that require each nonbank financial company supervised by the Board of Governors and bank holding companies described in subsection (a) to maintain a minimum amount of contingent capital that is convertible to equity in times of financial stress."	Board of Governors	July 22, 2012 (Subsequent to submission by the Financial Stability Oversight Council of a report to Congress. Report required within two years after enactment.)
Section 165(d)(1)(D)	Requires the collection of information regarding "rapid and orderly resolution in the event of material financial distress or failure," which shall include certain items as well as any other information jointly specified "by rule or order."	Board of Governors and the Federal Deposit Insurance Corporation	January 22, 2012 (Per Section 168, unless otherwise specified, Board of Governors' final rules in subtitles A and C must be issued within 18 months of the act's effective date.)
Section 165(e)(3)(F)	The definition of "credit exposure" includes "any other similar transactions that the Board of Governors, by regulation, determines to be a credit exposure for purposes of this section."	Board of Governors	January 22, 2012 (Per Section 168, unless otherwise specified, Board of Governors' final rules in subtitles A and C must be issued within 18 months of the act's effective date.) Per Section 165(e)(7), the rules cannot take effect for at least three years after the date of enactment.
Section 165(e)(5)	."...may issue such regulations and orders, including definitions consistent with this section, as may be necessary to administer and carry out this subsection" (on "Concentration Limits").	Board of Governors	January 22, 2012 (Per Section 168, unless otherwise specified, Board of Governors' final rules in subtitles A and C must be issued within 18 months of the act's effective date.) Per Section 165(e)(7), the rules cannot take effect for at least three years after the date of enactment.

Table B-1. (Continued).

Section	Text of the Provision	Agency	Deadline
Section 165(e)(6)	"…may, by regulation or order, exempt transactions, in whole or in part, from the definition of the term 'credit exposure' for purposes of this subsection, if the Board of Governors finds that the exemption is in the public interest and is consistent with the purpose of this subsection."	Board of Governors	January 22, 2012 (Per Section 168, unless otherwise specified, Board of Governors' final rules in subtitles A and C must be issued within 18 months of the act's effective date.) Per Section 165(e)(7), the rules cannot take effect for at least three years after the date of enactment.
Section 165(f)	" … may prescribe, by regulation, periodic public disclosures by nonbank financial companies supervised by the Board of Governors and bank holding companies described in subsection (a) in order to support market evaluation of the risk profile, capital adequacy, and risk management capabilities thereof."	Board of Governors	January 22, 2012 (Per Section 168, unless otherwise specified, Board of Governors' final rules in subtitles A and C must be issued within 18 months of the act's effective date.)
Section 165(g)(1)	" … may, by regulation, prescribe a limit on the amount of short-term debt, including off-balance sheet exposures, that may be accumulated by any bank holding company described in subsection (a) and any nonbank financial company supervised by the Board of Governors."	Board of Governors	January 22, 2012 (Per Section 168, unless otherwise specified, Board of Governors' final rules in subtitles A and C must be issued within 18 months of the act's effective date.)
Section 165(g)(3)	"For purposes of this subsection, the term 'short-term debt' means such liabilities with short-dated maturity that the Board of Governors identifies, by regulation, except that such term does not include insured deposits."	Board of Governors	January 22, 2012 (Per Section 168, unless otherwise specified, Board of Governors' final rules in subtitles A and C must be issued within 18 months of the act's effective date.)
Section 165(g)(4)	" … may prescribe such regulations, including definitions consistent with this subsection, and issue such orders, as may be necessary to carry out this subsection."	Board of Governors	January 22, 2012 (Per Section 168, unless otherwise specified, Board of Governors' final rules in subtitles A and C must be issued within 18 months of the act's effective date.)
Section 165(h)(2)(B)	(Under the heading "Permissive Regulations") "… may require each bank holding company that is a publicly traded company and that has total consolidated assets of less than $10,000,000,000 to establish a risk committee, as set forth in paragraph (3), as determined necessary or appropriate by the Board of Governors to promote sound risk management practices."	Board of Governors	January 22, 2012 (Per Section 168, unless otherwise specified, Board of Governors' final rules in subtitles A and C must be issued within 18 months of the act's effective date.)

Section	Text of the Provision	Agency	Deadline
Section 165(k)(3)	"The term 'off-balance-sheet activities' means an existing liability of a company that is not currently a balance sheet liability, but may become one upon ... such other activities or transactions as the Board of Governors may, by rule, define."	Board of Governors	January 22, 2012 (Per Section 168, unless otherwise specified, Board of Governors' final rules in subtitles A and C must be issued within 18 months of the act's effective date.)
Section 167(b)(1)(A)	"... may require (certain companies) to establish and conduct all or a portion of such activities that are determined to be financial in nature or incidental thereto in or through an intermediate holding company established pursuant to regulation of the Board of Governors, not later than 90 days (or such longer period as the Board of Governors may deem appropriate) after the date on which the nonbank financial company supervised by the Board of Governors is notified of the determination of the Board of Governors under this section."	Board of Governors	January 22, 2012 (Per Section 168, unless otherwise specified, Board of Governors' final rules in subtitles A and C must be issued within 18 months of the act's effective date.)
Section 167(c)(2)	"... may promulgate regulations to establish any restrictions or limitations on transactions between an intermediate holding company or a nonbank financial company supervised by the Board of Governors and its affiliates, as necessary to prevent unsafe and unsound practices in connection with transactions between such company, or any subsidiary thereof, and its parent company or affiliates that are not subsidiaries of such company...."	Board of Governors	January 22, 2012 (Per Section 168, unless otherwise specified, Board of Governors' final rules in subtitles A and C must be issued within 18 months of the act's effective date.)
Section 202(d)(5)	"... may issue regulations governing the termination of receiverships under this title."	Federal Deposit Insurance Corporation	None
Section 209	"... shall ... prescribe such rules or regulations as the Corporation considers necessary or appropriate to implement this title...."	Federal Deposit Insurance Corporation, in consultation with the Financial Stability Oversight Council	None
Section 210(a)(7)(d)	"... may prescribe such rules, including definitions of terms, as the Corporation deems appropriate to establish an interest rate for or to make payments of post-insolvency interest to creditors holding proven claims against the receivership estate of a covered financial company, except that no such interest shall be paid until the Corporation as receiver has satisfied the principal amount of all creditor claims."	Federal Deposit Insurance Corporation	None

Table B-1. (Continued).

Section	Text of the Provision	Agency	Deadline
Section 210 (a)(16)(D)(i)	" ... shall prescribe such regulations and establish such retention schedules as are necessary to maintain the documents and records of the Corporation generated in exercising the authorities of this title and the records of a covered financial company for which the Corporation is appointed receiver, with due regard for—(I) the avoidance of duplicative record retention; and (II) the expected evidentiary needs of the Corporation as receiver for a covered financial company and the public regarding the records of covered financial companies."	Federal Deposit Insurance Corporation	None
Section 210(c)(3)(E)	" ... may, by rule or regulation, prescribe that actual direct compensatory damages shall be no less than the estimated value of the claim as of the date the Corporation was appointed receiver of the covered financial company..."	Federal Deposit Insurance Corporation	None
Section 210 (c)(8)(D)(i)	"The term 'qualified financial contract' means any securities contract, commodity contract, forward contract, repurchase agreement, swap agreement, and any similar agreement that the Corporation determines by regulation, resolution, or order to be a qualified financial contract for purposes of this paragraph."	Federal Deposit Insurance Corporation	None
Section 210 (c)(8)(D)(ii)(II)	The term "securities contract" "does not include any purchase, sale, or repurchase obligation under a participation in a commercial mortgage loan unless the Corporation determines by regulation, resolution, or order to include any such agreement within the meaning of such term."	Federal Deposit Insurance Corporation	None
Section 210 (c)(8)(D)(v)(I)	The term "qualified foreign government securities" has certain meanings "as determined by regulation or order ...."	Board of Governors	None
Section 210 (c)(8)(D)(v)(II)	The term "repurchase agreement" does not include any repurchase obligation under a participation in a commercial mortgage loan, unless so determined "by regulation, resolution, or order...."	Board of Governors	None
Section 210 (c)(9)(D)(i)	"...the term 'financial institution' means a broker or dealer, a depository institution, a futures commission merchant, a bridge financial company, or any other institution determined by the Corporation, by regulation, to be a financial institution."	Federal Deposit Insurance Corporation	None

Section	Text of the Provision	Agency	Deadline
Section 355 (amending Section 106(b)(1) of the Bank Holding Company Act Amendments of 1970 (12 U.S.C. 1972(1))	" ... (may) issue such regulations as are necessary to carry out this section."	Board of Governors	None
Section 369(4) (amending the Home Owners' Loan Act (12 U.S.C. 1461 et seq.))	" ... may prescribe regulations with respect to savings associations, as the Comptroller determines to be appropriate to carry out the purposes of this Act."	Comptroller of the Currency	None
Section 369(5) (amending the Home Owners' Loan Act (12 U.S.C. 1461 et seq.))	" ... may issue such regulations, and the appropriate Federal banking agency may issue such orders, including those issued pursuant to section 8 of the Federal Deposit Insurance Act, as may be necessary to administer and carry out this paragraph and to prevent evasion of this paragraph."	Comptroller of the Currency	None
Section 402(a) (amending Section 202(a) of the Investment Advisers Act of 1940 (15 U.S.C. 80b-2(a)))	The term "foreign private advisor" means (among other things) "has aggregate assets under management attributable to clients in the United States and investors in the United States in private funds advised by the investment adviser of less than $25,000,000, or such higher amount as the Commission may, by rule, deem appropriate in accordance with the purposes of this title."	Securities and Exchange Commission	None
Section 404(2) (amending Section 204 of the Investment Advisers Act of 1940 (15 U.S.C. 80b-4))	"An investment adviser registered under this title shall maintain such records of private funds advised by the investment adviser for such period or periods as the Commission, by rule, may prescribe as necessary and appropriate in the public interest and for the protection of investors, or for the assessment of systemic risk."	Securities and Exchange Commission	None
Section 408 (amending Section 203 of the Investment Advisers Act of 1940 (15 U.S.C. 80b-3))	"In prescribing regulations to carry out the requirements of this section with respect to investment advisers acting as investment advisers to mid-sized private funds, the Commission shall take into account the size, governance, and investment strategy of such funds to determine whether they pose systemic risk, and shall provide for registration and examination procedures with respect to the investment advisers of such funds which reflect the level of systemic risk posed by such funds."	Securities and Exchange Commission	None
Section 411 (amending the Investment Advisers Act of 1940 (15 U.S.C. 80b-1 et seq.))	"An investment adviser registered under this title shall take such steps to safeguard client assets over which such adviser has custody, including, without limitation, verification of such assets by an independent public accountant, as the Commission may, by rule, prescribe."	Securities and Exchange Commission	None

Table B-1. (Continued).

Section	Text of the Provision	Agency	Deadline
Section 413(b)(1)(B)	" ... may, by notice and comment rulemaking, make such adjustments to the definition of the term 'accredited investor' ... as the Commission may deem appropriate for the protection of investors, in the public interest, and in light of the economy."	Securities and Exchange Commission	None (Rules may be issued after completion of a discretionary review.)
Section 413(b)(2)(B)	" ... may, by notice and comment rulemaking, make such adjustments to the definition of the term 'accredited investor' ... as the Commission may deem appropriate for the protection of investors, in the public interest, and in light of the economy."	Securities and Exchange Commission	July 21, 2014 (Rules may be issued after completion of a review, which can be done no earlier than four years after the date of enactment.)
Section 502(a)(3) (amending Subchapter I of chapter 3 of subtitle I of title 31, United States Code)	" ... may issue orders, regulations, policies, and procedures to implement this section."	Secretary of the Treasury	None
Section 608(a) (amending Section 23A of the Federal Reserve Act (12 U.S.C. 371c))	" ... may issue such regulations or interpretations as the Board determines are necessary or appropriate with respect to the manner in which a netting agreement may be taken into account in determining the amount of a covered transaction between a member bank or a subsidiary and an affiliate...."	Board of Governors	None
Section 615(a) (amending Section 18 of the Federal Deposit Insurance Act (12 U.S.C. 1828))	" ... may issue such rules as may be necessary to define terms and to carry out the purposes this subsection."	Board of Governors, after consulting with the Comptroller of the Currency and the Corporation	None
Section 618(b)(2)(A)	"A securities holding company that elects to be subject to comprehensive consolidated supervision shall register by filing with the Board of Governors such information and documents as the Board of Governors, by regulation, may prescribe as necessary or appropriate in furtherance of the purposes of this section."	Board of Governors	None
Section 618(e)(2)	"Except as the Board of Governors may otherwise provide by regulation or order, a supervised securities holding company shall be subject to the provisions of the Bank Holding Company Act of 1956 (12 U.S.C. 1841 et seq.) in the same manner and to the same extent a bank holding company is subject to such provisions...."	Board of Governors	None

Rulemaking Requirements and Authorities...

Section	Text of the Provision	Agency	Deadline
Section 619 (amending the Bank Holding Company Act of 1956 (12 U.S.C. 1841 et seq.), new Section 13)	Section requires certain entities to bring their activities and investments into compliance within two years of the requirements taking effect or the entity becomes supervised. Also states that "The Board may, by rule or order, extend this two-year period for not more than one year at a time, if, in the judgment of the Board, such an extension is consistent with the purposes of this section and would not be detrimental to the public interest."	Board of Governors	None
Section 619 (amending the Bank Holding Company Act of 1956 (12 U.S.C. 1841 et seq.))	Agencies may permit specific activities, as well as "such other activity as (the agencies) determine, by rule, as provided in subsection (b)(2), would promote and protect the safety and soundness of the banking entity and the financial stability of the United States."	"Appropriate Federal banking agencies," the Securities and Exchange Commission, and the Commodity Futures Trading Commission.	None
Section 623(a) (amending Section 18(c) of the Federal Deposit Insurance Act (12 U.S.C. 1828(c)))	The term "home state" means... "with respect to a Federal savings association, the State in which the home office (as defined by the regulations of the Director of the Office of Thrift Supervision, or, on and after the transfer date, the Comptroller of the Currency) of the Federal savings association is located."	Director of the Office of Thrift Supervision (before transfer date) or Comptroller of the Currency (after transfer date)	None
Section 623(b) (amending Section 2(o)(4) of the Bank Holding Company Act of 1956 (12 U.S.C. 1841(o)(4)))	The term "home state" means... "with respect to a Federal savings association, the State in which the home office (as defined by the regulations of the Director of the Office of Thrift Supervision, or, on and after the transfer date, the Comptroller of the Currency) of the Federal savings association is located."	Director of the Office of Thrift Supervision (before transfer date) or Comptroller of the Currency (after transfer date)	None
Section 623(c) (amending Section 10(e)(2) of the Home Owners' Loan Act (12 U.S.C. 1467a(e)(2)))	The term "home state" means... "with respect to a Federal savings association, the State in which the home office (as defined by the regulations of the Director of the Office of Thrift Supervision, or, on and after the transfer date, the Comptroller of the Currency) of the Federal savings association is located."	Director of the Office of Thrift Supervision (before transfer date) or Comptroller of the Currency (after transfer date)	None
Section 626 (amending Home Owners' Loan Act (12 U.S.C. 1461 et seq.)	"If a grandfathered unitary savings and loan holding company conducts activities other than financial activities, the Board may require such company to establish and conduct all or a portion of such financial activities in or through an intermediate holding company, which shall be a savings and loan holding company, established pursuant to regulations of the Board...."	Board of Governors	October 19, 2011 (Within 90 days after the transfer date, or later, if the Board deems it appropriate.)

Table B-1. (Continued).

Section	Text of the Provision	Agency	Deadline
Section 626 (creating a new Section 10A on "Intermediate Holding Companies" to the Homeowners' Loan Act)	" ... may promulgate regulations to establish any restrictions or limitations on transactions between an intermediate holding company or a parent of such company and its affiliates, as necessary to prevent unsafe and unsound practices in connection with transactions between the intermediate holding company, or any subsidiary thereof, and its parent company or affiliates that are not subsidiaries of the intermediate holding company, except that such regulations shall not restrict or limit any transaction in connection with the bona fide acquisition or lease by an unaffiliated person of assets, goods, or services."	Board of Governors	None
Section 712(d)(2)(A)	"..., shall jointly adopt such other rules regarding such definitions as the Commodity Futures Trading Commission and the Securities and Exchange Commission determine are necessary and appropriate, in the public interest, and for the protection of investors."	Commodity Futures Trading Commission and the Securities and Exchange Commission, in consultation with the Board of Governors	None
Section 712(f)	" ... may promulgate rules, regulations, or orders permitted or required by this Act."	Commodity Futures Trading Commission and the Securities and Exchange Commission	July 16, 2011 (Section 712(e) requires that all mandatory Title VII CFTC and SEC rules (other than those issued jointly) be promulgated within 360 days after the date of enactment, unless another provision states otherwise.)
Section 714	"...may, by rule or order (1) collect information as may be necessary concerning the markets for any types of (A) swap (as defined in section 1a of the Commodity Exchange Act (7 U.S.C. 1a)); or (B) security-based swap (as defined in section 1a of the Commodity Exchange Act (7 U.S.C. 1a))...."	Commodity Futures Trading Commission or the Securities and Exchange Commission, or both	July 16, 2011 (Section 712(e) requires that all mandatory Title VII CFTC and SEC rules (other than those issued jointly) be promulgated within 360 days after the date of enactment, unless another provision states otherwise.)
Section 719(d)(1)(B)	"If the Commissions determine that stable value contracts fall within the definition of a swap, the Commissions jointly shall determine if an exemption for stable value contracts from the definition of swap is appropriate and in the public interest. The Commissions shall issue regulations implementing the determinations required under this paragraph."	Commodity Futures Trading Commission and the Securities and Exchange Commission	None (Study leading to the regulation is to be conducted within 15 months of the date of enactment (i.e., by October 21, 2011). No prescribed date for the regulation.)

Rulemaking Requirements and Authorities...

Section	Text of the Provision	Agency	Deadline
Section 721(a)(5) (amending Section 1a of the Commodity Exchange Act (7 U.S.C. 1a))	" ... by rule or regulation, may include within, or exclude from, the term 'commodity pool' any investment trust, syndicate, or similar form of enterprise if the Commission determines that the rule or regulation will effectuate the purposes of this Act."	Commodity Futures Trading Commission	None
Section 721(a)(10) (amending Section 1a of the Commodity Exchange Act (7 U.S.C. 1a))	" ... by rule or regulation, may include within, or exclude from, the term 'floor broker' any person in or surrounding any pit, ring, post, or other place provided by a contract market for the meeting of persons similarly engaged who trades for any other person if the Commission determines that the rule or regulation will effectuate the purposes of this Act."	Commodity Futures Trading Commission	None
Section 721(a)(13) (amending Section 1a of the Commodity Exchange Act (7 U.S.C. 1a))	" ... by rule or regulation, may include within, or exclude from, the term 'futures commission merchant' any person who...."	Commodity Futures Trading Commission	None
Section 721(a)(15) (amending Section 1a of the Commodity Exchange Act (7 U.S.C. 1a))	" ... by rule or regulation, may include within, or exclude from, the term 'introducing broker' any person who...."	Commodity Futures Trading Commission	None
Section 721(a)(21)	" ... all foreign exchange swaps and foreign exchange forwards shall be reported to either a swap data repository, or, if there is no swap data repository that would accept such swaps or forwards, to the Commission pursuant to section 4r within such time period as the Commission may by rule or regulation prescribe."	Commodity Futures Trading Commission	None
Section 721(b)	" ... may adopt a rule to define—(1) the term 'commercial risk'; and (2) any other term included in an amendment to the Commodity Exchange Act (7 U.S.C. 1 et seq.) made by this subtitle."	Commodity Futures Trading Commission	None
Section 721(d) (amending the	" ... may by rule, regulation, or order jointly exclude any agreement, contract, or transaction from section 2(a)(1)(D)) if the Commissions determine that the exemption would be consistent with the public interest."	Commodity Futures Trading Commission and the Securities and Exchange Commission	None
Section 723(a)(3) (amending Section 2 of the Commodity Exchange Act (7 U.S.C. 2))	"...shall prescribe rules under this subsection (and issue interpretations of rules prescribed under this subsection) as determined by the Commission to be necessary to prevent evasions of the mandatory clearing requirements under this Act."	Commodity Futures Trading Commission	None

Table B-1. (Continued).

Section	Text of the Provision	Agency	Deadline
Section 723(a)(3) (amending Section 2 of the Commodity Exchange Act (7 U.S.C. 2))	"Swaps entered into on or after such date of enactment shall be reported to a registered swap data repository or the Commission no later than … such other time after entering into the swap as the Commission may prescribe by rule or regulation."	Commodity Futures Trading Commission	None
Section 723(a)(3) (amending Section 2 of the Commodity Exchange Act (7 U.S.C. 2))	"…may prescribe such rules or issue interpretations of the rules as the Commission determines to be necessary to prevent abuse of the exceptions described in this paragraph."	Commodity Futures Trading Commission	None
Section 724(a) (amending Section 4d of the Commodity Exchange Act (7 U.S.C. 6d))	" … in accordance with such terms and conditions as the Commission may prescribe by rule, regulation, or order, any money, securities, or property of the swaps customers of a futures commission merchant … may be commingled and deposited in customer accounts.…"	Commodity Futures Trading Commission	None
Section 724(a) (amending Section 4d of the Commodity Exchange Act (7 U.S.C. 6d))	"Money described in paragraph (2) may be invested in obligations of the United States, in … any other investment that the Commission may by rule or regulation prescribe, and such investments shall be made in accordance with such rules and regulations and subject to such conditions as the Commission may prescribe."	Commodity Futures Trading Commission	None
Section 724(c)	Swap dealers or major swap participants must maintain certain funds or other property in a segregated account "in accordance with such rules and regulations as the Commission may promulgate."	Commodity Futures Trading Commission	None
Section 725(b) (amending Section 5b of the Commodity Exchange Act (7 U.S.C. 7a-1))	"In accordance with rules prescribed by the Commission, the chief compliance officer shall annually prepare and sign a report that contains a description of.…"	Commodity Futures Trading Commission	None
Section 725(c) (amending Section 5b(c) of the Commodity Exchange Act (7 U.S.C. 7a-1(c)))	" … a derivatives clearing organization shall comply with each core principle described in this paragraph and any requirement that the Commission may impose by rule or regulation."	Commodity Futures Trading Commission	None
Section 727 (amending Section 2(a) of the Commodity Exchange Act (7 U.S.C. 2(a)))	" … may, by rule, regulation, or order, delegate the public reporting responsibilities of the Commission under this paragraph in accordance with such terms and conditions as the Commission determines to be appropriate and in the public interest."	Commodity Futures Trading Commission	None

Rulemaking Requirements and Authorities...

Section	Text of the Provision	Agency	Deadline
Section 728 (amending the Commodity Exchange Act after section 20 (7 U.S.C. 24))	"To be registered ... the swap data repository shall comply with... any requirement that the Commission may impose by rule or regulation pursuant to section 8a(5)."	Commodity Futures Trading Commission	None
Section 728 (amending the Commodity Exchange Act after section 20 (7 U.S.C. 24))	"In accordance with rules prescribed by the Commission, the chief compliance officer shall annually prepare and sign a report that contains a description of...."	Commodity Futures Trading Commission	None
Section 729 (amending the Commodity Exchange Act by inserting after section 4q (7 U.S.C. 6o-1))	"Each swap that is not accepted for clearing by any derivatives clearing organization shall be reported to ... the Commission pursuant to this section within such time period as the Commission may by rule or regulation prescribe."	Commodity Futures Trading Commission	None
Section 730 (amending the Commodity Exchange Act (7 U.S.C. 1 et seq.))	"Books and records described in subsection (a)(2)(B) shall ... show such complete details concerning all transactions and positions as the Commission may prescribe by rule or regulation."	Commodity Futures Trading Commission	None
Section 730 (amending the Commodity Exchange Act (7 U.S.C. 1 et seq.))	Large swap trader reporting requirements "shall not apply if (A) the person files or causes to be filed with the properly designated officer of the Commission such reports regarding any transactions or positions described in subparagraphs (A) and (B) of paragraph (1) as the Commission may require by rule or regulation."	Commodity Futures Trading Commission	None
Section 731 (amending the Commodity Exchange Act (7 U.S.C. 1 et seq.))	" ... may prescribe rules applicable to swap dealers and major swap participants, including rules that limit the activities of swap dealers and major swap participants."	Commodity Futures Trading Commission	None
Section 731 (amending the Commodity Exchange Act (7 U.S.C. 1 et seq.))	Registered swap dealers and major swap participant must make such reports and keep books and records "as are required by the Commission by rule or regulation...."	Commodity Futures Trading Commission	None
Section 731 (amending the Commodity Exchange Act (7 U.S.C. 1 et seq.))	"Each registered swap dealer and major swap participant shall conform with such business conduct standards as prescribed in paragraph (3) and as may be prescribed by the Commission by rule or regulation...."	Commodity Futures Trading Commission	None
Section 733 (amending the Commodity Exchange Act by inserting a new section after section 5g (7 U.S.C. 7b-2))	"In accordance with rules prescribed by the Commission, the chief compliance officer shall annually prepare and sign a report that contains a description of...."	Commodity Futures Trading Commission	None

Table B-1. (Continued).

Section	Text of the Provision	Agency	Deadline
Section 733 (amending the Commodity Exchange Act by inserting a new section after section 5g (7 U.S.C. 7b-2))	" ... may promulgate rules defining the universe of swaps that can be executed on a swap execution facility."	Securities and Exchange Commission and Commodity Futures Trading Commission	None
Section 738(a)(4) (amending Section 4(b) of the Commodity Exchange Act (7 U.S.C. 6(b)))	" ... may adopt rules and regulations requiring registration with the Commission for a foreign board of trade that provides the members of the foreign board of trade or other participants located in the United States with direct access to the electronic trading and order matching system of the foreign board of trade, including rules and regulations prescribing procedures and requirements applicable to the registration of such foreign boards of trade."	Commodity Futures Trading Commission	None
Section 742(a)(2) (amending Section 2(c) of the Commodity Exchange Act (7 U.S.C. 2(c)))	Certain requirements do not apply to certain agreements, securities, and contracts if delivered within 28 days "or such other longer period as the Commission may determine by rule or regulation...."	Commodity Futures Trading Commission	None
Section 745(b) (amending Section 5c of the Commodity Exchange Act (7 U.S.C. 7a-2))	The Commission may determine that certain "agreements, contracts, or transactions are contrary to the public interest " if "determined by the Commission, by rule or regulation, to be contrary to the public interest.."	Commodity Futures Trading Commission	None
Section 747 (amending Section 4c(a) of the Commodity Exchange Act (7 U.S.C. 6c(a)))	"...may make and promulgate such rules and regulations as, in the judgment of the Commission, are reasonably necessary to prohibit the trading practices described in paragraph (5) and any other trading practice that is disruptive of fair and equitable trading."	Commodity Futures Trading Commission	None
Section 748 (amending the Commodity Exchange Act (7 U.S.C. 1 et seq.))	"The term 'whistleblower' means any individual, or 2 or more individuals acting jointly, who provides information relating to a violation of this Act to the Commission, in a manner established by rule or regulation by the Commission." (Also several other provisions regarding whistleblowers that may be established by rule or regulation.)	Commodity Futures Trading Commission	April 17, 2011 (Within 270 days after the date of enactment.)

Section	Text of the Provision	Agency	Deadline
Section 748 (amending the Commodity Exchange Act (7 U.S.C. 1 et seq.)) Section 761(b)	"...shall have the authority to issue such rules and regulations as may be necessary or appropriate to implement the provisions of this section consistent with the purposes of this section." "...may, by rule, further define (1) the term 'commercial risk'; (2) any other term included in an amendment to the Securities Exchange Act of 1934 (15 U.S.C. 78c(a)) made by this subtitle; and (3) the terms 'security-based swap', 'security-based swap dealer', 'major security-based swap participant', and 'eligible contract participant', with regard to security-based swaps (as such terms are defined in the amendments made by subsection (a)) for the purpose of including transactions and entities that have been structured to evade this subtitle or the amendments made by this subtitle."	Commodity Futures Trading Commission Securities and Exchange Commission	April 17, 2011 (Within 270 days after the date of enactment.) None
Section 763(a) (amending the Securities Exchange Act of 1934 (15 U.S.C. 78a et seq.))	"...shall prescribe rules under this section (and issue interpretations of rules prescribed under this section), as determined by the Commission to be necessary to prevent evasions of the mandatory clearing requirements under this Act."	Securities and Exchange Commission	None
Section 763(a) (amending the Securities Exchange Act of 1934 (15 U.S.C. 78a et seq.))	Security-based swaps entered into on or after the date of enactment must be reported within 90 days or "such other time after entering into the security-based swap as the Commission may prescribe by rule or regulation."	Securities and Exchange Commission	None
Section 763(a) (amending the Securities Exchange Act of 1934 (15 U.S.C. 78a et seq.))	"...may prescribe such rules or issue interpretations of the rules as the Commission determines to be necessary to prevent abuse of the exceptions described in this subsection."	Securities and Exchange Commission	None
Section 763(a) (amending the Securities Exchange Act of 1934 (15 U.S.C. 78a et seq.))	"In accordance with rules prescribed by the Commission, the chief compliance officer shall annually prepare and sign a report that contains a description of ...."	Securities and Exchange Commission	None
Section 763(b) (amending Section 17A of the Securities Exchange Act of 1934 (15 U.S.C. 78q-1))	"To be registered and to maintain registration as a clearing agency that clears security-based swap transactions, a clearing agency shall comply with such standards as the Commission may establish by rule."	Securities and Exchange Commission	None

Table B-1. (Continued).

Section	Text of the Provision	Agency	Deadline
Section 763(c) (amending the Securities Exchange Act of 1934 (15 U.S.C. 78a et seq.))	"To be registered, and maintain registration, as a security-based swap execution facility, the security-based swap execution facility shall comply with … any requirement that the Commission may impose by rule or regulation."	Securities and Exchange Commission	None
Section 763(c) (amending the Securities Exchange Act of 1934 (15 U.S.C. 78a et seq.))	"In accordance with rules prescribed by the Commission, the chief compliance officer shall annually prepare and sign a report that contains a description of…."	Securities and Exchange Commission	None
Section 763(d) (amending the Securities Exchange Act of 1934 (15 U.S.C. 78a et seq.))	"…in accordance with such terms and conditions as the Commission may prescribe by rule, regulation, or order, any money, securities, or property of the security-based swaps customer of a broker, dealer, or security-based swap dealer described in subsection (b) may be commingled and deposited as provided in this section with any other money, securities, or property received by the broker, dealer, or security-based swap dealer and required by the Commission to be separately accounted for and treated and dealt with as belonging to the security-based swaps customer of the broker, dealer, or security-based swap dealer."	Securities and Exchange Commission	None
Section 763(d) (amending the Securities Exchange Act of 1934 (15 U.S.C. 78a et seq.))	Certain funds may be invested in certain vehicles or "in any other investment that the Commission may by rule or regulation prescribe, and such investments shall be made in accordance with such rules and regulations and subject to such conditions as the Commission may prescribe."	Securities and Exchange Commission	None
Section 763(h) (amending the Securities Exchange Act of 1934 after section 10A (15 U.S.C. 78j-1))	"…shall, by rule or regulation, as necessary or appropriate in the public interest or for the protection of investors, establish limits (including related hedge exemption provisions) on the size of positions in any security-based swap that may be held by any person."	Securities and Exchange Commission	None
Section 763(h) (amending the Securities Exchange Act of 1934 after section 10A (15 U.S.C. 78j-1))	"…by rule, regulation, or order, may conditionally or unconditionally exempt any person or class of persons, any security-based swap or class of security-based swaps, or any transaction or class of transactions from any requirement the Commission may establish under this section with respect to position limits."	Securities and Exchange Commission	None

Rulemaking Requirements and Authorities...

Section	Text of the Provision	Agency	Deadline
Section 763(h) (amending the Securities Exchange Act of 1934 after section 10A (15 U.S.C. 78j-1))	"...by rule, regulation, or order, as necessary or appropriate in the public interest, for the protection of investors, or otherwise in furtherance of the purposes of this title, may direct a self-regulatory organization (A) to adopt rules regarding the size of positions in any security-based swap that may be held by...."	Securities and Exchange Commission	None
Section 763(h) (amending the Securities Exchange Act of 1934 after section 10A (15 U.S.C. 78j-1))	"...by rule or regulation, may require any person that effects transactions for such person's own account or the account of others in any securities-based swap or uncleared security-based swap and any security or loan or group or narrow-based security index of securities or loans as set forth in paragraphs (1) and (2) of subsection (a) under this section to report such information as the Commission may prescribe regarding...."	Securities and Exchange Commission	None
Section 763(i) (amending Section 13 of the Securities Exchange Act of 1934 (15 U.S.C. 78m))	"...is authorized to provide by rule for the public availability of security-based swap transaction, volume, and pricing data as follows...."	Securities and Exchange Commission	None
Section 763(i) (amending Section 13 of the Securities Exchange Act of 1934 (15 U.S.C. 78m))	"...may, by rule, regulation, or order, delegate the public reporting responsibilities of the Commission under this paragraph in accordance with such terms and conditions as the Commission determines to be appropriate and in the public interest."	Securities and Exchange Commission	None
Section 763(i) (amending Section 13 of the Securities Exchange Act of 1934 (15 U.S.C. 78m))	"In accordance with rules prescribed by the Commission, the chief compliance officer shall annually prepare and sign a report that contains a description of...."	Securities and Exchange Commission	None
Section 764(a) (amending the Securities Exchange Act of 1934 (15 U.S.C. 78a et seq.) after section 15E (15 U.S.C. 78o-7))	"Each registration under this section shall expire at such time as the Commission may prescribe by rule or regulation."	Securities and Exchange Commission	None
Section 764 (amending the Securities Exchange Act of 1934 (15 U.S.C. 78a et seq.))	" ... may prescribe rules applicable to security-based swap dealers and major security-based swap participants, including rules that limit the activities of non-bank security-based swap dealers and major security-based swap participants."	Securities and Exchange Commission	None

Table B-1. (Continued).

Section	Text of the Provision	Agency	Deadline
Section 805(a)(2)(A)	"…may each prescribe regulations… containing risk management standards … for those designated clearing entities and financial institutions engaged in designated activities for which each is the Supervisory Agency or the appropriate financial regulator…."	Commodity Futures Trading Commission and the Securities and Exchange Commission	None
Section 806(b)	"…discounts and borrowing privileges shall be subject to such other limitations, restrictions, and regulations as the Board of Governors may prescribe."	Board of Governors	None
Section 809(b)(3)	"…may … prescribe regulations under this section that impose a recordkeeping or reporting requirement on designated clearing entities or financial institutions engaged in designated activities that are subject to standards that have been prescribed under section 805(a)(2)."	Board of Governors, upon an affirmative vote by a majority of the Financial Stability Oversight Council	None
Section 810	"…are authorized to prescribe such rules and issue such orders as may be necessary to administer and carry out their respective authorities and duties granted under this title (on 'Payment, Clearing, and Settlement Supervision') and prevent evasions thereof."	Board of Governors, the supervisory agencies, and the Financial Stability Oversight Council	None
Section 913(f)	"…may commence a rulemaking, as necessary or appropriate in the public interest and for the protection of retail customers … to address the legal or regulatory standards of care for brokers, dealers, investment advisers, persons associated with brokers or dealers, and persons associated with investment advisers for providing personalized investment advice about securities to such retail customers."	Securities and Exchange Commission	None
Section 913(g)(1) (amending Section 15 of the Securities Exchange Act of 1934 (15 U.S.C. 78o))	" … may promulgate rules to provide that, with respect to a broker or dealer, when providing personalized investment advice about securities to a retail customer (and such other customers as he Commission may by rule provide), the standard of conduct for such broker or dealer with respect to such customer shall be the same as the standard of conduct applicable to an investment adviser under section 211 of the Investment Advisers Act of 1940."	Securities and Exchange Commission	None
Section 913(g)(1) (amending Section 15 of the Securities Exchange Act of 1934 (15 U.S.C. 78o))	"…may by rule require that (certain brokers or dealers)…provide notice to each retail customer and obtain the consent or acknowledgment of the customer."	Securities and Exchange Commission	None

Section	Text of the Provision	Agency	Deadline
Section 913(g)(1) (amending Section 15 of the Securities Exchange Act of 1934 (15 U.S.C. 78o))	"…shall…where appropriate, promulgate rules prohibiting or restricting certain sales practices, conflicts of interest, and compensation schemes for brokers, dealers, and investment advisers that the Commission deems contrary to the public interest and the protection of investors."	Securities and Exchange Commission	None
Section 913(g)(2) (amending Section 211 of the Investment Advisers Act of 1940)	"…may promulgate rules to provide that the standard of conduct for all brokers, dealers, and investment advisers, when providing personalized investment advice about securities to retail customers … shall be to act in the best interest of the customer without regard to the financial or other interest of the broker, dealer, or investment adviser providing the advice."	Securities and Exchange Commission	None
Section 913(g)(2) (amending Section 211 of the Investment Advisers Act of 1940)	"…where appropriate, promulgate rules prohibiting or restricting certain sales practices, conflicts of interest, and compensation schemes for brokers, dealers, and investment advisers that the Commission deems contrary to the public interest and the protection of investors."	Securities and Exchange Commission	None
Section 916(a) (amending Section 19(b) of the Securities Exchange Act of 1934 (15 U.S.C. 78s(b)))	"…shall approve a proposed rule change of a self-regulatory organization if it finds that such proposed rule change is consistent with the requirements of this title and the rules and regulations issued under this title that are applicable to such organization."	Securities and Exchange Commission	None
Section 919 (amending Section 15 of the Securities Exchange Act of 1934 (15 U.S.C. 78o))	" … may issue rules designating documents or information that shall be provided by a broker or dealer to a retail investor before the purchase of an investment product or service by the retail investor." (Goes on to detail contents)	Securities and Exchange Commission	None
Section 921(a) (amending Section 15 of the Securities Exchange Act of 1934 (15 U.S.C. 78o)) (Note: same provision in Section 921(b), amending Section 205 of the Investment Advisers Act of 1940 (15 U.S.C. 80b-5)).	"…by rule, may prohibit, or impose conditions or limitations on the use of, agreements that require customers or clients of any broker, dealer, or municipal securities dealer to arbitrate any future dispute between them arising under the Federal securities laws …"	Securities and Exchange Commission	None

Table B-1. (Continued).

Section	Text of the Provision	Agency	Deadline
Section 922(a) (amending the Securities Exchange Act of 1934 (15 U.S.C. 78a et seq.))	"The term 'whistleblower' means any individual who provides … information relating to a violation of the securities laws to the Commission, in a manner established, by rule or regulation, by the Commission." Also, awards are to be paid "under regulations prescribed by the Commission." Finally, the Commission is given the authority to issue "such rules and regulations as may be necessary or appropriate to implement the provisions of this section consistent with the purposes of this section."	Securities and Exchange Commission	None
Section 929D(2) (amending Section 17(f)(1) of the Securities Exchange Act of 1934 (15 U.S.C. 78q(f)(1)))	"…stolen, cancelled, or reported in such other manner as the Commission, by rule, may prescribe."	Securities and Exchange Commission	None
Section 929Q(a) (amending Section 31 of the Investment Company Act of 1940 (15 U.S.C. 80a-30))	"…shall maintain and preserve all records that relate to the custody or use by such person of the securities, deposits, or credits of the registered investment company for such period or periods as the Commission, by rule or regulation, may prescribe, as necessary or appropriate in the public interest or for the protection of investors.…" (Note: Same requirement in Section 929Q(b), amending Section 16(a) of the Securities Exchange Act of 1934 (15 U.S.C. 78p(a)))	Securities and Exchange Commission	None
Section 929R(a) (amending Section 13 of the Securities Exchange Act of 1934 (15 U.S.C. 78m))	Beneficial ownership and short-swing profit reporting is required within 10 days "or within such shorter time as the Commission may establish by rule."	Securities and Exchange Commission	None
Section 929W (amending Section 17A of the Securities Exchange Act of 1934 (15 U.S.C. 78q-1))	"…shall adopt such rules, regulations, and orders necessary to implement this subsection.… In proposing such rules, the Commission shall seek to minimize disruptions to current systems used by or on behalf of paying agents to process payment to account holders and avoid requiring multiple paying agents to send written notification to a missing security holder regarding the same not yet negotiated check."	Securities and Exchange Commission	July 21, 2011 (Within one year of the date of enactment (i.e., by July 21, 2011.)
Section 929X(b)(2) (amending Section 9 of the Securities Exchange Act of 1934 (15 U.S.C. 78i))	"…shall issue such other rules as are necessary or appropriate to ensure that the appropriate enforcement options and remedies are available for violations of this subsection (on short-selling enforcement) in the public interest or for the protection of investors."	Securities and Exchange Commission	None

Rulemaking Requirements and Authorities...

Section	Text of the Provision	Agency	Deadline
Section 929X(c)(2) (amending Section 15 of the Securities Exchange Act of 1934 (15 U.S.C. 78o)) Section 939F(d)	"…by rule, as it deems necessary or appropriate in the public interest and for the protection of investors, may prescribe the form, content, time, and manner of delivery of any notice required under this paragraph." "…shall, by rule, as the Commission determines is necessary or appropriate in the public interest or for the protection of investors, establish a system for the assignment of nationally recognized statistical rating organizations to determine the initial credit ratings of structured finance products.…"	Securities and Exchange Commission Securities and Exchange Commission	None July 21, 2012 (After submission of a report, which is required within 24 months after the date of enactment.)
Section 941(a) (amending Section 3(a) of the Securities Exchange Act of 1934 (15 U.S.C. 78c(a)))	An "asset-backed security" means (among other things) "a security that the Commission, by rule, determines to be an asset-backed security for purposes of this section."	Securities and Exchange Commission	None
Section 942(a)(3) (amending Section 15(d) of the Securities Exchange Act of 1934 (15 U.S.C. 78o(d))	"…may, by rule or regulation, provide for the suspension or termination of the duty to file under this subsection for any class of asset-backed security, on such terms and conditions and for such period or periods as the Commission deems necessary or appropriate in the public interest or for the protection of investors."	Securities and Exchange Commission	None
Section 951 (amending the Securities Exchange Act of 1934 (15 U.S.C. 78a et seq.))	"…may, by rule or order, exempt an issuer or class of issuers from the requirement under subsection (a) or (b)."	Securities and Exchange Commission	None
Section 956(e)(2)(G)	"The term 'covered financial institution' means … any other financial institution that the appropriate Federal regulators, jointly, by rule, determine should be treated as a covered financial institution for purposes of this section."	The "appropriate Federal regulators"	None
Section 957(2) (amending Section 6(b) of the Securities Exchange Act of 1934 (15 U.S.C. 78f(b)))	"A shareholder vote described in this subparagraph is a shareholder vote with respect to the election of a member of the board of directors of an issuer, executive compensation, or any other significant matter, as determined by the Commission, by rule."	Securities and Exchange Commission	None
Section 971(a) (amending Section 14(a) of the Securities Exchange Act of 1934 (15 U.S.C. 78n(a)))	"The rules and regulations prescribed by the Commission under paragraph (1) (on 'Proxy Access') may include (A) a requirement that a solicitation of proxy, consent, or authorization by (or on behalf of) an issuer include a nominee submitted by a shareholder to serve on the board of directors of the issuer."	Securities and Exchange Commission	None

Table B-1. (Continued).

Section	Text of the Provision	Agency	Deadline
Section 971(b) and (c)	" ... may issue rules permitting the use by a shareholder of proxy solicitation materials supplied by an issuer of securities for the purpose of nominating individuals to membership on the board of directors of the issuer...." Also, the Commission "may, by rule or order, exempt an issuer or class of issuers from the requirement made by this section or an amendment made by this section."	Securities and Exchange Commission	None
Section 982(e)	"...may, by rule, conduct and require a program of inspection in accordance with paragraph (1), on a basis to be determined by the Board, of registered public accounting firms that provide one or more audit reports for a broker or dealer."	Public Company Accounting Oversight Board	None
Section 984(a) (amending Section 10 of the Securities Exchange Act of 1934 (15 U.S.C. 78j))	Prohibits "borrowing of securities in contravention of such rules and regulations as the Commission may prescribe as necessary or appropriate in the public interest or for the protection of investors."	Securities and Exchange Commission	None
Section 985(b)(5) (amending Section 15 of the Securities Exchange Act of 1934 (15 U.S.C. 78a et seq.))	"The order granting registration shall not be effective until such broker or dealer has become a member of a registered securities association, or until such broker or dealer has become a member of a national securities exchange, if such broker or dealer effects transactions solely on that exchange, unless the Commission has exempted such broker or dealer, by rule or order, from such membership."	Securities and Exchange Commission	None
Section 1002(9)	The term "deposit-taking activity" includes "the receipt of funds or the equivalent thereof, as the Bureau may determine by rule or order, received or held by a covered person (or an agent for a covered person) for the purpose of facilitating a payment or transferring funds or value of funds between a consumer and a third party."	Consumer Financial Protection Bureau	None
Section 1002(15)(A)	The definition of the term "financial product or service" includes "...such other financial product or service as may be defined by the Bureau, by regulation, for purposes of this title...."	Consumer Financial Protection Bureau	None
Section 1002(25)	The definition of a "related person" includes "any shareholder, consultant, joint venture partner, or other person, as determined by the Bureau (by rule or on a case-by-case basis) who materially participates in the conduct of the affairs of such covered person."	Consumer Financial Protection Bureau	None

Section	Text of the Provision	Agency	Deadline
Section 1022(b)(1)	"…may prescribe rules and issue orders and guidance, as may be necessary or appropriate to enable the Bureau to administer and carry out the purposes and objectives of the Federal consumer financial laws, and to prevent evasions thereof."	Consumer Financial Protection Bureau	None
Section 1022(b)(3)(A)	"…by rule, may conditionally or unconditionally exempt any class of covered persons, service providers, or consumer financial products or services, from any provision of this title, or from any rule issued under this title, as the Bureau determines necessary or appropriate to carry out the purposes and objectives of this title, taking into consideration the factors in subparagraph (B)."	Consumer Financial Protection Bureau	None
Section 1022(c)(4)(B)	"…may … require covered persons and service providers participating in consumer financial services markets to file with the Bureau, under oath or otherwise, in such form and within such reasonable period of time as the Bureau may prescribe by rule or order, annual or special reports, or answers in writing to specific questions…."	Consumer Financial Protection Bureau	None
Section 1022(c)(5)	"In order to assess whether a nondepository is a covered person, as defined in section 1002, the Bureau may require such nondepository to file with the Bureau, under oath or otherwise, in such form and within such reasonable period of time as the Bureau may prescribe by rule or order, annual or special reports, or answers in writing to specific questions."	Consumer Financial Protection Bureau	None
Section 1022(c)(7)(A)	"…may prescribe rules regarding registration requirements applicable to a covered person, other than an insured depository institution, insured credit union, or related person."	Consumer Financial Protection Bureau	None
Section 1024(b)(7)(C)	"…may prescribe rules regarding a person described in subsection (a)(1), to ensure that such persons are legitimate entities and are able to perform their obligations to consumers. Such requirements may include background checks for principals, officers, directors, or key personnel and bonding or other appropriate financial requirements."	Consumer Financial Protection Bureau	None
Section 1027(b)(2)	"…may exercise rulemaking, supervisory, enforcement, or other authority under this title with respect to a person described in paragraph (1) when such person is (A) engaged in an activity of offering or providing any consumer financial product or service … or (B) otherwise subject to any enumerated consumer law or any law for which authorities are transferred under subtitle F or H…."	Consumer Financial Protection Bureau	None

Table B-1. (Continued).

Section	Text of the Provision	Agency	Deadline
Section 1027(g)(3)(B)(iii)	"Subject to a request or response pursuant to clause (i) or clause (ii) by the agencies made under this subparagraph (Departments of the Treasury and Labor), the Bureau may exercise rulemaking authority, and may act to enforce a rule prescribed pursuant to such request or response, in accordance with the provisions of this title."	Consumer Financial Protection Bureau	None
Section 1028(b)	"...by regulation, may prohibit or impose conditions or limitations on the use of an agreement between a covered person and a consumer for a consumer financial product or service providing for arbitration of any future dispute between the parties...."	Consumer Financial Protection Bureau	None
Section 1031(b)	"...may prescribe rules applicable to a covered person or service provider identifying as unlawful unfair, deceptive, or abusive acts or practices in connection with any transaction with a consumer for a consumer financial product or service, or the offering of a consumer financial product or service."	Consumer Financial Protection Bureau	None
Section 1032(a)	"...may prescribe rules to ensure that the features of any consumer financial product or service, both initially and over the term of the product or service, are fully, accurately, and effectively disclosed to consumers in a manner that permits consumers to understand the costs, benefits, and risks associated with the product or service, in light of the facts and circumstances."	Consumer Financial Protection Bureau	None
Section 1057(d)(3)	"...an arbitration provision in a collective bargaining agreement shall be enforceable as to disputes arising under subsection (a)(4), unless the Bureau determines, by rule, that such provision is inconsistent with the purposes of this title."	Consumer Financial Protection Bureau	None
Section 1071(a) (amending the Equal Credit Opportunity Act (15 U.S.C. 1691 et seq.))	"...shall prescribe such rules and issue such guidance as may be necessary to carry out, enforce, and compile data pursuant to this section" (on small business data collection).	Consumer Financial Protection Bureau	None
Section 1071(a) (amending the Equal Credit Opportunity Act (15 U.S.C. 1691 et seq.))	"...by rule or order, may adopt exceptions to any requirement of this section (on small business data collection) and may, conditionally or unconditionally, exempt any financial institution or class of financial institutions from the requirements of this section, as the Bureau deems necessary or appropriate to carry out the purposes of this section."	Consumer Financial Protection Bureau	None

Rulemaking Requirements and Authorities...

Section	Text of the Provision	Agency	Deadline
Section 1073(a)(4) (amending the Electronic Fund Transfer Act (15 U.S.C. 1693 et seq.)	"If the Board determines that a recipient nation does not legally allow, or the method by which transactions are made in the recipient country do not allow, a remittance transfer provider to know the amount of currency that will be received by the designated recipient, the Board may prescribe rules ... addressing the issue...."	Board of Governors	January 21, 2012 (Within 18 months after the date of enactment.)
Section 1075(a)(2) (amending the Electronic Fund Transfer Act (15 U.S.C. 1693 et seq.), creating a new Section 920	"...may prescribe regulations, pursuant to section 553 of title 5, United States Code, regarding any interchange transaction fee that an issuer may receive or charge with respect to an electronic debit transaction, to implement this subsection (including related definitions), and to prevent circumvention or evasion of this subsection."	Board of Governors	None
Section 1075(a)(2) (amending the Electronic Fund Transfer Act (15 U.S.C. 1693 et seq.), creating a new Section 920	" ... may, by regulation prescribed pursuant to section 553 of title 5, United States Code, increase the amount of the dollar value listed in subparagraph (A)(i)(II)."	Board of Governors	None
Section 1075(a)(2) (amending the Electronic Fund Transfer Act (15 U.S.C. 1693 et seq.), creating a new Section 920 Section 1075(a)(2) (amending the Electronic Fund Transfer Act (15 U.S.C. 1693 et seq.), creating a new Section 920	"The Board may allow for an adjustment to the fee amount received or charged by an issuer under paragraph (2), if (certain conditions are met).... The Board shall prescribe regulations ... to establish standards for making adjustments under this paragraph." "...may prescribe regulations, pursuant to section 553 of title 5, United States Code, regarding any network fee" (subject to certain limitations).	Board of Governors Board of Governors	April 21, 2011 (Any regulations must be issued in final form within nine months after the date of enactment.) April 21, 2011 (Any regulations must be issued in final form within nine months after the date of enactment.)
Section 1075(a)(2) (amending the Electronic Fund Transfer Act (15 U.S.C. 1693 et seq.), creating a new Section 920	"...may, by regulation prescribed pursuant to section 553 of title 5, United States Code, increase the amount of the dollar value listed in subparagraph (A)(i)(II)" ($10 minimum dollar value for acceptance of credit cards).	Board of Governors	None
Section 1076(b)	The Bureau should issue rules if it "determines through the study required under subsection (a) (on reverse mortgage transactions) that conditions or limitations on reverse mortgage transactions are necessary or appropriate for accomplishing the purposes and objectives of this title...."	Consumer Financial Protection Bureau	None (Study must be conducted within one year of enactment (i.e., by July 21, 2011), but no deadline established for possible regulations.)

Table B-1. (Continued).

Section	Text of the Provision	Agency	Deadline
Section 1084(3)(A)	"…shall have sole authority to prescribe rules (A) to carry out the purposes of this title with respect to a person described in section 1029(a) of the Consumer Financial Protection Act of 2010; and (B) to carry out the purposes of section 920."	Board of Governors	None
Section 1088(a) (amending the Fair Credit Reporting Act (15 U.S.C. 1681 et seq.))	Prohibits the treatment of information as a consumer report if it is disclosed as "…determined to be necessary and appropriate, by regulation or order, by the Bureau or the applicable State insurance authority (with respect to any person engaged in providing insurance or annuities)."	Consumer Financial Protection Bureau or applicable state insurance authorities	None
Section 1088(a)(4)(B) (amending the Fair Credit Reporting Act (15 U.S.C. 1681 et seq.))	"…may, after notice and opportunity for comment, prescribe regulations that permit transactions under paragraph (2) that are determined to be necessary and appropriate to protect legitimate operational, transactional, risk, consumer, and other needs…."	Consumer Financial Protection Bureau	None
Section 1088(a)(10)(E) (amending the Fair Credit Reporting Act (15 U.S.C. 1681 et seq.))	"…shall prescribe such regulations as are necessary to carry out the purposes of this title, except with respect to sections 615(e) and 628. The Bureau may prescribe regulations as may be necessary or appropriate to administer and carry out the purposes and objectives of this title, and to prevent evasions thereof or to facilitate compliance therewith."	Consumer Financial Protection Bureau	None
Section 1089(4) (amending the Fair Debt Collection Practices Act (15 U.S.C. 1692 et seq.))	"Except as provided in section 1029(a) of the Consumer Financial Protection Act of 2010, the Bureau may prescribe rules with respect to the collection of debts by debt collectors, as defined in this title."	Consumer Financial Protection Bureau	None
Section 1093(3)(A) (amending Title V of the Gramm-Leach-Bliley Act (15 U.S.C. 6801 et seq.))	"…shall have authority to prescribe such regulations as may be necessary to carry out the purposes of this subtitle with respect to financial institutions and other persons subject to their respective jurisdiction under section 505,…except that the Bureau of Consumer Financial Protection shall not have authority to prescribe regulations with respect to the standards under section 501."	Consumer Financial Protection Bureau and the Securities and Exchange Commission	None
Section 1093(3)(A) (amending Title V of the Gramm-Leach-Bliley Act (15 U.S.C. 6801 et seq.))	"…shall have authority to prescribe such regulations as may be necessary to carry out the purposes of this subtitle with respect to financial institutions and other persons subject to the jurisdiction of the Commodity Futures Trading Commission under section 5g of the Commodity Exchange Act."	Commodity Futures Trading Commission	None

Table B-1. (Continued).

Section	Text of the Provision	Agency	Deadline
Section 1093(3)(A) (amending Title V of the Gramm-Leach-Bliley Act (15 U.S.C. 6801 et seq.))	"…shall have authority to prescribe such regulations as may be necessary to carry out the purposes of this subtitle with respect to any financial institution that is a person described in section 1029(a) of the Consumer Financial Protection Act of 2010."	Federal Trade Commission	None
Section 1094(5) (amending the Home Mortgage Disclosure Act of 1975 (12 U.S.C. 2801 et seq.).	" … may, by regulation, exempt from the requirements of this title any State-chartered repository institution within any State or subdivision thereof, if the agency determines that, under the law of such State or subdivision, that institution is subject to requirements that are substantially similar to those imposed under this title, and that such law contains adequate provisions for enforcement."	Consumer Financial Protection Bureau	None
Section 1097(1) (amending Section 626 of the Omnibus Appropriations Act, 2009 (15 U.S.C. 1638 note)).	"…shall have authority to prescribe rules with respect to mortgage loans in accordance with section 553 of title 5, United States Code. Such rulemaking shall relate to unfair or deceptive acts or practices regarding mortgage loans, which may include unfair or deceptive acts or practices involving loan modification and foreclosure rescue services."	Consumer Financial Protection Bureau	None
Section 1100(6)(B) (amending the S.A.F.E. Mortgage Licensing Act of 2008 (12 U.S.C. 5101 et seq.))	"…is authorized to promulgate regulations setting minimum net worth or surety bond requirements for residential mortgage loan originators and minimum requirements for recovery funds paid into by loan originators."	Consumer Financial Protection Bureau	None
Section 1204(b)	"Subject to regulations prescribed by the Secretary under this title, 1 or more eligible entities may participate in 1 or several programs established under subsection (a)" (e.g., grants and cooperative agreements).	Secretary of the Treasury	None
Section 1209	"…is authorized to promulgate regulations to implement and administer the grant programs and undertakings authorized by this title."	Secretary of the Treasury	None
Section 1405(a) (amending Section 129B of the Truth in Lending Act)	"…shall, by regulations, prohibit or condition terms, acts or practices relating to residential mortgage loans that the Board finds to be abusive, unfair, deceptive, predatory, necessary or proper to ensure that responsible, affordable mortgage credit remains available to consumers in a manner consistent with the purposes of this section and section 129C…."	Board of Governors	None

Table B-1. (Continued).

Section	Text of the Provision	Agency	Deadline
Section 1405(b)	"…may, by rule, exempt from or modify disclosure requirements, in whole or in part, for any class of residential mortgage loans if the Board determines that such exemption or modification is in the interest of consumers and in the public interest."	Board of Governors	None
Section 1412 (amending the Truth in Lending Act (15 U.S.C. 1631 et seq.))	" … may, by regulation, provide that the term 'qualified mortgage' includes a balloon loan... (that meets several specified criteria and conditions)."	Board of Governors	None
Section 1412 (amending the Truth in Lending Act (15 U.S.C. 1631 et seq.))	"…may prescribe regulations that revise, add to, or subtract from the criteria that define a qualified mortgage upon a finding that such regulations are necessary or proper to ensure that responsible, affordable mortgage credit remains available to consumers in a manner consistent with the purposes of this section…."	Board of Governors	None
Section 1420 (amending Section 128 of the Truth in Lending Act (15 U.S.C. 1638))	"The creditor, assignee, or servicer with respect to any residential mortgage loan shall transmit to the obligor, for each billing cycle, a statement setting forth (a list of items and) … such other information as the Board may prescribe in regulations."	Board of Governors	None
Section 1433(e) (amending Section 129 of the Truth in Lending Act (15 U.S.C. 1639) Section 1461(a) (amending Chapter 2 of the Truth in Lending Act (15 U.S.C. 1631 et seq.))	"…may prescribe such regulations as the Board determines to be appropriate to carry out the requirements of paragraph (1)" (on pre-loan counseling). "…may, by regulation, exempt from the requirements of subsection (a) a creditor that (1) operates predominantly in rural or underserved areas; (2) together with all affiliates, has total annual mortgage loan originations that do not exceed a limit set by the Board; (3) retains its mortgage loan originations in portfolio; and (4) meets any asset size threshold and any other criteria the Board may establish, consistent with the purposes of this subtitle."	Board of Governors Board of Governors	None None
Section 1461(a) (amending Chapter 2 of the Truth in Lending Act (15 U.S.C. 1631 et seq.), by adding a new Section 129D)	" … may, by regulation, exempt from the requirements of subsection (a) ("Escrow or Impound Accounts") a creditor that—(1) operates predominantly in rural or underserved areas; (2) together with all affiliates, has total annual mortgage loan originations that do not exceed a limit set by the Board; (3) retains its mortgage loan originations in portfolio; and (4) meets any asset size threshold and any other criteria the Board may establish, consistent with the purposes of this subtitle."	Board of Governors	None

Rulemaking Requirements and Authorities...   311

Section	Text of the Provision	Agency	Deadline
Section 1461(b)	"…may prescribe rules that revise, add to, or subtract from the criteria of section 129D(b) of the Truth in Lending Act if the Board determines that such rules are in the interest of consumers and in the public interest."	Board of Governors	None
Section 1472(a) (amending Chapter 2 of the Truth in Lending Act (15 U.S.C. 1631 et seq.)	"…may jointly issue rules, interpretive guidelines, and general statements of policy with respect to acts or practices that violate appraisal independence in the provision of mortgage lending services for a consumer credit transaction secured by the principal dwelling of the consumer and mortgage brokerage services for such a transaction, within the meaning of subsections (a), (b), (c), (d), (e), (f), (h), and (i)."	Board of Governors, the Comptroller of the Currency, the Federal Deposit Insurance Corporation, the National Credit Union Administration Board, the Federal Housing Finance Agency, and the Consumer Financial Protection Bureau	None
Section 1472(a) (amending Chapter 2 of the Truth in Lending Act (15 U.S.C. 1631 et seq.)	"…may jointly issue regulations that address the issue of appraisal report portability, including regulations that ensure the portability of the appraisal report between lenders for a consumer credit transaction secured by a 1-4 unit single family residence that is the principal dwelling of the consumer, or mortgage brokerage services for such a transaction."	Board of Governors, the Comptroller of the Currency, the Federal Deposit Insurance Corporation, the National Credit Union Administration Board, the Federal Housing Finance Agency, and the Consumer Financial Protection Bureau	None
Section 1473(d) (amending Section 1106 of the Financial Institutions Reform, Recovery, and Enforcement Act of 1989 (12 U.S.C. 3335))	Allows the appraisal subcommittee to "prescribe regulations in accordance with (the Administrative Procedure Act) after notice and opportunity for comment" regarding "temporary practice, national registry, information sharing, and enforcement." Requires the appraisal subcommittee to "establish an advisory committee of industry participants, including appraisers, lenders, consumer advocates, real estate agents, and government agencies, and hold meetings as necessary to support the development of regulations."	Appraisal Subcommittee	None
Section 1503(d)(2)	"… is authorized to issue such rules or regulations as are necessary or appropriate for the protection of investors and to carry out the purposes of this section."	Securities and Exchange Commission	None

End Notes

[1] For more information on the Dodd-Frank Act, see CRS Report R41350, *The Dodd-Frank Wall Street Reform and Consumer Protection Act: Issues and Summary*, coordinated by Baird Webel. For more information on the CFPB, see CRS Report R41338, *The Dodd-Frank Wall Street Reform and Consumer Protection Act: Title X, The Consumer Financial Protection Bureau*, by David H. Carpenter.

[2] Gretchen Morgenson, "After U.S. Financial Reform Bill, the Hard Work Begins," *International Herald Tribune*, August 30, 2010, p. 17.

[3] Lorraine Mirabella, "Lawyers Await Regulations to Spring from Financial Reform," *McClatchy-Tribune Business News*, July 27, 2010, quoting Cindy Allner, a principal with Miles & Stockbridge in Baltimore.

[4] "The Uncertainty Principle: Dodd-Frank Will Require at Least 243 New Federal Rule-makings," *Wall Street Journal*, July 14, 2010, available at http://online.wsj.com/article/SB 100014240527 48704288204 575363162664835780.html.

[5] Binyamin Appelbaum, "On Finance Bill, Lobbying Shifts to Regulations," *New York Times*, June 27, 2010, p. A1.

[6] Jeremy L. Siegel, "For Good and Bad, Financial Overhaul Law to Affect Many," *Washington Post*, October 3, 2010, p. G3.

[7] See http://www.davispolk.com/files/Publication/7084f9fe-6580-413b-b870-b7c025ed2ecf/Presentation/ PublicationAttachment/1d4495c7-0be0-4e9a-ba77-f786fb90464a/070910_Financial_Reform_Summary.pdf.

[8] The Chamber of Commerce's Center for Capital Markets Competitiveness said that the Dodd-Frank Act "will lead to 520 rulemakings." See Thomas Quaadman, "Dodd-Frank: Governance Issues Galore and Not Limited to Financial Institutions, *The Metropolitan Corporate Counsel*, August 2010, p. 18, available at http://www.metrocorpcounsel.com/current.php?artType=view&artMonth=August&artYear=2010&EntryNo=1 1258.

[9] CRS Report R41380, *The Dodd-Frank Wall Street Reform and Consumer Protection Act: Regulations to be Issued by the Consumer Financial Protection Bureau*, by Curtis W. Copeland.

[10] On September 21, 2010, the SEC issued a final rule rescinding the rules that had been issued to administer a program under the statutory provision that was removed by Section 922. See U.S. Securities and Exchange Commission, "Rescission of Rules Pertaining to the Payment of Bounties for Information Leading to the Recovery of Civil Penalties for Insider Trading," 75 *Federal Register* 57384, September 21, 2010.

[11] See, for example, Section 618(d)(1), Section 737(a)(4), and Section 805(a)(1) in Appendix A of this report. Similar constructions include "by rule or order" and "by regulation and order."

[12] For example, Title VII of the Dodd-Frank Act establishes a regulatory structure for derivatives that had not previously existed, and that title contains numerous provisions requiring or authorizing the issuance of rules.

[13] Many reviewing courts and scholars divide agency-issued documents into two categories: (1) "legislative rules," which are required to conform to the notice-and-comment requirements in Section 553 of the Administrative Procedure Act (5 U.S.C. § 551 *et seq.*), and therefore, have the full force and effect of law; and (2) so-called "nonlegislative rules," which are exempt from the requirements of Section 553 and not legally binding. Judicial inquiry in this area, however, is extremely fact intensive and is done on a case-by-case basis with emphasis placed on the specific terms used in the document at issue. For a summary of these cases, see Jeffrey S. Lubbers, *A Guide to Federal Agency Rulemaking*, 4th edition (Chicago: American Bar Association, 2006), pp. 73-105.

[14] CRS Report R41346, *PPACA Regulations Issued During the First Four Months of the Act's Implementation*, by Curtis W. Copeland.

[15] Others listed in these seven provisions are the Comptroller of the Currency, the FDIC, the National Credit Union Administration Board, and the Federal Housing Finance Agency. Other multiple agency provisions are to be implemented by "the appropriate federal regulators" and "each federal primary financial regulatory agency," so they may also include these agencies.

[16] The same requirement appears in Sections 623(b) and 623(c) of the act, with the three provisions amending three different underlying statutes. The three sections were all treated as one rulemaking requirement in this report. The Secretary of the Treasury has announced that the transfer date will be July 21, 2011 (the one-year anniversary of the Dodd-Frank Act). See Bureau of Consumer Financial Protection, "Designated Transfer Date," 75 *Federal Register* 57252, September 20, 2010.

[17] 5 U.S.C. §553(b)(3)(B). The agency must conclude that notice and comment is "impracticable, unnecessary, or contrary to the public interest," and must incorporate the finding and a brief explanation in the rule being issued.

[18] Interim final rulemaking has been used for some time, and has been recommended by the Administrative Conference of the United States for noncontroversial and expedited rulemaking. To view this recommendation, see http://www.law.fsu.edu/library/admin/acus/305954.html.

[19] See "FDIC Announces Open Door Policy for Regulatory Reform Rulemaking," available at http://www.fdic.gov/news/news/press/2010/pr10187.html; and Mary L. Shapiro, "Moving Forward: The Next Phase in Financial Reform," available at http://www.sec.gov/news/speech. See also, Edward Wyatt, "SEC Expands Process for Public Comments on New Financial Rules," *New York Times*, July 28, 2010, p. B8; and R. Christian Bruce, "Changes in the Works for Rulewriting as Dodd-Frank Moves to Implementation," BNA Daily Report for Executives, July 30, 2010, p. EE-6.

[20] Sewell Chan, "Regulators to Write New Financial Rules in the Open," *New York Times*, August 14, 2010, p. B2.

[21] Ibid.

[22] Chris Frates, "Watchdog: Wall Streeters Fill CFTC's Dance Card," *Politico*, October 19, 2010, p. 15.

[23] ACUS Recommendation 78-3, available at http://www.law.fsu.edu/library/admin/acus/305783.html.

[24] For a summary of these cases, see Jeffrey S. Lubbers, *A Guide to Federal Agency Rulemaking*, 4th edition (Chicago: American Bar Association, 2006), pp. 111-113.

[25] Bureau of Consumer Financial Protection, "Designated Transfer Date," 75 *Federal Register* 57252, September 20, 2010.

[26] As noted later in this report, this interim final rule has been issued. See U.S. Commodity Futures Trading Commission, "Interim Final Rule for Reporting Pre-Enactment Swap Transactions," 75 *Federal Register* 6380, October 14, 2010.

[27] As noted later in this report, this interim final rule has been issued. See U.S. Securities and Exchange Commission, "Reporting of Security-Based Swap Transaction Data," 75 *Federal Register* 64643, October 20, 2010.

[28] As noted later in this report, this interim final rule has been issued. See U.S. Securities and Exchange Commission, "Removal from Regulation FD of the Exemption for Credit Rating Agencies," 75 *Federal Register* 6150, October 4, 2010.

[29] As noted later in this report, although this interim final rule had not been published in the *Federal Register* as of October 20, 2010, the Board of Governors had published a version of the rule on the agency's website and requested comments. See http://www.federalreserve.gov/newsevents/press/bcreg/20101018a.htm.

[30] Speech before New York University's Stern School of Business, August 2, 2010, available at http://www.treasury.gov/press/releases/tg808.htm.

[31] Glenn Hubbard and Hal S. Scott, "Geithner's Hollow 'Speed' Pledge to Business," *Wall Street Journal* (Online), August 4, 2010, available at http://online.wsj.com/article/SB10001424052748704017 90457540946 1883624210.html.

[32] U.S. Federal Deposit Insurance Corporation, "Deposit Insurance Regulations; Permanent Increase in Standard Coverage Amount; Advertisement of Membership; International Banking; Foreign Banks," 75 *Federal Register* 49363, August 13, 2010.

[33] U.S. National Credit Union Administration, "Display of Official Sign; Permanent Increase in Standard Maximum Share Insurance Amount," 75 *Federal Register* 53841, September 2, 2010.

[34] U.S. Securities and Exchange Commission, "Temporary Registration of Municipal Advisors," 75 *Federal Register* 54465, September 8, 2010.

[35] U.S. Commodity Futures Trading Commission, "Regulation of Off-Exchange Retail Foreign Exchange Transactions and Intermediaries," 75 U.S. Commodity Futures Trading Commission, "Regulation of Off-Exchange Retail Foreign Exchange Transactions and Intermediaries," 75 *Federal Register* 55410, September 10, 2010.

[36] U.S. Securities and Exchange Commission, "Internal Control Over Financial Reporting in Exchange Act Periodic Reports of Non-Accelerated Filers," 75 *Federal Register* 57385, September 21, 2010.

[37] U.S. Securities and Exchange Commission, "Rescission of Rules Pertaining to the Payment of Bounties for Information Leading to the Recovery of Civil Penalties for Insider Trading," 75 *Federal Register* 57384, September 21, 2010.

[38] U.S. Securities and Exchange Commission, "Removal from Regulation FD of the Exemption for Credit Rating Agencies," 75 *Federal Register* 6150, October 4, 2010.

[39] U.S. Securities and Exchange Commission, "Delegation of Authority to the Director of the Division of Trading and Markets," 75 *Federal Register* 62466, October 12, 2010.

[40] U.S. Commodity Futures Trading Commission, "Interim Final Rule for Reporting Pre-Enactment Swap Transactions," 75 *Federal Register* 6380, October 14, 2010.

[41] U.S. Securities and Exchange Commission, "Reporting of Security-Based Swap Transaction Data," 75 *Federal Register* 64643, October 20, 2010.

[42] See http://www.federalreserve.gov/newsevents/press/bcreg/20101018a.htm.

[43] See, for example, U.S. National Credit Union Administration, "Corporate Credit Unions," 75 *Federal Register* 64786, October 20, 2010, in which the agency noted that certain sections of the Dodd-Frank Act would affect the rule being issued, but those changes would be made in the future.

[44] See, for example, U.S. Securities and Exchange Commission, "Disclosure for Asset-Backed Securities Required by Section 943 of the Dodd-Frank Wall Street Reform and Consumer Protection Act," 75 *Federal Register* 62718, October 13, 2010; and U.S. Federal Deposit Insurance Corporation, "Notice of Proposed Rulemaking Implementing Certain Orderly Liquidation Authority Provisions of the Dodd-Frank Wall Street Reform and Consumer Protection Act," 75 *Federal Register* 64173.

[45] For more information on these and other rulemaking statutes, see CRS Report RL32240, *The Federal Rulemaking Process: An Overview*, by Curtis W. Copeland.

[46] The President, Executive Order 12866, "Regulatory Planning and Review," 58 *Federal Register* 51735, October 4, 1993, Section 6(a). A "significant" regulatory action is defined in Section 3(f) as "Any regulatory action that is likely to result in a rule that may (1) have an annual effect on the economy of $100 million or more or adversely affect in a material way the economy, a sector of the economy, productivity, competition, jobs, the environment, public health or safety, or State, local, or tribal governments or communities; (2) create a serious inconsistency or otherwise interfere with an action taken or planned by another agency; (3) materially alter the budgetary impact of entitlements, grants, user fees, or loan programs or the rights and obligations of recipients thereof; or (4) raise novel legal or policy issues arising out of legal mandates, the President's priorities, or the principles set forth in the Executive order." For more information on OIRA and its review process, see CRS Report RL32397, *Federal Rulemaking: The Role of the Office of Information and Regulatory Affairs*, by Curtis W. Copeland.

[47] Section 1(b)(6) of Executive Order 12866. As the executive order and OMB Circular A-4 make clear, even under this standard, the monetized benefits of a rule are not required to exceed the monetized costs of the rule before the agency can issue the rule, only that the costs of the rule be "justified" by the benefits (quantitative or non-quantitative).

[48] Section 6(a)(3)(C) of Executive Order 12866.

[49] Section 6(a)(3)(C)(iii) of Executive Order 12866.

[50] 44 U.S.C. 3508.

[51] 5 U.S.C. 553.

[52] 5 U.S.C. 553(b)(3(B). These requirements also do not apply to interpretative rules, general statements of policy, or rules of agency organization, procedure, or practice (5 U.S.C. 553(b)(A)).

[53] 5 U.S.C. 553(d).

[54] These rules were the FDIC's August 13, 2010, rule; the National Credit Union Administration's September 2, 2010, rule; the CFTC's October 14, 2010, rule; and the SEC's rules of September 8, September 21 (two rules), October 4, and October 20, 2010.

[55] This rule was the SEC's October 12, 2010, rule on "Delegation of Authority to the Director of the Division of Trading and Markets."

[56] This was the CFTC's September 10, 2010, rule on "Regulation of Off-Exchange Retail Foreign Exchange Transactions and Intermediaries." The January 20, 2010, proposed rule was issued in response to the CFTC Reauthorization Act of 2008 (CRA, P.L. 110-246). CFTC noted in the final rule that the Dodd-Frank Act dealt with some of the same issues, so the final rule was being issued pursuant to both the CRA and the Dodd-Frank Act.

[57] For more information on the RFA, see CRS Report RL34355, *The Regulatory Flexibility Act: Implementation Issues and Proposed Reforms*, by Curtis W. Copeland.

[58] Agencies' interpretations of these phrases are, however, subject to judicial review (5 U.S.C. 611).

[59] See 5 U.S.C. 603(a), which states that agencies must prepare initial regulatory flexibility analyses "whenever an agency is required...to publish a general notice of proposed rulemaking for any proposed rule." See also 5 U.S.C. 604(a), which requires agencies to prepare a final regulatory flexibility analysis when an agency publishes a final rule "after being required...to publish a general notice of proposed rulemaking."

[60] These were the FDIC rule of August 13, 2010; the National Credit Union Administration rule of September 2, 2010; the CFTC rule of September 10, 2010; and the SEC rule of October 20, 2010.

[61] These were the SEC's rules of September 21, 2010, (two rules) and October 4, 2010; and the CFTC rule of October 14, 2010.

[62] This was the SEC's October 12, 2010, rule on "Delegation of Authority to the Director of the Division of Trading and Markets."

[63] This was the SEC's September 8, 2010, final rule on "Temporary Registration of Municipal Advisors."

[64] As used in this report, the term "independent regulatory agencies" refers to the boards and commissions identified as such in the Paperwork Reduction Act (44 U.S.C. §3502(5)). Independent regulatory agencies are generally established to be more independent of presidential direction and control than Cabinet departments and other agencies. For more information, see Paul R. Verkuil, "The Purposes and Limits of Independent Agencies," *Duke Law Journal*, vol. 37 (1988), pp. 257-279.

[65] Certain planning requirements in Section 4(b) and Section 4(c) regarding the "unified regulatory agenda" and the "regulatory plan" apply to independent regulatory agencies. Generally, however, the executive order does not apply to independent regulatory agencies.

[66] Other sections of the Dodd-Frank Act require agencies to study certain issues, including the costs and benefits of certain actions. (See, for example, Section 929Y, a study on extraterritorial private rights of action.) However, those studies are not in the context of rulemaking.

[67] 44 U.S.C. 3507(f)(1).

[68] See, for example, U.S. General Accounting Office, *Unfunded Mandates: Analysis of Reform Act Coverage*, GAO-04-637, May 12, 2004.

[69] CRS Report RL34354, *Congressional Influence on Rulemaking and Regulation Through Appropriations Restrictions*, by Curtis W. Copeland.

[70] Others, however, take the view that even these non-appropriated funds must be at least figuratively deposited into the Treasury, and that "all spending in the name of the United States must be pursuant to legislative appropriation." Kate Stith, "Congress' Power of the Purse," *The Yale Law Journal*, vol. 97 (1988), p. 1345.

[71] See http://www.federalreserve.gov/generalinfo/faq/faqfrs.htm#6. Other sources of income are the interest on foreign currency investments held by the system; fees received for services provided to depository institutions, such as check clearing, funds transfers, and automated clearinghouse operations; and interest on loans to depository institutions (the rate on which is the so-called discount rate). After paying its expenses, the Federal Reserve turns the rest of its earnings over to the U.S. Treasury.

[72] Section 1017. However, if the director of the CFPB determines that these non-appropriated funds are insufficient, the Dodd-Frank Act authorizes appropriations of up to $200 million per year for FY2010 through FY2014. Appropriations restrictions could be added to any such appropriated funds.

[73] As noted in CRS Report R40801, *Financial Services and General Government (FSGG): FY2010 Appropriations*, coordinated by Garrett Hatch, the SEC's budget is set through the normal appropriations process, but funds for the agency come from fees that are imposed on sales of stock, new issues of stocks and bonds, corporate mergers, and other securities market transactions. When the fees are collected, they go to a special offsetting account available to appropriators, not to the Treasury's general fund. The SEC is required to adjust the fee rates periodically in order to make the amount collected approximately equal to target amounts set in statute.

[74] See U.S. General Accounting Office, *Principles of Appropriations Law, Third Edition, Volume I*, GAO-04-261SP, (January 2004), p. 2-34, which states that "Since an appropriation act is made for a particular fiscal year, the starting presumption is that everything contained in the act is effective only for the fiscal year covered. Thus, the rule is: A provision contained in an annual appropriation act is not to be construed to be permanent legislation unless the language used therein or the nature of the provision makes it clear that Congress intended it to be permanent."

[75] The Unified Agenda is available at http://www.reginfo.gov/public/do/eAgendaMain.

[76] CRS Report R40713, *The Unified Agenda: Implications for Rulemaking Transparency and Participation*, by Curtis W. Copeland.

[77] E-mail from Therese A. Taylor, Regulatory Information Service Center, General Services Administration, October 18, 2010.

[78] In *Sierra Club v. Costle* (657 F.2d 298, D.C. Cir. 1981), the D.C. Circuit concluded (at 409) that it was "entirely proper for congressional representatives vigorously to represent the interests of their constituents before administrative agencies engaged in informal, general policy rulemaking, so long as the individual Members of Congress do not frustrate the intent of Congress as a whole as expressed in statute, nor undermine applicable rules of procedure."

[79] Dominique Custos, "The Rulemaking Power of Independent Regulatory Agencies," *The American Journal of Comparative Law*, vol. 54 (Fall 2006), p. 633.

[80] A complete list of these GAO studies is available from the author of this report.

[81] See *GAO's Congressional Protocols*, available at http://www.gao.gov/new.items/d04310g.pdf.

[82] Joint statement of House and Senate Sponsors, 142 *Cong. Rec.* E571, at E571 (daily ed. April 19, 1996); 142 *Cong. Rec.* S3683, at S3683 (daily ed. April 18, 1996).

[83] If a rule is considered "major" (e.g., has a $100 million annual effect on the economy), then the CRA generally prohibits it from taking effect until 60 days after the date that it is submitted to Congress.

[84] For a detailed discussion of CRA procedures, see CRS Report RL31160, *Disapproval of Regulations by Congress: Procedure Under the Congressional Review Act*, by Richard S. Beth.

[85] For more on the potential scope of the definition of a "rule" under the CRA, see CRS Report RL30116, *Congressional Review of Agency Rulemaking: An Update and Assessment of The Congressional Review Act after a Decade*, by Morton Rosenberg.

[86] The rule overturned in March 2001 was the Occupational Safety and Health Administration's ergonomics standard. This reversal was the result of a unique set of circumstances in which the incoming President (George W. Bush) did not veto the resolution disapproving the outgoing President's (William J. Clinton's) rule. See CRS Report RL30116, *Congressional Review of Agency Rulemaking: An Update and Assessment of The Congressional Review Act after a Decade*, by Morton Rosenberg, for a description of several possible factors affecting the CRA's use, and for other effects that the act may have on agency rulemaking.

[87] See CRS Report RL30116, *Congressional Review of Agency Rulemaking: An Update and Assessment of The Congressional Review Act after a Decade*, by Morton Rosenberg, for a description of instances in which the filing of a resolution of disapproval had an effect on agencies' decisions.

In: The Dodd-Frank Wall Street Reform...
Editors: Nathan L. Morris and Philip O. Price

ISBN: 978-1-61324-101-1
© 2011 Nova Science Publishers, Inc.

Chapter 14

THE DODD-FRANK WALL STREET REFORM AND CONSUMER PROTECTION ACT CHANGES TO THE REGULATION OF DERIVATIVES AND THEIR IMPACT ON AGRIBUSINESS[*]

Michael K. Adjemian and Gerald E. Plato

ABSTRACT

The Dodd-Frank Wall Street Reform and Consumer Protection Act makes significant changes to Federal regulation of the U.S. over-the-counter (OTC) derivatives markets. With the goals of improving market transparency and reducing systemic default risk, the act calls for swaps to be centrally cleared and traded on an exchange or execution facility and for dealers and major participants that trade these derivatives to be subject to collateral requirements. Although the act exempts certain types of swaps and traders from these clearing, collateral, and trading venue requirements in order to preserve market efficiency, all swaps will be subject to new recordkeeping and reporting rules. In this article, we review some important features of the new law and discuss their potential impact on agribusiness, much of which will depend on how the rules are written and implemented by regulators.

ACKNOWLEDGMENTS

The authors received helpful comments from Erik Dohlman, Ron Durst, Andrew Morton, and Linwood Hoffman of USDA's Economic Research Service; Steve Neff, formerly of USDA's Farm Services Agency; Thomas Worth of USDA's Risk Management Agency; David Stallings of USDA's World Agricultural Outlook Board; and Eugene Kunda of the

---

[*] This is an edited, reformatted and augmented version of a Report from the Economic Research Services publication, dated November 2010.

Office for Futures and Options Research at the University of Illinois, Urbana-Champaign. Thanks also to Courtney Knauth and Susan DeGeorge for editorial and design assistance.

INTRODUCTION

A severe credit crunch in the United States in 2007 marked the beginning of a global financial crisis, which was symbolized by a series of surprising bank acquisitions and failures.[1] In spite of repeated efforts by the United States Federal Reserve Board and Federal Open Markets Committee to boost liquidity by lowering the primary credit rate and the Federal funds rate target, the American economy slid into a deep recession beginning in December 2007 (National Bureau of Economic Research, 2008). In 2008, Bear Stearns and Merrill Lynch, two investment banks in business for a century, collapsed and were bought out. In September of that year, the financial services firm Lehman Brothers, founded in 1850, filed for Chapter 11 bankruptcy protection. Because the Federal National Mortgage Corporation (Fannie Mae) and the Federal Home Loan Mortgage Corporation (Freddie Mac) were deeply involved in the home mortgage derivatives market, which lay at the heart of the financial crisis, the Federal Government took conservatorship of both, and it acquired an ownership stake in American International Group (AIG) to provide confidence to the financial system. In the agricultural sector, the credit squeeze, in combination with a concurrent price boom in commodities markets, may have contributed to difficulties for some established cotton merchants to finance *margin calls*,[2] forcing them into bankruptcy or mergers.

On July 21, 2010, President Obama signed the Dodd-Frank Wall Street Reform and Consumer Protection Act (2010) (hereafter referred to either as "the act" or "Dodd-Frank"), with the aim of confronting problems that precipitated the financial crisis. Among the provisions in the legislation, Congress mandated a tightening of financial market regulation, to improve transparency and reduce *systemic default risk* in the over-the-counter (OTC) derivatives trade. Such derivatives, which will be subject to enhanced regulation under the act, are a major component of the *hedging* activities of modern agribusiness. In this article, we review some important features of the new law and discuss their potential impact.

DERIVATIVES MARKETS

A derivative is a financial instrument whose value is based on the value of an underlying asset (Hull, 1993). In the United States, the history of deriva-tives is closely tied to agriculture. Initially established as a *cash market* in 1848, the Chicago Mercantile Exchange (CME) Group's Chicago Board of Trade (CBOT) recorded the earliest forward contract, for the future delivery of 3,000 bushels of corn, in 1851 (Chicago Board of Trade, 2006).[3] Forward contracts for wheat and other commodities soon followed. In 1864, the CBOT traded the first standardized "exchange-traded" forwards, which were called "*futures contracts*." Following the success of futures trading in agri-cultural markets, derivatives trading eventually expanded to minerals, metals, and, beginning in the 1970s, financial instruments.

Today, derivatives markets serve two essential economic functions for the global economy: *price discovery* and risk management.

Market participants trade derivatives for a variety of reasons. Commercial firms that deal in the underlying commodity use derivatives in hedging operations both as temporary substitutes for a cash transaction that will occur later and to manage price risk (Peck, 1985), effectively reducing the firms' exposure to shifts in the commodity price level.[4] *Speculators,* in contrast, attempt to benefit from the same price-level changes that *hedgers* avoid.[5] Through this profit-seeking behavior, speculators provide the market with essential liquidity, willingly taking the opposite side of contracts that hedgers may otherwise have difficulty establishing, making the market much more efficient. By determining a commodity price competitively, liquid exchange-traded derivatives markets instantaneously transmit fundamental economic information worldwide. In general, derivatives do not magnify or reduce risk, but spread it among the parties most willing to shoulder the variations in the price of the underlying asset (Hieronymus, 1977). For example, a derivatives market does not make grain production any more or less variable, but it does allow producers to insulate themselves from, say, a falling price of corn.[6]

Examples of derivatives contracts include *forwards, futures, options,* and *swaps,* summarized below. In each case, the contract is established between two willing parties, and the returns are zero-sum, before transaction costs. Gains for one side offset losses to the other.

- *Forward contracts* are agreements to exchange a specified asset for a certain price at a future date; they are typically made between private parties and, for commodities, generally result in *physical delivery.*
- *Futures contracts* are similar to forward contracts, except that their terms, such as quality and delivery location, are standardized to facilitate rapid trading on an exchange. Further, the terms of futures contracts specify whether they are cash settled or instead settled by physical delivery at contract expiration, although most are offset by an opposite position prior to expiration. Futures contracts also require that daily contract losses and gains from price changes be paid and received each day to guard against the risk that one of the firms that enters the contract will not perform its obligations (also known as counterparty default risk).
- *Options*—In contrast to futures and forward contracts, which carry the obligation to trade an asset for an agreed-upon price—an option represents the right to purchase or sell an instrument for a previously determined *strike price*. The buyer of a *put (call) option* has the right, but not the obligation, to sell (buy) the underlying asset at the strike price regardless of the asset's market price. To purchase this right, the buyer pays a premium to the writer of the option contract, who is responsible for satisfying the contract if it is exercised.
- *Swaps* are agreements to exchange assets, usually cash flows (Bailey, 2005). The most common, a "plain vanilla" swap, involves the exchange of a fixed interest payment for a variable one, with the difference to be paid in cash at contract *settlement*. A *commodity swap* is one in which the payout is based on the price of a commodity or the level of a commodity index.

Derivatives can be traded on a regulated, organized exchange or through a less formal dealer network. If search costs are not prohibitive, two willing parties can even write and trade derivatives without the aid of a dealer. Trades that are not executed on an organized exchange are said to occur in the over-the-counter (OTC) market. Swaps and hybrid *"swaptions,"* which are options on swap agreements, are the most common off-exchange derivatives (Lang, 2009).[7] As shown in figure 1, the *notional amount* of outstanding OTC derivatives is estimated to be about $615 trillion worldwide (Bank for International Settlements, 2010) (fig. 1), of which $300 trillion is in the United States alone (FCIC, 2010).[8] In comparison, the entire gross domestic product of the United States is less than $15 trillion (Bureau of Economic Analysis, 2010). Nonmetal commodity derivatives, including those for agricultural crops, amounted to almost $2.5 trillion in notional value last year (Bank for International Settlements, 2010).

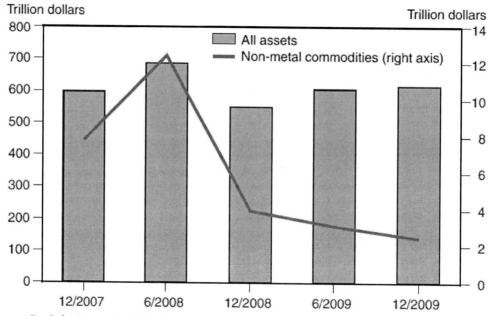

Source: Bank for International Settlements, 2010.

Figure 1. Size of the OTC derivatives market.

Once transacted by a buyer and seller, futures and options contracts must be registered with and processed by a *clearing member*, who assumes the default risk of the original parties, and cleared by a *clearing house* (a financial entity that splits the original contract, acting as buyer to all sellers and seller to all buyers) that stands between the counterparties until the contract is settled. The clearing house pools the risk that a clearing member will default on a contract among all its members and requires them to provide collateral in the form of a *margin* account, from which daily gains or losses are posted (clearing members, who are *Futures Commission Merchants*, in turn, collect margin from their nonmember customers, or from their own funds if they are trading on their own account). Daily gains and losses are calculated through a process known as *marking to market*, bringing trading *positions* in line with their current market value.[9]

The role of the clearing house is to remain adequately capitalized, so that it can cancel a contract in case a clearing member cannot meet its margin requirements and remunerate the counterparty, centralizing default risk. Because it concentrates the default risk of all counterparties, the stability of the clearing house is essential to a well-functioning clearing system. A stable clearing house that maintains adequate access to financial resources reduces the counterparty default risk faced by nonmember traders, and can ultimately lower systemic default risk by guaranteeing performance of member contracts (Squam Lake Working Group on Financial Regulation, 2009). Another advantage of the clearing house is that it monitors all trades, which increases market transparency, and nets[10] them so that credit exposure is reduced. Before the act, there was no legal requirement for clearing OTC swaps. The traders could, however, volunteer OTC derivatives contracts to firms with a clearing house function like CME or IntercontinentalExchange (ICE) for clearing, provided the firm agreed to assume the default risk responsibility.[11]

Clearing highly customized OTC derivatives is more time-consuming and expensive than for traditional, standardized exchange-traded derivatives. Moreover, the clearing system is not without its drawbacks, which are discussed in detail by Pirrong (2010). For example, clearing reduces the potential for counterparty defaults as well as the losses associated with those defaults, improving the allocation of default risk—but those benefits may lead to an expansion of trading and a greater level of risk-taking. This is referred to by economists as a *moral hazard*: even partial insulation from default risk makes a trader more likely to engage in riskier trading. Moral hazard can be limited by the clearing house by increasing margin or setting *position limits* (capping the number of contracts a member may hold), but these tools may result in a less efficient situation than existed in the original, bilateral OTC market. Another concern about the clearing process is that if it is fragmented through the establishment of multiple specialized clearing houses, the benefits of netting are reduced, while counterparty and systemic default risks are increased (Squam Lake Working Group on Financial Regulation, 2009).

OTC derivatives offer some unique advantages over exchange-traded instruments. To facilitate trading expediency, exchanges standardize futures and options contracts. OTC swaps, on the other hand are more flexible because they can be customized to meet the risk management desires of the individual traders. In the past, OTC swaps had lower margin requirements—and less frequent, if any, marking-to-market requirements—which may be more convenient for those who face constraints on their access to capital. Finally, parties to OTC derivatives have greater freedom to bargain contract terms, including collateral and price, based on the creditworthiness of the traders. In contrast, futures trades must be executed at the current market price. Although many swaps are priced with respect to a related futures contract, some do not have a corresponding exchange-traded counterpart and represent an entirely new market. *Swap dealers* bridge the OTC and exchange-traded markets, using futures contracts to manage the risks they incur by trading customized swaps (CFTC, 2008).

Derivatives in U.S. Agriculture

Many American agribusinesses use derivatives to manage the risks associated with their commercial interests. Millers and packers hedge against a rise in grain or livestock prices, since these are production inputs. Similarly, large grain and livestock producers, concerned that prices may fall before they can sell their output, hedge against commodity price decreases and rising fuel prices. Fertilizer, herbicide, biotechnology, and farm machinery firms use derivatives to shield their returns. For example, a tractor exporter can use currency instruments to hedge against an adverse change in exchange rates. Few small farmers use exchange-traded derivatives to hedge price risk because of the cost of trading, including the risk of margin calls and production uncertainty (Pannell et al., 2008), although some pool together into cooperatives to buy and sell futures and options. Many individual producers prefer to avoid margin calls and basis risk, contracting their production forward with grain elevators, processors, and packers, who in turn assume the price risk originally faced by producers.[12]

Derivatives for agricultural commodities tend to be uniquely designed around crop features. For example, five futures contracts for corn and five for wheat are traded on the CBOT each calendar year, expiring around planting time, during the growing season, and bracketing the harvest. Rather than being cash-settled, agricultural futures contracts generally specify physical settlement (delivery of the underlying commodity), directly tying together the cash and futures markets. Delivery points are selected based on the commodity flow, and contract specifications usually call for a specific grade of the product and method of delivery. Futures and options contracts for certain agricultural commodities are subject to CFTC-mandated limits for speculative positions. Traders who do not possess a *hedging exemption* are limited to a specified number of contracts, aggregated across futures and options, for each single contract month and all months combined. OTC *agricultural swaps* tend to be highly customized derivatives, with terms based on the commercial interests of the traders. For example, a soybean producer can enter into a swap agreement with a grain elevator operator, securing a fixed payment of $350 per metric ton to be paid at harvest. At expiration, the swap is settled by cash payment; the farmer will pay the elevator operator the difference if the agreed-upon benchmark price per ton of soybeans is more than $350, and if the price is lower, the operator will pay the farmer. In the end, each party realizes a price of $350 and is free to purchase or sell grain in the local *cash market*.

Important Dodd-Frank Reforms for Agribusiness

The financial reform act makes significant changes to the regulation of derivatives (table 1). We describe those changes below, as well as their potential effects on agribusiness. Throughout, we stress that much of the act's impact will depend on the implementation of the law in the form of regulatory rule-making. Because this article is concerned with agribusiness and its related commodities, the relevant regulator is the CFTC. The CFTC's rulemaking process is open to the public; like other agencies responsible for rulemaking prescribed in Dodd-Frank, CFTC includes public commentary in its draft and final rulemaking efforts. The process is further described in the box, "Federal Rulemaking Procedures." Successful regulation will strike the right balance between increasing transparency while protecting market participants against systemic default risk and maintaining the efficiency of OTC markets.

Regulation of Swaps

Before Dodd-Frank was passed, no formal regulatory structure or recording mechanism existed for swap derivatives. The act mandates that security-based swaps be regulated by the Securities and Exchange Commission (SEC). Most other swaps (which the law refers to as simply "swaps"—we use the same designation) fall under CFTC jurisdiction; swaps and security-based swaps are defined in the act.[13] CFTC and SEC are to cooperate to ensure regulatory consistency. Title VII of the act gives CFTC the responsibility of reviewing all groups, categories, types, or classes of swaps to determine whether they should be cleared. This review process can be initiated by the derivatives-clearing organization (DCO), or by CFTC itself. The act does not alter rules pertaining to other derivatives, i.e., forward contracts or exchange-traded futures and options. Various sections of the act stipulate that information regarding swap transactions be reported to CFTC after being recorded by a DCO, a board of trade, a swap execution facility, or a swap data repository, each of which must register with CFTC. In addition, the act calls for CFTC and SEC to conduct a study on international swap regulations, identifying similar areas of regulation, including those where U.S rules could be harmonized with those of other countries.

Federal Rulemaking Procedures

The Dodd-Frank Act expresses the intent of Congress concerning financial market regulation. Federal agencies tasked with implementing the act must draft specific rules and regulations according to the Administrative Procedures Act. Proposed rules and regulations must be posted in the Federal Register for public comment. After the public comment period, and after weighing the comments and congressional intent, the agencies involved draft final rules and regulations, which are also posted in the Federal Register. Final rules and regulations, which are subject to judicial and congressional review, often include input both from the public comments and from public meetings sponsored by the agencies involved.

Public participation in the rulemaking process has increased as the Internet has lowered search costs and made information easier to obtain; agency websites and the regulation.gov website are used to solicit public comments and to track the rulemaking activities (Reilly, 2010).

Rulemaking in support of Dodd-Frank can be followed on http://www.regulation. gov, including requests for comments, meeting notices, proposed rules, and final rules. The CFTC posts topics, attendees, and summaries of all meetings that its staff has with outside groups regarding implementation of the act, public comments, and updates to its rulemaking efforts on its website, at http://wwwcftc.gov/.

Table 1. Potenial impact of the Dodd-Frank derivatives regulation on agribusiness.

	Before Dodd-Frank	Dodd-Frank legislation	Potential benefits	Potential costs
Regulation of swaps	Very little regulatory authority.	CFTC is responsible for all (non-security-based) swaps and will determine which swaps must be cleared. Cleared swaps will trade on a contract market or swap facility.[1] Regardless of the clearing requirement, all swaps must be reported.	The law brings oversight and transparency to an unregulated market. Establishing CFTC as the single regulator central-izes rulemaking.	If highly customized deriva-tives are forced to clear, OTC trades may be hampered. Reporting and recordkeeping increases transparency, although it may be more expensive for certain swaps.
Clearing and collateral requirements	Clearing and margin were mandatory for exchange-traded derivatives, but were not required in the OTC markets.	Margin accounts must be created for cleared swaps, but will not be required for end users who exercise a clearing exemption. How-ever, their counterparties are often swap dealers and major swap participants, who will still need to post collateral.	Clearing and margin requirements increase market transparency, reduce counterparty risk, provide for collateral to cover losses, and ulti-mately may help lower systemic default risk.	Clearing requirements may be inefficient, and can increase systemic risk if not well-de-signed. Overly strict clearing and/or collateral requirements may make certain OTC deriva-tives less attractive for swap dealers and other counterpar-ties to traditional hedgers, reducing market liquidity.

	Before Dodd-Frank	Dodd-Frank legislation	Potential benefits	Potential costs
Position limits	CFTC set position limits for non-hedgers of exchange-traded ag. commodities, but no limits existed for OTC derivatives. Certain nontraditional financial traders were granted hedging exemptions.	CFTC is responsible for setting aggregate position limits across derivative types (including OTC) for the same commodity. Position limits are still exempted for bona fide hedgers.	Position limits are intended to prevent market concentration, manipulation, and "excessive speculation," although empirical evidence of their benefits is sparse.	Limiting the ability of the largest speculators to trade derivatives can decrease liquidity, making trading—and risk management efforts—more expensive.
Hedging exemptions	Part 1 of the CFTC regulations defined a bona fide hedge. CFTC granted hedging exemptions to some nontraditional financial traders in agricultural markets.	The Commodity Exchange Act is amended to add a similar definition.	CFTC may be less likely to give hedge exemptions to nontraditional financial traders, enforcing a more narrowly defined bona fide hedge.	Combined with position limits, more stringent rules for hedge exemptions could force large financials overseas and/or into domestic commodity cash markets.
Agricultural swaps	Agricultural swaps were allowed between "eligible swap participants," as defined by Part 35 of the CFTC regulations. There was no clearing or margin requirement for these swaps.	Agricultural swaps can be made only by eligible contract participants, or as otherwise expressly permitted by CFTC rules. All other trade in such swaps is banned.	Continuing to limit agricultural swaps to eligible contract participants guarantees that the market is available only to "informed" traders.	Constraining the agricultural swaps market limits risk management options of participants who do not meet trading threshholds.

[1] Unless a hedging exemption is excercised, or no transaction facility will accept the swap for clearing.

Making CFTC the swap regulator centralizes rulemaking and brings oversight to what was essentially an unregulated market. Although OTC derivatives serve an important risk management role, amounting to trillions of dollars in value, until now regulators had no authority to monitor the market and set or alter trading rules. The comprehensive reporting and recordkeeping requirements are intended to enhance market transparency, providing CFTC a real-time surveillance of trends in the swap market. The law further requires CFTC to provide reports on transaction and pricing data for OTC derivatives, keeping the general public informed about market developments, as is currently the case for other derivatives like futures and options. The act authorizes the CFTC to decide the timing and manner in which the swap transactions data are made available to the public, with the intention of enhancing price discovery.

Although the law sets guidelines, CFTC is responsible for rulemaking that will establish regulatory oversight and directly affect the efficiency of the swap markets. The benefits of improved market transparency must be weighed against the possibility that burdensome new trading rules could reduce the attractiveness of OTC derivatives and limit their usefulness for hedging. Real-time public reporting of cleared swap transactions may increase the competitiveness and efficiency of swap markets, but could increase costs for dealers, who may choose to pass those costs on to end- users (Ackerman, 2010). Conversely, a long delay in the publication of swaps transactions will produce only modest gains in market transparency. In the short term, until the practice becomes routine, recordkeeping for customized derivatives may be more expensive than for standardized transactions made on an exchange. One goal of the review process for new OTC derivatives will be to avoid slowing innovation in and development of new risk management products.

Clearing and Collateral Requirements

OTC markets did not have mandatory clearing or margin rules for swaps before passage of the act. Now, once CFTC determines which types of swaps must clear, these must be cleared through a derivatives-clearing organization—if one is available—that stands between the counterparties and guarantees trades. The DCO must establish capital and margin requirements for swaps it clears, such as marking them to market at least once per day, to protect its own financial integrity and the integrity of the transactions it clears in case a large participant defaults.

As nonfinancial firms with a bona fide commercial hedging interest in the underlying asset, end users may be exempted from the new mandatory clearing requirements. To gain this exemption, they must demonstrate to CFTC how they meet financial obligations associated with trading uncleared swaps, although they can volunteer a swap for clearing at the DCO of their choosing. An example of an agribusiness end-user could be a producer that uses interest rate swaps to hedge against financial risks it encounters in the course of its normal commercial business.[14]

A swap can also go uncleared if no derivatives-clearing organization chooses to clear it. When trading uncleared swaps, swap dealers and other major swap participants must meet minimum capital and margin requirements set by CFTC; the act specifies that these participants are to register with the regulator within a year of enactment. When trading cleared swaps, swap dealers and other major swap participants are to follow the capital and margin guidelines set by the derivatives-clearing organization.

Clearing and margin requirements can act as safeguards for the performance of the OTC derivatives markets. Ideally, clearing eliminates counterparty credit risk between the original traders. As a result, market participants may be more confident in their ability to manage risk, which, in turn, should improve market liquidity and lower transaction costs. Moreover, requiring margin accounts to be sufficient to cover potential losses could reduce systemic default risk. Given adequate collateral requirements, a default by one trader is less likely to lead to a domino effect of cascading, market-wide defaults on derivative contracts.

The clearing process has some drawbacks, however. It may be that clearing did not develop organically in the OTC market for many swaps because of informational problems that make clearing less efficient than bilateral execution for these types of derivatives (Pirrong, 2010). Moreover, forcing swaps to clear could actually increase systemic default risk. According to Duffie et al. (2010), the clearing house should maintain adequate financial resources to cover a broader set of risks than just a default by its largest participant, such as the ability to offset potential losses equal to the market's largest historical price swing. If it cannot cover its losses, the likelihood of which may be heightened by moral hazard or the difficulty of clearing highly customized derivatives, a clearing house poses a risk to the financial system overall.

Provided they meet the definition of an end user, agribusinesses and other nonfinancial firms that use swaps to hedge commercial risks are exempt from clearing and margin requirements (Dodd and Lincoln, 2010). Swap dealers and other major swap participants, who often take the other side of these OTC trades, will, however, need to post collateral before trading uncleared swaps with exempted parties. At the option of the end user, that collateral will be segregated with an independent third party. If the margin requirements are too stringent, swap dealers and major swap participants may find certain highly customized derivatives—like agricultural swaps—less attractive. In that case, reduced market liquidity would increase transaction costs for agribusinesses engaged in customized swap trading.

Position Limits and Hedging Exemptions

Among agricultural commodities, CFTC previously set position limits only for derivatives traded on an exchange. Title VII of the act authorizes CFTC to set aggregate position limits across derivatives that are based on the same underlying commodity. This regulation includes swaps that perform a significant price discovery function, as defined in the law. Bona fide hedgers are exempt from these limits if they can demonstrate a commercial interest to CFTC. The act revises the Commodity Exchange Act to include the existing definition of a bona fide hedger in CFTC regulations. CFTC is also charged with conducting a study on the impact of position limits on "excessive speculation" and the movement of transactions from domestic to international markets.

Limits on the size of trading positions are intended to prevent market concentration, manipulation, and "excessive speculation." By establishing position limits, the CFTC attempts to cap the net positions for traders who do not have a direct commercial interest in the underlying commodity. Speculators reduce transaction costs to hedgers by boosting trading volume, spreading the fixed costs of market operation across many more trades. A derivatives market composed only of hedgers would make risk management much more expensive (Working, 1970). Although tight position limits can be effective at preventing market manipulation (Kyle, 1984), they can also constrict the ability of the largest speculators to trade derivatives, decreasing market liquidity. Empirical evidence of the effect of position limits is thin, but Irwin et al. (2007) conclude that price volatility in CBOT corn, soybeans, and wheat did not measurably increase after speculative limits on these contracts were relaxed in 2005.

Market liquidity may also be decreased if Congress intends for CFTC to apply the hedging exemption more scrupulously. Since the late 1980s, the exemption has been interpreted to apply to nontraditional financial firms, like swap dealers and commodity index fund traders. For example, swap dealers have been able to obtain an exemption from position limits for futures markets in order to manage the risks they incurred in the OTC markets, and index funds have obtained an exemption if they tracked an index of commodity prices. Under new rules, tighter hedge exemptions, combined with position limits, could drive index funds into cash markets (Irwin and Sanders, 2010) or into overseas derivatives markets. The spirit of position limits could be indirectly circumvented if tighter hedging exemptions were to cause large financial traders to split into numerous smaller funds, leaving the total speculative position in place, but losing economies of scale and increasing trading costs to fund participants.

Agricultural Swaps

Before Dodd-Frank's passage, agricultural swaps were permitted for trading between eligible swap participants under Part 35 of CFTC regulations, which was adopted pursuant to section 4(c) of the Commodity Exchange Act (CEA). The Part 35 provision allows the CFTC to exempt transactions from the exchange-trading requirement or other provisions of the CEA. Title VII of Dodd-Frank expressly bans all transactions in agricultural swaps, unless they are pursuant to an exemption under CEA section 4(c). In addition, a swap execution facility must follow to-be-determined rules before it can list an agricultural swap for trading. Under Dodd-Frank, swap transactions are limited to *eligible contract participants* (ECPs)—that is, to large investors, like a commodity pool, an insurance company, or an individual with over $10 million in assets. The ECP category most likely to apply to agricultural producers includes a corporation, partnership, proprietorship, organization, trust, or other entity that has a net worth exceeding $1 million and is hedging. Ongoing trade in agricultural commodity swaps under current Part 35 is grandfathered under the act, although future CFTC revisions to Part 35 will presumably affect regulation of these swaps (Heitman, 2010). Currently, trade in agricultural swaps is permitted only to relatively informed traders with access to capital. Market participants who do not meet these eligibility requirements are unable to engage in agricultural swaps for investment or risk management, but may still engage in forward contracts for commercial purposes.

CONCLUSIONS

The Dodd-Frank Wall Street Reform and Consumer Protection Act makes important regulatory changes that will affect the operation and efficiency of OTC derivatives markets, which serve as an important hedging forum for modern agribusiness. Although the act provides a general guide to the derivative reforms, much of the impact on agribusiness will become known only after the rules are written and implemented by the regulators. There are clearly benefits to improving market transparency and attempting to reduce the likelihood of systemic default. The goal for the regulating agencies will be to balance those benefits against the potential costs associated with mandating clearing, establishing capital and margin requirements, limiting contract positions, and instituting standards for reporting and recordkeeping in the OTC markets.

REFERENCES

Ackerman, A. "CFTC, SEC Roundtable Considers Lags for Reporting Big Swaps Trades." *The Bond Buyer*, September 15, 2010.

Bailey, R. E. *The Economics of Financial Markets.* Cambridge, MA: Cambridge University Press, 2005.

Bank for International Settlements. "Semiannual OTC derivatives statistics at end-December 2009," on 7/12/2010. Web Address: http://www.bis.org/ statistics/derstats.htm. 2010.

Bureau of Economic Analysis. *Gross Domestic Product: First Quarter 2010 (Third Estimate).* U.S. Department of Commerce, Washington, DC, 2010.

Carter, C. A., and J. P. Janzen. *The 2008 Cotton Price Spike and Extraordinary Hedging Costs.* ARE Update 13, no. 2. University of California at Berkeley: Giannini Foundation of Agricultural Economics, 2009.

Commodity Futures Trading Commission (CFTC). *Commodity Swap Dealers & Index Traders with Commission Recommendations.* CFTC Staff Report. Washington, DC, September 2008.

Commodity Futures Trading Commission (CFTC). *Staff Report on Cotton Futures and Options Market Activity During the Week of March 3, 2008.* CFTC Staff Report. Washington, DC, 2010.

Chicago Board of Trade. *Handbook of Futures and Options.* New York: McGraw-Hill, 2006.

Dodd, C., and B. Lincoln. Letter from the Chairmen of the Senate Financial Services and Agriculture Committees to the Chairmen of the House Financial Services and Agriculture Committees, 6/30/2010.

Dodd-Frank Wall Street Reform and Consumer Protection Act. *Public Law No. 111-203.* 111th United States Congress, 2010.

Duffie, D., A. Li, and T. Lubke. *Policy Perspectives on OTC Derivatives Market Infrastructure.* Federal Reserve Bank of New York Staff Reports, 2010.

FCIC. "Testimony of CFTC Chairman Gary Gensler Before the Financial Crisis Inquiry Commission," 7/1/2010 Hearing, www.fcic.gov.

Harwood, J., R. Heifner, K. Coble, J. Perry, and A. Somwaru. *Managing Risk in Farming: Concepts, Research and Analysis.* USDA, Economic Research Service, Agricultural

Economics Report No. 774. Washington, DC, 1999, http://www.ers.usda.gov/Publications/AER774/.

Heitman, D. "Agriculture and the Dodd-Frank Bill," a presentation before the CFTC Agricultural Advisory Committee, City Futures Trading Commission, 8/5/2010, Washington, DC.

Hieronymus, T. A. *Economics of Futures Trading for Commercial and Personal Profit, 2nd ed.* New York, NY: Commodity Research Bureau, 1977.

Hull, J. C. *Options, Futures, and Other Derivative Securities.* Upper Saddle River, New Jersey: Prentice Hall, 1993.

Irwin, S. H., P. Garcia, and D. L. Good. "The Performance of Chicago Board of Trade Corn, Soybean, and Wheat Futures Contracts after Recent Changes in Speculative Limits." Presentation at American Agricultural Economics Association Annual Meeting, July 29-31, 2007, Portland, OR.

Irwin, S. H., and D. R. Sanders. *The Impacts of Index and Swap Funds in Commodity Futures Markets.* Organization for Economic Co-Operation and Development Technical Report. Washington, DC, 2010.

Kyle, A. S. "A Theory of Futures Market Manipulations," in *The Industrial Organization of Futures Markets*, ed. R. W. Anderson. Lexington, MA: D.C. Heath, 1984.

Lang, I. "Financial Derivatives: Pricing and Risk Management," in the *Robert W. Kolb Series*, ed. R. W. Kolb and J. A. Overdahl. Hoboken, NJ: John Wiley & Sons Inc., 2009.

MacDonald, J. M., and P. Korb. *Agricultural Contracting Update.* USDA, Economic Research Service, Economic Information Bulletin No. 35, 2005, http://www.ers.usda.gov/publications/eib35/.

Morrison, J. "The Operational Challenges of OTC Clearing," *Futures Industry Magazine*, June 2010:27-30.

National Bureau of Economic Research. *Determination of the December 2007 Peak in Economic Activity.* Cambridge, MA, 2008.

Pannell, D. J., G. Hailu, S. Weersink, and A. Burt. "More Reasons Why Farmers Have so Little Interest in Futures Markets," *Agricultural Economics* 39(1):41-60, 2008.

Peck, A. E. "The Economic Role of Traditional Commodity Futures Markets," in *Futures Markets: Their Economic Role*, ed. A. E. Peck. Washington, DC: American Enterprise Institute for Public Policy Research, pp. 1-81, 1985.

Pirrong, C. *The Inefficiency of Clearing Mandates.* Cato Policy Analysis No. 665. Washington, DC: The Cato Institute, 2010.

Reilly, S. "Future of rule making: Pilot project aims to increase public participation," *FederalTimes.com*, August 23, 2010.

Squam Lake Working Group on Financial Regulation. "Credit Default Swaps, Clearing houses, and Exchanges." Working paper, Council on Foreign Relations, Center for Geoeconomic Studies, 2009.Working, H. "Economic Functions of Futures Markets," in *Futures Trading in Livestock: Origins and Concepts*, ed. H. Bakken. Madison, WI: Chicago Mercantile Exchange, 1970.

GLOSSARY

Abbreviations

CBOT	Chicago Board of Trade
CEA	Commodity Exchange Act
CFTC	Commodity Futures Trading Commission CME – Chicago Mercantile Exchange.
DCO	Derivatives Clearing Organization ECP – Eligible contract participant
ICE	IntercontinentalExchange
OTC	Over-the counter
SEC	Securities and Exchange Commission

Glossary[1]

Agricultural swap—A commodity swap in which the payout to at least one counterparty is based on the price of an agricultural commodity or the level of an agricultural commodity index.*

Basis—The difference between the spot or cash price of a commodity and the price of the nearest futures contract for the same or a related commodity (typically calculated as cash minus futures). Basis is usually computed in relation to the futures contract due to expire next and may reflect different time periods, product forms, grades, or locations.

Basis risk —The risk associated with an unexpected widening or narrowing of the basis between the time a hedge position is established and the time that it is lifted.

Cash settlement—A method of settling futures options and other derivatives whereby the seller (or *short*) pays the buyer (or *long*) the cash value of the underlying commodity or a cash amount based on the level of an index or price according to a procedure specified in the contract. Also called financial settlement.

Call option —An *option* contract that gives the buyer the right, but not the obligation, to purchase a commodity or other asset or to enter into a long derivatives position at a specified price on or prior to a specified expiration date

Cash market—The market for the cash commodity (as contrasted to a derivatives contract) taking the form of: (1) an organized, self-regulated central market (e.g., a commodity exchange); (2) a decentralized over-the-counter market; or (3) a local organization, such as a grain elevator or meat processor, that provides a market for a small region.

Clearing house—An entity through which futures and other derivative transactions are cleared and settled. It is also charged with assuring the proper conduct of each contract's delivery procedures and the adequate financing of trading. A clearing house may be a division of a particular exchange, an adjunct or affiliate thereof, or a freestanding entity. Also called a clearing organization, multilateral clearing organization, centralized counterparty, or clearing association.

Clearing member—A member of a clearing organization. All trades of a non-clearing member must be processed and eventually settled through a clearing member.

Commodity Index—An index of a specified set of (physical) commodity prices or commodity futures prices.

Commodity Index fund—An investment fund that enters into futures or commodity swap positions for the purpose of replicating the return of an index of commodity prices or commodity futures prices.

Commodity swap—A swap in which the payout to at least one counterparty is based on the price of a commodity or the level of a commodity index.

Derivative—A financial instrument, traded on or off an exchange, the price of which is directly dependent upon (i.e., "derived from") the value of one or more underlying securities, equity indices, debt instruments, commodities, other derivative instruments, or any agreed-upon pricing index or arrangement.

Efficient market —In economic theory, an efficient market is one in which market prices adjust rapidly to reflect new information.

Eligible Contract Participant—An entity, such as a financial institution, insurance company, or commodity pool, that is classified by the Commodity Exchange Act as an eligible contract participant based upon its regulated status or amount of assets. This classification permits these persons to engage in transactions not generally available to non-eligible contract participants.

Forward contract—A cash transaction common in many industries, including commodity merchandising, in which a commercial buyer and seller agree upon delivery of a specified quality and quantity of goods at a specified future date. Terms may be more "personalized" than is the case with standardized futures contracts (i.e., delivery time and amount are as determined between seller and buyer). A price may be agreed upon in advance, or there may be agreement that the price will be determined at the time of delivery.

Futures Commission Merchant—Individuals, associations, partnerships, corporations, and trusts that solicit or accept orders for the purchase or sale of any commodity for future delivery on or subject to the rules of any exchange and that accept payment from or extend credit to those whose orders are accepted.

Futures contract—An agreement to purchase or sell a commodity for delivery in the future (1) at a price that is determined at initiation of the contract; (2) that obligates each party to the contract to fulfill the contract at the specified price; (3) that is used to assume or shift price risk; and (4) that may be satisfied by delivery or offset.

Hedger—A trader who participates in hedging.

Hedging—The act of entering into positions in a derivatives market, opposite to positions held in a cash market, to minimize the risk of financial loss from an adverse price change, or the act of purchasing or selling derivatives as a temporary substitute for a cash transaction that will occur later. Cash market positions, whether *long* or *short,* can be hedged.

Hedging exemption—An exemption from speculative position limits for bona fide hedgers and certain other persons who meet the requirements of exchange and regulator rules.

Long—The buying side of an open futures contract, a market position that obligates the holder to take delivery of the underlying asset.

Margin—The amount of money or collateral deposited by a customer with his broker, by a nonmember broker with a *clearing member*, or by a clearing member with a clearing organization. The margin is not partial payment on a purchase. There are two main kinds

Changes to the Regulation of Derivatives and Their Impact on Agribusiness 333

of margins: (1) Initial margin is the amount of margin required by the broker when a futures position is opened; (2) Maintenance margin is an amount that must be maintained on deposit at all times. If the equity in a customer's account drops to or below the level of maintenance margin because of adverse price movement, the broker must issue a *margin call* to restore the customer's equity to the maintenance level. Exchanges specify levels of initial margin and maintenance margin for each futures contract, but futures commission merchants may require their customers to post margin at higher levels than those specified by the exchange.

Margin call—(1) A request from a *futures commission merchant* to a customer to bring margin deposits up to maintenance levels; (2) a request by the clearing organization to a *clearing member* to make a deposit of original margin, or a daily or intra-day variation margin payment because of adverse price movement, based on *positions* carried by the clearing member.

Marking to market—Part of the daily cash flow system used by an exchange to maintain a minimum level of margin equity for a given derivatives contract *position.* The level is determined by calculating the gain or loss in each contract position resulting from changes in the price of the derivatives contracts at the end of each trading session. These amounts are added or subtracted to each account balance.

Moral hazard—The possibility that insulation from risk will affect agent behavior.*

Net position—The difference between the open *long* contracts and the open *short* contracts held by a trader in any one commodity.

Notional amount—The notional amount outstanding is a snapshot of the face value of the underlying asset upon which the derivative is based.*

Option—A contract that gives the buyer the right, but not the obligation, to buy or sell a specified quantity of a commodity or other instrument at a specific price within a specified period of time, regardless of the market price of that instrument. Also see *call option* and *put option.*

Over-the-Counter (OTC)—The trading of commodities, contracts, or other instruments not listed on any exchange. OTC transactions can occur electronically or over the telephone. Also referred to as Off-Exchange.

Physical delivery—A provision in a futures contract or other derivative for delivery of the actual commodity to satisfy the contract.

Position—An interest in the market, either *long* or *short,* in the form of one or more open contracts.

Position limit—The maximum *position*, either net *long* or net *short*, in one commodity future (or option) or in all futures (or options) of one commodity combined that may be held or controlled by one person (other than a person eligible for a *hedge exemption*), as prescribed by an exchange and/or by the market regulator.

Price discovery —The process of determining the price level for a commodity based on supply and demand conditions. Price discovery may occur in a derivatives market or cash market.

Put option—An *option* contract that gives the holder the right but not the obligation to sell a specified quantity of a particular commodity, security, or other asset or to enter into a *short* derivatives position at a given price (the *strike price*) prior to or on a specified expiration date.

Settlement—The act of fulfilling the delivery requirements of a derivatives contract.

Short—The selling side of an open futures contract.

Speculator—In commodity derivatives, a trader who does not hedge, but who trades with the objective of achieving profits through the successful anticipation of price movements.

Strike price—The price, specified in the option contract, at which the underlying futures contract, security, or commodity will move from seller to buyer when the option is exercised.

Swap—In general, the exchange of one asset or liability for a similar asset or liability for the purpose of lengthening or shortening maturities, or otherwise shifting risks. This may entail selling one securities issue and buying another in foreign currency; it may entail buying a currency on the spot market and simultaneously selling it forward. Swaps also may involve exchanging income flows; for example, exchanging the fixed rate coupon stream of a bond for a variable rate payment stream, or vice versa, while not swapping the principal component of the bond. Swaps are generally traded *over-the-counter*.

Swap dealer—An entity such as a bank or investment bank that markets swaps to end users. Swap dealers often hedge their swap positions in futures markets. Alternatively, an entity that declares itself a "Swap/Derivatives Dealer" on CFTC Form 40.

Swaption—An option to enter into a swap—i.e., the right, but not the obligation, to enter into a specified type of swap at a specified future date.

Systemic default risk—The risk that a default by one market participant will have repercussions on other participants due to the interlocking nature of financial markets. For example, customer A's default in X market may affect intermediary B's ability to fulfill its obligations in markets X, Y, and Z.

End Notes

[1] See the Federal Reserve Bank of St. Louis website for a thorough timeline of the financial crisis.

[2] The Commodity Futures Trading Commission (CFTC, 2010) makes this point in a staff report on the March 2008 cotton price spike, although other factors covered in the report and by Carter and Janzen (2009) may be more directly tied to observed defaults; Note: *Margin calls* and other italicized terms are defined in the Glossary at the end ot the report.

[3] Modern CBOT corn contracts are traded in 5,000-bushel units.

[4] Hedging is done to manage risks rather than to avoid them. Even if fully hedged, a commercial firm is exposed to basis risk, from which it seeks to profit. *Basis risk* is the unanticipated change in the difference between cash and derivative prices. To avoid risk entirely, the firm would operate only in the cash market as it established forward contracts for its output.

[5] Many traders cannot easily be classified as either hedgers or speculators, but blend features of both and operate on a continuum between the two categories.

[6] There is no free lunch, though. Whether in the form of an option premium or an opportunity cost, derivatives are not costless.

[7] Throughout the text, the terms "swaps" and "OTC derivatives" are used interchangeably, since swaps are such a prominent component of the OTC market. Title VII of the act includes swaptions in its definition of swaps.

[8] The notional amount outstanding is the face value, in dollars, of the underlying asset upon which the derivative is based. The value of funds at risk is a considerably smaller figure.

[9] Marking to market is sometimes done more frequently than once per day.

[10] Netting is the process of calculating a trader's actual position in a commodity. For example, a net position in corn futures equals the number of long minus short contracts. Margin requirements are based on the net position.

[11] See Morrison (2010) for an overview of existing OTC clearing houses and the types of derivatives in which they currently specialize or are planning to implement.

[12] Harwood et al. (1999) describe the tools and strategies that farmers use to manage risk. MacDonald and Korb (2005) provide results of a related USDA survey.

[13] Dodd-Frank defines "mixed swaps" as a third class of transactions that share features of both swaps and security-based swaps. SEC and CFTC share regulatory and rulemaking authority over these swaps.

[14] Because specific rules have yet to be written, this is only a potential example.

[15] Unless otherwise noted with an asterisk (*), these definitions are drawn from the CFTC glossary, which can be found on the web at http://www.cftc. gov/ConsumerProtection/EducationCenter/CFTCGlossary/index.htm

CHAPTER SOURCES

Chapter 1 - This This is an edited, reformatted and augmented version of a Congressional Research Services publication, R41350, dated July 29, 2010.

Chapter 3 - This is an edited, reformatted and augmented version of a Congressional Research Services publication, R41384, dated August 27, 2010.

Chapter 4 - This is an edited, reformatted and augmented version of a Congressional Research Services publication, R41339, dated July 23, 2010.

Chapter 5 - This is an edited, reformatted and augmented version of a Congressional Research Services publication, R40783, dated July 16, 2010.

Chapter 6 - This is an edited, reformatted and augmented version of a Congressional Research Services publication, R41380, dated August 25, 2010.

Chapter 7 - This is an edited, reformatted and augmented version of a Congressional Research Services publication, R41398, dated August 30, 2010.

Chapter 8 - This is an edited, reformatted and augmented version of a Congressional Research Services publication, R41529, dated December 10, 2010.

Chapter 9 - This is an edited, reformatted and augmented version of a Congressional Research Services publication, R41503, dated November 24, 2010.

Chapter 10 - This is an edited, reformatted and augmented version of a Congressional Research Services publication, R41319, dated November 9, 2010.

Chapter 11 - This is an edited, reformatted and augmented version of a Congressional Research Services publication, R41338, dated July 21, 2010.

Chapter 12 - This is an edited, reformatted and augmented version of a Congressional Research Services publication, R41381, dated August 19, 2010.

Chapter 13 - This is an edited, reformatted and augmented version of a Congressional Research Services publication, R41472, dated November 3, 2010.

Chapter 14 - This is an edited, reformatted and augmented version of a Report from the Economic Research Services publication, AIS-89, dated November 2010.

INDEX

A

abuse, 141, 296, 299

access, 15, 17, 19, 20, 24, 31, 32, 33, 41, 42, 45, 49, 63, 68, 85, 88, 101, 139, 142, 145, 146, 151, 156, 179, 192, 199, 213, 216, 218, 261, 298, 323, 330

accommodations, 167

accountability, vii, 16, 23, 24, 66, 188, 201

accounting, 16, 17, 19, 31, 52, 59, 96, 194, 199, 200, 201, 207, 246, 306

accounting standards, 31, 52, 199

acquisitions, x, 47, 66, 72, 73, 81, 84, 320

adjustment, 309

Administrative Procedure Act (APA), 98, 105, 106, 108, 113, 128, 217, 218, 224, 238, 246, 254, 255, 313, 314

administrators, 196

adverse effects, 7, 27, 54, 57

advocacy, 108

age, 214

agency actions, 239

agricultural market, 327

agricultural producers, 330

agricultural sector, x, 320

agriculture, 60, 135, 320

alters, 27, 69

American Stock Exchange, 155

amortization, 13

analytical framework, 169

antitrust, 84

appraisals, 102

appropriations, 17, 59, 94, 95, 105, 108, 130, 184, 202, 214, 238, 257, 258, 260, 317

arbitrage, 10, 32, 66

arbitration, 123, 187, 196, 222, 228, 308

armed groups, 35

assessment, 10, 20, 33, 69, 70, 90, 101, 105, 114, 121, 188, 195, 196, 254, 262, 264, 265, 278, 291

assets, vii, viii, 1, 3, 7, 8, 9, 10, 11, 18, 19, 20, 24, 27, 30, 33, 40, 41, 42, 45, 46, 47, 52, 53, 54, 56, 60, 62, 69, 72, 73, 76, 77, 79, 81, 82, 90, 91, 128, 135, 141, 144, 145, 146, 148, 149, 158, 190, 191, 192, 193, 194, 206, 213, 216, 235, 242, 252, 262, 뱀264, 266, 268, 276, 288, 291, 294, 321, 330, 334

audit, 6, 17, 27, 59, 60, 140, 160, 189, 199, 246, 306

audits, 184

authenticity, 160

authorities, x, 11, 32, 59, 83, 94, 95, 97, 98, 101, 102, 106, 110, 111, 114, 117, 122, 124, 128, 129, 151, 153, 160, 169, 197, 212, 213, 214, 215, 217, 222, 237, 240, 243, 278, 290, 302, 307, 310

Automobile, 217

automobiles, 217

avoidance, 290

awareness, 220

B

background information, 179

bail, 23, 145

balance sheet, 5, 8, 13, 42, 56, 62, 76, 145, 191, 288, 289

bank charter, 70

bank debt, 45

bank failure, 62, 63, 200

Bank Secrecy Act, 160

banking, 6, 8, 10, 11, 12, 17, 19, 20, 21, 22, 25, 29, 31, 37, 40, 44, 45, 49, 56, 57, 58, 60, 65, 66, 67, 69, 71, 72, 74, 75, 76, 77, 78, 79, 80, 81, 82, 84, 94, 103, 109, 110, 111, 117, 140, 145, 152, 153, 159, 160, 161, 162, 164, 165, 167, 169, 175, 178, 181, 182, 191, 192, 194,

201, 211, 212, 219, 223, 224, 240, 242, 243,
244, 265, 266, 276, 281, 291, 293
banking industry, 60, 66
banking sector, 19
bankruptcies, 6
bankruptcy, x, 3, 6, 7, 27, 42, 47, 54, 56, 137,
151, 206, 320
banks, vii, 1, 4, 8, 9, 10, 11, 19, 20, 22, 23, 24,
25, 26, 27, 28, 32, 35, 38, 40, 44, 45, 46, 47,
48, 49, 57, 59, 60, 61, 62, 66, 67, 69, 71, 73,
74, 75, 83, 84, 94, 143, 145, 147, 155, 156,
161, 162, 174, 175, 176, 181, 191, 210, 211,
212, 213, 216, 220, 221, 222, 224, 241, 265
base, 3, 10, 20, 69, 264
Belgium, 157, 178, 181
beneficiaries, 86, 87
benefits, 18, 24, 68, 103, 105, 107, 123, 130, 179,
186, 194, 219, 220, 254, 256, 308, 316, 317,
323, 326, 327, 328, 331
bias, 187, 243
biotechnology, 324
blame, 188, 212
blind spot, 44
board members, 18, 198
bonding, 122, 307
bonds, 15, 22, 135, 149, 155, 157, 162, 183, 188,
190, 317
bonuses, 29, 193
borrowers, 6, 8, 9, 13, 14, 29, 44, 56, 60, 62, 115,
223, 279
branching, 67, 75, 84
breakdown, 5, 41, 43, 61, 152
business ethics, 230
business model, 140
businesses, vii, 8, 9, 23, 24, 25, 29, 70, 84, 135,
188, 192, 211
buyer, 3, 155, 159, 321, 322, 333, 334, 335, 336
buyers, 8, 40, 42, 43, 151, 191, 322

C

Cabinet, 257, 317
caliber, 197
candidates, 19, 184, 197
capital markets, 197
cash, 55, 133, 135, 139, 153, 163, 173, 177, 179,
188, 320, 321, 324, 327, 330, 333, 334, 335,
336
cash flow, 321, 335
central bank, 3, 45, 156, 160, 162, 169, 172
certification, 80, 195, 274
Chamber of Commerce, 129, 239, 314
chaos, 137
charities, 218

Chicago, 157, 314, 315, 320, 331, 332, 333
Chicago Mercantile Exchange, 157, 320, 332,
333
circulation, 153, 234
City, 332
clarity, 253
classes, 2, 9, 39, 103, 147, 185, 191, 263, 325
classification, 334
clients, 17, 18, 78, 86, 87, 88, 89, 90, 91, 184,
187, 230, 234, 235, 259, 291, 303
coercion, 102
collaboration, 115
collateral, 3, 14, 45, 59, 60, 119, 136, 137, 160,
163, 166, 173, 285, 319, 322, 323, 326, 329,
334
collective bargaining, 123, 308
commerce, 60, 229, 234, 235
commercial, 5, 9, 15, 32, 34, 40, 42, 46, 56, 57,
61, 62, 65, 71, 82, 83, 84, 95, 134, 140, 141,
143, 149, 151, 154, 155, 162, 172, 175, 177,
189, 192, 211, 217, 286, 290, 295, 299, 324,
328, 329, 330, 334, 336
commercial bank, 5, 9, 15, 46, 62
commodity, 14, 22, 55, 76, 84, 90, 134, 135, 140,
146, 148, 164, 165, 198, 243, 271, 290, 295,
321, 322, 324, 327, 329, 330, 333, 334, 335,
336
commodity futures, 14, 165, 334
communication, 195, 242
communities, 20, 24, 32, 130, 316
community, 20, 39, 144
compensation, ix, 2, 7, 14, 17, 18, 19, 24, 31, 54,
87, 89, 183, 184, 186, 189, 192, 193, 194,
196, 205, 206, 207, 208, 229, 233, 234, 238,
253, 264, 277, 278, 303, 305
compensation package, 206
competition, 10, 13, 44, 130, 139, 219, 316
competitiveness, 52, 328
complexity, 8, 25, 26, 191
compliance, 10, 11, 30, 59, 66, 72, 74, 75, 80, 99,
106, 124, 137, 140, 159, 167, 170, 185, 189,
196, 197, 201, 212, 213, 232, 249, 255, 259,
277, 282, 283, 293, 296, 297, 299, 300, 301,
310
composition, 198
computer, 159
conference, ix, 1, 2, 145, 186, 205, 206, 209, 210,
231
confidentiality, 90, 187, 199
conflict, 11, 15, 35, 77, 81, 168, 189, 212, 220,
234, 235, 244, 266, 286
conflict of interest, 15, 77, 81, 189, 235, 266
Congo, 35

consensus, 245

consent, 59, 67, 95, 109, 190, 213, 233, 234, 235, 253, 277, 302, 305

consolidation, 10, 72, 159, 206, 228

constituents, 112, 131, 259, 317

Constitution, 220, 224

constitutional law, 220

construction, 80, 87, 135, 240

consulting, 167, 243, 244, 252, 261, 292

consumer advocates, 223, 313

consumer choice, 13

consumer education, 214

consumer protection, viii, ix, 2, 10, 11, 12, 20, 24, 58, 66, 93, 94, 95, 96, 103, 104, 110, 111, 115, 118, 209, 210, 211, 212, 213, 214, 216, 220, 221, 224, 238, 279, 284

consumers, 4, 8, 9, 11, 12, 13, 23, 24, 29, 33, 60, 77, 94, 98, 99, 101, 102, 103, 114, 116, 120, 122, 123, 186, 192, 212, 213, 215, 216, 217, 218, 219, 220, 221, 259, 278, 279, 280, 282, 307, 308, 311, 312, 313

consumption, 4

controversial, ix, 143, 183, 184, 187

cooperation, 68, 196

cooperative agreements, 311

coordination, 52, 66, 67, 150, 151, 163, 168, 169, 262

corporate governance, 19, 205

correlation, 158

cost, 6, 11, 14, 20, 26, 27, 29, 32, 41, 42, 46, 60, 62, 73, 94, 105, 107, 108, 143, 187, 201, 213, 254, 256, 280, 324, 336

cost saving, 187

cost-benefit analysis, 94, 105, 254

cotton, x, 320, 336

counsel, 193, 206

counseling, 14, 29, 283, 312

Court of Appeals, viii, 85, 87

covering, 240, 241

cracks, 25

credit market, 134

credit rating, 2, 8, 15, 16, 24, 30, 31, 137, 183, 184, 189, 190, 191, 251, 253, 275, 276, 305

Credit Rating Agency Reform Act, 22, 189

credit squeeze, x, 320

creditors, viii, 6, 7, 27, 40, 41, 42, 47, 54, 118, 133, 284, 289

creditworthiness, 4, 15, 135, 136, 323

creep, 40

crises, 3, 5, 38, 40, 158, 212

criticism, 43, 146, 231

crop, 324

crops, 322

CRS report, 258

cure, 50, 207

currency, 149, 154, 177, 253, 309, 317, 324, 336

customers, 16, 33, 68, 78, 79, 135, 139, 155, 158, 172, 175, 178, 179, 185, 186, 187, 188, 200, 227, 229, 232, 233, 234, 267, 272, 296, 302, 303, 322, 335

D

damages, iv, 7, 29, 54, 189, 229, 290

danger, 7, 53, 54, 71, 81

data center, 161

data collection, 28, 100, 123, 308

debts, 124, 310

deduction, 79

defects, 207

deficiencies, 193, 201

deficiency, 201

delinquency, 13

Democratic Republic of Congo, 21, 35

Department of Education, 115

deposit accounts, 167

depository institutions, vii, 2, 5, 7, 10, 11, 15, 19, 44, 45, 48, 53, 56, 57, 65, 66, 67, 69, 71, 73, 74, 81, 84, 103, 141, 144, 145, 155, 156, 161, 167, 172, 173, 179, 200, 208, 211, 212, 213, 215, 216, 220, 223, 249, 282, 317

deposits, 6, 32, 40, 41, 42, 46, 48, 53, 55, 62, 69, 71, 81, 84, 133, 222, 288, 304, 335

depression, 230

depth, 21

derivatives, viii, x, 2, 3, 4, 14, 24, 28, 38, 39, 41, 43, 44, 55, 56, 133, 134, 135, 137, 138, 139, 140, 141, 142, 143, 145, 146, 147, 149, 150, 151, 152, 153, 154, 155, 157, 159, 160, 161, 162, 163, 164, 165, 169, 170, 182, 198, 199, 238, 252, 268, 270, 296, 297, 314, 319, 320, 321, 322, 323, 324, 325, 326, 327, 328, 329, 330, 331, 333, 334, 335, 336

destruction, 39

detection, 101, 114, 278

direct action, 57, 72

directors, 6, 19, 27, 28, 31, 54, 60, 82, 122, 184, 189, 193, 195, 197, 206, 207, 252, 264, 277, 278, 305, 306, 307

disability, 70

disbursement, 172

disclosure, 2, 6, 16, 17, 19, 34, 38, 60, 88, 99, 102, 117, 129, 185, 190, 192, 207, 219, 222, 223, 230, 234, 235, 252, 274, 281, 312

discrimination, 60

disequilibrium, 44

disposition, 78, 80, 87, 206

342 Index

distortions, 40
distress, 3, 52, 57
distribution, 56, 134, 246, 264
District of Columbia, 87
diversification, 39
diversity, 29, 70, 184
divestiture, 77, 252
donations, 218
draft, 99, 110, 182, 324, 325

E

earnings, 59, 95, 108, 167, 190, 193, 214, 257, 317
economic downturn, 205
economic fundamentals, 44, 146
economic growth, 71
economic theory, 50, 334
economics, 41
economies of scale, 330
education, 30, 115
educational materials, 200
election, 305
electronic systems, 140
eligibility criteria, 83
e-mail, 247
emergency, 2, 5, 6, 27, 28, 38, 45, 46, 47, 56, 57, 59, 62, 140, 167, 251, 282
Emergency Economic Stabilization Act, 57
emergency rule, 140
employees, viii, 19, 30, 59, 65, 68, 84, 114, 129, 189, 193, 194, 195, 196, 198, 200, 207, 213, 249, 279, 282
employment, 29, 49, 70
end-users, 56, 134, 141, 143, 178
energy, 135, 146
energy prices, 135
enforcement, viii, 5, 10, 11, 12, 24, 32, 55, 58, 60, 66, 68, 73, 74, 76, 82, 83, 93, 95, 101, 110, 117, 122, 125, 128, 150, 167, 168, 182, 187, 188, 193, 195, 197, 210, 211, 213, 214, 215, 216, 217, 218, 222, 228, 233, 257, 258, 304, 307, 311, 313
engineering, 18, 135
environment, 44, 130, 316
Environmental Protection Agency, 108
Equal Credit Opportunity Act, 98, 100, 115, 116, 123, 128, 214, 279, 280, 281, 308
equipment, 201
equities, 145, 155, 157, 162, 176
equity, 5, 10, 15, 17, 18, 26, 29, 38, 42, 54, 56, 57, 66, 67, 69, 76, 77, 79, 144, 157, 185, 206, 207, 266, 268, 277, 287, 334, 335
ergonomics, 131, 318

ethical standards, 230
European Central Bank, 61
evidence, 47, 50, 220, 221, 327, 330
examinations, 58, 72, 73, 90, 128, 167, 183, 195, 196, 197, 211, 212, 213, 216, 232
exchange rate, 324
exclusion, 164, 232
execution, 55, 56, 84, 134, 139, 140, 164, 166, 220, 229, 252, 268, 271, 272, 298, 300, 319, 325, 329, 330
executive branch, 40, 94, 95, 110
Executive Order, 94, 105, 106, 110, 112, 130, 238, 254, 256, 316
exercise, 21, 35, 98, 101, 107, 114, 122, 129, 167, 168, 169, 221, 234, 256, 263, 278, 307, 308, 326
expenditures, 78
expertise, 25, 30, 50, 51, 86, 109, 139, 196, 197, 199, 245
exporter, 324
exposure, 4, 5, 32, 41, 44, 46, 53, 55, 74, 75, 76, 77, 90, 134, 165, 245, 287, 288, 321, 323
extraction, 21, 286

F

facilitators, 102, 116, 280
fairness, 195, 199
faith, 110, 111, 230, 234, 235, 283
families, 20, 24, 214, 223
farmers, 324, 337
FDI, 75, 76
fear, 38, 45
fears, 39, 46
federal agency, 55, 90, 157, 165, 170, 190, 215, 239
federal assistance, 15, 145
federal funds, 162, 172
Federal funds, x, 154, 320
federal government, 110, 153, 155, 173, 180, 220
Federal Government, x, 286, 320
federal law, 10, 15, 24, 51, 57, 72, 210, 211, 220, 221
Federal Register, 95, 103, 105, 106, 110, 113, 129, 130, 182, 238, 246, 253, 254, 255, 314, 315, 316, 325
federal regulations, 206
Federal Reserve Board, x, 7, 25, 28, 54, 58, 60, 62, 94, 161, 165, 166, 320
Federal Trade Commission Act, 128, 129, 217
financial condition, vii, 1, 40, 53, 81, 87, 134
financial crisis, vii, viii, ix, x, 4, 6, 13, 18, 19, 23, 27, 37, 38, 39, 48, 50, 59, 66, 85, 94, 133,

134, 135, 149, 159, 163, 183, 184, 188, 193, 198, 209, 210, 238, 320, 336
financial data, 11, 25, 58, 212, 215
financial distress, 75, 263, 287
financial incentives, 29
financial innovation, 13, 45, 50, 134
financial institutions, ix, 2, 4, 6, 7, 11, 19, 20, 24, 26, 31, 39, 45, 46, 47, 54, 56, 61, 94, 95, 123, 125, 134, 136, 143, 144, 145, 149, 150, 152, 153, 154, 155, 158, 159, 160, 163, 164, 165, 166, 167, 169, 170, 171, 175, 176, 178, 179, 182, 183, 194, 205, 211, 212, 223, 245, 250, 278, 302, 308, 310
financial intermediaries, 62, 151, 159, 178
financial markets, 2, 3, 4, 18, 38, 44, 49, 151, 157, 158, 161, 166, 167, 336
financial oversight, 201
financial performance, 19, 194, 207
financial planning, 186
financial regulation, vii, 2
financial resources, 9, 28, 170, 323, 329
financial sector, 8, 42, 44, 146, 159, 201, 238, 239
Financial Services Authority, 150, 162
financial shocks, 11, 212
financial stability, 7, 8, 13, 25, 26, 27, 28, 38, 51, 52, 53, 54, 57, 72, 77, 78, 79, 80, 133, 163, 166, 167, 168, 245, 261, 266, 293
financial system, vii, viii, x, 1, 2, 3, 4, 7, 12, 13, 23, 25, 26, 29, 37, 38, 39, 41, 44, 46, 49, 50, 51, 53, 56, 58, 61, 80, 84, 85, 94, 109, 110, 111, 134, 143, 145, 149, 150, 151, 157, 158, 160, 161, 163, 165, 166, 167, 168, 182, 219, 267, 271, 320, 329
fixed costs, 329
fixed rate, 336
flexibility, 74, 106, 108, 130, 142, 184, 202, 255, 256, 316
flight, 43
force, 183, 201, 248, 285, 314, 327
foreclosure, 12, 13, 24, 29, 34, 100, 101, 125, 215, 311
foreign banks, 94, 174, 175, 211
foreign exchange, 48, 55, 135, 144, 151, 154, 157, 162, 164, 177, 295
foreign firms, 55
formation, 156
formula, 10
fragility, 1
France, 181
fraud, 24, 43, 183, 187, 188, 195, 227, 229, 230, 235
freedom, 323

freezing, 134, 191
fuel prices, 324
funding, 7, 8, 16, 17, 54, 57, 68, 107, 163, 180, 196, 197, 199, 210, 211, 257

G

GATS, 63
General Accounting Office (GAO), 2, 6, 27, 28, 33, 59, 60, 62, 71, 112, 113, 130, 186, 195, 196, 198, 201, 259, 260, 317
Germany, 181
Glass-Steagall Act, 63
global economy, 321
globalization, 159
goods and services, 153
governance, 28, 60, 184, 196, 197, 291
government intervention, 38
government securities, 145, 155, 156, 157, 257, 290
grades, 15, 333
grading, 15
Gramm-Leach-Bliley Act, 49, 62, 63, 98, 125, 214, 234, 245, 310, 311
grant programs, 311
grants, 34, 102, 130, 138, 200, 245, 311, 316
Great Depression, vii, ix, 3, 4, 23, 94, 209, 210, 238
Great Recession, 212
gross domestic product, 21, 322
Gross Domestic Product, 35, 331
groupthink, 44
growth, 5, 26, 31, 50, 135, 239
GSA, 62, 63
guidance, 12, 19, 58, 78, 98, 100, 113, 120, 123, 143, 158, 182, 213, 218, 260, 307, 308
guidelines, 48, 97, 117, 126, 161, 194, 278, 281, 313, 328, 329
guilty, 235

H

harmonization, 233
health, 43, 130, 243
health care, 130, 243
hedging, 9, 55, 78, 81, 135, 143, 145, 320, 321, 324, 327, 328, 330, 331, 334
herbicide, 324
high school, 70
higher education, 115
hiring, 33, 197
history, 87, 230, 235, 320
holding company, 10, 32, 43, 46, 48, 49, 52, 53, 54, 57, 58, 60, 61, 68, 71, 72, 73, 75, 76, 81,

82, 83, 120, 148, 194, 208, 234, 245, 250, 252, 262, 263, 267, 268, 287, 288, 289, 292, 293, 294

home ownership, 34

homeowners, 13, 34

homes, 4, 12, 217

honesty, 234

House, ix, 1, 2, 3, 21, 59, 66, 68, 80, 84, 95, 96, 103, 108, 110, 131, 138, 140, 143, 147, 148, 152, 154, 157, 163, 174, 175, 179, 181, 182, 186, 205, 206, 209, 210, 214, 222, 225, 228, 231, 232, 239, 257, 259, 318, 331

House of Representatives, ix, 96, 103, 148, 152, 163, 209, 210, 239

housing, vii, 4, 8, 13, 14, 15, 23, 29, 44, 47, 50, 135, 188

Housing and Urban Development, 9, 24, 117, 128, 213, 244, 276, 281, 283

HUD, 9, 29, 34, 191, 201

hybrid, 322

I

identification, 20, 286

identity, 60, 97, 223

illiquid asset, 6, 45, 77

image, 55, 133

imbalances, 49

income, 9, 12, 13, 21, 32, 34, 35, 202, 217, 257, 317, 336

income tax, 12, 217

independence, 10, 31, 58, 102, 126, 193, 206, 213, 247, 251, 285, 313

Independence, 23, 206

individuals, 18, 20, 24, 160, 185, 186, 187, 197, 199, 211, 214, 223, 247, 252, 278, 298, 306

industries, 334

industry, 18, 32, 39, 40, 46, 49, 60, 86, 151, 160, 184, 186, 187, 196, 198, 223, 228, 230, 231, 313

inefficiency, 59, 95, 213

inflation, 45, 188, 222

information sharing, 52, 313

informed consent, 234

infrastructure, viii, 39, 139, 149, 150, 151, 152, 153, 156, 157, 158, 160, 161, 162, 163, 170

initiation, 334

injure, 230

inspections, 195, 197

inspectors, 201

institutions, 3, 6, 7, 9, 10, 11, 12, 15, 18, 22, 29, 38, 41, 42, 43, 45, 46, 47, 48, 52, 53, 54, 56, 57, 58, 59, 65, 67, 68, 69, 71, 78, 81, 84, 94, 115, 128, 136, 141, 145, 147, 148, 149, 151,

152, 154, 155, 156, 158, 160, 161, 164, 167, 168, 172, 173, 174, 175, 177, 179, 190, 192, 194, 211, 212, 213, 216, 223, 249, 282, 317

insulation, 323, 335

integrity, 16, 17, 30, 59, 136, 142, 185, 188, 328

interest groups, 257

interest rates, 13, 14, 42, 44, 49, 50, 135, 145, 156

interface, 154

intermediaries, 140, 154, 164, 198

internal controls, 6, 59, 201, 274

internal processes, 159

Internal Revenue Service, 187

International Monetary Fund (IMF), 21, 35, 41, 61, 158, 180, 182

international standards, 161, 166, 273

intervention, 21, 51, 61, 133

investment, vii, ix, x, 1, 2, 4, 16, 17, 18, 19, 22, 26, 29, 30, 31, 33, 40, 42, 43, 44, 46, 47, 55, 61, 65, 71, 75, 76, 77, 78, 79, 80, 83, 84, 86, 87, 88, 89, 90, 91, 145, 148, 164, 184, 185, 186, 189, 190, 194, 196, 198, 201, 202, 206, 208, 227, 228, 229, 230, 231, 232, 233, 234, 235, 242, 259, 265, 268, 291, 295, 296, 300, 302, 303, 304, 320, 330, 334, 336

investment bank, vii, x, 1, 42, 43, 44, 46, 47, 61, 75, 320, 336

investments, 5, 21, 26, 55, 67, 72, 76, 78, 79, 80, 82, 88, 89, 185, 229, 231, 293, 296, 300, 317

investors, ix, 2, 4, 8, 9, 15, 16, 17, 18, 23, 24, 30, 31, 33, 40, 42, 44, 46, 79, 81, 86, 87, 88, 90, 91, 151, 155, 180, 184, 185, 186, 187, 188, 189, 190, 191, 192, 193, 197, 198, 199, 202, 227, 228, 229, 233, 234, 246, 252, 265, 275, 278, 291, 292, 294, 300, 301, 303, 304, 305, 306, 313, 330

isolation, 41

issues, vii, ix, 2, 17, 20, 38, 45, 47, 49, 51, 58, 66, 71, 94, 108, 162, 183, 184, 185, 186, 209, 210, 219, 220, 222, 227, 228, 234, 242, 243, 245, 246, 247, 266, 316, 317

Italy, 181

J

Japan, 181

jurisdiction, 5, 12, 59, 60, 68, 125, 138, 141, 161, 165, 213, 215, 217, 219, 220, 242, 245, 260, 261, 310, 325

L

landscape, 238

law enforcement, 187

law suits, 68

laws, ix, 10, 11, 12, 19, 20, 58, 59, 66, 72, 79, 84, 86, 88, 93, 94, 95, 98, 104, 120, 128, 129, 159, 165, 179, 183, 185, 199, 210, 211, 212, 213, 214, 215, 216, 218, 219, 220, 221, 224, 230, 241, 303, 304, 307

laws and regulations, 11, 20, 199, 213, 214, 216, 224

lawyers, 25

lead, 10, 19, 38, 39, 41, 44, 49, 50, 58, 62, 73, 129, 156, 158, 159, 194, 208, 242, 314, 323, 329

legislation, vii, ix, 1, 2, 4, 6, 11, 14, 19, 20, 38, 55, 57, 58, 60, 66, 68, 76, 82, 83, 84, 94, 96, 97, 104, 105, 110, 113, 117, 130, 140, 144, 145, 146, 163, 184, 186, 187, 197, 205, 206, 220, 228, 231, 238, 243, 245, 249, 251, 253, 258, 260, 317, 320, 326, 327

legislative authority, 110

lender of last resort, 152, 161

lending, 3, 5, 6, 8, 13, 27, 28, 32, 38, 45, 46, 47, 56, 59, 60, 67, 71, 74, 75, 119, 126, 151, 179, 188, 223, 224, 247, 251, 259, 282, 285, 313

light, 11, 45, 88, 123, 152, 195, 246, 253, 292, 308

limited liability, 6, 178

liquidate, 23, 27, 40

liquidity, x, 3, 4, 5, 8, 16, 18, 25, 26, 37, 40, 41, 43, 44, 45, 46, 47, 50, 53, 56, 57, 76, 77, 81, 135, 138, 145, 149, 158, 159, 163, 165, 199, 320, 321, 326, 327, 329, 330

literacy, 214

litigation, 188, 248

livestock, 324

loans, 6, 8, 9, 12, 13, 14, 20, 21, 27, 29, 33, 34, 35, 40, 42, 47, 59, 60, 62, 66, 71, 74, 75, 80, 83, 84, 100, 101, 102, 115, 117, 118, 125, 145, 151, 154, 172, 191, 192, 193, 215, 223, 279, 282, 283, 284, 301, 311, 312, 317

local government, 29, 199

loyalty, 233, 235

M

machinery, 324

majority, 18, 27, 28, 34, 55, 103, 107, 115, 155, 157, 167, 184, 198, 211, 220, 239, 256, 257, 279, 302

malfeasance, 59, 95, 213

man, 327

management, 7, 18, 26, 27, 31, 33, 54, 70, 90, 102, 119, 160, 166, 184, 195, 196, 197, 201, 206, 234, 235, 267, 271, 285, 291

manipulation, 24, 139, 146, 329

manufactured goods, 141

manufacturing, 35, 65, 82, 83

market capitalization, 201

market concentration, 327, 329

market discipline, 48, 189

market position, 142, 334

market segment, 41

market structure, 137

marketing, 16, 186, 200, 275

marketplace, 17, 135, 136, 188

Maryland, 220

materials, 19, 21, 35, 72, 186, 190, 197, 201, 207, 253, 306

matrix, 27

matter, iv, 58, 213, 222, 305

meat, 333

media, viii, 85, 86

median, 194, 207

membership, 17, 162, 182, 197, 306

merchandise, 141

mergers, x, 53, 66, 73, 317, 320

messages, 160, 178

metals, 145, 320

methodology, 189

military, 214

minorities, 32

mission, 40, 51, 105

models, 119, 135, 188, 189, 275, 285

modifications, 38, 57

monetary policy, 10, 37, 49, 50, 59, 152, 156, 161

money laundering, 84

money supply, 156

moral hazard, 38, 41, 42, 45, 47, 51, 323, 329

moratorium, 10, 71

mortgage-backed securities, 8, 15, 33, 137, 154, 162, 175, 191

motivation, 195

N

national origin, 60

natural gas, 34, 286

negative effects, 13, 25

neglect, 59, 95, 213

Netherlands, 178, 181

New York Stock Exchange, 18, 155, 228

nominee, 197, 305

O

Obama, ix, 3, 11, 38, 91, 158, 160, 163, 209, 210, 212, 222

346   Index

Obama Administration, ix, 3, 11, 38, 91, 158,
160, 163, 209, 210, 212, 222
Office of Management and Budget, 94, 128, 129,
202, 254
officials, 50, 248
oil, 34, 286
omission, 227, 229
Omnibus Appropriations Act,, 98, 100, 125, 215,
311
opacity, 4, 14
open market operations, 6, 45, 59, 60, 156, 173,
257
operational independence, 259
operations, 11, 26, 48, 49, 56, 59, 67, 94, 134,
145, 150, 157, 161, 166, 167, 169, 188, 197,
211, 212, 220, 273, 317, 321
opportunities, 247
organ, 79
organize, 79, 80, 191
overlap, 17, 153, 234
oversight, 2, 5, 9, 16, 20, 24, 38, 51, 94, 109, 112,
151, 152, 160, 161, 162, 163, 164, 168, 169,
170, 186, 196, 197, 199, 232, 238, 243, 259,
260, 267, 271, 326, 328
ownership, x, 55, 76, 77, 79, 80, 84, 154, 223,
304, 320

P

parallel, 72, 138, 142
participants, 2, 4, 14, 15, 22, 28, 39, 42, 43, 47,
50, 56, 57, 59, 85, 86, 115, 134, 137, 139,
140, 143, 145, 147, 151, 157, 158, 160, 163,
172, 173, 174, 175, 176, 179, 180, 191, 269,
270, 271, 273, 296, 297, 298, 301, 313, 319,
321, 325, 326, 327, 328, 329, 330, 334, 336
payroll, 149, 153, 174, 175
peer review, 201
penalties, 13, 14, 29, 214, 275
Pension Benefit Guaranty Corporation, 201
permit, viii, x, 16, 70, 75, 79, 80, 93, 96, 97, 99,
100, 102, 104, 110, 111, 117, 124, 139, 189,
192, 193, 194, 237, 239, 242, 246, 247, 249,
258, 283, 286, 293, 310
platform, 136, 139
Plato, vi, 319
policy, 3, 4, 6, 10, 11, 18, 19, 20, 28, 47, 48, 49,
50, 51, 60, 63, 85, 97, 113, 126, 130, 131,
157, 161, 162, 180, 181, 182, 202, 207, 212,
260, 313, 316, 317
policy issues, 130, 316
policy options, 4, 6, 47
policymakers, vii, 6, 10, 14, 37, 42, 44, 47
political parties, 257

pollution, 258
pools, 22, 135, 187, 322
portability, 126, 313
portfolio, 55, 82, 87, 177, 200, 235, 312
portfolio investment, 55
positive externalities, 41
potential benefits, 98, 107, 218, 256
precedent, 220
preparation, iv, 116, 280
preservation, 34
President, ix, 1, 7, 24, 27, 28, 48, 51, 54, 57, 59,
60, 67, 85, 91, 95, 105, 109, 110, 113, 130,
131, 181, 205, 206, 209, 210, 213, 231, 254,
260, 316, 318, 320
President Obama, 1, 85, 209, 210, 320
prevention, 34, 223
price changes, 321
price manipulation, 146
primary function, 49, 53
principles, 130, 139, 161, 221, 316
private education, 115, 214, 279
probability, 191
producers, 321, 324
professionals, 39, 184, 185, 199, 228, 231
profit, 11, 106, 193, 212, 230, 255, 304, 321, 336
profitability, 232
project, 332
proposed regulations, 170
proprietary trading activities, 5
protection, ix, x, 10, 11, 20, 38, 43, 58, 59, 84,
91, 93, 94, 95, 103, 110, 128, 151, 183, 184,
187, 196, 197, 200, 202, 211, 212, 213, 214,
220, 221, 223, 232, 233, 234, 246, 265, 275,
291, 292, 294, 300, 301, 302, 303, 304, 305,
306, 313, 320
prudential regulation, vii, 2, 47, 65, 66, 143
Public Company Accounting Oversight Board,
199, 246, 306
public debt, 21, 35
public health, 130, 316
public interest, 34, 74, 90, 91, 99, 106, 118, 141,
187, 189, 192, 233, 234, 246, 255, 265, 275,
284, 288, 291, 292, 293, 294, 295, 296, 298,
300, 301, 302, 303, 304, 305, 306, 312, 313,
314
public resources, 6
publishing, 100, 106, 108, 109

Q

quality control, 119, 285

Index

R

race, 44, 60
rating agencies, 2, 15, 16, 188, 190
real estate, vii, 1, 11, 12, 58, 62, 101, 154, 172, 212, 215, 217, 224, 313
real time, 155, 156
reality, 238
reasoning, 110, 221
recession, x, 4, 320
recognition, 230
recommendations, iv, 16, 25, 26, 28, 49, 52, 55, 77, 80, 81, 100, 108, 109, 152, 162, 185, 199, 200, 229, 231, 232, 242, 267, 273
recovery, 101, 125, 311
recruiting, 70
recurrence, 3
reform, vii, ix, 1, 2, 3, 4, 14, 20, 21, 38, 39, 51, 61, 65, 85, 88, 96, 130, 137, 152, 163, 182, 188, 197, 205, 206, 209, 210, 228, 231, 238, 324
Reform, 1, iii, v, vi, vii, viii, ix, 1, 2, 3, 16, 21, 22, 23, 29, 33, 37, 38, 51, 61, 63, 65, 66, 91, 93, 94, 96, 105, 107, 119, 128, 129, 130, 133, 146, 147, 150, 163, 179, 180, 181, 182, 183, 184, 197, 202, 205, 206, 209, 210, 215, 222, 227, 228, 229, 231, 237, 238, 246, 254, 257, 285, 313, 314, 315, 316, 317, 319, 320, 331
reforms, ix, 2, 20, 32, 85, 133, 136, 158, 209, 210, 223, 242, 243, 331
regional integration, 159
regulatory agencies, 5, 16, 29, 51, 67, 76, 85, 88, 94, 106, 107, 108, 110, 112, 128, 130, 161, 238, 242, 244, 248, 252, 256, 257, 259, 260, 261, 263, 274, 317
regulatory bodies, 199
regulatory changes, 52, 331
regulatory framework, 66, 71, 149, 150, 152, 163, 164, 170
regulatory oversight, viii, 19, 28, 93, 94, 96, 106, 109, 152, 163, 165, 256, 328
regulatory requirements, 152, 232
regulatory systems, 46
rehabilitation, 78
reinsurance, 20, 32
reliability, 17, 191
relief, 12, 101, 215
remediation, 53, 263
repair, 217
repo, 41, 43, 149, 160, 163, 173
Republic of the Congo, 286
reputation, 159

resale, 187
reserves, 41, 69, 220
resilience, 161
resolution, 2, 6, 7, 20, 21, 38, 51, 52, 53, 54, 57, 62, 63, 103, 112, 113, 115, 131, 193, 220, 260, 279, 287, 290, 318
resources, 16, 30, 33, 84, 139, 140, 184, 188, 199, 232
response, 3, 57, 59, 60, 86, 122, 195, 273, 308, 316
restitution, 7, 54
restrictions, vii, 2, 14, 19, 26, 67, 72, 73, 75, 77, 78, 80, 82, 94, 108, 112, 130, 187, 189, 217, 238, 257, 258, 260, 289, 294, 302, 317
restructuring, 147, 197
retail, 2, 17, 20, 71, 151, 152, 153, 154, 162, 179, 185, 231, 232, 233, 253, 302, 303
retail deposit, 71
retained earnings, 79
retaliation, 114, 279
retirement, 4, 68
revenue, 158
rewards, 33
risk management, 6, 25, 26, 53, 55, 57, 61, 73, 76, 159, 161, 163, 164, 166, 168, 169, 170, 171, 192, 266, 273, 288, 302, 321, 323, 327, 328, 330
risk profile, 288
risks, 2, 3, 8, 12, 14, 18, 25, 26, 28, 39, 42, 43, 47, 48, 51, 56, 57, 72, 78, 80, 81, 99, 101, 114, 123, 134, 135, 152, 157, 158, 159, 160, 161, 162, 166, 167, 180, 182, 193, 194, 202, 215, 219, 235, 238, 240, 245, 262, 266, 278, 308, 323, 324, 328, 329, 330, 램336
risk-taking, 28, 39, 50, 323
root, 49
roots, 4
rural areas, 98, 218

S

safety, 3, 5, 9, 10, 11, 12, 19, 21, 25, 37, 38, 46, 47, 49, 52, 56, 58, 67, 75, 76, 77, 78, 79, 80, 84, 94, 103, 109, 111, 118, 130, 145, 158, 162, 208, 212, 219, 220, 266, 284, 293, 316
sanctions, 159, 187
Sarbanes-Oxley Act, 17, 22, 195, 201, 203, 253
savings, vii, viii, 3, 4, 20, 22, 23, 60, 61, 62, 65, 66, 68, 70, 71, 72, 73, 74, 75, 81, 82, 83, 94, 147, 161, 175, 181, 211, 241, 245, 251, 264, 265, 267, 291, 293
savings account, 4, 20
scarcity, 43

scope, 46, 49, 52, 76, 97, 105, 131, 150, 166, 167, 170, 184, 216, 218, 219, 261, 318

Secretary of the Treasury, 7, 27, 38, 49, 51, 84, 95, 109, 165, 167, 213, 215, 243, 244, 249, 251, 253, 261, 262, 263, 264, 282, 286, 292, 311, 314

Securities Act of 1933, 81, 89, 190, 198, 202, 230, 252, 265, 266, 276

Securities Exchange Act, 61, 75, 83, 89, 185, 187, 190, 206, 207, 208, 227, 229, 230, 233, 234, 241, 247, 251, 252, 267, 271, 272, 273, 274, 275, 276, 277, 278, 286, 299, 300, 301, 302, 303, 304, 305, 306

securities firms, 46, 49, 186, 227, 228

security, 8, 14, 15, 16, 22, 30, 43, 55, 56, 57, 59, 62, 76, 81, 87, 134, 135, 138, 139, 140, 141, 142, 143, 145, 147, 148, 154, 159, 160, 164, 180, 189, 191, 192, 193, 200, 207, 208, 228, 234, 247, 251, 252, 254, 272, 273, 274, 275, 276, 277, 294, 299, 300, 301, 304, 305, 325, 326, 335, 336, 337

self-interest, 77

seller, 12, 155, 159, 186, 217, 322, 333, 334, 336

sellers, 12, 40, 191, 217, 322

Senate, ix, 1, 2, 24, 59, 60, 61, 62, 66, 68, 80, 84, 95, 96, 103, 108, 109, 110, 112, 113, 131, 138, 140, 142, 143, 144, 145, 147, 148, 163, 182, 186, 189, 205, 206, 209, 210, 213, 214, 228, 231, 232, 239, 257, 259, 260, 318, 331

service provider, 17, 99, 121, 122, 182, 185, 223, 233, 234, 307, 308

settlements, 154, 175

sex, 60

shareholder value, 205

shareholders, 7, 19, 24, 31, 54, 86, 87, 184, 193, 194, 197, 206, 208, 277

shock, 3, 4, 9, 134

short-term liabilities, 62

showing, 55, 207

signs, 49

skin, 8, 31, 183, 191

small businesses, 12, 83, 106, 217, 223, 255, 259

small firms, 56

Social Security, 174

solution, 44

soybeans, 324, 330

specialists, 25

specifications, 324

speculation, 50, 146, 327, 329

speech, 21, 50, 63, 235, 315

spending, 202, 317

spillover effects, 158

spin, 3, 145

spot market, 336

Spring, 128, 314

stability, 3, 4, 12, 14, 23, 25, 31, 44, 52, 58, 77, 78, 137, 158, 160, 165, 219, 239, 323

stabilization, 251

staff members, 247

state, viii, 9, 10, 15, 17, 18, 20, 25, 29, 30, 32, 44, 49, 65, 66, 68, 70, 71, 73, 74, 75, 78, 79, 80, 83, 84, 86, 87, 94, 107, 113, 124, 145, 161, 166, 168, 173, 181, 185, 187, 189, 196, 199, 202, 210, 211, 216, 218, 220, 221, 222, 223, 224, 229, 232, 241, 257, 293, 310

state laws, 75, 220, 222, 223

state regulators, 211, 222

states, 5, 7, 10, 18, 19, 26, 54, 62, 83, 89, 95, 96, 97, 99, 100, 101, 102, 103, 104, 107, 108, 110, 111, 113, 130, 190, 200, 202, 220, 223, 228, 232, 234, 235, 239, 240, 241, 242, 245, 246, 248, 249, 250, 251, 252, 254, 256, 257, 267, 268, 269, 270, 271, 272, 273, 293, 294, 316, 317

statistics, 331

statutes, 16, 101, 102, 105, 108, 129, 164, 184, 221, 230, 239, 243, 254, 314, 316

statutory authority, 86, 160, 161, 242

statutory provisions, 190

stock exchange, 19, 193, 194

stock price, 135

stockholders, 48

storage, 55, 173

stress, 5, 42, 48, 53, 133, 151, 159, 160, 191, 262, 287, 324

structural changes, 45, 46

structure, vii, 26, 48, 65, 67, 78, 89, 194, 195, 196, 197, 198, 210, 211, 212, 314, 325

subprime loans, 29

subsidy, 48

substitutes, 70, 153, 321

substitution, 190

supervision, 10, 11, 23, 26, 28, 30, 32, 48, 52, 60, 61, 66, 75, 83, 101, 102, 112, 114, 150, 152, 158, 161, 168, 169, 170, 200, 211, 212, 243, 259, 263, 278, 292

supervisor, 11, 12, 47, 58, 71, 109, 160, 168, 212, 215, 216

supervisors, 25, 109, 150, 195, 211

suppliers, 153

Supreme Court, 87, 88, 220, 222, 230

surplus, 20, 32, 245

surveillance, 191, 328

Sweden, 181

Switzerland, 179, 180, 181, 182

Index

systemic risk, vii, viii, 3, 4, 5, 6, 11, 18, 20, 21, 23, 26, 30, 32, 37, 38, 39, 40, 42, 43, 44, 45, 46, 47, 48, 49, 50, 51, 52, 57, 58, 61, 62, 88, 90, 133, 139, 151, 152, 158, 159, 163, 168, 180, 212, 265, 291, 326

T

takeover, 193
target, x, 317, 320
taxation, 220
taxpayers, 23, 26, 27, 57, 59, 77, 145
technical assistance, 29, 167, 213
technological advances, 197
technologies, 170
technology, 159, 201
teeth, 238
telecommunications, 156, 159
telephone, 140, 174, 335
tenants, 34
theft, 223
threats, 38, 52, 261
thrifts, viii, 9, 10, 22, 35, 43, 47, 57, 60, 65, 66, 71, 83, 94, 210, 211, 216, 220, 221, 222, 224
time constraints, 106
time periods, 166, 333
Title I, v, vii, ix, 7, 8, 10, 16, 17, 18, 19, 20, 51, 52, 53, 56, 60, 65, 66, 67, 68, 70, 85, 88, 107, 136, 181, 183, 184, 206, 208, 219, 224, 257, 265
Title II, vii, 7, 10, 20, 53, 60, 65, 66, 67, 68, 70, 107, 136, 181, 208, 219, 224, 257
Title IV, 18, 85, 88, 265
Title V, v, 10, 20, 53, 54, 55, 56, 57, 58, 61, 65, 67, 71, 125, 133, 138, 143, 146, 149, 150, 151, 152, 153, 156, 159, 160, 163, 164, 165, 166, 167, 168, 169, 170, 179, 182, 245, 250, 267, 268, 269, 270, 271, 272, 273, 294, 310, 311, 314, 325, 329, 330, 336
trade, 15, 22, 35, 43, 55, 56, 136, 137, 139, 140, 147, 153, 155, 158, 164, 166, 179, 217, 219, 252, 268, 298, 319, 320, 321, 322, 325, 326, 327, 330
trading partners, viii, 56, 133, 134, 179
training, 189, 201, 275
tranches, 9
transaction costs, 321, 329
transaction value, 154
transition period, 68
transmission, 158, 159
transparency, 4, 15, 24, 28, 43, 137, 139, 140, 146, 151, 188, 199, 247, 278, 319, 320, 323, 325, 326, 328, 331

Treasury, viii, 1, 3, 5, 6, 7, 17, 20, 21, 25, 27, 28, 32, 38, 43, 46, 51, 52, 54, 55, 56, 57, 61, 62, 63, 65, 67, 68, 70, 109, 122, 137, 153, 156, 172, 173, 182, 201, 202, 244, 261, 282, 308, 317
Treasury Secretary, 1, 3, 5, 6, 21, 25, 27, 28, 38, 51, 52, 54, 55, 56, 57
treatment, 20, 47, 68, 84, 101, 114, 124, 129, 139, 266, 278, 310
triggers, 29
trust fund, 84
turnover, 147, 195

U

U.S. Department of Commerce, 331
U.S. Department of the Treasury, 22, 62, 151, 158, 160, 178, 179, 180, 181, 182, 222
U.S. economy, 50, 149, 152
U.S. Treasury, 21, 155, 156, 172, 173, 177, 180, 317
unacceptable risk, 74
underwriting, 8, 9, 44, 78, 192, 193
unforeseen circumstances, 41
uniform, 26, 32, 163, 168, 186
unions, viii, 9, 10, 19, 20, 22, 24, 35, 47, 65, 69, 94, 141, 147, 175, 211, 216
United, x, 6, 7, 9, 10, 12, 13, 25, 26, 32, 41, 46, 52, 53, 54, 55, 58, 61, 77, 78, 79, 80, 81, 84, 87, 88, 90, 91, 100, 109, 110, 125, 129, 147, 149, 150, 151, 152, 153, 154, 155, 156, 157, 160, 162, 165, 166, 167, 172, 178, 181, 192, 219, 224, 227, 228, 230, 234, 245, 248, 267, 271, 291, 292, 293, 296, 298, 309, 311, 315, 317, 320, 322, 331
United Kingdom (UK), 150, 162, 181
United States (USA), x, 6, 7, 9, 10, 12, 13, 25, 26, 32, 41, 46, 52, 53, 54, 55, 58, 61, 77, 78, 79, 80, 81, 84, 87, 88, 90, 91, 100, 109, 110, 125, 129, 147, 149, 151, 152, 153, 154, 155, 156, 157, 160, 165, 166, 167, 172, 178, 181, 192, 219, 224, 227, 228, 230, 234, 245, 248, 267, 271, 291, 292, 293, 296, 298, 309, 311, 315, 317, 320, 322, 331
universe, 298
updating, 23
USA PATRIOT Act, 160
USDA, 319, 331, 332, 337

V

valuation, 90, 119, 191, 285
variables, 135
variations, 321

vehicles, 8, 18, 89, 217, 300
venture capital, 18, 90, 265
venue, 319
veto, 113, 131, 260, 318
victims, 214
volatility, 56, 134, 146, 330
Volcker Rule, 21, 26, 31, 76, 83, 84
vote, 2, 5, 19, 24, 25, 28, 31, 52, 55, 94, 107, 110, 111, 113, 165, 166, 167, 170, 193, 206, 208, 250, 256, 257, 260, 261, 302, 305
voters, 206
voting, 51, 52, 71, 72, 89, 110, 130, 206, 208, 252, 268
vulnerability, viii, 149

W

waiver, 82

Washington, 60, 61, 62, 63, 66, 128, 151, 179, 180, 181, 182, 314, 331, 332
weakness, 133
web, 22, 91, 180, 222, 337
websites, 21, 61, 178, 325
wholesale, 96, 153, 154, 156, 159, 160, 162, 179
withdrawal, 40, 41
workforce, 29, 70
workplace, 197
World Bank, 182
worldwide, 321, 322
worry, 136
writing process, 253

Y

yield, 29